*Cambridge studies in medieval life and thought*

# LAND AND POWER IN LATE
# MEDIEVAL FERRARA

# Cambridge studies in medieval life and thought
## Fourth series

General Editor:
### J. C. HOLT
*Professor of Medieval History and*
*Master of Fitzwilliam College, University of Cambridge*

Advisory Editors:
### C. N. L. BROOKE
*Dixie Professor of Ecclesiastical History and*
*Fellow of Gonville and Caius College,*
*University of Cambridge*

### D. E. LUSCOMBE
*Professor of Medieval History, University of Sheffield*

The series Cambridge Studies in Medieval Life and Thought was inaugurated by G. G. Coulton in 1920. Professor J. C. Holt now acts as General Editor of a Fourth Series, with Professor C. N. L. Brooke and Professor D. E. Luscombe as Advisory Editors. The series aims to bring together outstanding work by medieval scholars over a wide range of human endeavour extending from political economy to the history of ideas.

*Titles in the series*

# LAND AND POWER IN LATE MEDIEVAL FERRARA

## The Rule of the Este, 1350–1450

### TREVOR DEAN

*Fellow of Wolfson College, Oxford*

The right of the
University of Cambridge
to print and sell
all manner of books
was granted by
Henry VIII in 1534.
The University has printed
and published continuously
since 1584.

## CAMBRIDGE UNIVERSITY PRESS

### CAMBRIDGE

NEW YORK   NEW ROCHELLE   MELBOURNE   SYDNEY

Published by the Press Syndicate of the University of Cambridge
The Pitt Building, Trumpington Street, Cambridge CB2 1RP
32 East 57th Street, New York, NY10022, USA
10 Stamford Road, Oakleigh, Melbourne 3166, Australia

First published 1988

Printed in Great Britain at the University Press, Cambridge

*British Library cataloguing in publication data*
Dean, Trevor
Land and power in late medieval Ferrara:
the rule of the Este, 1350–1450. –
(Cambridge studies in medieval life and
thought. Fourth series; 7).
1. Ferrara (Italy) – History
I. Title
945'.45  DG975.F4

*Library of Congress cataloguing in publication data*
Dean, Trevor.
Land and power in late medieval Ferrara.
(Cambridge studies in medieval life and thought.
4th ser., 7)
Based on the author's thesis (doctoral) –
University of Oxford, 1982.
Bibliography.
1. Land tenure – Italy – Ferrara (Province) – History.
2. Land tenure – Italy – Emilia – Romagna – History.
3. Ferrara (Italy: Province) – History.  4. Emilia-
Romagna (Italy) – History.  5. Este family.  I. Title.
II. Series.
HD679.F47D43 1988  333.3'0945'45  87–6583

ISBN 0 521 33127 7

HD
679
.F47
D43
1988

# CONTENTS

# MAPS

# PREFACE

This book began life as a doctoral thesis submitted to the University of Oxford in 1982. In rewriting it after four years, I have made many changes: all the chapters have, to some extent, been rearranged and rewritten; new material has been introduced and the bibliography updated; the footnotes have been reduced and I have tried to enliven the rather dull and awkward style in which I found the thesis had been written. None of these changes has altered the overall or detailed argument of the thesis and I hope that none has generated unwitting errors. I have especially altered the material of chapter 6, but remain grateful to the editors of the *English Historical Review* for their permission to reproduce parts of an article published in that journal in 1985.

In carrying out the original research and in revising the thesis now, many debts have been incurred, of both a professional and personal nature. I hope that, in recording those below, others not mentioned will consider themselves included in my gratitude. Greatest of all is my debt to Dr P. J. Jones, who first awakened in me an interest in Italian history, who suggested the Este as a research topic and who supervised the writing of the thesis. I owe more to his vision and trust than can be recorded here. I have debts also to Brasenose College, Oxford, for generously electing me to a Senior Scholarship which enabled me to spend more time in the Modenese archives; to the British School in Rome for also awarding me a Scholarship and for its hospitality; and to Mr M. H. Keen for his support in the early years of my research.

I am very grateful to Mike Knapton and Charles MacKay for supplying intellectual stimulation during lengthy research trips in Italy. I owe much to St Anne's, Wolfson and Lincoln Colleges, Oxford and to the History Departments of Sheffield and Lancaster Universities for sustaining and employing me since the thesis was written. Also to Ms M. Elford for her loving support in a lean year. The process of turning thesis into book has been assisted by the comments, made at various stages and in various circumstances, of Professors J. L. Larner, J. C. Holt and D. E. Luscombe and of Drs D. M. Bueno de Mesquita, G. Holmes, C. Wickham, R. G. Lewis, H. Mayr-Harting and A. Grant (to whose inspiration are due the scattered Scottish references). I was assisted, in the final stages of preparing the book, by a grant from the Twenty-Seven Foundation. Finally, I should like to thank the staffs of the following archives and libraries for their assistance and helpful service: Archivio di Stato, Modena; Archivio di Stato, Ferrara; Archivio Comunale, Ferrara; Biblioteca comunale Ariostea, Ferrara; Biblioteca Estense, Modena; Archivio Vaticano; Archivio di Stato, Venice; Bodleian Library, Oxford and British Library, London.

# ABBREVIATIONS

## ARCHIVES

| | |
|---|---|
| ACF | Archivio comunale, Ferrara |
| ANF | Archivio notarile, Ferrara |
| ASE | Archivio segreto estense |
| ASF | Archivio di Stato, Ferrara |
| ASM | Archivio di Stato, Modena |
| ASMn | Archivio di Stato, Mantua |
| ASV | Archivio segreto vaticano |
| ASVe | Archivio di Stato, Venice |
| AV | Archivio vaticano |
| BCF | Biblioteca comunale (ariostea), Ferrara |
| BEM | Biblioteca estense, Modena |

## MANUSCRIPT SERIES

| | |
|---|---|
| Archivio Pomposa | ASM, Camera Ducale, Cancelleria, Pomposa |
| Cam. Duc. | ASM, Camera Ducale |
| Casa e Stato | ASM, ASE, Documenti riguardanti la Casa e lo Stato |
| Leggi e Decreti | ASM, ASE, Cancelleria, Leggi e Decreti (also known as *Registra litterarum decretorumque*) |
| Not. Cam. | ASM, Camera Ducale, Notai camerali |
| RL | ASV, Registri Laterani |
| RV | ASV, Registri Vaticani |

## PERIODICALS

| | |
|---|---|
| *AHR* | *American Historical Review* |
| *AMF* | *Atti e Memorie della deputazione ferrarese di Storia Patria* |

# List of abbreviations

| | |
|---|---|
| AMMo | Atti e Memorie della Deputazione di Storia Patria per le provincie modenesi |
| AMRo | Atti e Memorie della Deputazione di Storia Patria per la Romagna |
| ASI | Archivio Storico Italiano |
| ASL | Archivio Storico Lombardo |
| ASPP | Archivio Storico per le provincie parmensi |
| AV | Archivio Veneto |
| BIHR | Bulletin of the Institute of Historical Research |
| BISI | Bollettino dell'Istituto Storico Italiano |
| BU | Bollettino della Deputazione di Storia Patria per l'Umbria |
| EcHR | Economic History Review |
| EHR | English Historical Review |
| JMH | Journal of Medieval History |
| JMRS | Journal of Medieval and Renaissance Studies |
| MA | Le Moyen Age |
| MEFR | Mélanges de l'Ecole française de Rome |
| MGH | Monumenta Germaniae Historica, Hannover, 1826– |
| NAV | Nuovo Archivio Veneto |
| NRHD | Nouvelle Revue Historique de Droit (français et étranger) |
| NRS | Nuova Rivista Storica |
| QS | Quaderni Storici |
| RHDF | Revue Historique de Droit français et étranger |
| RIS | Rerum Italicarum Scriptores, ed. L. A. Muratori, Milan, 1723–51 |
| RIS² | Rerum Italicarum Scriptores, Città di Castello, 1900– |
| RSDI | Rivista della Storia del Diritto Italiano |
| RSI | Rivista Storica Italiana |
| SM | Studi Medievali |
| SR | Studi Romagnoli |
| TRHS | Transactions of the Royal Historical Society |

# NOTE ON SOURCES

Any history of Este land-management has to start with the *Catastri delle Investiture* in ASM, a mixed series of registers or cartularies, written at various periods from the second half of the thirteenth century to the late sixteenth. Most of the volumes from before 1450 form two separate series: the first, (*Catastri* C–G) contains a systematic review and confirmation of all the Ferrarese fiefs held of the marquis in the late thirteenth century (the *confessioni di vassallaggio*); the second (*Catastro* H onwards), constitutes a fairly continuous series of investitures running by date from 1393 into the sixteenth century and subdivided according to type of tenure (fiefs, leases (*livelli*) and two peculiar Ferrarese forms of leasehold (*usi* and *terratici*)).[1] This second series was compiled from earlier records in the 1430s in a deliberate reorganisation of the records of the camera, the office which managed the marquis' lands and revenues. Previous cameral land registers, also called *catastri*, had certainly existed and are not infrequently referred to in the late fourteenth century, but none apparently survives. The records, on the other hand, of the cameral notaries, from which the *Catastri delle Investiture* were compiled, do in large part survive: there are sixty volumes covering the period from the 1330s to the 1440s (*Camera Ducale, Notai Camerali*). From the start, these contain large numbers of feudal grants. Supplementing these, and to some extent filling the gap between the *confessioni* and the notarial registers, is a further collection of *Investiture di Feudi, Usi e Livelli*, individual charters which, after the 1330s, duplicate the notarial registers.

These, however, form only a small part of the Este archive. The notarial registers themselves contain not only grants of land, but the whole range of business transacted by the camera: farms of the gabelles and other revenues, with relevant correspondence and enactments; appointments to a wide range of patrimonial and public offices throughout the Este 'state'; territorial acquisitions by the Este and so on. And similar material is to be found in the series of *Mandati*, mandates issued to the camera by the marquises, and in the correspondence between the camera and the local financial officials (*Amministrazione finanziaria dei paesi*). In addition to the cameral records, the Este chancery kept two series of registers of letters and decrees (*Leggi e Decreti*), which run from the 1360s, as well as leaving other records which are today divided into various series (*Rettori dello Stato; Carteggi di Referendari* and so on).

Other archives have also been consulted in order to discover more about certain individuals, families and monasteries and to avoid over-reliance on the records of the central administration in Ferrara: the Contrari documents in the Archivio Boncompagni in the Vatican and the Gozzadini archive in Bologna; material from the Pomposa and Vangadizza archives in Modena; the Ferrarese notarial archive and other collections in Ferrara and Modena for Ferrarese lay society; various state and private documents in Venice.

---

[1] Fiefs are contained in Catastri H, N, R and BC; *usi* in Catastri K and S; *livelli* and *terratici* in Catastri L, O, P, U and X. Catastro A contains documents regarding Este relations with the church and Catastro B diplomatic documents of the commune in the thirteenth century.

# NOTES ON MONEY, MEASUREMENTS
# AND TERMS

## MONEY

Various units of currency were in use in Ferrara in the later Middle
Ages. I have avoided frequent use of monetary terms, but the
following notes might assist comprehension where they are used.
Venetian ducats and Florentine florins, as international currencies,
were used in Ferrara, but the main units were, by the late fourteenth
century, the *Lira marchesana* (expressed in text as L.) and its con-
stituent parts. The *lira* was notionally divided into 20s. and 240d.,
but the only coins actually issued were the *soldo* (1s.), the *quattrino*
(2d) and the *bagattino* ($\frac{1}{2}$d). The rate of the *lira* against the ducat
declined throughout our period: 1 ducat standing at 34s. in 1381 and
at 46s. in 1441. For rough calculation, then, L.2 = 1 ducat. (See V.
Bellini, *Delle monete di Ferrara*, (Ferrara, 1761), pp. 97–116).

## MEASUREMENTS

Each city of late medieval Italy had its own measurements for surface
area, volume and weight. The following equivalents are taken from
A. Martini, *Manuale di metrologia*, (Turin, 1883). For the most part in
the text, surface area is given in hectares (1 hectare = 10,000 sq.
metres) and it should be remembered that 1 hectare = 2.471 acres.

Ferrara: 1 *staio* = 1,087 sq. m
Modena: 1 *biolca* = 2,836 sq. m
Reggio: 1 *biolca* = 2,922 sq. m
Rovigo: 1 *campo* = 4,464 sq. m
Padua: 1 *campo*= = 3,862 sq. m
Bologna: 1 *tornatura* = 2,080 sq. m.

## TERMS

I provide here the brief definitions of certain terms found frequently in the text.

Camera ('chamber'): the name given to the office which administered the Este lords' private affairs (their estates, revenues, households &c).

*Contadini*: literally, and technically, those living in the countryside, but often, by extension, peasants.

*Contado* (Latin *comitatus*): the countryside around the city and dependent on it.

Emphyteusis: A specific form of lease for three generations.

*Fattori generali*: the two officials who headed the camera.

*Giudice dei Savi*: see *Savi*

*Massaro*: a city official responsible for the collection and handling of communal revenues.

*Merum et mixtum imperium*: full powers of public jurisdiction.

*Podestà*: chief judicial official of a city or rural district (in a rural district, the *podestà*, often known as the *visconte*, would also have general executive and governmental powers).

*Raccomandato*: client serving lord under terms of *accomandigia* (see chapter 6).

*Savi* (literally, 'the wise'): elected or appointed councillors in the communal council. At Ferrara, the council of twelve *savi* was presided over by a *Giudice dei Savi*.

*Signore, signoria*: lord, lordship of a town and its *contado*.

*Valli*: large stretches of water or water and marsh.

*Visconte*: see *podestà*.

Chapter 1

# INTRODUCTION

## FEUDALISM: NORTH AND SOUTH

A strange inversion is currently taking place in the historiography of medieval Europe. For a long time, the political history of northern Europe was dominated by a feudal version of history: historians wrote confidently of a 'feudal system', of 'feudal society' and of 'feudal monarchy'. What they meant by the use of these terms was that society was organised by feudal bonds and that feudalism defined political and social structures. Homage, fealty and feudal service were the ubiquitous signs of a true 'system' which embraced almost the whole of society (from princes to peasants) and nearly all social activity (warfare and political action, agriculture and social discipline). Only towns and trade remained isolated from the system's comprehensiveness. The situation in Italy was always different, as we shall see, but the historiography of feudalism has for some time seemed to be moving in different directions north and south of the Alps. While in northern Europe historians have been reducing the significance of feudalism, even propounding the rewriting of medieval history without it,[1] Italian historians have been revising their medieval history specifically to include it.[2] In northern Europe, decades of social history have taught us the importance of other, non-feudal social bonds, such as kinship, lordship and community, to the point where feudo-vassalic bonds have faded into the background. Feudalism is no longer on such

[1] E. Brown, 'The tyranny of a construct: feudalism and historians of medieval Europe', *AHR*, 79 (1974); S. Reynolds, *Kingdoms and Communities in Western Europe, 900–1300* (Oxford, 1984), pp. 9, 220–3, 259; W. H. Dunham, review of B. D. Lyon, *From Fief to Indenture*, in *Speculum*, 33 (1958), 304.

[2] G. Tabacco, review of H. Keller, *Adelsherrschaft und städtische Gesellschaft in Oberitalien*, in *RSI*, 93 (1981), 852–5; G. Tabacco, 'Fief et seigneurie dans l'Italie communale', *MA*, 75 (1969); *Structures féodales et féodalisme dans l'occident mediterranéen (Xe-XIIIe siècles)*, in *Collection de l'Ecole française de Rome*, 44 (1980); and review by S. Gasparri in *Studi storici*, 22 (1981).

I

historians' agenda,[3] and the vocabulary of feudalism is dismissed as 'meaningless' and 'unhelpful in understanding medieval society'.[4] In northern Europe, it is now a textbook statement that 'feudalism' was not the basis of royal or princely power and that it is utterly inadequate to describe society as 'feudal'.[5] But in Italy, it has for some time been accepted as commonplace that 'feudalism' played an important, indeed underrated, part in the history of *signorie*, both urban and rural.[6] More recently, those works which have attempted to provide a firmer feudal dimension to Italian medieval history have attracted great attention.[7] In particular, there has been a confident reaction against the dominance of a 'classical model' of feudalism imported from France and against vigorous old prejudices which dismissed Italian feudalism as superficial and of no account because confined to the countryside. A process of what is awkwardly called 'historiographical decolonization' is now well in progress and interest in feudalism is robustly continuing.[8]

What can explain this divergence? Leaving aside the continuing use of feudalism in a socio-economic sense,[9] it is certainly not the case that the term 'feudalism' is differently understood north and south of the Alps: whether dismissing or embracing it, historians

---

[3] B. Guenée, 'Les tendances actuelles de l'histoire politique du moyen âge français', *Politique et histoire au Moyen Age* (Paris, 1981).

[4] Reynolds, *Kingdoms and Communities*, p. 9.

[5] E. M. Hallam, *Capetian France 987–1328* (London, 1980), pp. 17–18, 94–7, 169–73; Reynolds, *Kingdoms and Communities*, p. 277; Guenée, 'Les tendances actuelles', pp. 187–9.

[6] D. Waley, *The Italian City-Republics* (2nd edn, London, 1978), pp. 128–33; J. Larner, *Italy in the Age of Dante and Petrarch 1216–1380* (London, 1980), pp. 137–9.

[7] See note 2 and also: G Chittolini, 'Infeudazioni e politica feudale nel ducato visconteo-sforzesco', *QS*, 19 (1972); P. J. Jones, 'Economia e società nell'Italia medievale: la leggenda della borghesia', in *Storia d'Italia Einaudi, Annali*, vol. 1 (Turin, 1978); S. Polica, 'Basso Medioevo e Rinascimento: "rifeudalizzazione" e "transizione"', *BISI*, 88 (1979); C. Mozzarelli and P. Malanima, 'A proposito degli "Annali" della "Storia d'Italia": Dal feudalesimo al capitalismo', *Società e Storia*, 7 (1980); M. Nobili, 'L'equazione città antica – città comunale ed il "mancato sviluppo italiano" nel saggio di Philip Jones', *Società e Storia*, 10 (1980); R. Bordone, 'Tema cittadino e "ritorno alla terra" nella storiografia comunale recente', *QS*, 52 (1983).

[8] *Structures féodales* and review by Gasparri (see note 2); C. M. de la Roncière, 'Fidélités, patronages, clientèles dans le contado florentin au XIV siècle. Les seigneuries féodales, le cas des comtes Guidi', *Ricerche Storiche*, 15 (1985).

[9] B. Figliuolo, in a review of *Structures féodales* (*Archivio storico per le provincie napoletane*, s. 3, 20 (1981)), usefully distinguishes between *feodalità*, the ensemble of feudo-vassalic bonds, and *feodalismo*, the socio-economic 'system', a distinction which would seem to have much to commend it, were it not for the unfamiliarity of the English word 'feudality'.

are, by and large, talking about the same thing. Although much of the criticism has been directed at obvious targets, such as the ideas of a 'feudal pyramid' or of 'feudal society', both Italian and northern European historians ultimately have in mind feudo-vassalic bonds, in which fiefs are granted by lords, under the peculiar terms of feudal custom, in return for homage, fealty and service. The divergence seems, rather, to derive from different historiographical traditions and their revision in both cases. In northern Europe, mainstream historiography was for long focused on feudal relationships, on feudal service and on feudal disputes. Bound up with this were ideas of government and hierarchy which stressed the vertical structure of society and the formal acts (homage, investiture) by which that structure was created. To the revisionists, that picture now looks artificial. From Duby's study of the Mâconnais onwards, it has been argued that we have to look outside the formal political structure in order to understand the relationships that bound medieval society together. Most recently, it has been advanced that medieval society was a vast collection of groups or 'collectivities' and that it is the solidarities within these groups that are the key to understanding that society: in such an interpretation, it is claimed, feudalism has no place.[10]

In Italy, by contrast, it was precisely the (presumed) 'non-feudal' aspects of medieval history that for long drew much attention: the high levels of urbanisation and of commercial/industrial activity and wealth; cities under republican rule (Florence, Venice etc.); and a culture which it is easy to interpret as 'bourgeois'. It has, however, been shown that the emphasis placed on these was disproportionate and that it is questionable how 'non-feudal' they really were.[11] This radical revision of basic interpretations, as it affects feudalism, need be only briefly outlined here. According to an older orthodoxy, a 'feudal age' in Italy was presented as coming to an end in the early twelfth century, succumbing to the attacks of allegedly merchant-dominated communes, which challenged the powers of the feudal nobility in the interests of commercial convenience and profit. Castles were seized, nobles forced to reside in the cities and the 'feudal economy' undermined. In the thirteenth century, the guilds and artisans, grouped together as the *popolo*, heightened this attack

---

[10] G. Duby, *La société aux XIe et XIIe siècles dans la région mâconnaise* (Paris, 1953); S. Reynolds, *Kingdoms and Communities*.

[11] P. J. Jones, 'Economia e società nell'Italia medievale: il mito della borghesia', in P. J. Jones, *Economia e società nell'Italia medievale* (Turin, 1980), *passim*.

on noble privilege and lawlessness by passing laws against unruly 'magnates' and the means by which they fomented unrest. Among the instruments of noble power that were attacked was the fief: prohibitions were issued on the granting of fiefs, on the wearing of devices (which advertised vassalic dependence) and on the drafting of vassals into the city in support of nobles' political pretensions.[12] Because these 'anti-magnate' campaigns were seen as largely successful, feudalism came to be disregarded after the twelfth century. Feudalism was pushed to the margins of Italian historiography, as it was indeed in the geographical margins alone that it was recognised as surviving, on the peripheries of the emergent regional states of the fourteenth century and in the hill-country of Emilia and Romagna.[13] Fourteenth-century feudalism in Italy was for long dismissed as a mere 'relic', and the feudatories solely as creatures of the countryside, obstacles to state control – 'feudatories' in the historian's vocabulary came to denote troublesome rural lords, irredeemable backwoodsmen.[14]

That Italian medieval history is not to be written in terms of a conflict between cities and feudalism is now a commonplace and the re-evaluation of the social and political importance of landed society has gone a long way ('the return to the land').[15] This has invested all aspects of medieval Italian history, from agrarian organisation, agriculture and trade to the political structure of the countryside and culture. The large presence of the non-mercantile aristocracy, the continuing reality of magnate power and the crucial importance of a

---

[12] G. Fasoli, 'Ricerche sulla legislazione antimagnatizia nei comuni dell'alta e media Italia', *RSDI*, 12 (1939).

[13] J. Heers, *Le clan familial au Moyen Age* (Paris, 1974), pp. 43–5, 181; G. Cherubini, *Una comunità dell'Appennino dal XIII al XV secolo* (Florence, 1972), p. 133; F. Ercole, 'Impero e papato nel diritto pubblico del Rinascimento', in his *Dal comune al principato* (Florence, 1929), p. 313; S. Bertelli, *Il potere oligarchico nello stato-città medievale*, (Florence, 1978), pp. 25–32; and *cf.* G. Chittolini, *La formazione dello stato regionale e le istituzioni del contado* (Turin, 1979), p. x.

[14] A. Palmieri, 'Feudatari e popolo della montagna bolognese (periodo comunale)', *AMRo*, s. 4, 4 (1913–14), 407–8; A. Palmieri, *La montagna bolognese del medio evo* (Bologna, 1929), pp. 13, 46, 252, 455–6; N. Tamassia, *La famiglia italiana nei secoli decimoquinto e decimosesto* (1910), p. 14; U. Petronio, 'Giurisdizioni feudali e ideologia giuridica nel ducato di Milano', *QS*, 26 (1974), 399; G. Fasoli, 'Lineamenti di politica e di legislazione feudale veneziana in terraferma', *RSDI*, 25 (1952), 62–3; G. Fasoli, 'Legislazione antimagnatizia', pp. 152ff, 166, 242–3; G. Magni, *Il tramonto del feudo lombardo* (Milan, 1937), pp. 65, 108ff; J. K. Laurent, 'Feudalismo e signoria', *ASI*, 137 (1979), 174–5; D. M. Bueno de Mesquita, 'Ludovico Sforza and his vassals', in *Italian Renaissance Studies*, ed. E. F. Jacob (London, 1960); *cf.* Chittolini, 'Infeudazioni', now in *La formazione*, p. 36.

[15] Jones, 'Mito', p. 5 and *passim*.

4

feudal aristocracy that was also urban have been recognised.[16] Too often, nobles were portrayed as 'losing' their 'feudal' character on transferring residence into the city;[17] but, as the 'anti-magnate' and 'anti-feudal' legislation shows only too clearly, feudal clientage, along with fortified houses, aristocratic lawlessness and fights for power, were all imported from the countryside into the town. And most towns ended by appointing a feudal lord as *signore*. The 'feudal age' obviously did not draw to a close in the twelfth century: the power of feudal lords endured, alongside, when not in charge of, the city communes;[18] fiefs cannot be confined geographically to peripheral or mountainous regions;[19] all the earlier *signori* were feudal lords and, as will be seen in the case of Ferrara, feudal bonds could be used to support urban *signoria*. The presence of the fief in the city is now widely accepted and older assumptions regarding the chronology and significance of feudalism in Italy have been revised.[20]

Feudal lordship is thus seen to have a reality in Italy which runs counter to the trend in northern Europe to minimise its significance or to write as if fiefs and vassals had never existed. The total

[16] Ibid., pp. 6–15, 51–64, 74–5, 123; E. Cristiani, *Nobiltà e popolo nel comune di Pisa*, (Naples, 1962); Petronio, 'Giurisdizioni', p. 399; P. J. Jones, 'Communes and despots: the city-state in late medieval Italy', *TRHS*, 15 (1965), 75–8; G. Luzzatto, 'Tramonto e sopravivenza del feudalismo nei comuni italiani del Medio Evo', *SM*, s. 3, 3 (1962), 411; E. Fiumi, *Storia economica e sociale di San Gimignano*, (Florence, 1961), pp. 45–51; C. Wickham, *Early Medieval Italy* (London, 1981), pp. 86–8, 176.

[17] A. Ventura, *Nobiltà e popolo nella società veneta del '400 e '500* (Bari, 1964), p. 108; E. Guidoni, 'Residenza, casa e proprietà nei patti tra feudalità e comuni', in *Structures féodales*; cf. Cristiani, *Nobiltà e popolo*, pp. 70–1.

[18] Tabacco, 'Fief', p. 212; E. Sestan, 'Le origini delle signorie cittadine: un problema storico esaurito?', in his *Italia medievale* (Naples, 1968), pp. 209–10; Jones, 'Mito', pp. 111–12, 121; G. Fasoli, 'Città e feudalità', in *Structures féodales*, pp. 371–2.

[19] That the fief persisted in vast parts of the countryside is commonly asserted: Ercole, 'Impero e papato', p. 313; Luzzatto, 'Tramonto', p. 418; Ventura, *Nobiltà e popolo*, pp. 7, 108; E. Fiumi, 'Fioritura e decadenza dell'economia fiorentina', *ASI*, 115 (1957), 420, 428; Fasoli, 'Città e feudalità', pp. 373–5; D. Waley, 'The army of the Florentine republic from the twelfth to the fourteenth century', in *Florentine Studies*, ed. N. Rubinstein (London, 1968), pp. 93–4.

[20] 'Il n'y a pas *un* modèle féodal. Il n'existe que des espèces locales qu'il faut prendre et comprendre pour elle-mêmes': P. Toubert, *Les structures du Latium médiéval* (Rome, 1973), p. 1136; G. Rippe, 'Feudum sine fidelitate. Formes féodales et structures sociales dans la région de Padoue à l'époque de la première commune (1131–1236)', *MEFR*, 87 (1975), 189; Tabacco, 'Fief', pp. 6–9, 13–19, 25–8, 35, 215–16; *Structures féodales*, pp. 241, 520, 526; Jones, 'Mito', pp. 4–5; G. Chittolini, 'Città e contado nella tarda età comunale', *NRS*, 53 (1969). Cf. Duby, *La société . . . mâconnaise*, pp. 186–8, 192, 195; T. Evergates, *Feudal Society in the Bailliage of Troyes under the Counts of Champagne 1152–1284* (Baltimore, 1975), pp. 62–3, 80–2, 90, 120.

repudiation of feudal vocabulary is surely an unnecessarily extreme position. It is obviously undeniable that the space given to 'feudalism' in the past was excessive and that the word had a currency that went far beyond its usefulness. But this does not mean that we need go beyond merely reducing feudalism to its only useful meaning: the practice of granting fiefs in return for fealty and service and a political structure incorporating (though not necessarily based on) feudo-vassalic bonds. Against this view, it can of course be argued, from both ends of the Middle Ages, that the period when real lord–man relations coincided with the structures that are reconstructed from feudal records was in fact a brief one, that such coincidence as there was was never total and that the real object of study should not be 'feudalism', but lordship and the practical realities of leadership and authority. That feudal bonds are only part of the picture is, again, undeniable, but it is to establish precisely how large that part is, in one medieval state, that this book is directed. For in Italy at the end of the Middle Ages, it is clear that rulers did conceive of relationships with their territorial nobilities in feudal terms. As Chittolini has amply demonstrated, the Dukes of Milan in the fifteenth century were insisting anew on the feudal dependence of their rural nobles (feudal service, subjection to feudal law, etc.). Fiefs formed a major part of the structure of authority: it was as a papal fief that the Este sought to hold Ferrara and it was in fief that they held Reggio from the Dukes of Milan (after 1421). These were clearly not inherited, arcane relationships, of no relevance to the way that rulers thought of their position relative to other rulers: they both created and expressed ideas of territorial and political hierarchy.

## BASTARD FEUDALISM AND REFEUDALISATION

Another sign of the divide separating Italian and northern European historiographies is the absence in Italy of debate over the precise nature of late-medieval feudalism and over the emergence of non- or post-feudal bonds in political society.[21] In essence, that debate has focused on the separation of political relationships of alliance and dependence from land and the tenure of land. Although the whole

---

[21] B. D. Lyon, *From Fief to Indenture* (Cambridge, Mass., 1957), pp. 252–3 and the bibliography there; C. Carpenter, 'The Beauchamp affinity: a study of bastard feudalism at work', *EHR*, 95 (1980); P. S. Lewis, 'Decayed and non-feudalism in later medieval France', *BIHR*, 37 (1964); J. Wormald, *Lords and Men in Scotland: Bonds of Manrent, 1442–1603* (Edinburgh, 1985), ch. 1.

structure of land-holding in return for homage, fealty and service remained nominally intact, it had by 1500 long parted company with the realities of lordship. The alienability of fiefs and the development of a land market eroded the element of personal dependence; homage and fealty were vitiated by multiple lordship; service was commuted, neglected or refused. All that was left (in England at least) was a formal structure in law and the lord's claim to certain 'incidents' (relief, marriage, wardship). As landed feudalism lost its close functional relationship with political groupings, so real social and political relations were created and defined by other forms of bond or contract – ones which gave to the dependant not land in heredity, but a pension or a promise of protection by the lord, both of which could be more easily revoked.

Such bonds took many different forms: bonds of manrent in Scotland, indentures of retinue in England, *alliances* in parts of France and, as we shall see, *accomandigia* in Italy. Whether such contracts may or may not be called 'feudal' has attracted much attention and debate, suggesting to one recent commentator that the major concern of historians has been over the appropriateness of a mere label, to the exclusion of deeper and fuller study of medieval political and social structures.[22] Part of the difficulty is that there are clear problems with the suggested transition from 'feudal' to 'non-feudal' (or 'bastard-feudal') society. Nowhere was the transition clear-cut. First of all, of course, personal dependence was eroded from the earliest times, as fiefs were transmitted to the sons (or other relatives) of the first recipients and as the recipients tried to absorb fiefs into their private patrimonies.[23] On the other hand, landed fiefs long continued to be granted by rulers to their intimates in reward or expectation of service. Secondly, the transition from landed fiefs to money 'fees' was blurred by the existence of money fiefs (*fief-rentes*) alongside ordinary fiefs: in France, we are told, non-feudal bonds evolved quietly out of decayed money fiefs. Thirdly, the separation of political relations from the structure of land tenure was not total: in England, pensions to a lord's local retainers (some of whom would also be his tenants) might be assigned on the revenues of the local manor;[24] and generally in late medieval Europe, it is easy

22 Ibid., pp. 7–8.
23 F. L Ganshof, *Feudalism* (3rd edn, London, 1964), pp. 37, 44–6.
24 A. J. Pollard, 'The Richmondshire community of gentry during the Wars of the Roses', in *Patronage, Pedigree and Power in Later Medieval England*, ed. C. Ross (Gloucester, 1979), pp. 52–4; N. Saul, *Knights and Esquires: The Gloucestershire Gentry in the Fourteenth Century* (Oxford, 1981), pp. 69–82.

enough to find examples of fief-holding serving as the basis of military forces or duties deployed or required by lords.[25] And although the new types of bond do look like other, non-feudal contracts (of friendship, brotherhood or alliance),[26] they neverthe-less used a feudal vocabulary and both the type of relationship created and the loyalty and service expected look very feudal too.[27] It might in fact be argued that all that the new contracts achieved was to restore to lords the flexibility in attaching and dismissing supporters, in shaping and controlling their entourage, that they had enjoyed before the development of a feudal land law which protected tenants' rights. In England, the transition to more flexible relations between lords and men has been held responsible for the collapse of political solidarities in the later fifteenth century, despite the fact that flexi-bility in recruiting and mobilising military forces through fees and friendship was certainly available, to the king at least, in earlier (and less disturbed) centuries.[28] 'Bastard feudalism', it might be argued, was more akin to earlier feudalism than the thirteenth-century model from which it was supposed to have degenerated.

This raises the possibility of dissolving the period of late-medieval feudalism into the long pre-industrial history of political relations between lords and men. In this case, historical enquiry is directed away from the question of feudalism and towards the specific political structures of different societies. The problem is then that we still have to make sense of fiefs and of the obligations that they created or reflected. Fiefs did, after all, greatly exercise the minds of late medieval (and early modern) rulers and their officials – in the issuing of charters, the compiling of registers of holdings and services, the writing of books of feudal law. If, as suggested above, there was not a clear point when all this activity passed into the area of legal fiction, of redundancy at a practical level, then we still have to assess, for each local society, the significance of fiefs and of feudal

---

25 P. S. Lewis, *Later Medieval France: The Polity* (London, 1968), p. 198; C. T. Allmand, *Lancastrian Normandy 1415–50* (Oxford, 1983), pp. 52ff; M. E. James, 'The first earl of Cumberland (1493–1542) and the decline of northern feudalism', *Northern History*, 1 (1966), 48–50; A Scufflaire, *Les fiefs directs des comtes de Hainaut de 1349 à 1504* (Brussels, 1978), pp. 158–77; but *cf.* R. Vaughan, *Charles the Bold* (London, 1973), pp. 218–19.
26 Wormald, *Bonds of Manrent*, pp. 35–41; M. H. Keen, 'Brotherhood in arms', *History*, 47 (1962); G. Leseur, *Histoire de Gaston IV, comte de Foix*, ed. H. Courteault (2 vols., Paris, 1893–6), vol. 2, pp. 308–9.
27 Dunham, review of Lyon, pp. 302–4; but *cf.* Wormald, *Bonds of Manrent*, pp. 14–33.
28 R. L. Storey, *The End of the House of Lancaster* (London, 1966), pp. 9–17; J. O. Prestwich, 'The military household of the Norman kings', *EHR*, 96 (1981).

8

bonds. This, in general terms, is one of the objects of this book.

As we shall see, there is in late medieval Italy a parallel to the 'new feudalisms' of northern Europe. But this 'refeudalisation' has a much wider meaning in current Italian historiography than 'bastard feudalism' has in England. On one level, it refers to the revived use by Italian states of the feudal grant of land to attach men, often military commanders, to their service or to define a territorial and political relationship. But this specific and technical meaning is only a part of a much broader trend which is perceived in later medieval Italy – a trend away from the innovative social and economic effects of the commercial revolution of the preceding centuries. 'Refeudalisation' meant the shift of capital from trade to land, the advance of aristocratic values and the undoing of the achievements of economic and urban growth. These technical and general meanings obviously harmonise: a revival of landed feudalism calls into question the extent of the commercialisation of land-ownership and land-tenure in the preceding period. On a broader level still, re-feudalisation is one answer to the problem of Italy's failure to develop economically in the early modern period (the *mancato sviluppo*). Why, as one historian has put it, was Italy the 'first economic power of the fourteenth century, but the last of the eighteenth'?[29]

Interest in this problem has been stimulated by the publication in 1978 of the first volume of *Annali* annexed to the Einaudi *Storia d'Italia* (entitled *Dal Feudalesimo al Capitalismo*). The obvious implications of the title parallel similar debates in England on the transition from feudalism to capitalism.[30] Discussion of the complex issues would be out of place here, but suffice it to say that part of the debate in Italy has focused on the nature of the Italian city-states and on the scale and incidence of social and political change brought about by economic growth. The achievements of (some of) the city-states in terms of wealth creation, republican government, social mobility and the development of an urban culture are impressive and undeniable.[31] The question is whether all this was 'capitalistic' and modern in some sense or still dominated by aristocratic values and demands. In support of the latter view, it has been argued that the greatest commercial profits came from providing luxury goods and services to a small, aristocratic market, while the bulk of trade in

[29] Nobili, 'L'equazione', p. 891.
[30] *The Transition from Feudalism to Capitalism*, ed. R. H. Hilton (London, 1978); *The Brenner Debate*, ed. T. H. Aston (Cambridge, 1985).
[31] P. J. Jones, 'La storia economica', in *Storia d'Italia Einaudi*, vol. 2 (Turin, 1974).

volume was in basic commodities, mainly agricultural; that bourgeois culture was in fact permeated and led by aristocratic and chivalric values; and that republican government, for many cities, was short-lived and turbulent.[32] Rather than being progressive states pointing towards modernity, the Italian cities were conservative, looking backwards to classical antiquity.[33]

## FERRARA AND THE ESTE

In all this, Ferrara is important because of its eccentricity: the first city of north and central Italy to produce a stable *signoria*; a city where feudo-vassalic bonds had a continuing presence and importance; and an urban economy which failed to generate the social and political framework typical of cities of its size and economic function.[34] Although the economic history of Ferrara awaits modern study, the conventional account would see a firm connection between Ferrara's socio-economic and its political structures, both in the conditions which generated *signoria* and in the reinforcement of those conditions after the establishment of the Este as *signori* in the mid-thirteenth century. Both economic and political feudalism, *feudalismo* and *feudalità*, seem to lie at the origins of *signoria* in Ferrara and both were, it is argued, reinforced by the Este after 1240. There are, however, problems here. The nature of Ferrara's economy in the century before the Este *signoria* and the precise nature of its failure is an intriguing puzzle. It is claimed that, in the quickening of economic exchanges from the eleventh century onwards, Ferrara had become a prosperous centre of distribution owing to its geographical location: not far from the coast, between Bologna and Venice, and commanding the zone where the Po divided into several branches. Ferrara was thus at the point of contact between interior and maritime trade and apparently rivalled Venice for the transit traffic from the Adriatic, its two annual fairs possibly attracting merchants from all over Italy. However, and here lies the paradox, a mercantile aristocracy failed to develop in Ferrara;[35] the guilds were not politically active nor at all prominent;[36] and there was no

[32] Jones, 'Mito'.  [33] Nobili, 'L'equazione'.  [34] Sestan, 'Origini'.
[35] *Statuta Ferrariae de anno 1287*, ed. W. Montorsi (Ferrara, 1955), pp. lxxxviii–ix; Sestan, 'Origini', pp. 201–2; F. Bocchi, 'Patti e rappresaglie fra Bologna e Ferrara dal 1193 al 1255', *AMRo*, 23 (1972), 74; A. L. Trombetti Budriesi, 'Vassalli e feudi a Ferrara e nel Ferrarese dall'età precomunale alla signoria estense', *AMF*, s. 3, 28 (1980), 22–3, 229; Jones, 'Mito', p. 29.
[36] A. Sitta, 'Le università delle arti a Ferrara dal secolo xii al xviii,', *AMF*, 8 (1896).

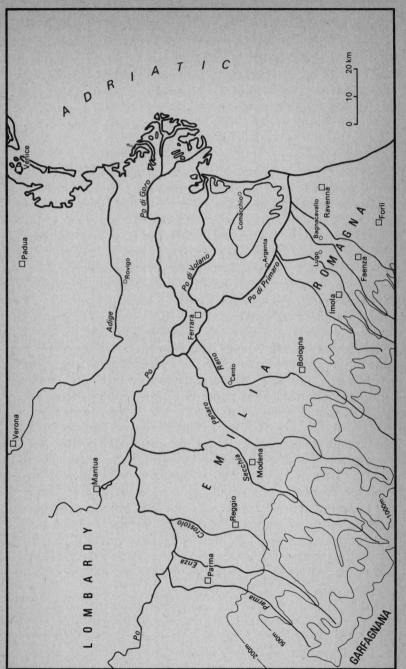

Map 1  General map of north-east Italy

organised *popolo* and consequently no popular, 'anti-magnate' or
'anti-feudal' legislation.[37] It may of course be that either or both
parts of the paradox are falsely stated: that Ferrarese commercial
prosperity has been exaggerated or that merchants and guilds were
more prominent than has been thought (or than the evidence allows
us to see), but as yet the paradox stands.[38] Similar problems attend
the alleged reinforcement of this failure to develop after 1240: it is
usually noted that it was the Este who allowed Venice to stifle
Ferrara's trade and to divert it to Venice, in return for Venetian
political support in the installation of the *signoria*.[39] But how full and
secure Venetian economic domination turned out to be is open to
question,[40] and the Este seem before long to have favoured and
protected Ferrarese traders against Venetians. There are thus complex problems surrounding the question of 'economic feudalism' at
Ferrara and its value as an explanation for the rise of *signoria*. No such
problems surround the question of 'political feudalism': as we shall
see, its role is clear in Ferrara's swift and straightforward transition
from aristocracy to *signoria*.[41]

In other respects too, Ferrara was perhaps atypical. As elsewhere
in Byzantine Italy in the eighth to tenth centuries, the nobility had
remained urban and rural lordships based on castles had failed to
develop. Power remained concentrated in the city and in the courts
(*curie*) of the major churches (especially the Archbishopric of
Ravenna), not dispersed in large rural possessions organised around
a castle. Although noble patrimonies did develop in the eleventh and
twelfth centuries, the firm hold on power of the regional lords (the
Canossa) and of the churches of Rome and Ravenna impeded the
construction of rural lordships.[42] One reason for this was perhaps

[37] Fasoli, 'Legislazione antimagnatizia', pp. 107–8; *Statuta Ferrariae*, pp. lxxix,
lxxxvii–ix; Sestan, 'Origini', pp. 204–6; Jones, 'Mito', pp. 140, 146.
[38] T. Dean, 'Venetian economic hegemony: the case of Ferrara, 1200–1500', *Studi
Veneziani*, forthcoming; G. Zanella, *Riccobaldo e dintorni* (Ferrara, 1980), pp. 82–3.
[39] B. Ghetti, *I patti tra Venezia e Ferrara dal 1191 al 1313*, (Rome, 1907), pp. 88–126; R.
Cessi, *La repubblica di Venezia e il problema adriatico* (Naples, 1953), pp. 42, 56–7,
60–2, 67–8, 75–6.
[40] Dean, 'Venetian economic hegemony'.
[41] Sestan, 'Origini', pp. 204–5; Jones, 'Storia economica', p. 1798; A. Castagnetti,
'Enti ecclesiastici, Canossa, Estensi, famiglie signorili e vassalatiche a Verona e
Ferrara', in *Structures féodales*, p. 412; A. Castagnetti, *Società e politica a Ferrara
dall'età postcarolingia alla signoria estense* (Bologna, 1985), ch. 9; Trombetti, 'Vassalli', pp. 67–77. Whether the Torelli supremacy, or that of the Estensi before 1264,
may be considered *signoria* is questioned by Zanella, *Riccobaldo*, p. 89.
[42] A. Castagnetti, *L'organizzazione del territorio rurale nel Medioevo* (Turin, 1979),
pp. 208, 211–12, 218–22, 227; A. Castagnetti, 'Enti', pp. 399–411; Trombetti,

geographical: contemporaries and later historians have noted the absence of large numbers of castles in the Ferrarese *contado*. In a flat region, much of which was below sea-level and covered, permanently or seasonally, by marsh and crossed by rivers liable to flood, the number of fortifiable positions was not great and the environment dictated a very different type of military architecture.[43] Consequently, the consular commune, which developed in a union of town and bishop against Ravenna, faced no 'nest of petty lords' in the *contado* against which it had to struggle to establish its dominance.[44] The scene was therefore set for the polarisation of power in the late twelfth century between two city families and their supporters: the Torelli and the Adelardi (soon to be replaced by the Estensi). Despite their large landed possessions, other noble families apparently did not have the military bases in the *contado* to challenge the domination of these two families, nor to prevent the early establishment of *signoria*.[45]

It was the 1180s which saw the first development of a substantial Este interest in Ferrara. This family of marquises (*marchesi*) had in preceding centuries held wide lands throughout north and central Italy. But from the second half of the twelfth century, they had taken up residence at Este in the Padovano (from then they were known as the *marchesi d'Este*), supported by their large landed possessions in the southern Padovano and in the area to the north of Ferrara (the *Polesine di Rovigo*).[46] In the late twelfth and early thirteenth centuries, their interests and ambitions were not limited to a single city, but extended across the *Marca Trevigiana*. Here they were active as political and military leaders of the faction which took their name

---

'Vassalli', pp. 17–20; A. Vasina, 'Il territorio ferrarese nell'alto medioevo', in *Insediamenti nel ferrarese* (Florence, 1976), pp. 85ff.

[43] 'Non sunt magna castra in dicto comitatu, ymo modica, sed sunt ville . . .': A. Theiner, *Codex diplomaticus Dominii temporalis Sanctae Sedis* (3 vols., Rome, 1861–2), vol. 2, p. 538; Castagnetti, *L'organizzazione*, p. 231; Vasina, 'Territorio', p. 89. No noble families at Ferrara derived their name from a castle in the *contado*: Castagnetti, 'Enti', pp. 399–400.

[44] L. Simeoni, 'L'azione del comune nel comitato', in *Verona e il suo territorio*, vol. 2 (Verona, 1954), p. 318; L. Simeoni, 'Il comune rurale nel territorio veronese', *NAV*, 42 (1921), 184; Jones, 'Mito', pp. 14–15, 125–6.

[45] Sestan, 'Origini', pp. 207–9; Bertelli, *Il potere oligarchico*, pp. 52–3; Trombetti, 'Vassalli', pp. 8–9; Castagnetti, 'Enti', p. 411.

[46] E. Zorzi, *Il territorio padovano nel periodo di trapasso da comitato a comune* (Venice, 1929), pp. 162–84; I. Alessi, *Ricerche istorico-critiche delle antichità di Este*, vol. 1 (Padua, 1776), pp. 524–97. For the narrative sections that follow: *Chronicon Estense, RIS*, 15; Jacobus de Delayto, *Annales Estenses, RIS*, 18; L. A. Muratori, *Delle Antichità Estensi ed Italiane* (2 vols., Modena, 1717–40); A. Frizzi, *Memorie per la storia di Ferrara* (2nd edn, Ferrara, 1847–8).

(the *pars Marchionis*). However, when the last of the Adelardi died without male heirs, the Estensi intervened in Ferrara, taking over their lands and assuming the leadership of Adelardi supporters. This marked a substantial shift in the direction of Este ambitions and was followed in time by a slow withdrawal from the *Marca*: in the late thirteenth century, the Este acquisition of Modena and Reggio in Emilia led to a relaxation of Este control in the Polesine and by 1500 both the Polesine and Este lands in the Padovano had been surrendered to Venice.[47]

## THE COURSE OF EVENTS, 1200–1393

For some years, the Estensi and Torelli seem to have accepted positions of equal eminence and power in Ferrara. Members of both families served as *podestà* and there were some years of concord. But the rivalry for supremacy soon led to open conflict, which was played out on the larger stage of opposing alliances within north-east Italy. Two decades of repeated disputes between Estensi and Torelli left Salinguerra Torelli in control of Ferrara from 1224. But Salinguerra's alliance with Emperor Frederick II in 1236 led to the formation of a powerful league against him of Venice, Bologna, the Estensi and the papal legate. These were the forces which besieged and took Ferrara in 1240, expelling Salinguerra and allowing the installation of an Este lordship.[48] From this date, Este control of Ferrara continued, with minor interruptions, until 1597. No other *signoria*, established so early, lasted so long.

For the first decades, Azzo d'Este's power remained informal and was challenged at times by noble opposition and conspiracy (1251, 1261, 1270). But Azzo carefully advanced his power and that of his supporters: lands were taken from political opponents and from the Church and redistributed, as we shall see; nobles who had supported Salinguerra were won over with fiefs. Consequently, on Azzo's death in 1264, the *signoria* was formalised for his grandson (Obizzo II). This event was carefully stage-managed: the city was cleared of

[47] A. L. Trombetti Budriesi, 'Beni estensi nel Padovano: da un codice di Albertino Mussato del 1293', *SM*, s. 3, 21 (1980), 168–70; V. Lazzarini, 'Beni carraresi e proprietari veneziani', in *Studi in onore di Gino Luzzatto* (Milan, 1949), vol. 1, p. 277; R. Gallo, 'Una famiglia patrizia, i Pisani ed i palazzi di S. Stefano e di Stra', *AV*, s. 5, 24–5 (1944), 72.

[48] G. Marchetti Longhi, 'La legazione in Lombardia di Gregorio da Monte Longo', *Archivio della Società Romana di Storia Patria*, 36 (1913); P. Rocca, 'Filippo, vescovo di Ferrara, arcivescovo di Ravenna', *AMF*, s. 3, 2 (1966), 17–60.

opponents, an armed guard was installed and weighty political support was drafted in from north-east Italy. Under these conditions, a group of Ferrarese nobles 'elected' Obizzo hereditary lord of Ferrara.[49] Although the true nature of this 'election' is clear enough, there has in the past been some support for the notion of popular involvement, but this is to confuse acclamation with real participation.[50] The determining force in the creation of the *signoria* was, here as elsewhere, the relationship between the *signore* and the local nobility. Este support among the Ferrarese nobility was substantial: perhaps a dozen families supported Azzo against the Torelli. Foremost among these were the Giocoli (Joculi) and the Turchi, both with large landed property to the north-east of the city, and also the Costabili, Contrari, Signorelli, Bocchimpani and Pagani. Some of the former Torelli partisans made accommodations with the Este in the years immediately following 1240, but rebelled later in the century (the Fontana, Mainardi).[51] Major Torelli supporters such as the Ramberti went into exile, their property seized by the Este and distributed in fief among their followers.[52]

In the 1260s and early 1270s, in response to further noble disturbances, the marquis issued a number of enactments to break the power of remaining opposition. Most of these measures dealt with military and feudal control of the city: regulating the picked militia of 100 cavalry and 800 infantry (who were to wear Este devices); forbidding others, at times of civil unrest, to take up arms or to assemble in large groups; forbidding movement into Ferrara from the *contado* during such disturbances; banning contacts between exiles and their families remaining in Ferrara.[53] Above all, as we shall see, the marquis sought to preserve the feudal basis of his power and to seal it off from the influence of other nobles (below, pp. 116–17). For fiefs and vassalage were essential to the structure of faction and of factional lordship in Ferrara. Referring to the period of Este–Torelli rivalry, the chronicler Riccobaldo noted the use of fiefs by the

---

[49] 'Gubernator et rector et generalis et perpetuus dominus': Muratori, *Antichità*, vol. 2, pp. 25–6.

[50] W. Gundersheimer, *Ferrara: the Style of a Renaissance Despotism* (Princeton, 1973), pp. 25–8; J. K. Laurent, 'The signory and its supporters: the Este of Ferrara', *JMH*, 3 (1977).

[51] *Chronica Parva Ferrariensis, RIS*, 8, 487; Frizzi, *Memorie*, vol. 3, pp. 191–7; J. K. Laurent, 'The Este and their vassals: a study in signorial politics', Brown University D.Phil thesis, 1976, pp. 140–1.

[52] Trombetti, 'Vassalli', pp. 69–70.

[53] *Statuta Ferrariae*, Liber I, xi, a, c, e, g, h, i, l, m, p; xiii, a, c, d, e; xiv, a, b, c, d; *Chron. Est.*, 385.

politically ambitious to bind men to them and the Este faction in Ferrara was maintained through feudal grants of the property of the Adelardi, Ramberti and others.[54] The factional importance of fiefs is revealed in Este insistence that fiefs with female succession should pass to women only if the husband was 'of the marquis' faction'.[55] And the element of personal dependence was reinforced and, above all, publicly demonstrated, in feudal assemblies (*curie vassallorum*) held by the Este with the clear intention of over-awing their opponents.[56] Moreover, in 1264 the terms of feudal fealty formed the basis of a general oath sworn by all the citizens to their new lord.[57] The Este *signoria* in Ferrara was thus from the outset feudal: it was created and maintained by feudal means and its history was in part determined by feudal disputes.[58]

Following the consolidation of their lordship of Ferrara, the Estensi turned their ambitions to the neighbouring cities of Emilia: Bologna, Modena and Reggio. At Bologna, as will be seen, a party was created of Este supporters, but it was never strong enough to confer the *signoria*. Greater success was had at Modena and Reggio. Here, as in other cities from around 1200, dominance of the city had earlier been disputed among the local nobility. Factional struggle pitted against each other groups within an aristocracy that was both rural and urban, combining control of castles and river routes in the *contado* with political ambitions focused on the city.[59] Unlike Ferrara, there was at Modena and Reggio no single family powerful enough to turn temporary superiority into permanent *signoria* and it was eventually to an outside lord that one of the factions turned to defeat its opponents. It was thus that in 1288 the nobles of several Modenese families (the Rangoni, Boschetti and Guidoni) delivered the city into the hands of Obizzo II d'Este. Their example was followed in Reggio in 1290. But this acceptance of foreign *signoria* had a price. The demands of the dominant faction had to be satisfied.

---

[54] *Chronica Parva*, 480; Trombetti, 'Vassalli', pp. 12–13, 68–73, 81; Jones, 'Mito', p. 152.
[55] Laurent, 'Vassals', p. 65.
[56] Trombetti, 'Vassalli', pp. 43–4, 55, 66.
[57] *Statuta Ferrariae*, Liber I, ii; Frizzi, *Memorie*, vol. 3, p. 148.
[58] In 1308 conflict arose from Azzo VIII's attempt to demise to his grandson, Folco, the *dominium* of all his 'feuda et concessiones' and with them control of all Este personal dependants ('nostris militibus et aliis personis'): A. Gaudenzi, 'Il testamento di Azzo VIII d'Este e la pace del 1326 tra Modena e Bologna', in *Miscellanea Tassoniana* (Bologna, 1908), p. 111.
[59] L. Simeoni, 'Ricerche sulle origini della signoria estense a Modena', *AMMo*, s. 5, 12 (1919).

At Modena in 1288 this involved cash payments, the firm banishment of political opponents and the arranging of an Este marriage for one of the Rangoni. Similar conditions attended the Este recovery of Modena in 1336, thirty years after their power there had collapsed (see below, chapter 6).

Elsewhere, Obizzo II made a number of other territorial gains. In 1285 he secured control of Lendinara, a small town of some strategic importance on the Adige and an object of Paduan territorial expansion.[60] He maintained the uncertain Este hold on Argenta, another small town commanding an important riverine position. And further south, Este designs were directed on Bologna: such designs, and the responding Bolognese fears, formed part of the prelude to war between Bologna and Ferrara in the late thirteenth century.[61] These ambitions in fact continued throughout the fourteenth and fifteenth centuries. In 1360–1 there were detailed negotiations between the papal legate and the marquis Aldrovandino about the possible grant of Bologna in vicariate and rumours of this revived in the 1370s.[62] In 1389 Alberto d'Este, one of his officials and a number of his Bolognese vassals were under suspicion in Bologna of conspiring against the regime and pro-Este plots, originating in the Este faction, continued in the fifteenth century.[63]

Territorial expansiveness to the west and south was, however, offset by losses to the north. From early in the thirteenth century there had been Paduan pressure on the Este lands in the Padovano and on the Polesine. As the Este became more detached from Paduan society, so Paduan tolerance of Este military and landed power in the

[60] B. Cessi, *Venezia e Padova e il Polesine di Rovigo* (Città di Castello, 1904), pp. 20–1; Trombetti, 'Beni estensi', p. 147, n. 22; J. K. Hyde, 'Lendinara, Vangadizza e le relazioni fra gli Estensi e il comune di Padova', *Bollettino del Museo Civico di Padova*, 52 (1963).

[61] A. Gorreta, *La lotta fra il comune bolognese e la signoria estense (1293–1303)* (Bologna, 1906), pp. 27–8; V. Vitale, *Il dominio della parte guelfa in Bologna (1280–1327)* (Bologna, 1902), pp. 66–7, 80–101; M. T. Ferrer i Mallal, 'Mercenaris catalans a Ferrara (1307–1317)', *Anuario de estudios medievales*, 2 (1965), 157–8.

[62] F. Filippini, *Il Cardinale Egidio Albornoz* (Bologna, 1933), pp. 255–6; Frizzi, *Memorie*, vol. 3, p. 355; G. Tiraboschi, *Storia dell'augusta badia di Nonantola*, vol. 1 (Modena, 1785), p. 162.

[63] A. Palmieri, 'La congiura per sottomettere Bologna al conte di Virtu', *AMRo*, s. 4, 6 (1916), 210–12; G. Gozzadini, *Nanne Gozzadini e Baldassare Cossa poi Giovanni XXIII* (Bologna, 1880), pp. 460–4; B. della Pugliola, *Historia miscella bononiensis, RIS*, 18, 586; M. Griffoni, *Memoriale historicum de rebus bononiensium, RIS²*, vol. 18, pt. 2, p. 94; M. Sanudo, *Vite de' duche di Venezia, RIS*, 22, 882–3; *Gli atti cancellereschi viscontei*, ed. G. Vittani, vol. 2 (Milan, 1929), p. 595; F. Forti, 'Bologna e Ferrara nel 1465 in un dialogo di Ludovico Carbone', *AMRo*, 22 (1971), 68.

*contado* diminished. In the 1290s, an inheritance dispute among the Este enabled Padua to extract major territorial concessions from one of the marquises, to defeat Este defending forces and to dismantle a number of Este castles.[64]

This was the beginning of a troubled period for the Este and the early years of the fourteenth century were the nadir of their fortunes in the later Middle Ages. War with Bologna in the last years of the thirteenth century was followed by the loss of Modena and Reggio in 1306 and a serious succession dispute following the death of Azzo VIII in 1308.[65] Azzo's attempt to transfer his lands and lordships to his grandson, Folco, provoked a rebellion from Azzo's brothers, who turned for support to Padua and the Papacy. Hard-pressed by this alliance, Folco negotiated the cession of Ferrara to Venice, whose intervention brought it into direct conflict with the Papacy, eager to establish its own control of Ferrara. The Venetians, having established a military presence in Ferrara, were unable to break the papal siege and finally surrendered (1310). The Papacy then enforced its direct rule of the city and, with the return of the Torelli and their supporters (the Ramberti and Menabuoi), there were considerable disorders. Francesco d'Este was killed, his brother Aldrovandino was arrested and Este property was seized (1312). A pro-Este revolt in 1317 eventually restored to power the sons of Francesco and Aldrovandino d'Este (as we shall see, below, p. 53).

It took some years, however, before the Este won acceptance of their position in Ferrara from the Papacy, which was now more active in defence of its rights in the region. For Ferrara was indisputably part of the Papal State, although the Papacy had been slow to assert its claims in an area so far from Rome. For much of the later Middle Ages the Popes did little to challenge the power of the Este in Ferrara, but the early decades of the fourteenth century saw a series of aggressive campaigns to make papal lordship effective: the successful recovery of Ferrara from Venice, the prosecution of the re-established Estensi as heretics (1321) and a direct attack on Ferrara by the papal legate in 1333.[66] During the 1320s, however, aggressive

---

[64] Trombetti, 'Beni estensi', pp. 177–80.
[65] Gorreta, *La lotta*; G. Soranzo, *La guerra fra Venezia e la Santa Sede per il dominio di Ferrara* (Città di Castello, 1905); Gaudenzi, 'Testamento'; Ferrer i Mallal, 'Mercenaris', pp. 175–95.
[66] F. Bock, 'Der Este-Prozess von 1321', *Archivum fratrum praedicatorum*, 7 (1937); N. Housley, *The Italian Crusades*, (Oxford, 1982), pp. 24–9; L. Ciaccio, 'Il Cardinal legato Bertrando del Poggetto in Bologna (1327–1334)', *AMRo*, s. 3, 23 (1904–5), 471–81.

moves were accompanied by negotiation, which resulted in 1329 in the grant to the marquises of a papal vicariate of Ferrara for ten years.[67] The price was high for the Este: a single payment of 30,000 florins, an annual *census* of 10,000 florins, military service at the Pope's request and the surrender of Argenta to the Archbishop of Ravenna. As we shall see, the Este baulked at this last condition, but for the rest of the fourteenth century the *census* was fully (if irregularly) paid and the military service performed. The vicariate was granted first for periods of years and only later for life, but with it the Este secured the sort of legitimation of their rule from the superior lord which other *signori* were likewise obtaining from the Emperor.

From the 1320s, Este power recovered under the able leadership of Rinaldo and Obizzo III d'Este. In 1325 they finally secured the town of Comacchio, near the coast, which they had disputed with the Polenta lords of Ravenna. Comacchio was important for the natural resources (fish and salt) of its *valli*: farms of these became the largest single source of Este revenue.[68] Este efforts to recover Modena resumed in 1332 and were eventually successful in 1336. Following this, the marquises went on to retake Argenta and San Felice, a small town on the river Panaro (1346). Indicative of the scale of Este ambitions was their acquisition of the lordship of Parma in 1344 with the support of a number of its noble families. But Parma proved untenable in the face of opposition from the Gonzaga, lords of Mantua and Reggio, and the Visconti, ever eager to expand their Lombard lordship into Emilia.

On the death of Obizzo III in 1352, his son Aldrovandino was proclaimed *signore*, but was immediately opposed by Francesco di Bertoldo d'Este. His revolt triggered a reaction among the Ferrarese nobility against the power at court of some of the marquis' advisers. As in previous family disputes, it was difficult to prevent the intervention of other, hostile lords looking to expand their territory at Este expense. Francesco secured assistance at first from other *signori* (the Malatesta, Gonzaga, Carrara) and more lastingly from the Visconti, in whose service he remained in the following decades. The Carrara, lords of Padua, like the Paduan commune before them,

---

[67] ASM, Camera Ducale, Catastri delle Investiture, Catastro A, *passim*; Theiner, *Codex*, vol. 1, pp. 562–6; G. de Vergottini, 'Di un vicariato imperiale degli Estensi a Ferrara sotto Ludovico IV', *RSDI*, 11 (1938); P. Partner, *The Papal State under Martin V* (London, 1958), pp. 186–92.

[68] L. Bellini, 'La legislazione speciale delle valli di Comacchio', *AMF*, s. 3, 1 (1965); L. Chiappini, *Gli Estensi* (Varese, 1967), pp. 333–6; and see below.

were quick to exploit divisions among the Estensi to advance their own territorial designs – in the peace settlement that ended Francesco's rebellion in 1354, Aldrovandino d'Este was obliged to cede to the Carrara the castle of Vighizzolo in the Padovano.[69]

The period from the mid-1350s saw a succession of wars in northern Italy, in which the struggle between the Este and the Visconti for the cities and territories of central Emilia played an important part. The general pattern of these wars was of an alliance of the Este, the papal legate of Bologna, other *signori* (the Gonzaga, Malatesta and Carrara) and various members of the local nobilities of central Emilia (for example, the Boiardi and Fogliani) contesting control of this area with the Visconti and their local supporters, who included the Pio, Pico and Correggio families. Short wars in 1362–3, 1368 and 1370 were followed in the early 1370s by major political changes which increased the Visconti threat to Este and papal positions. In 1371 Niccolo II d'Este (who had succeeded Aldrovandino in 1361) took Reggio from its lord Feltrino Gonzaga, but immediately lost it to Bernabò Visconti.[70] With Reggio held directly by the Visconti from then until 1402, the pressure increased both on Este supporters in the Reggiano and on Modena. The Sassuolo, Fogliani and Pio became active Visconti supporters and although peace was restored in 1374, the succession dispute which opened up on the death of Alberto d'Este in 1393 brought a fresh wave of rebellions in the Modenese, with the suspicion of Visconti interference.

But from the mid-1370s, the Este began to reap the reward for their long and close alliance with the Papacy. In 1376 the Archbishop of Ravenna had ceded them Lugo in the Romagna and in the following year the papal legate sold the Romagnol city of Faenza to Niccolo II d'Este (though he failed to hold it against its local lords, the Manfredi). These acquisitions began a long (but chequered) period of Este penetration of the Romagna and by 1450 they had control of Lugo, Conselice, Bagnacavallo, Massalombarda and Fusignano.[71] Internally, however, the 1380s were not an easy period for the Este: a serious tax revolt broke out in Ferrara in 1385, damaging Este confidence in their power there[72] and this was

[69] B. Cessi, 'Un trattato fra Carraresi ed Estensi', *NAV*, 7 (1904).
[70] N. Grimaldi, *La signoria di Barnabo Visconti e di Regina della Scala in Reggio 1371–85* (Reggio, 1921), pp. 1–76.
[71] A. Vasina, 'La Romagna estense', *SR*, 21 (1970).
[72] J. E. Law, 'Popular unrest in Ferrara in 1385', in *The Renaissance in Ferrara and its European Horizons*, ed. J. Salmons and W. Moretti (Cardiff and Ravenna, 1985).

followed in 1388 by yet another family conspiracy, against Niccolo II's successor, Alberto d'Este. Alberto's short reign (1388–93) was marked by a diplomatic volte-face in his alliance with the Visconti, which brought its reward in the brief recovery of Este itself in 1389, a town the marquises had lost to Padua in the preceding century. Despite his alliance with the Visconti, Alberto did not lose the friendship of the Pope: indeed, during his pilgrimage to Rome in 1391 he obtained two important favours from Pope Boniface IX – the establishment of a university in Ferrara and the relaxation of control of Ferrarese churches over their lay tenants (see below, pp. 44–5).

In the first century and a half of Este rule in Ferrara, two themes stand out as relevant to the argument of this book. First comes the establishment of political control in Ferrara itself. This was achieved by the 1320s: the marquises survived early dissensions and revolts among the Ferrarese nobility and rapidly recovered from their expulsion between 1310 and 1317. Already from the late thirteenth century, the major threat to the stability of their lordship came from quarrels within the Este family (as we shall see) and not from internal noble opposition. Ferrara was quickly, within two generations, turned into an Este stronghold. In looking for the explanations of this, it is the argument of this book that Este landed power and their use of fiefs and feudo-vassalic bonds were of crucial importance. The second theme of interest is the scale and direction of Este ambitions following their securing of Ferrara. Doubtless there was much opportunism in their shift away from the *Marca Trevigiana* and from their established connections and reputation there, but the aggressive confidence they displayed in their designs on the towns and cities of Emilia and Romagna is indicative of their material resources, powers of command and skills of leadership. But why were the Este attractive to the local nobilities of Emilia and Romagna? In answer to this question, it will be suggested that the Este consciously maintained a network of friendships and alliances centred on their court in Ferrara and based at least in part on the enfeoffment of land to those useful to their territorial ambitions.

## FROM SIGNORIA TO PRINCIPALITY

The second half of the fourteenth century saw a number of developments in Este government of Ferrara, which together marked the beginnings of a transition from *signoria* to principality. The common feature of these developments was the identification of government with the person of the lord and with his officials. The setting-up of a university in Ferrara in 1391 has already been mentioned (though it was many years before it was properly constituted and financed). Indicative also of the lord's concern for the welfare of his subjects was the delegation to his council in 1418 of special jurisdiction in legal cases involving widows and children.[73] More graphic were the changes in the Ferrarese coinage: the replacement of the old *ferrarini* by *marchesini* in 1381 and the appearance on coins of images of the Este lords in the mid-fifteenth century.[74]

Pointing in the same direction was the growth of central administrative offices: the camera (chamber, for finance) and the chancery (for letters and decrees).[75] The camera was at first combined with the chancery, in business and personnel, but slowly separated from it and took over some of the financial business of the Ferrarese commune. Detailed analysis of this process is presented in chapter 2. Of the two offices, the chancery was the more dependent on the marquis, its director (the *referendario*, later *secretario*) following the marquis in his more or less continuous movements around the *contado*. The chancery was staffed by a number of notaries, who were employed also as representatives of the marquises in a wide variety of political and diplomatic business. The camera, directed by two *fattori generali*, had secondary offices in the major centres of the state (at Modena, Reggio, Este, San Felice, Rovigo, Finale and Lendinara).

In the major cities under Este rule, the governing council (the *regimen*) consisted of three officials: the *podestà*, the military captain and the cameral official (*massaro*). These shared the government of the city with the local commune (represented by a small council of *savi* or *anziani*). At Ferrara, because of the presence of the marquis and of the central officers, the structure was more complex. Military and financial affairs were dealt with directly by the central officers. The communal council of twelve *savi* was headed by a president (*Giudice dei Savi*) appointed by the Este. In addition to the *podestà*,

---

73 ACF, Deliberazioni, Libro C, fol. 20 and see my forthcoming paper 'Sovereignty and paternalism in Ferrara'.
74 V. Bellini, *Delle monete di Ferrara* (Ferrara, 1761), pp. 97–9, 108, 118, 123.
75 F. Valenti, 'Note storiche sulla cancelleria degli Estensi a Ferrara dalle origini alla metà del secolo XVI', *Bollettino dell'Archivio Paleografico Italiano*, n.s., 2–3 (1956–7); P. di Pietro, 'La cancelleria degli Estensi nel periodo ferrarese', *AMMo*, s. 10, 10 (1975).

judicial matters were also dealt with by judges attached to the Este court (*judices curie*). In Ferrara at least, the role of the local commune was largely confined to the maintenance of fortifications, roads and dykes, the regulation of food supply and the assessment and administration of direct taxation.[76] In the minor centres, for example Adria or Lendinara, the *podestà* (or *visconte*) combined military and judicial offices. The rest of the Ferrarese countryside was divided into a number of *podesterie*, whose incumbents had very limited civil and criminal jurisdiction. The major cases were reserved to city officials. In the Modenese and Reggiano the right to appoint the local *podestà* was often held by the local noble family (invested with *merum et mixtum imperium*), but in the Ferrarese there is little evidence of such private jurisdiction.

The period from the 1360s also saw the development of the lord's council in Ferrara. It is in that decade that the term 'counsellor' began to be applied to the marquis' political advisers and judicial and financial officials.[77] A formal council, however, did not appear until the 1390s, in the form of a regency council for Alberto d'Este's infant son, Niccolo III. This council consisted of four permanent members from Alberto's entourage and six members 'on behalf of the commune and people' who were changed every two months. Although the communal representatives soon ceased to be appointed and the permanent membership was changed, the formal council lasted until Niccolo's majority. It seems that informal use of the term 'counsellor' then revived, at least until 1418 when a formal council was reconstituted, with a fixed membership of officials and major political figures, and with delegated jurisdiction as well as frequent *ad hoc* commissions.[78]

### THE COURSE OF EVENTS 1393–1450

The first fifteen years of Niccolo III's reign (1393–1441) were seriously disturbed by wars and revolts. His succession was immediately challenged by Azzo, son of the exiled Francesco (above, p. 19), who seems to have drawn considerable support from nobles and others close to the court. There were numerous executions in

[76] ACF, Deliberazioni, *passim*.
[77] F. Valenti, 'I consigli di governo presso gli Estensi dalle origini alla devoluzione di Ferrara', in *Studi in onore di R. Filangieri* (Naples, 1959), who underrates the activity of the council in the 1420s.
[78] ASM, Leggi e Decreti, B IV, fol. 114.

Ferrara, while in the Modenese Azzo d'Este was supported by members of the local nobility (Francesco da Sassuolo, Atto da Roteglia and Giordano da Savignano). Niccolo retained, however, the loyalty of the Pio, Boiardi and Roberti, received military aid from most of the cities of northern Italy and finally defeated and captured Azzo in 1395. Azzo did not, however, entirely disappear from the scene: he was held in custody, first by Astorgio Manfredi, lord of Faenza, and then by Venice and was used as a puppet leader when Venice attacked Ferrara in 1405. Nor was the problem of the Modenese rebels settled: Francesco da Sassuolo and Atto da Roteglia continued in revolt, becoming adherents of Ottobuono Terzi in his brief period as lord of Reggio. In 1404, Venice saw the value of negotiating with various Modenese nobles in order to weaken Niccolo's position.[79]

Partly interlocking with Azzo's challenge were disturbances in the Frignano, the southernmost part of the Modenese. These had started in the 1380s with an inheritance dispute within the Montecuccoli family and continued intermittently into the early fifteenth century.[80] Este control of this remote region was not strong, as we shall see (chapter 6) and rested on the two major families, Montegarullo and Montecuccolo. The most troublesome of these was Obizzo da Montegarullo, against whom Niccolo could, in the 1390s, do little: his frequent rebellions, covered by Florentine protection, were not effectively dealt with and his power was, on the contrary, confirmed and increased. In 1398 he was appointed governor of the *podesteria* of Sestola, the only directly-controlled Este base in the region. However, a successful campaign against him in 1406 captured all but three of his castles, and those three he was forced to surrender in 1408. Montecuccoli power was also reduced in the early decades of the fifteenth century, but with the disappearance of the Montegarullo, they remained the most powerful family of the region.

Territorially, these early years of Niccolo's reign saw considerable reversals of the gains of the previous decades: Nonantola and Bazzano (castles on the Modenese border with Bologna) were ceded to Bologna; Cotignola and Bagnacavallo in the Romagna were made

[79] ASVe, Senato, Secreta, reg. 2, fol. 54. For Niccolo III's early years: Cessi, *Venezia e Padova*, pp. 51ff; A. Manni, *L'età minore di Nicolo d'Este marchese di Ferrara (1393–1402)*, (Reggio, 1910).

[80] G. Tiraboschi, *Memorie storiche modenesi* (3 vols., Modena, 1793–5), vol. 3, pp. 157–77; C. Campori, *Notizie storiche del Frignano* (Modena, 1886), pp. 40–60.

over to the lords of Ravenna; the Polesine di Rovigo was mortgaged to Venice and the village of Mellara in the Ferrarese to the Gonzaga; the revenues of Migliaro, also in the Ferrarese, were assigned to Astorgio Manfredi (to cover the costs of his custody of Azzo d'Este). But from 1402, with his majority, Niccolo began to play a more active and aggressive role and to repair much of the damage. The combination of Niccolo's restless powers of leadership and the military skills of his right-hand man, Uguccione Contrari, was soon making its mark on north Italian politics. As Venice commented, 'the marquis is young and, as appears from his actions, highly desirous to see and do something new every day', while he also 'does nothing but what Uguccione wishes'.[81] Already in 1402, Venice was trying to restrain Niccolo's appetite for acquisitive ventures directed at Reggio and Parma, but in 1404 Uguccione Contrari managed temporarily to occupy Reggio, with the aid of Niccolo Roberti and Gerardo Boiardi, and in 1405 Uguccione was seeking Venetian sponsorship for an attack on Piacenza.[82] From the papal legate, Baldassare Cossa, Niccolo received promises of the return of Nonantola and Bazzano and of aid to mount the conquest of Reggio and Parma. But Cossa was 'liberal in making promises, meagre in keeping them' (Delayto) and when in 1404 Niccolo joined Francesco da Carrara in his defence of Padua against Venetian attack, Cossa entered negotiations with Venice aimed at toppling Niccolo. In the war that followed, Niccolo reoccupied the Polesine, but was forced to a settlement by Venice in 1405 which not only restored the lands he had occupied, but also entailed concessions to Venetian economic interests. More successful was Niccolo's campaign from 1407 against Ottobuono Terzi, who had become lord of Reggio and Parma in the disintegration of Visconti territories after the death of Giangaleazzo Visconti in 1402. Backed by a general alliance against the Terzi and supported by some powerful Parma nobles (the Rossi, San Vitali, Rolando Pallavicino), Niccolo had Ottobuono assassinated at a 'peace-meeting' near Rubiera in 1409 and rapidly conquered Reggio and Parma.[83] This campaign also had the effect of reinforcing the Este *signoria* in central Emilia: Niccolo took the opportunity

[81] ASVe, Senato, Secreta, reg. 1, fol. 30v (8 Nov. 1401); reg. 2, fol. 68v (29 Oct. 1404).
[82] Ibid., reg. 1, fol. 74; reg. 2, fol. 161.
[83] A. Pezzana, *Storia della città di Parma*, vol. 2 (Parma, 1842), pp. 91–134; A. Manni, 'Terzi ed Estensi 1402–21', *AMF*, 25 (1925). For the later notoriety of this episode: Aeneas Sylvius Piccolomineus, *De viris illustribus*, (Stuttgart, 1842), p. 15; Ludovico Ariosto, *Orlando furioso*, iii, 43.

to seize the castles of the Fogliani and Montegarullo and this demonstration of military power persuaded many of the nobles of the Modenese and Reggiano to reaffirm their loyalty to the marquis.

The period from 1393 to 1409 thus saw great difficulties skilfully overcome. Financially, the mortgaging of the Polesine was only the start of Niccolo's huge indebtedness to Venice, which had reached by 1407 the sum of 116,000 ducats (on Venetian calculation), but Venice had great difficulty in securing even partial repayment.[84] Territorially, the disintegration of Este lordship, especially in the Modenese, was effectively countered, although Venice retained the Polesine until 1438 and Niccolo was forced to surrender Parma to Filippo Maria Visconti in 1421. Nevertheless, the territorial assemblage of Ferrara, Adria, Comacchio, Modena and Reggio, with points of expansion in the Romagna and Garfagnana, was that which the Este lordship retained into the sixteenth century. Politically, Niccolo had first been drawn towards Milan, but the Pope had warned him that he would appoint a different vicar in Ferrara unless Niccolo joined the papal-Florentine alliance; he was then threatened by Venice and torn between Venice and Padua, being forced to witness the destruction of his father-in-law, Francesco da Carrara; and had finally survived Cossa's attempt to partition Este territories with Venice.

The remaining years of Niccolo's reign were not marked by events as threatening as these. Despite their earlier conflict, his relations with Cossa were good after Cossa's election as Pope (John XXIII): Uguccione Contrari became papal captain-general; Niccolo secured the appointment of his candidate to the important Archbishopric of Ravenna and the grant of palatine counties for a number of Ferrarese nobles (see below, chapter 5). In the 1420s and 1430s, Niccolo promoted himself as an arbiter and peacemaker in conflicts among the Italian states and he assumed, with age, the role of elder statesman in Italian diplomacy. He was host (briefly) to the Church Council of 1438 attended by the Greek Emperor and Patriarchs, before it moved to Florence. Territorially, the loss of Parma was offset by the recovery of the Polesine from Venice in 1438, the military occupation of lands in the Garfagnana in the 1420s and the purchase of Bagnacavallo and Massalombarda in the Romagna.[85]

[84] ASVe, Senato, Secreta, reg. 1, fols. 106–10, 114, 119; reg. 3, fols. 77v–8; reg. 4, fols. 73–v, 81v.
[85] D. Pacchi, *Ricerche istoriche sulla provincia della Garfagnana* (Modena, 1785); C. de Stefani, 'Storia dei comuni di Garfagnana', *AMMo*, s. 7, 2 (1923).

Niccolo is best remembered for his many mistresses and illegitimate offspring and for his brutal reaction to the adultery of his third wife, Parisina Malatesta, with his bastard son, Ugo. Niccolo was recorded by Pope Pius II as 'fat, jocund and given up to pleasure' and has been likened by one historian to the sixteenth-century king of England, Henry VIII.[86] He genuinely seems to fit the image of the *signore* in contemporary *novelle*: capricious, strong-willed and quick to anger, yet generous and open to counsel.[87]

Niccolo died in 1441 and was succeeded by his eldest son, Leonello, who was to rule until his sudden death in 1450. Leonello had in fact had charge of internal administration since the early 1430s and his more active, paternalistic style of government was already displayed in those years. After 1441, he completed Niccolo's foundation of the church of S. Maria degli Angeli (di Belfiore), stimulated the reorganisation and revival of the university, sponsored the building and endowment of the hospital of S. Anna and issued sumptuary legislation. In external affairs, he continued Niccolo's policies of close alliance with Milan, combined with intervention as mediator and negotiator. Leonello, whom Eugenius IV apparently thought would make a good priest, has been most renowned for his erudition and his classical tastes in literature and the decorative arts.[88]

The reigns of Niccolo III and Leonello saw in the Este 'state', as elsewhere in Italy, the achievement of greater territorial and political stability. With the papal vicariate now extended to life terms, with a developing bureaucracy and with increasing control over outlying areas (for example, the Frignano), the marquis' collection of lands and lordships began to take on its enduring shape.[89] But, in the construction of this 'Renaissance principality', as earlier in the construction of the *signoria* at Ferrara, success depended in large part on the accumulation and distribution of land and on the manipulation by these means of the internal power structure of areas slowly brought under Este control. The lordships of Modena and Reggio rested on the support and cooperation of the local nobility and in ensuring that support, it is argued here, fiefs and feudal (or semi-feudal) bonds were of great importance.

---

[86] Aeneas Sylvius, *De viris illustribus*, p. 15; Gundersheimer, *Ferrara*, p. 90.
[87] F. Sacchetti, *Il Trecentonovelle; Facezie di Lodovico Carbone*, ed. A. Salza (Livorno, 1900), nos. 8, 12, 68, 88, 98.
[88] Ibid., p. 18; Gundersheimer, *Ferrara*, pp. 92–126.
[89] Chittolini, *La formazione*, pp. vii–xv.

*Chapter 2*

# THE ESTE PATRIMONY

'It is as landowners that they first appear and landowners they all remained.'[1] This, written of the Malatesta of Rimini, could be applied to most of the *signori* of late medieval Italy. Indeed, so far were the *signori* identified with the land and landed society, that it is possible to speak of their rise as the victory of the countryside over the city.[2] Yet the landed resources of these families have not attracted much scholarly attention, largely because *signorie* have continued to be considered primarily as urban lordships. However, the recent trends in Italian medieval historiography examined above, in conducting a re-evaluation of the relationship between town and country, have pointed the way towards analysis of this dimension of urban *signorie*.

Tracing the origin of Este possessions in the Ferrarese *contado* and the Polesine would take us back to the tenth century, but we need go back no further than the late twelfth, when Este political involvement in Ferrara intensified following their succession to the Adelardi as landowners and leaders of faction.[3] The story of this major acquisition has been frequently told: the death of the Adelardi brothers, Guglielmo and Adelardo, without male heirs; the seizure of Adelardo's young daughter from her appointed husband; her delivery and possible marriage to Obizzo d'Este and his resulting entry into possession of the inheritance.[4] Despite the dubious legality of these proceedings, Obizzo was able to persuade Ferrarese ecclesiastical lords to invest him with Adelardi property, while the

[1] P. J. Jones, *The Malatesta of Rimini and the Papal State* (Cambridge, 1974), p. 290 (amended).
[2] Jones, 'Mito', p. 112; Bordone, 'Tema cittadino', p. 263.
[3] Zorzi, *Territorio padovano*, pp. 165ff; Alessi, *Ricerche*, vol. 1, pp. 447–9; Castagnetti, *Organizzazione*, p. 134; Castagnetti, 'Enti', pp. 403–9.
[4] *Chron. Parva*, 481; Muratori, *Antichità*, vol. 1, pp. 354–5; and most recently see G. Zanella, *Riccobaldo e dintorni* (Ferrara, 1980), p. 66–73, with full bibliography.

other heirs stood aside. Although the size of this inheritance is not known, it was clearly spread over a wide area and the Adelardi, as one of the chief noble families of the city, had an important following of vassals and clients. That the Este held on to much of this heritage is improbable: it was later claimed that they had distributed most of it as fiefs among their supporters and this would explain their alleged wealth of support, but lack of money, in the city in the early thirteenth century.[5]

In the period between the succession to the Adelardi and the establishment of the Este *signoria* after 1240, we largely lose sight of Este landholdings, but the fact that, once constituted, the Este *signoria* appears as a feudal regime forces us to recognise the primary importance of land. For the two centuries following 1240, it will be seen how Este property was expanded by two means (often overlapping): acquisitions from the Church and the absorption of the lands of defeated opponents and 'rebels'. Much of this was transferred by the Este to their nobles and subjects and the continuing distribution of land to reward support and service will be analysed. The Este also, however, retained significant blocks of land for themselves and it will be shown how the management of this private patrimony merged with their direction of public affairs as an Este 'state' was constructed.

## CHURCH LANDS

Rulers helping themselves to Church property is a recurrent feature of medieval government.[6] That the Italian *signori* were hugely fortified by resources plundered from the Church has been frequently noted,[7] but less often systematically examined. For some *signori*, from the powerful Visconti in Milan to the humbler Casali in Cortona, control of the local bishopric was turned to vital political

---

[5] ASM, Manoscritti della biblioteca, 136, Pellegrino Prisciani, Collectanea, ii, fol. 3v; Muratori, *Antiquitates*, vol. 3, 159–60; *Chron. Parva*, 481.

[6] F. L. Ganshof, *The Carolingians and the Frankish Monarchy* (London, 1971), pp. 95, 219; H. Fichtenau, *The Carolingian Empire* (Oxford, 1957), pp. 132–3; K. Leyser, 'The German aristocracy from the ninth to the early twelfth century', *Past and Present*, 41 (1968), 47–8; B. Arnold, *German Knighthood 1050–1300* (Oxford, 1985), p. 150.

[7] Jones, 'Mito', p. 116; C. M. Cipolla, 'Une crise ignorée. Comment s'est perdue la propriété ecclésiastique dans l'Italie du nord entre le xie et le xve siècle', *Annales*, 2 (1947); A. Vasina, 'L'abbazia di Pomposa nel duecento', *Analecta Pomposiana*, 1 (1965), 180.

importance.[8] Others invaded cathedral chapters with their kinsmen and friends[9] or obliged bishops and abbots to grant them and their supporters fiefs, often on favourable terms.[10] Kinsmen were appointed to key monasteries and churches' military resources and judicial powers were commandeered.[11] Violence was applied to both churchmen and church property, while ecclesiastical vassals were propelled into dependence on *signori*.[12] The institution of aristocratic advocates, intended to protect churches from oppression, was often turned into an instrument of oppression itself. The advocate's duties of ceremonially installing the new prelate in his benefice and of supervising the administration of church property and church jurisdiction, could take on more the character of ownership of the church.[13] The cumulative results could be overwhelming. In 1406, for example, the new Venetian rulers of Verona found ecclesiastical property 'in tatters' after decades of signorial exploitation.[14] But it was not, of course, only under *signori* that the opportunities for secular profit offered by the Church were seized upon.[15]

Many of the forms of exploitation described above were used in Ferrara, as we shall see, where the Este were perhaps assisted by the rather crowded ecclesiastical presence in the areas under their control (see Map 2). The diocesan map did not coincide with political boundaries. The Archbishopric of Ravenna retained, from an earlier

---

[8] *Storia di Milano* (16 vols., Milan, 1955), vol. 5, pp. 104, 225, 292; F. Cardini, 'Una signoria cittadina "minore" in Toscana: i Casali di Cortona', *ASI*, 131 (1973).

[9] S. Collodo, 'Per la storia della signoria carrarese: lo sfruttamento dei benefici canonicali di Padova nel XIV secolo', *Passatopresente*, 1 (1981), 97–109. Niccolo II d'Este's wife, Verde della Scala, made compensation in her will for two clerics denied canonries at Ferrara by her intervention in favour of others: ASVe, Procuratori di S. Marco, Commissarie miste, 98A.

[10] G. M. Varanini, 'Un esempio di ristrutturazione agraria quattrocentesca nella bassa veronese: il monastero di S. Maria in Organo e le terre di Roncanova', *Studi Storici Veronesi*, 30–1 (1980–1), 41–2; G. B. Picotti, *I Caminesi e la loro signoria in Treviso dal 1283 al 1312* (Livorno, 1905), p. 63; G. Galli, 'La dominazione viscontea a Verona (1387–1404)', *ASL*, 54 (1927), 490–1, 496.

[11] Collodo, 'Signoria carrarese'; F. S. Dondi Orologio, *Dissertazioni sopra l'istoria ecclesiastica di Padova* (9 vols, Padua, 1802–17), vol. 8, pp. 136–8; Cherubini, *Comunità*, pp. 135–8.

[12] Dondi Orologio, *Dissertazioni*, vol. 8, p. 64, doc. 70; Cherubini, *Comunità*, pp. 135–8; *cf.* Arnold, *German Knighthood*, pp. 150, 228–34.

[13] For the duties of advocates: Dondi Orologio, *Dissertazioni*, vol. 8, doc. 6, pp. 14–15; *cf.* Arnold, *German Knighthood*, pp. 159–60.

[14] A. Stella, 'La proprietà ecclesiastica nella Repubblicca di Venezia dal secolo XV al XVII', *NRS*, 42 (1958), 54.

[15] Tangheroni, *Politica, commercio, agricoltura*, pp. 164–7; R. Bizzocchi, 'Chiesa e aristocrazia nella Firenze del Quattrocento', *ASI*, 142 (1984).

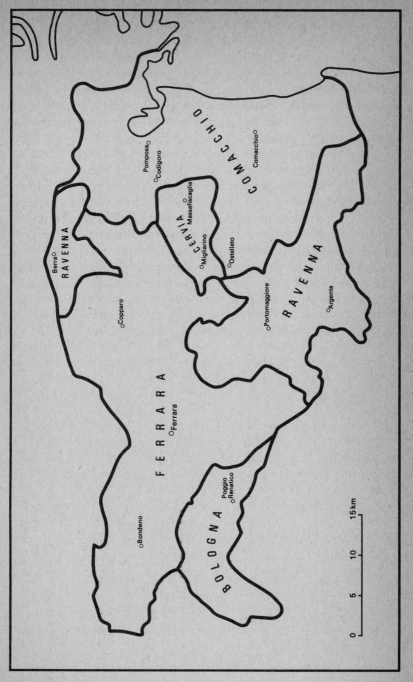

Map 2 Diocesan boundaries (based on Bellini, 'Comacchio', tav. III)

preponderance, the large parish of Portomaggiore and a strip along the Po from Cologna to the Po di Goro at Ariano; while the area around Migliarino and Massafiscaglia formed part of the bishopric of Cervia. Beyond these, to the East, the area from Ostellato and Comacchio to Ariano and Mesola and from there northwards into the Polesine was subject to the bishops of Comacchio and Adria and to the abbot of Pomposa. This left to the bishop of Ferrara a broad strip south of the Po from Bondeno to Copparo and Formignana (and the marshes beyond) and a block immediately south of the city towards the Po di Primaro. In addition to the religious houses in Ferrara itself, the region also included two major rural abbeys: the Camaldolese community at Vangadizza (at Badia Polesine) and the Benedictine house at Pomposa, both ancient and wealthy founda-tions. All these institutions, as well as more distant churches in Venice and Ravenna, owned properties both urban and rural, that were vulnerable to secular invasion.[16]

Of the two major abbeys, that of Vangadizza had had connections with the Estensi from early in its history (their benefactions are recorded from the eleventh century) and in the thirteenth century some of the family were buried there.[17] Papal confirmations of the Abbey's property in the twelfth century reveal it to have been spread across the Este heartland in the southern Padovano and the Polesine di Rovigo, but especially along the Adige towards Rovigo (see map 3).[18] These lands were of some importance, controlling the zone where the Adigetto branched off from the Adige and the Abbey had both temporal jurisdiction and the right to levy river tolls.[19] Throughout the fourteenth and early fifteenth centuries, the abbey retained control of estates in a number of places in the Polesine, both around the small town of Badia itself (Salvaterra, Villafora, Francavilla), around Rovigo (Borsea, Costa, Mardimago, S. Apol-linare) and in the Padovano (Este, Masi) where it had two dependent priories (at Este and Monselice).[20] These estates remained of some size and value. Surveys of the abbey's holdings at Villa Valle in 1415 and 1420 give totals approaching 90 hectares (200 *campi*) and the

---

[16] For foreign churches with lands in the Ferrarese, see A. Samaritani, 'L'estimo del clero a Ferrara nel 1410', *AMF*, s. 3, 27 (1980).

[17] Bocchi, *Sede*, pp. 221–2.

[18] ASM, Archivi privati, Archivio d'Espagnac, b. 18, no. 68 and fol. 437; Bocchi, *Sede*, pp. 222–3; Alessi, *Ricerche*, vol. 1, pp. 573–4.

[19] Bocchi, *Sede*, p. 223; Trombetti, 'Beni Estensi', pp. 169–70.

[20] Archivio d'Espagnac, bb. 2 and 19 *passim*.

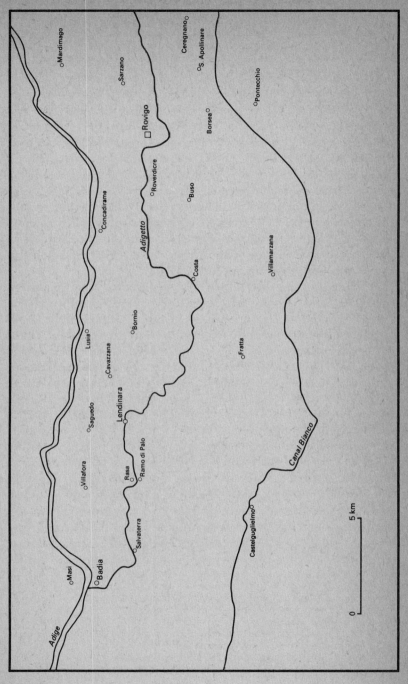

Map 3  The Polesine di Rovigo

Masi
Badia
Villafora
Saguedo
Lusia
Cavazzana
Lendinara
Rasa
Ramo di Palo
Salvaterra
Bornio
Concadirame
Mardimago
Sarzano
Rovigo
Roverdicre
Buso
Costa
Fratta
Villamarzana
Borsea
Ceregnano
S. Apollinare
Pontecchio
Castelguglielmo

Adige
Adigetto
Canal Bianco

0        5 km

abbey had over fifty tenants at Salvaterra.[21] Occasional leases of blocks of the abbey's property brought in large sums,[22] and the abbey had close financial dealings with the commune of Badia, which rented from it some tithes, woodland and a house for the *podestà*.[23] The abbey's estates and privileges were protected by agreements with the successive lords of the Polesine (Padua, the Este, Venice), who recognised the abbot's jurisdiction, possessions and tax immunities. This did not stop Vangadizza's privileges becoming a source of occasional dispute.[24]

However, by the late fourteenth century, much had already passed to the Estensi. In addition to fiefs held since the twelfth century, the abbot in 1216 granted a lease to Azzo d'Este of 100 *mansi* of land at Mardimago.[25] In 1270 the abbot accepted the protection of Obizzo II by appointing him advocate of the abbey, with the condition that the abbot was to make no alienations of land without Obizzo's consent.[26] Badia was included in an imperial investiture to Obizzo in 1286 and three years later the abbot surrendered his temporal jurisdiction as well.[27] Este control of the fortifications at Badia probably dates from these years and by 1400 the Este had the full range of civil and military officials there.[28] An early attempt to make the abbey subject to taxation by the commune of Rovigo failed under the weight of ecclesiastical reaction, but by the early fifteenth century a fixed tax (*terraticum*) had been imposed, though now paid to the camera in Ferrara.[29] Also, in 1289 the abbot made a division with the marquis of the *valli* at Pontecchio and Borsea, but the Estensi eventually took control of the abbot's share as well.[30] By the second half of the fifteenth century, the abbey looks very much on the defensive, seeking frequent arbitration of border disputes and

---

[21] Ibid., bb. 19 and 40; *cf.* C. Corrain, 'Alcuni registri di terratici ed affitti del Monastero della Vangadizza', *Atti e Memorie del Sodalizio Vangadiciense*, 1 (1972–3) for late-thirteenth-century registers.

[22] Archivio d'Espagnac, b. 2, no. 26 and b. 19, reg. 'No 4', fol. 53v.

[23] Ibid., b. 40, reg. 'B', fols. 54v–5v.

[24] Ibid., b. 18, fols. 473–4 and b. 25; Bocchi, *Sede*, p. 224; Trombetti, 'Beni Estensi', pp. 170–1.

[25] Muratori, *Antiquitates*, vol. 3, 161–2.

[26] Ibid., vol. 5, 287–90; Bocchi, *Sede*, p. 223.

[27] A. Nicolio, *Historia . . . dell'origine et antichità di Rovigo* (Brescia, 1584), p. 110. This jurisdiction was transferred to Padua from 1298 to 1318.

[28] Archivio d'Espagnac, b. 40, reg. 'B', fols. 10v–12.

[29] Under Venetian rule at the end of the fifteenth century, the abbey claimed that this payment had not been made since 1289, a claim belied by the abbey's own registers: ibid., bb. 25 and 40.

[30] Ibid., b. 25 (1289, 1464, 1468).

using violence in attempts to sequestrate the crops of tenants among the Ferrarese nobility who were refusing to pay their rents.[31]

The more important abbey of Pomposa, near the coast on the Po di Volano (see Map 4) preserved its lands and jurisdictions much longer. As it was removed from the immediate neighbourhood of Este possessions, Este pressure was applied only slowly, through infiltration, local alliances and underhand attempts to influence abbatial elections.[32] Imperial and papal diplomas of the twelfth and thirteenth centuries had confirmed to the abbey the *isola pomposiana*, along with Lagosanto, Ostellato, Massenzatica, the banks of the Po di Goro and the Po outlet at Volano, forming a block between Ferrara and the coast, to the north of the Valli di Comacchio.[33] Throughout the later Middle Ages, the abbot retained civil jurisdiction here and his right to appoint the *podestà* of the *isola* was several times recognised.[34] The *isola* itself was largely covered by woods and *valli*, but the abbey continued to control the settlements at Codigoro, Massenzatica, Lagosanto and Ostellato.[35] A renewal of leases at Codigoro in 1438, for example, revealed a total of perhaps 100 hectares (484 *tornature*) held of the abbey there.[36] A detailed picture of the abbey's possessions was drawn up in the 1490s prior to the division of the property.[37]

The process of Este encroachment on this compact ecclesiastical lordship began in the mid-twelfth century and was finally complete in the later fifteenth, with the transfer of the monks to Padua and of much of their lands, in bulk, to the Estensi. In 1196, while Azzo d'Este was *podestà* of Ferrara, a long dispute, spanning three generations, was finally settled between the abbot and the Estensi in the

---

[31] Ibid., b. 25.

[32] Ibid., b. 25; A. Ostoja, 'Vicende della commenda pomposiana in relazione al piano di assorbimento della signoria estense', *Analecta Pomposiana*, 1965, pp. 195–6; A. Samaritani, 'Statuta Pomposiae annis MCCXC et MCCCXXXVIII–LXXXIII', *AMF*, Serie Monumenti, 4 (1958), 13.

[33] ASM, Archivio Pomposa, b. 8 (1177, 1195, 1202, 1263); M. Zucchini, *L'agricoltura ferrarese attraverso i secoli* (Rome, 1967), pp. 34–5. The financially valuable *portus* at Volano was disputed between Pomposa and Ravenna until the latter recognised Pomposa's claim in 1388: Archivio Pomposa, b. 8.

[34] ASM, Archivio Pomposa, b. 3, no. N and b. 8; ASV, A. A. Arm., i–xviii, 4799; Samaritani, 'Statuta', pp. 11–12; M. Roberti, 'Pomposa', *Annuario della libera università di Ferrara*, 1905–6, pp. 22–3, 41.

[35] M. Zucchini, 'Pomposa e la bonifica ferrarese', *AMF*, n.s., 29 (1964), 435–6; G. Gurrieri, 'Notizie e problemi della storia economica di Pomposa nei sec. X–XIV', ibid., p. 150. In a financial account of 1338, half the abbey's revenue came from the forests.

[36] ASM, Archivio Pomposa, b. 8.         [37] See Appendix 5.

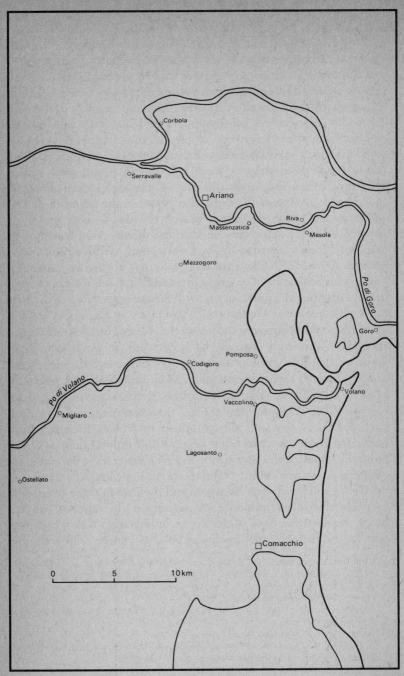

Map 4 Possessions of the Abbey of Pomposa

latters' favour. At issue had been lands in the Polesine, the former
fiefs of Guglielmo Adelardi and of another Ferrarese magnate,
Casotto, and bequests made to the abbey by Obizzo I's daughter. It
was indicative of rising Este power that Azzo should have secured
investiture of all this property in fief without fealty (*sine fidelitate*).[38]
There was further dispute between abbot and marquis in the early
thirteenth century over Lagosanto and evidence of Este penetration
of abbey lands at Gragnano, where we find the abbot trying to
dispossess men who claimed to be vassals of the marquis and who
had intruded themselves by force.[39] With Este power predominant
at Ferrara from mid-century, the pace of invasion quickened. In 1264
the woods at Mesola were divided between the abbot and Azzo
VII,[40] and in 1270 the abbot placed the whole *isola* under the
protection of the marquises. In 1290 the monks complained to the
Pope of secular interference in the election of the abbot and of
alienations made to the Estensi.[41] In 1293, apparently unable to
enforce his authority over Codigoro and Ostellato, the abbot granted the marquis the position of 'lord' (*dominus generalis*) of the *isola*,
with jurisdiction at Codigoro.[42] The value to the abbey of Este
protection was apparently shown by the collapse of Este authority in
the early fourteenth century: in 1317 a bull of Pope John XXII
recorded that many nobles and 'potentes' of the area had obstructed
abbey officials, forced the monks, 'by intimidation and threats' to
appoint an abbot of their choosing and, by the same means, forced
vassals of the abbey to obey them.[43] It was probably as a result of
such pressures that the abbey looked to Venice for protection,
obtaining Venetian citizenship in 1315 and immediately soliciting
from the Doge a letter of warning to Ferrara to respect the rights and
property of its new citizen.[44] But it was the Pope himself, arbitrating
another dispute between Pomposa and the Este in these years, who
awarded to Aldrovandino d'Este possession of a number of places
along the northern bank of the Po, including areas which commanded the important canal from Corbola to Venice.[45] In following

[38] Muratori, *Antiquitates*, vol. 4, 46, 71–2; Muratori, *Antichità*, vol. 1, pp. 368–9;
Alessi, *Ricerche*, vol. 1, pp. 634–5. On *feuda sine fidelitate*, see below p. 126.
[39] ASM, Archivio Pomposa, b. 8; Ostoja, 'Vicende', p. 196.
[40] Gurrieri, 'Storia economica', p. 157.
[41] Muratori, *Antichità*, vol. 2, pp. 30, 46–7; Ostoja, 'Vicende', pp. 199–200.
[42] Samaritani, 'Statuta', p. 12.
[43] ASM, Archivio Pomposa, b. 8 (1317).
[44] A. S. Minotto, *Documenta ad Ferrariam, Rhodigium, Policinium ac Marchiones Estenses
spectantia* (2 vols., Venice, 1873–4), vol. 2, pp. 50, 52.
[45] ASF, Archivio Tassoni, III/17, 18.

years Este usurpations, and abbatial complaints, continued.[46] The marquis' position as advocate of Pomposa remained of some importance in these years, being exercised, for example, in 1336, when Obizzo III ceremonially placed the abbot in possession of the abbey and the abbot acknowledged and confirmed Este 'protection'.[47] By the late fourteenth century, the marquis had control of some of the abbey's property at Ostellato (which had become subject to the Este *podestà* at Migliaro),[48] and early in the fifteenth century Niccolo III assumed control of all the abbey's property in four other localities.[49] At some stage the Este even imposed a tribute on the communes of the *isola*.[50]

The early fifteenth century saw the first major step towards direct control of the abbey: in 1405 Pandolfo Malatesta had been appointed its administrator and in 1407 he agreed with Niccolo d'Este to renounce his office (in return for the revenues of some other benefices) and to support Niccolo's nomination of a successor. Pandolfo also, it seems, surrendered control of the abbey revenues, for Niccolo immediately appointed an agent to collect them.[51] It is not clear how effective this agreement was, but in 1413 Niccolo obtained from the Pope, as part of the price of his entry into the Florentine-Papal league, a promise to grant Pomposa *in commendam* to Baldassare Sala, brother of one of Niccolo's favourites and already Niccolo's administrator of the church of S. Giorgio near Ferrara.[52] Baldassare was not a mere Este placeman: he was active in resuming usurped property, even when held by powerful men such as Uguccione Contrari,[53] but his appointment as a lay governor, closely associated with the court, was a major step towards complete control.[54] One of his successors as commendatory abbot was one of Niccolo's own sons, Rinaldo.

Pomposa was a model of the gradual collapse of ecclesiastical

---

[46] Gurrieri, 'Storia economica', pp. 158–9.
[47] ASM, Not. Cam., P. Fabro, fol. 29; *cf.* Francesco da Carrara's exercise of his advocacy of the bishopric of Padua in 1374: Dondi Orologio, *Dissertazioni*, vol. 8, doc. 124, p. 115.
[48] ASM, Not. Cam., M. Conte, fol. 127; Archivio Pomposa, b. 8.
[49] To secure repayment of the abbey's debts to the camera: ASM, Leggi e Decreti, B III, fol. 171.
[50] 161 cartloads of staves: ASM, Mandati, i, fol. 165v.
[51] ANF, R. Jacobelli, pacco 1, 12 Apr. 1407; Ostoja, 'Vicende', pp. 203–4, 211–14.
[52] ASM, Leggi e Decreti, B. III, fol. 188; S. Busmanti, *Pomposa*, (Imola, 1881), p. 13; Ostoja, 'Vicende', p. 207.
[53] ANF, U. Rossetti, 5 Mar. 1448; ASF, Archivio Tassoni, VII/39.
[54] Ostoja, 'Vicende', pp. 206, 208.

property; the only real problem is why it took so long. Part of the answer lies in the political history of the Este *signoria* in Ferrara: their expulsion in the early fourteenth century, their prosecution for heresy in the 1320s, the attack on Ferrara by the papal legate in 1333 and the political and financial crises of the late fourteenth century, all probably retarded their displacement of the abbot. Also, of course, their position as papal vicars obliged them to protect and defend church property and the chorus of ecclesiastical protest to the Pope, which showed exactly what sort of protection this was, cannot have gone unheard.[55] And finally, other families had their eyes on Pomposa too: in 1400 the Gozzadini, a powerful Bolognese family, successfully lobbied at the papal court for, as Gabbione di Nanne wrote 'two of the most celebrated abbeys in Italy' – Pomposa for Battista Gozzadini and Nonantola (Modena) for Dalfino – 'to improve and advance the honour and profit of our house'.[56]

Other monasteries added further property to the Este patrimony. Azzo d'Este had been granted the advocacy of San Romano (Ferrara) in 1188, along with the former Adelardi fiefs in Ferrara, Denore and Villanova.[57] By the late fourteenth century, the marquis, as advocate, was able to appoint agents to collect the monastery's revenues.[58] In the Padovano in 1293, the nuns of S. Maria di Fistomba won a legal action against Obizzo II's sons, alleging that he had occupied their lands at Baone for many years.[59] The abbey of Gavello in the Polesine, an early Benedictine foundation, had, it seems, already by the mid-eleventh century lost its territory to the Estensi. And in 1425 it was suppressed and placed at the disposition of the bishop of Adria, whose first appointment as commendatory abbot was Jacopo Pritati, a kinsman of the marquis' favourite, Pietro Pritati. The following two commendatory abbots were members of the Este family (first, Niccolo III's son Gurone Maria, then Gurone's own son, Niccolo Maria).[60] Early in the fifteenth century, the Este estates office (camera) seems to have had control of the property of the monastery of S. Bartolo on account of its tax debts, while in 1410

[55] Jones, *Malatesta*, pp. 276, 300–1 n. 12.
[56] 'due le piu notabili abadie da ytalia', 'de fare bene et de vantagiare l'onore e l'utile dela chaxa': Biblioteca comunale, Bologna, Archivio Gozzadini, b. 41, 18 May 1400.
[57] Muratori, *Antichità*, vol. 1, p. 353.
[58] ASM, Leggi e Decreti, A 2, fol. 227 and B III, fol. 59. The receipts were ostensibly to be applied to repairs.
[59] Dondi Orologio, *Dissertazioni*, vol. 8, p. 18.
[60] Bocchi, *Sede*, pp. 189–91.

Uguccione Contrari was seeking to lease all the property of the monastery of S. Giorgio from its cardinal commendatories.[61] *Valli* were leased from the monastery of San Giacobo di Cella Volana, the prior of which from the 1420s was Biagio Novelli, from a family prominent in Este financial administration.[62] The commendatory abbot of S. Bartolo in the early fifteenth century was the former bishop of Padua, then titular Patriarch of Jerusalem, Ugo Roberti, whose family had dominated Ferrarese political life in the early years of Niccolo III. From the early fifteenth century, it seems, the Este, their friends and others with access to Este power were increasing their hold on Church property.

The bishoprics with extensive possessions in or around the Ferrarese *contado* came under varying degrees of Este influence. As with the abbey of Vangadizza, Este penetration of the bishop of Adria's lands was rapid. Already in the twelfth century the two centres of Rovigo and Ariano had been appropriated and were secured by an imperial grant in 1221.[63] By restoring to the church the rights to some tithes in the Polesine, Azzo d'Este obtained the *castrum et curia Adriani* in fief from the bishop. This transfer of lordship from the bishop led to a dispute between the marquis and the local commune of Ariano, but this was settled in Azzo's favour and his lordship was in fact extended to cover the important woodland in the area (the *nemus Adriani*), which had been specifically omitted from the bishop's grant.[64] In the thirteenth century, Adria itself passed to the marquises: an Este official (*visconte*) appeared there from the 1220s and in 1270 a statute incorporated Adria, for tax purposes, in the Ferrarese *contado*.[65] Further episcopal grants followed: in 1253 the tithes of Massafiscaglia, in 1265 all the bishop's fiefs in the Polesine, in 1339 the tithes of Lendinara and its surrounding villages.[66] These

---

[61] ASM, Not. Cam., N. Delaito, B, fols. 36, 57v and P. Bononia, fol. 93v.
[62] ASM, Not. Cam., P. Sardi, F, fol. 89v (1414) and D. Dulcini, D, fol. 40 (1437).
[63] Bocchi, *Sede*, pp. 11–12, 175.
[64] Muratori, *Antiquitates*, vol. 3, 209–12; Muratori, *Antichità*, vol. 1, p. 367; A. Speroni, *Adriensium Episcoporum Series*, (Padua, 1788), pp. 85–95; Bocchi, *Sede*, pp. xxxviii, 11, 176–7; J. Zennari, *Adria e il suo territorio attraverso i secoli*, (Adria, 1931), p. 223.
[65] Speroni, *Series*, p. 121; Zennari, *Adria*, pp. 210–11; A. Gaudenzi, 'Il testamento di Azzo VIII d'Este e la pace del 1326 tra Modena e Bologna', in *Miscellanea Tassoniana*, (Bologna, 1908), p. 112. The bishop seems to have retained criminal jurisdiction within the castle of Adria itself: ASVe, Provveditori sopra camere, A1, 19, fol. 19v.
[66] Muratori, *Antichità*, vol. 2, pp. 10, 30; Speroni, *Series*, pp. 110, 131, 133; Bocchi, *Sede*, p. 15; ASM, Casa e Stato, 13/5; Not. Cam., D. Dulcini, B, fol. 90.

accumulating transfers quickly, it seems, overreached the bishop, who complained in 1305 of usurpation of his rights by the *visconte* and who by the early fifteenth century was even without a residence in Adria (to obtain one from the marquis he had to surrender the tithe of new assarts at Corbola, an area Niccolo d'Este was busy reclaiming).[67]

Occasional evidence from other bishoprics indicates a similar trend. In the early fourteenth century, the bishop of Comacchio is found appealing to the papal governor of Ferrara against Este violations of his territory and jurisdictions. Comacchio itself passed definitively to the marquises in 1325 and from early in the fifteenth century there was an uninterrupted succession of Ferraresi as bishops.[68] The bishopric of Cervia too at one point lost control of its revenues in Ferrarese territory to the marquis.[69]

At Ferrara itself, by the fourteenth century the Estensi seem to have had a large measure of influence over both the episcopal lands and the appointment of the bishop. In the late fourteenth century and into the early fifteenth there was a succession of bishops from important court families: Aldrovandino d'Este, Niccolo Roberti, Pietro Boiardi, though after Boiardi's resignation in 1431 this connection seems to have been lost. Indeed, it was unusual for *signori* in the papal states to exercise much control over the appointment of the bishop.[70] Nevertheless, evidence does suggest a considerable degree of Este control over episcopal land: those who held land in fief of the marquis tended to hold the tithe due from that land in fief of the bishop.[71] The Este also directed large amounts of episcopal land to themselves. They were vassals of the bishop from the twelfth century, their fief (as described in 1332) comprising a number of *valli* towards the border with Bologna, formerly held by the Torelli and Ramberti, and the tithe or part of the tithe of sixteen localities (*fundi*), formerly the fief of the Adelardi.[72] To these were added in 1334 the tithes previously held by the Menabuoi,[73] and before 1334 a grant of

[67] L. Bellini, 'La legislazione speciale delle valli di Comacchio nella sua genesi storica nelle fonti e nell'applicazione', *AMF*, s. 3, 1 (1965), 27; Zennari, *Adria*, p. 211; Bocchi, *Sede*, p. 20; and see below pp. 65–7.

[68] A. Samaritani, 'I vescovi ferraresi di Comacchio nella storia della civiltà estense', *Palestra del Clero*, July 1963; L. Bellini, 'Sul territorio della diocesi di Comacchio', *AMF*, n.s., 8 (1953), 89.

[69] ASM, Leggi e Decreti, B III, fol. 43 (1402).

[70] Jones, *Malatesta*, pp. 300–1 n. 12; Frizzi, *Memorie*, vol. 3, pp. 361, 391, 417, 461–5.

[71] ASM, ASE, Giurisdizione sovrana, Vescovado di Ferrara, 250, *passim*.

[72] ASM, Casa e Stato, Controversie di Stato, 511; Trombetti, 'Vassalli', pp. 70–3.

[73] ASM, Not. Cam., P. Fabro, fol. 16.

Mellara, Bergantino, Bariano and Trecenta.[74] These settlements had been acquired by the bishop in the mid-twelfth century from the monastery of Nonantola and their passage to the Estensi marked a further step in the gradual Este penetration of episcopal lordships to the north-west of the city.[75] Nearby Bondeno had been partly acquired by the marquises in grants in 1239 and 1332.[76] By 1393 the bishop had further granted to the Estensi the tithe or part-tithe of another eleven *fundi*, some taken from other Ferrarese families.[77]

The archbishopric of Ravenna had in the tenth to twelfth centuries held large areas of the Ferrarese *contado*, which had then largely passed to the bishop of Ferrara and to the local abbeys, but the archbishop and other churches in Ravenna did retain property throughout the eastern part of the *contado*.[78] By 1251 the marquises had accumulated extensive holdings of the archbishopric: properties formerly held by the Adelardi and Costabili and lands across a wide area to the east of the city.[79] In 1393 were added tithes and a fraction of the jurisdiction of Crespino, Cologna and the surrounding places, previously held by the Turchi family,[80] followed in 1395 by the rich Medici inheritance of lands at Maiero and Consandalo.[81] As with

---

[74] ASM, Not. Cam., F. Sale, fol. 112.

[75] Muratori, *Antiquitates*, vol. 1, 725–8; Castagnetti, *Organizzazione*, p. 149. The bishop had substantial control of Mellara, Bergantino and Trecenta in the early fourteenth century, issuing statutes (BCF, Cl. 1, 126), appointing the *visconte* (ASE, Giurisdizione sovrana, 250, fols. 9, 11, 18, 62v), farming the *valli* (ibid., fols. 9, 63). See also A. Franceschini, 'Curie episcopali ferraresi nella traspadana (sec. X–XIV): Trecenta', *Ravennatensia*, 5 (1976).

[76] There was an Estense podestà at Bondeno from at least 1338: ASM, Not. Cam., P. Fabro, fol. 46; G. Ferraresi, *Storia di Bondeno raccolta di documenti* (Rovigo, 1963), pp. 148, 185–6, 195; Zucchini, *L'agricoltura*, p. 55.

[77] Half of the tithe of Quartesana, Viconovo, Albarea and Fossalta and two quarters of that of Corlo: ASM, Not. Cam., F. Tagliapetri, A, fol. 48 (11 Mar 1367); Casa e Stato, Controversie di Stato, 511; L. Barotti, *Serie dei vescovi e arcivescovi di Ferrara* (Ferrara, 1781), pp. 68–74; and see below p. 58.

[78] Bellini, 'Territorio di Comacchio', pp. 50–9; Castagnetti, *Organizzazione*, p. 224; Vasina, 'Territorio'; *Regesto della Chiesa di Ravenna. Le carte dell'archivio estense*, ed. V. Federici and G. Buzzi (2 vols., Rome, 1911–31), vol. 1, nos. 287, 291, 337; vol. 2, nos. 529, 545, 555, 570 etc. In the early fifteenth century, the archbishopric of Ravenna had a tax assessment at Ferrara larger than many of Ferrara's urban churches: Samaritani, 'L'estimo del clero', pp. 132, 138–41. In 1413 the archbishop leased all his property in the Ferrarese for 500 ducats p.a.: ASM, Not. Cam., P. Sardi, F, fol. 56.

[79] *Reg. Ch. Rav.*, vol. 2, appx ii, nos. 15, 17, pp. 342, 345–6; Muratori, *Antichità*, vol. 2, p. 10.

[80] A. Tarlazzi, *Appendice ai Monumenti Ravennati dei secoli di mezzo del conte M. Fantuzzi* (2 vols., Ravenna, 1869–76), vol. 2, doc. 195, pp. 364–7.

[81] Frizzi, *Memorie*, vol. 3, p. 399. Francesco and Guglielmo Medici had been invested in 1311 with parts of Dogato, near Ostellato and Galasso was later (1339–68)

Pomposa, control tightened in the early fifteenth century. In 1411 Niccolo III obtained from the Pope (John XXIII) appointment of his candidate as archbishop: Tommaso Perondoli, from a family prominent in Este service (he was the son of a former *fattore generale* and the brother of the then *Giudice dei Savi*). According to one chronicler, Tommaso was appointed 'to please the marquis', who signalled his pleasure by his presence at the new archbishop's first mass.[82] In 1425 Tommaso was elected to the marquis' new council and became one of its most assiduous members.[83] But, like Baldassare Sala, he did not wholly sacrifice ecclesiastical interests to those of the Estensi: he repeatedly pressed Niccolo about his arrears of rent on property held of the archbishopric and made a final settlement with the marquis of the long-standing dispute over the town of Argenta, which had been a source of conflict beween Ferrara and the archbishop for over two centuries. This town, on the Po di Primaro to the south east of Ferrara, was of some strategic interest, as it controlled one of the river routes to Bologna.[84] From early in the thirteenth century the commune of Ferrara had challenged the archbishop's jurisdiction there and in a large area to the north around Portomaggiore, by imposing oaths and levies and by usurping jurisdiction and *regalia*.[85] The archbishop's defence of Porto and Argenta, though tenacious, proved unequal to the task: in 1332 Porto and its surrounding villages were awarded to Ferrara[86] and Este possession of Argenta was fairly continuous from the early thirteenth century, despite occasional recoveries by the archbishop.[87] Indeed, in 1327 the Estensi attempted to deny Church sovereignty over Ferrara and Argenta altogether, by obtaining a grant of both from the Emperor; and whereas the papal reaction ensured that Ferrara was not again the object of imperial conferment, Argenta was included in subsequent

invested with lands at Consandolo and Maiero: *Reg. Ch. Rav.*, vol. 2, appendix i, pp. 283, 322, 323. On the Medici: Laurent, 'Vassals', pp. 84–5.

82  *Diario Ferrarese dall'anno 1419 sino al 1502 di autore incerto, RIS²*, vol. 24, pt 7, p. 10; G. Ferraresi, *Il beato Giovanni Tavelli da Tossignano e la riforma di Ferrara nel Quattrocento* (2 vols., Brescia, 1969), vol. 1, p. 143.

83  ASM, Leggi e Decreti, B IV, fol. 114 (26 Feb. 1425).

84  Theiner, *Codex*, vol. 2, p. 539; Tabanelli, *Romagna Estense*, pp. 37–8.

85  *Reg. Ch. Rav.*, vol. 1, nos. 147–8, 151, 155, 197.

86  Frizzi, *Memorie*, vol. 3, pp. 279–80, 282; F. L. Bertoldi, *Memorie storiche d'Argenta* (3 vols., Ferrara, 1787–1821), vol. 3, pt 2, pp. 35–6.

87  Bertoldi, *Argenta*, vol. 3, pt. 2, pp. 8–35; Muratori, *Antichità*, vol. 1, pp. 395, 402; vol. 2, pp. 30, 32, 65, 75; Muratori, *Antiquitates*, vol. 3, 227–8; G. Marchetti Longhi, 'La legazione in Lombardia di Gregorio da Monte Longo', *Archivio della Società Romana di Storia Patria*, 36 (1913), 601–2; Tabanelli, *Romagna Estense*, pp. 39–51.

imperial grants to the Estensi.[88] Despite this attempt to eliminate the archbishop's title, from 1344 the marquises held Argenta from the archbishop on short-term leases, the archbishop being unwilling to grant it at a longer term 'because', as he put it, 'of the marquises' power'.[89] But short-term leases were no restraint on Este pretensions and their control of transit traffic at Argenta brought them into conflict with the Church. Estensi claims to impose gabelles on Bolognese salt cargoes provoked protests from the Pope's legate in Bologna, on the grounds that the Estensi could not possibly tax the Pope in his own lands.[90] Until late in the fourteenth century, the Este had paid, if irregularly, the tribute (*census*) due for Argenta, but Niccolo III let the last short-term lease expire without renewing it and let the payments lapse too. To the archbishop's petitions that he resume payments, Niccolo drew the matter out, agreeing in principle, but refusing to pay the former rent, until in 1421 the archbishop granted him Argenta as a vicariate, with full jurisdiction at a rent of 200 ducats a year. In return, Niccolo assigned to the archbishop his estates and revenues at Paviole in the Ferrarese *contado*.[91]

It was not only the Este, of course, who held land from the church in Ferrara: ecclesiastical fiefs and leases formed a considerable part of most lay landholdings. The problems that arose from having the church as landlord were significantly eased in 1391 with a papal bull obtained by Alberto d'Este during a visit to Rome (the *bolla bonifaciana*). The importance of this bull may be gauged by the gratitude shown by the commune which had the text inscribed on the façade of the cathedral alongside the statue of Alberto himself.[92] The pre-

---

[88] ASM, Not. Cam., N. Abbatia, B, fol. 95; Casa e Stato, 22/18 (1354); Muratori, *Antichità*, vol. 2, pp. 79 (1327), 196 (1433).

[89] ASM, N. Abbatia, B, fol. 95. For the short-term leases of 1344, 1348, 1351, 1367 and 1394; Bertoldi, *Argenta*, vol. 3, pt 2, pp. 35–6; ASV, Arm. xlvi, vol. 21; ASM, Not. Cam., F. Tagliapetri, A, fols. 65v–7 and J. Delaito, fols. 101v–3.

[90] When the marquis' officials halted salt cargoes, the legate protested 'quod [Marchio] non habebat plus iuris quam Archiepiscopus et quod Archiepiscopus posset dominum nostrum gabellare absurdissimum erat. . .': Theiner, *Codex*, vol. 2, p. 539. For the 'Statuta daciorum et gabellarum comunis Argente' issued by the marquis in 1391: BL, MS 25595.

[91] The six *possessiones* at Paviola totalled 2,290 *starii*, 36,500 vines and 129 *opere*, with tax immunities for the tenants, the tithes and the inn: ASM, Not. Cam., N. Abbatia, B, fols. 95–107; and see Muratori, *Antichità*, vol. 2, p. 188; Bertoldi, *Argenta*, vol. 3, pt 2, p. 104.

[92] Muratori, *Antichità*, vol. 2, p. 158; Frizzi, *Memorie*, vol. 3, pp. 382–3; Zucchini, *L'agricoltura*, pp. 113–14; L. Borsari, *Il contratto d'enfiteusi* (Ferrara, 1850), pp. 728ff. For the text of the bull: ASM, Catastro I, fols. 24–6; *Statuta civitatis Ferrariae*

amble asserted that the marquis and the commune had complained of the 'many quarrels, grudges and enmities' arising from the 'undue demand for rent' and for reinvestiture made by the many churches of which Ferrarese citizens were tenants. It is difficult now to see how justified lay complaints were: most of the problems they identified centred on succession and inheritance, where, one may suspect, the churches, as undying institutions, were exercising a control that was too close for lay comfort. Hence the grievances listed: the refusal of churches to invest heirs, the inability of minors to prove previous payments of rent, denial by church lords of succession, unjustified reoccupations of property and high entry-fines. And hence the remedies provided by the Pope: removing the possibility of forfeiture for failure to pay rent or to obtain investiture; creating freedoms to alienate and ordering a general rent increase (by 10s.) and a round of new investitures. The effect of this legislation was, as the *Chronicon Estense* noted, the quasi-allodialisation of ecclesiastical tenancies.[93] A similar reform at Argenta in 1364 extracted from the archbishop by Niccolo II and the local commune had been highly praised by the local councillors, whose response was, doubtless, echoed at Ferrara thirty years later: one said that by this reform 'men could call their own the property that they had and could say that they had been released from servitude to liberty'.[94] The substantial benefits which accrued to lay tenants by such enactments, and the substantial loss of control imposed on church landlords, could together be interpreted as tantamount to disendowment of the church: a fitting gift to their subjects from *signori* who had exploited the church from the outset.

The chronology of that exploitation coincides roughly with the political history of the Este *signoria*: significant acquisitions in the years immediately following their succession to the Adelardi and again after 1240, but with a hiatus in the early fourteenth century. The period from the late fourteenth century then marked another

(Ferrara, 1476), fols. 72–3v; L. Borsari, *Collezione di leggi e ordinamenti per servire all'opera "Il contratto d'enfiteusi"* (Ferrara, 1854). For the celebrations attending Alberto's return to Ferrara: A. Stella, 'Testi volgari ferraresi del secondo trecento', *Studi di filologia italiana*, 26 (1968), 248–9.
[93] *Chron. Est.*, 521.
[94] '. . . homines possunt dicere esse bona sua que habent . . . et possunt dicere se esse conversi de servitudine in libertatem': Bertoldi, *Argenta*, vol. 3, pt 2, pp. 57–61. This speaker specifically mentioned the inability to transfer property to collateral kin ('ascendentibus nec collateralibus nec transversalibus nec aliquibus actinentibus') as a major grievance. *Cf.* a papal bull of 1413 secularising ecclesiastical land at Pesaro for tax purposes: Jones, *Malatesta*, p. 276 n. 3.

major advance: occupied lands were secured by regular grant, men close to the court (and later members of the family) were placed in key ecclesiastical offices, abbeys were converted to *commendae*.[95] In addition, property acquisitions by the churches were controlled by licences; the appointment of episcopal vicars became subject to Este approval; and all legal cases involving specific monasteries and churches were committed to Este-appointed judges-delegate.[96] And with the diversion *en bloc* of church property from church control by the *Bolla bonifaciana* in 1391, the marquises could be said to have fulfilled the proud threat attributed to them by the Pope in 1321: 'that the property which the churches hold is not the property of the churches, but of the men of Ferrara who gave it to them, and that if they gave it, so could they take it away . . .'[97]

### LANDS IN THE PADOVANO

In contrast to the gradual expansion of Este property in the Polesine and in the Ferrarese *contado*, the history of Este lands in the Padovano, the original lands of the family, is one of slow reduction and dispersion. In general outline, these Paduan possessions formed a compact strip along the Adige, uniting Montagnana and Merlara with Monselice and Vescovana (see Map 5), and including not only three of the four most populous towns of the Paduan *contado* (Monselice, Este and Montagnana), but also important castles, in those three places and at Cero, Calaone, Arqua and Vighizzolo.[98] For much of the twelfth century these lands were held in part from the Dukes of Bavaria, cousins of the Este, and then from 1184 from

---

[95] A. Prosperi, 'Le istituzioni ecclesiastiche e le idee religiosi', in *Il Rinascimento nelle corti padane. Società e cultura* (Bari, 1977), pp. 129–30.

[96] Obizzo II may have committed all Vangadizza cases to the *visconte* at Rovigo (Nicolio, *Rovigo*, p. 113). From the late fourteenth century, there are numerous examples of such judges: for Ravenna (Tarlazzi, *Appendice*, vol. 2, doc. 190, pp. 357–9), Vangadizza (ASM, Leggi e Decreti, B III, fols. 47, 169), the bishopric of Comacchio (ibid., fol. 47) and the monasteries of S. Bartolo (ibid., fol. 233) and S. Antonio in Polesine (ibid., fol. 97) etc.

[97] 'quod bona quae tenent ecclesiae non sunt bona ecclesiarum sed hominum de Ferraria qui dederunt dicta bona ecclesiis et si etiam dederunt ita possunt auferre': ASM, Manoscritti della biblioteca, 133, Pellegrino Prisciani, Historiae Ferrariae liber ix, fol. 7v. See also F. Bock, 'Der Este-Prozess von 1321', *Archivum Fratrum Praedicatorum*, 7 (1937); Jones, *Malatesta*, p. 46 nn. 1–2; and cf. M. Aston, '"Caim's castles": poverty, politics and disendowment', in *The Church, Politics and Patronage in the Fifteenth Century*, ed. B. Dobson (Gloucester, 1984).

[98] Muratori, *Antichità*, vol. 1, p. 427; J. K. Hyde, *Padua in the Age of Dante* (Manchester, 1966), p. 350.

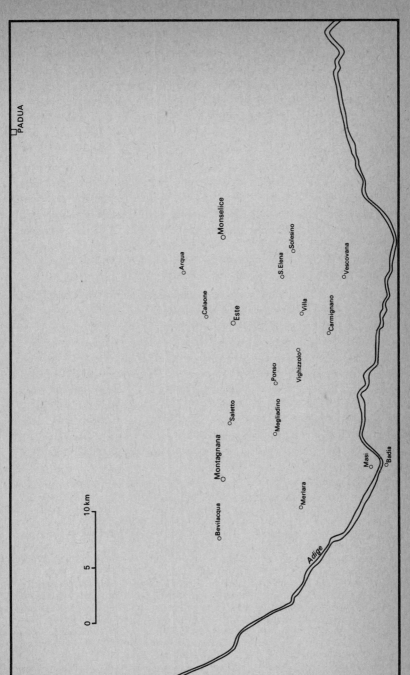

Map 5 The southern Padovano

the Emperor.[99] From the late twelfth century, the Estensi had to meet Paduan hostility to their jurisdictions and military bases (first that of the commune, later that of the *signori*, the da Carrara) and slowly, in a history at times both complicated and unclear, they were surrendered.[100] The marquises seem to have lost jurisdiction in the southern Padovano in 1213, but recovered it in the middle decades of the century, losing it again in 1294 after renewed conflict with Padua. In 1336 they recognised Carrara dominion over Monselice, Este and Montagnana and in 1354 ceded the castle of Vighizzolo. Though Este itself was briefly recovered in 1389 as a reward for joining the Milanese and Venetian attack on Francesco da Carrara, it was lost again in 1390 and thereafter Este attempts to recover their castles and jurisdictions in the Padovano were abandoned: in 1405 Este, with Padua, submitted to Venice.

The extent of Este lands, which they retained despite other losses, is well documented. An arbitrated settlement between Azzo VII and the commune of Este in 1204 calculated that Azzo held over 2,000 hectares (5,357 *campi*) of allodial property alone (not counting feudal property).[101] Two surveys, of the 1270s and 1290s, give an almost complete picture of these lands. That of the 1270s provides impressive documentation of the character and extent of this vast lordship, comprising castles, towers and *palatia*, mills and canals, pasture, woodland, *valli* and vineyards, demesne and tenants, vassals, jurisdiction and tithes. Only some of the property is measured and that alone totals over 6,250 hectares (16,183 *campi*).[102] The 1293 survey contains rather less in measured *campi* (4,300 hectares), but reveals it as concentrated, as in the 1270s, around Este, Megliadino, Montagnana, Solesino and Saletto. Of this land, less than one fifth was farmed directly, while over one third was infeudated, the rest being leased out in various forms of sharecropping contracts or at fixed money rents.[103] A further survey in the 1440s might appear to show the effects of the division of the property and the losses of the

[99] Muratori, *Antichità*, vol. 1, pp. 35–6, 341–2, 351; Alessi, *Ricerche*, vol. 1, pp. 467, 501–2, 512, 542–4, 590–4, 612–25; Zorzi, *Territorio padovano*, pp. 181–3.

[100] For what follows: *Chron. Est.*, 475, 478; Nicolio, *Rovigo*, pp. 135–42, 147, 167–71; Muratori, *Antichità*, vol. 1, pp. 410–13, 415, 427; vol. 2, pp. 6, 8, 9, 13–17, 32–3, 50, 119, 154–6; Muratori, *Antiquitates*, vol. 4, 1152–3, 1155–6; Alessi, *Ricerche*, vol. 1, pp. 701–2; G. Nuvolato, *Storia di Este e del suo territorio* (Este, 1851), pp. 424–6, 429–35; Zorzi, *Territorio padovano*, pp. 188–218; Zorzi 'Ordinamento', p. 85 ff; Cessi, *Venezia e Padova*, pp. 37, 46–7; Cessi, 'Trattato', pp. 415–16.

[101] Muratori, *Antiquitates*, vol. 4, 43–6.

[102] ASVe, Provveditori sopra camere, A 1, 2.

[103] BEM, MSS Lat., 1271; Trombetti, 'Beni Estensi', pp. 187–96.

castles: it contains a much reduced total of land – some 830 hectares (2,150 *campi*) – now for the most part leased out. This impression is slightly inacccurate, for the survey covered only the leasehold tenants of Leonello d'Este and therefore excluded both the fiefs held of him and the property held by the branch of the family which, excluded from Ferrara after 1352, had settled at Este itself.[104] But even taking account of these (the fiefs added over 1,100 *campi*), the total would not seem to reach the levels of the late thirteenth century.

The history of the Paduan properties between the thirteenth- and fifteenth-century surveys is unclear. Much was still held in common between the two branches of the family, despite their estrangement. In 1405 there were plans to divide between Niccolo III and Azzo di Francesco all fiefs and vassals that they held in common in the Padovano.[105] This followed two attempts by Azzo to dislodge Niccolo from the lordship of Ferrara by armed force. For whatever reason, the division was not made and instead Niccolo released to Azzo all his property at Este and Montagnana in return for 1,000 ducats a year.[106] Niccolo was clearly anxious not to lose these estates and he reoccupied them immediately on Azzo's death in 1415 (though he subsequently released them to Azzo's sons).[107] Of the lands held by Francesco, Azzo and his sons, little is known: some acquisitions by them are recorded, but from early in the fifteenth century their property was slowly mortgaged to Venice and to individual Venetians.[108] Finally, in 1466 on the death of Bertoldo di Taddeo, the last of the line, Venice foreclosed on the remaining estates (still amounting to thousands of *campi*) in repayment of Bertoldo's debts. The property was auctioned to the Pisani family,

---

[104] BEM, MSS Lat., 1273; L. A. Steer, 'Landownership and rural conditions in the Padovano during the later Middle Ages', Oxford University D.Phil. thesis, 1967, p. 228–9.

[105] ASM, Not. Cam., N. Abbatia, A, fols. 21v–2 (1406) and P. Bononia, fol. 73v (1407); A. Manni, *Un ramo della famiglia estense in esilio e le sue relazioni coi signori di Ferrara* (Novara, 1919), p. 11. For fiefs held of Niccolo III and Azzo jointly: ASM, Catastri delle Investiture, H, fol. 614 and N, fols. 109, 387, 418; Not. Cam., P. Sardi, D, fol. 10v.

[106] Muratori, *Antichità*, vol. 2, p. 173. *Cf.* Giangaleazzo Visconti's method of dealing with the sons of the displaced Bernabò – exile and pensions in return for renunciation of rights in the patrimony: M. Brunetti, 'Nuovi documenti viscontei tratti dall'Archivio di Stato di Venezia', *ASL*, s. 4, 11 (1909), 21–30.

[107] ASM, Not. Cam., P. Bononia, fol. 164 (30 Jan. 1415). This property had apparently been recovered by 1439: Not. Cam., D.Dulcini, D, fol. 91v.

[108] For acquisitions: ASM, Investiture di Feudi, 12/25; Casa e Stato, 23/15 and 23/42. For debts: ASVe, Senato, Secreta, reg. 4, fol. 73v (7 Nov. 1409); Museo Civico Correr, Venice, MSS P.D., C 666, no. 11 (19 July 1415).

despite the efforts of Borso d'Este to reclaim it. 'Never, never, never will the Venetians give you anything of this inheritance', reported despairingly the Este envoy in Venice.[109] A similar story might perhaps be told of the rights of the Estensi over various churches in the Padovano. In 1308 Aldrovandino and Francesco held patronage rights over S. Maria di Carceri, Este; S. Andrea, Villa; S. Giustina, Calaone; the priory of S. Elena; S. Maria, Solesino and S. Trinità, Tricontai.[110] By the fifteenth century, the Estensi were having to defend these rights against repeated challenge from the Paduan church. In 1399, Niccolo III successfully protested against the bishop of Padua's dismissal of the rector at Calaone on the grounds that it offended his patronage rights. In 1422 the bishop challenged Niccolo III's approval of the election of a new abbess for the abbey of Gemola and the fullness of Este patronage was compromised on arbitration. In the 1440s the canons of S. Giacomo, Monselice contested the right of Leonello and Taddeo d'Este to the tithes in the parish of S. Maria, Solesino, claiming that they had levied them 'by force' ('violenter') for a number of years.[111]

### THE DIVISION OF THE PATRIMONY AND THE FAMILY

The movement of the Estensi into Ferrara at the end of the twelfth century had coincided with the concentration of their possessions in the hands of Obizzo I.[112] At the same time, the family's territorial holdings had been simplified: references cease to their property in Tuscany, lands in the Lunigiana were ceded to the Malaspina and the Bavarian title to part of the Paduan estates was eliminated.[113] As lands now remote from the family's interests were disposed of, the Estensi came to concentrate their attention on the Padovano, Polesine and Ferrarese, planting increasingly firm territorial and

109 'volgio fare questo iudicio, che questi venetiani de questa hereditate mai mai e mai vi darano alcuna cossa . . .': ASM, Amministrazione finanziaria dei paesi, Polesine Di Rovigo (Camarlengheria di Este), letters of 1466. See also V. Lazzarini, 'Beni carraresi e proprietari veneziani', in *Studi in onore di G. Luzzatto* (Milan, 1949) p. 277; R. Gallo, 'Una famiglia patrizia, i Pisani ed i Palazzi di S. Stefano e di Stra', *AV*, s. 5, 24–5 (1944), 72; ASVe, Dieci, Misto, reg. 22, fols. 227–8.
110 ASM, Casa e Stato, 8/21 (24 Feb. 1308).
111 Dondi Orologio, *Dissertazioni*, vol. 8, p. 138 and vol. 9, p. 19; A. Rigon, *S. Giacomo di Monselice nel Medio Evo*, (Padua, 1972), pp. 121–2. Note that the Venetians were creating an atmosphere of aggressive reassertion of ecclesiastical rights in the Terraferma: Varanini, 'Il monastero di S. Maria in Organo'.
112 Muratori, *Antichità*, vol. 1, pp. 355, 360ff; Alessi, *Ricerche*, vol. 1, pp. 586–97; Zorzi, *Territorio padovano*, pp. 181–4.
113 Zanella, *Riccobaldo*, pp. 66–7, 79–80; Muratori, *Antichità*, vol. 1, pp. 175–83.

social roots there. During the thirteenth century, the patrimony seems to have remained largely intact, by virtue of a succession of single sons and deaths without male issue.[114] But the history of the family's political and territorial interests in the following two centuries illustrates well the recurrent conflicts that were generated by tensions between the concentration of land and power within linear descent groups and the pressure from other kinsmen for inclusion in the exercise and profits of authority. There was, on the one hand, a definite trend towards primogeniture and, on the other, a more pragmatic recognition of the benefits of condominium, with repeated proposals to divide up Este territories. The result was a series of violent and costly succession disputes and the successive exclusion of certain branches of the family from the patrimony and from power.

The unity of the patrimony inherited by Obizzo II in 1264 was largely the result of biological accident and already in 1282 he was contemplating the alienation of all his Paduan lands to his son Francesco.[115] Within weeks of Obizzo II's death in 1293, his three sons were fighting among themselves, as the younger sons tried to appropriate segments of Este lordships (Modena, the Polesine).[116] This conflict was pacified, but only perhaps as a result of the highly aggressive and expansionist policies adopted by Azzo VIII, who dominated the family into the early fourteenth century. But Azzo's intention to promote his own children, in preference to his brothers, led to renewed dispute, as Francesco seized Lendinara and surrendered it to Padua in return for political support.[117] The family was thus already divided when Azzo VIII died in 1308, demising the main lordships out of the hands of his brothers: Modena to his father-in-law, Charles d'Anjou, and Ferrara to his grandson, Folco d'Este.[118]

Not for the first (or last) time in the family, the claims of primogeniture, legitimacy and seniority came into conflict. On the day of Azzo's death, his brothers Francesco and Aldrovandino agreed to combine to recover 'their' inheritance, though within a few weeks Aldrovandino transferred to his own sons (Rinaldo and Obizzo III) nearly all the property he held in common with Francesco, reaching a formal division of the rest with Francesco in

[114] Muratori, *Antichità*, vol. 1, pp. 396–9; vol. 2, p. 24.
[115] Ibid., vol. 2, pp. 36–7.  [116] Frizzi, *Memorie*, vol. 3, pp. 215–18.
[117] Ibid., pp. 232–9.  [118] Gaudenzi, 'Il testamento'.

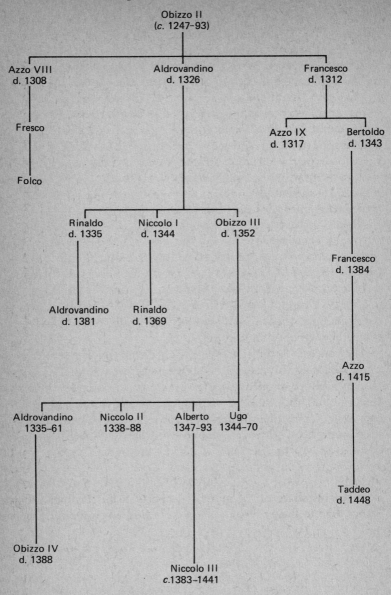

Fig. 1 Simplified genealogical table of the Este family

1310.[119] These two transactions cover substantial landed property in the Padovano, Polesine and Ferrarese, including castles and jurisdiction, arable, woodland and *valli*, tithes and patronage rights over churches. The ensuing conflict with Folco consumed everything that had been achieved since 1240: Modena and Reggio had already been lost before Azzo died, Rovigo and Lendinara were lost to Padua, and Folco, unable to resist the attacks of his kinsmen and their allies, surrendered Ferrara to Venice. Francesco was assassinated in 1312 and his sons took up residence in the Polesine. The scarring impact of these losses on the Ferrarese historical memory was made plain later: in 1352 the new Este lords of Ferrara were publicly entreated at their installation to remain united and to remember the earlier divisions which had almost destroyed their family.[120]

Already, however, the generation that returned to power in Ferrara in 1317 had showed that the lessons of division and disunity had been learned: the sons of Aldrovandino (Rinaldo, Niccolo and Obizzo III) and of Francesco (Azzo and Bertoldo) were all actively engaged in government, sharing the dangers and profits of lordship. There was careful attention to their participation and honour, through knighthood, military commands, favourable marriages into other signorial families and so on.[121]

The benefits of this joint enterprise were impressive: the recovery of Modena and Rovigo, the acquisition of Comacchio, Argenta and (briefly) Parma, the fending off of political and military attacks by the Pope and his legate and the papal grant of a vicariate for Ferrara. However, once again there were also clear trends towards concentration, now within the lineage of Aldrovandino and his eldest son Obizzo. From the 1320s, imperial and other investitures were made to the sons of Aldrovandino alone and it was they who received the papal vicariate in 1329.[122] Niccolo di Aldrovandino demised his share of his father's property to his brother Obizzo, rather than to his own son, Rinaldo.[123] And when Obizzo, the last

---

[119] See Appendix, docs. 1 & 2.      [120] *Chron. Est.*, 469.

[121] Frizzi, *Memorie*, vol. 3, pp. 262–308; *Chron. Est.*, 380–425; Muratori, *Antichità*, vol. 2, pp. 87, 103–4, 109.

[122] Muratori, *Antichità*, vol. 2, pp. 76–7, 80–1, 117; *cf.* the distinction among the Gonzaga between the holders of the imperial vicariate and the holders of the *capitaneato*, between, that is, the official and the real rulers: E. M. L. Waller, 'The diplomatic relations of the Gonzaga 1328–1407', Oxford B.Litt. thesis 1953, p. 247.

[123] ASM, Not. Cam., M. Benintendi, fol. 57 (15 Mar. 1352). The restitution of this property to Rinaldo di Niccolo, ordered in Obizzo's will, was not apparently complete until 1368: ASM, Casa e Stato, 18/1.

surviving of Aldrovandino's three sons, died in 1352, he named his own sons as his sole heirs, with the instruction that the eldest, Aldrovandino, should be *signore*.[124] The immediate reaction of Francesco di Bertoldo, Rinaldo di Niccolo and their Ferrarese supporters, combined with an atmosphere of violent intimidation created by Aldrovandino's Bolognese adviser, Bonifacio Ariosti, posed serious problems for Aldrovandino for several years. This time, however, none of the neighbouring states used the opportunity to intervene in Ferrara: Venice declared its neutrality, the lord of Verona was in close political alliance with Aldrovandino and the lord of Padua, though reviving Paduan designs on the Polesine, was satisfied with the surrender of the castle at Vighizzolo.[125] Francesco di Bertoldo was, however, honourably received by his wife's family, the Visconti lords of Milan, for whom he became a military captain in the wars against a league of north Italian states which included the Este. It was as a result of Visconti sponsorship that settlement of Francesco's rebellion was included on the agenda of the general peace settlement in 1358.[126] This, however, only facilitated the quiet dispossession of Francesco. Immediately on Francesco's flight from Ferrara in 1352, Aldrovandino had seized all his property in the *contado* and in the Polesine.[127] This was evidently the property that had fallen to Francesco's grandfather in the division of 1310 and constituted a large, almost separate lordship on the edge of the *contado*.[128] Although Francesco was allowed to take formal repossession of these properties, he then surrendered them all to Aldrovandino in a series of short-term leases which continued into the 1390s.[129] The large payments due under these leases were made

---

124  ASM, Not. Cam., M. Benintendi, fol. 57v. For the progress of ideas of primogeniture, see the fifteenth-century account of the succession of Azzo VIII in 1293: 'De Rebus Estensium', ed. C. Antolini, *AMF*, 12 (1900), 23. *Cf.* E. Sestan, 'La storia dei Gonzaga nel Rinascimento', in *Mantova e i Gonzaga nella civiltà del Rinascimento* (Mantua, 1977), p. 20; *Storia di Milano*, vol. 6, p. 69.

125  *Chron. Est.*, 470–81; Frizzi, *Memorie*, vol. 3, pp. 320–9; *Le deliberazioni del consiglio dei XL della repubblica di Venezia*, ed. A. Lombardo (3 vols., Venice, 1957–67), vol. 3, p. 14.

126  Muratori, *Antichità*, vol. 2, p. 127; Manni, *Un ramo*, p. 9; Chiappini, *Gli Estensi*, p. 67.

127  ASM, Not. Cam., M. Benintendi, fol. 68v (11 Dec. 1352).

128  See Appendix doc. 2. Bertoldo di Francesco is found exercising his 'plenitudo potestatis' in issuing statutes at Ariano in 1328: Frizzi, *Memorie*, vol. 3, p. 303. See also, for investitures by the bishop of Adria to Francesco: ASVe, Provveditori sopra camere, A 1, 19, fol. 23.

129  See Appendix doc. 3. For the leases: ASM, Casa e Stato, 14/46, 16/19, 18/17, 19/20; Not. Cam., R. Codegorio, B, fol. 9 and P. Arquada, fols. 4–v. Rents varied

regularly at times, but were suspended when Francesco rejoined the Visconti in the early 1370s. The Este in Ferrara refused to pay Francesco anything until he took up residence in neutral or friendly territory.[130] When Francesco's son, Azzo, in turn rebelled in 1393, the payments were abruptly stopped and never resumed.[131] Neither Francesco nor his descendants returned to Ferrara: Francesco died at Milan and his descendants resided, intermittently, at Este, from where they confined their interests to the Padovano and to Venetian military service.[132] After Azzo's death, the separation of the two branches of the family became almost complete: excluded from the *signoria*, then from direct control of their Ferrarese estates, the Este branch saw repeated, and ultimately successful efforts by Niccolo III to eliminate their claims on the *signori* altogether.

Meanwhile in Ferrara, the displacement of one branch did not bring a halt to disputes within the other. Aldrovandino died in 1361, naming his son, Obizzo, as his sole heir.[133] But Obizzo, who was still a child, was thrust aside by his uncles, who established a condominium reminiscent of the 1320s and 1330s. The papal vicariate was reissued to these three brothers, Niccolo II, Ugo and Alberto, who made and received joint investitures and participated jointly in political and military action.[134] Again family unity brought territorial expansion – this time into the Romagna[135] – but failed to prevent further internal disorder: a tax revolt erupted in 1385 and in 1388 Alberto had to deal with the rebellion of Obizzo di Aldrovandino and other members of the family.[136] When Alberto tried to pass the lordship of Ferrara to his own infant son in 1393, the result was a repetition of the events of the early fourteenth century. An invasion by Azzo di Francesco was backed by nobles of the

from 4,800 to 5,300 ducats p.a. Manni, *Un ramo*, p. 10, gives a confused picture. A further act of expropriation followed in 1367 when the bishop invested Niccolo II and his brothers with Francesco's half of the family's fief, alleging a failure to petition for investiture: ASM, Not. Cam., F. Tagliapetri, A, fol. 46.

130 ASM, Leggi e Decreti, A 1, fol. 178.
131 ASM, Leggi e Decreti, A 2, fol. 58.
132 Nuvolato, *Este*, pp. 477–82; M. Mallett, 'Venice and its condottieri 1404–54', in *Renaissance Venice*, ed. J. R. Hale (London, 1973), pp. 125–6; M. E. Mallett and J. R. Hale, *The Military Organisation of a Renaissance State: Venice c. 1400 to 1617* (Cambridge, 1984), pp. 30–1, 41, 44–6, 58.
133 ASM, Casa e Stato, b. 324 (fasc. 7/1960), i.
134 Frizzi, *Memorie*, vol. 3, pp. 331–75; J. C. Lünig, *Codex Italiae Diplomaticus* (4 vols., Frankfurt & Leipzig, 1725–35), vol. 1, 1601–16.
135 A. Vasina, 'La Romagna Estense', *SR*, 21 (1970).
136 *Chron. Est.*, 509–12, 517–18; Frizzi, *Memorie*, vol. 3, p. 377; J. E. Law, 'Popular unrest in Ferrara in 1385'.

Modenese *contado* who threw the region into confusion; the lord of Padua made an attempt to seize control in Ferrara; and a severe financial crisis compelled the mortgaging of both the Polesine and the territories in the Romagna in return for loans.[137] Full recovery from this crisis was slow, but Azzo was rapidly defeated and exiled, with a pension of 3,000 ducats a year which Niccolo III was not prompt in paying.[138]

Conflicts within the family over the distribution of property and power then ceased for the rest of Niccolo's reign (1393–1441), which witnessed another phase of territorial expansion, with the recovery of Reggio, the temporary acquisition of Parma (1409–21) and the retrieval of positions in the Romagna.[139] But with Niccolo's sons, the problems of combining individual leadership with satisfactory provision for other kinsmen revived. Again tensions between legitimacy and primogeniture were created by Niccolo's preference of his first-born (but illegitimate) son, Leonello, over his legitimate sons, Ercole and Sigismondo. Already in the 1430s, Niccolo had formally transferred to Leonello the internal administration of the lordships and in his will he directed that a strict rule of primogeniture should be observed after Leonello's death.[140] Stories that Niccolo had planned to divide up his territories among his sons were thus frustrated, but Leonello, as if aware of the hopes thus created, did assign the Polesine and castles in the Reggiano to Borso and later sent Borso, Ercole and Sigismondo away to Naples.[141] The brothers did not, however, allow Leonello's son to succeed to the lordship: he was displaced first by Borso (1450–71), then by Ercole (1471–1505) and reacted by launching an invasion of Ferrara in 1476.[142]

In all this, two points stand out. First, the remarkable extent to which the Estensi were able to prevent the partition of their ter-

---

[137] Frizzi, *Memorie*, vol. 3, pp. 394–415; B. Cessi, *Venezia e Padova e il Polesine di Rovigo* (Città di Castello, 1904), pp. 51 ff; A. Manni, *L'età minore di Niccolo d'Este Marchese di Ferrara (1393–1402)* (Reggio, 1910).

[138] The pension was partly in compensation for revenues from Azzo's estates seized by Niccolo III: ASM, Not.Cam., P. Bononia, fol. 70v; *Libri Commemoriali*, ix, nos. 195–6; Sanudo, *Vite*, 780. For Azzo's difficulties in obtaining payment: ASVe, Senato, Secreta, reg. 3, fols. 15 (22 Apr. 1406), 59 (17 Mar. 1407); ibid., reg. 4, fol. 73v (9 Oct. 1409); ASM, Casa e Stato, 22/65 (5 Dec. 1411). See also Nicolio, *Rovigo*, p. 173; Manni, *Un ramo*, pp. 14–15.

[139] Frizzi, *Memorie*, vol. 3, pp. 415ff.

[140] ASM, Casa e Stato, b. 324 (fasc. 10/1963), iii.

[141] Frizzi, *Memorie*, vol. 3, pp. 491, 499.

[142] A. Capelli, 'Niccolo di Lionello d'Este', *AMMo*, 5 (1868).

ritories and lordships. Neither formal division, as practised by the Visconti, nor informal division, as practised by the Malatesta, were adopted and other members did not create separate, hereditary lordships (*cf.* the Malatesta of Pesaro).[143] The second point, which was in contrast shared by all other *signori*, was the scant regard paid to legitimate succession: there was a persistent tendency for lineal descent to be contested, at times frustrated, by the power of collateral kinsmen.[144]

### THE LANDS OF EXILES AND REBELS

The ruthlessness with which the *signori* eliminated rivals was shown not only within the Este family: from the start, the Este patrimony was expanded by dispossession of Ferrarese noble families, first the Adelardi and Casotti, then, following 1240, the Torelli, Ramberti and other exiles.[145] The result, as the marquises acquired the property of both families that had previously dominated Ferrara, was that no other family could rival the Estensi in terms of landed power. This alone could explain the early success of the Este *signoria*.[146]

Acquisition of these properties was not altogether straight-forward, however, and the date and precise political context of their final passage to the Estensi is not always clear. As late as 1259, a group of Ferrarese exiles in Cremona still retained their estates in the Ferrarese *contado*, as the marquis agreed to release the crops to them.[147] But at about the same time, the bishop confiscated the fiefs of the Ramberti and others, which were later granted to Azzo d'Este 'to be distributed in fief among the men of his faction'.[148] In this case, the seizure of exiles' property was made secure by the church, but in other cases the process was more difficult. In the 1250s and 1260s,

---

[143] Jones, *Malatesta*, pp. 86, 102–3, 179, 267, 296–7.

[144] Ibid., pp. 165, 186n, 204, 247, 253.

[145] For the Casotti property, contested between Aldrovandino d'Este and Salinguerra Torelli and later to be found held by Este vassals: Castagnetti, 'Enti', p. 404; Muratori, *Antichità*, vol. 2, p. 2; Trombetti, 'Vassalli', nos. 95, 115, 130, 349. For the property of the Guattarelli and Partenopeo ('vir dives et potens', *Chron. Parva*, 480): ASM, Catastri, A, fol. 21v; Feudi Usi Livelli Affitti, 22.

[146] A. Castagnetti, *Società e politica a Ferrara*, pp. 216–17.

[147] *Documenti per la storia delle relazioni diplomatiche fra Verona e Mantova nel sec. XIII*, ed. C. Cipolla (Milan, 1901), p. 78.

[148] 'per feudum . . . inter factionis suae viros distribuendae': Trombetti, 'Vassalli', p. 70n. (This supplements the claim of *Chron. Parva*, 482). For the 1332 investiture of *valli* and *possessiones* towards the border with Bologna: ASM, Casa e Stato, Controversie di Stato, b. 511; Frizzi, *Memorie*, vol. 3, p. 131; Trombetti, 'Vassalli', pp. 70–3.

Azzo d'Este, in assuming and granting such lands, sometimes admitted his poor title, either explicitly or by granting in revocable form (*feudum ad voluntatem*).[149] In the 1270s, however, in accordance with statutes issued in the previous decade, special officials were appointed to pronounce on disputes arising from possession of exiles' lands.[150] Later, in the fourteenth century, there appeared a separate office dealing with rebel property (*camera rebellium*). This office was perhaps created during the period of direct papal rule of Ferrara (1310–17): certainly we later find the Pope confirming Este grants to a number of courtiers of rebel property confiscated during that period.[151] A separate official, for these rebel properties and other revenues, is recorded at times throughout the fourteenth century,[152] and though the office was eventually absorbed by the Este *camera*, cameral account books nevertheless long retained the original categories of property ('Usus Rambertorum', 'Usus Salinguerre', 'Usus rebellium'), which formed a small, but significant section of landed income.[153]

From the late thirteenth century, the passage to the *signori* of fiefs and leases previously held of the church by other noble families became frequent. When Manuele and Francesco Menabuoi died without legitimate male heirs in 1334, the tithes they had held in fief of the bishop were transferred to the Estensi.[154] In 1367 the bishop granted to the marquis the tithes which Francesco Medici, Filippo Pagani and members of the Costabili had held, claiming them as escheats because of their failure to obtain investiture (in fact, the Costabili had been executed by the Estensi).[155] Land which the Costabili had held followed in 1393.[156] Meanwhile, the bishop of Adria had invested the Estensi with tithes at and around Lendinara, an escheat from the Cattanei di Lendinara, and of rights at Raccano in

---

149 Trombetti, 'Vassalli', pp. 111 n. 20, 175. On *feuda ad voluntatem*, see below, chapter 4. Again in the 1330s, the Este were making grants *ad voluntatem* of rebels' property: ASM, Not. Cam., P. Fabro, fols. 54v, 62v, 66v, 68, 91.
150 'quod dominus Marchio vel cui commiserit habeat cognitionem de omnibus questionibus que essent vel esse possent occasione terrarum extrinsecorum propter guerram': *Stat Ferr. 1287*, Lib. I, ix. For such sentences in 1270s: Trombetti, 'Vassalli', pp. 109 n. 14, 116 n. 33, 121 n. 40.
151 ASV, RV, 253, fols. 36v–8v. Papal licences were later required to alienate this property: RV, 256, fol. 74v; 257, fols. 46v–7.
152 'iudex et officialis super bonis Sancte Romane Ecclesie, rebellium et terraticorum comunis Ferrarie': ASM, Investiture di Feudi, 11/22; Not. Cam., Diversorum.
153 ASM, Feudi Usi Affitti Livelli, 22, fols. 6–14v.
154 ASM, Not. Cam., P. Fabro, fol. 16.
155 ASM, Not. Cam., F. Tagliapetri, A, fols. 48–v (11 Mar. 1367).
156 ASM, Casa e Stato, Controversie di Stato, b. 511 (22 June 1393).

the Polesine formerly held by the da Fratta family.[157] And in addition to ecclesiastical property, allods were seized and fiefs previously granted by the Este themselves were resumed.[158]

GIFTS AND GRANTS

From the start, the Estensi had redistributed what they had inherited or grasped and their liberality continued long after the family itself was firmly established in the city. As elsewhere, the exercise of lordship was a continuing task, needing to be continually asserted and renewed. And giving was an important part of that process: liberality was not just a virtue, but a powerful means of establishing political relationships.[159] In addition to outright gifts of land or the conversion of fiefs to allods, the Este also continued to grant new fiefs to their servants and supporters (as we shall see). This contrasts with Visconti practice, by which gifts of land took the place of fiefs in rewarding courtiers and officials as the fief was reserved to grants of jurisdiction to the territorial nobility. At Ferrara, both fiefs and gifts continued to be used to reward those close to the marquises.[160]

Gifts of land are recorded in small numbers from the 1330s, but become frequent only in the early fifteenth century. Some of these gifts were large: those, for example, to Niccolo III's right-hand man, Uguccione Contrari,[161] to his physician, Ugo Benzi,[162] to his secretaries, Niccolo dell'Abbadia and Jacopo Giglioli[163] or to his

---

[157] Speroni, *Series*, pp. 139–40; ASM, Casa e Stato, 13/5. Raccano, with Polesella, Litigia and Guandiario, was held by the da Fratta family in the thirteenth century (Trombetti, 'Vassalli', pp. 112–4), but was allotted to Aldrovandino d'Este in the 1310 division (see Appendix, doc. 2) and it was a dispute between Aldrovandino's sons and their vassals at Raccano that occasioned the revolt in Ferrara in 1317: *Sette libri inediti del 'De Gestis Italicorum post Henricum VII' di Albertino Mussato*, ed. L. Padrin (Venice, 1903), pp. 9–13.

[158] See below, chapter 5.

[159] 'Cogli amici si vuole essere liberale, prestare, donare loro, quando achade': G. Rucellai, *Il Zibaldone Quaresimale*, ed. A. Perosa (London, 1960), p. 10 and generally for the importance of spending pp. 10–12. Cf. Lewis, *Later Medieval France*, p. 201.

[160] Chittolini, 'Infeudazioni', pp. 65–6. Cf. the long list of 'Doni facti per lo duca Borso' in Ugo Caleffini, 'Cronaca in rime', ed. A. Capelli, *AMMo*, 2 (1865), 293–301; Jones, *Malatesta*, pp. 295, 299.

[161] 565 *starii* at Porto: ASM, Not. Cam., A. Montani, fols. 56v–7v.

[162] 641 *campi* near Rovigo: ASM, Not. Cam., C. Lardi, A, fols. 58v–60. For other gifts to Ugo Benzi, 'medicorum princeps' (Aeneas Sylvius) and for his period as Niccolo's physician: D. P. Lockwood, *Ugo Benzi, Medical Philosopher and Physician 1376–1439* (Chicago, 1951), pp. 30, 169, 173–7, 192–3.

[163] Niccolo dell'Abbadia received 250 *campi* near Francavilla to be held of the abbey of

mistresses.[164] Some gifts consisted of entire blocks of property (*castalderie*), demesne lands and tenants, with revenues from local tolls, gabelles and tithes; others consisted of specific categories of revenue from named tenants. Officials and courtiers received large rewards of this type. In 1435, for example, Bartolomeo Pendaglia, in reward for his skilful management of Este revenues, received the *castalderia* of Consandolo, consisting of two *palatia* (one called 'el castello') and ancillary buildings, over 490 hectares (4,500 *starii*) and thousands of vines, with the inn, livestock and tax immunities both for himself and his *laboratores*.[165] Jurisdiction might be given to such men too: Francesco Ariosti received that at Cornacervina, Galasso Medici was given that at Comacchio.[166] Generally, however, gifts consisted of one or more farms (*possessiones*) in the *contado*, even small pieces or houses in the city.[167]

Such gifts frequently recorded the loyalty, services and merits of the recipient, especially 'for the state, conservation and honour of the marquis'. Some rewarded specific expenses incurred in Este service, for example those of the Boiardi in garrisoning Fiorano against rebels in the Modenese in the 1390s, or those of Aldrovandino Giocoli for ransom and other expenses when, as Niccolo's ambassador, he was seized and imprisoned for four years.[168] Not all gifts, however, were rewards of service: a number were, more or less explicitly, repayments of debts, a clear indication of Estensi liquidity

---

Vangadizza: ASM, Archivio d'Espagnac, b. 25; and the escheat of the Cattanei da Lusia: ASM, Not. Cam., A. Villa, fol. 73v. On Giglioli, see below chapter 5.

[164] Stella dell'Assassino, mother of Ugo, Leonello and Borso, received 292 *campi* at Saguedo and Barbuglio: ASM, Not. Cam., J. Delaito, fols. 182–5 (1402); Camilla a Tavola received lands in the Bolognese and Ferrarese: Not. Cam., C. Lardi, A, fol. 60 (1434) and A. Villa, fol. 68.

[165] ASM, Not. Cam., D. Dulcini, C, fols. 63–9 (13 Apr. 1435).

[166] Gift to Francesco Ariosti of 856 *starii* and 57,800 vines mainly at Cornacervina, with a 'palacium' and stables, the river-crossing and the 'potestaria dicte ville': ASM, Not. Cam., J. Sanvitale, fols. 9–15 (8 Nov. 1361); gift to Galassio Medici of Comacchio 'cum toto eius districtu et cum mero et mixto imperio': Not. Cam., M. Conte, fol. 12 (11 July 1352). The grant of Comacchio seems unique in Este control of the outlying territories towards the coast and might be connected with Este relations with Venice: see Dean, 'Venetian economic hegemony'.

[167] The ambassador Aldrovandino Giocoli received 448 *starii* and 6,000 vines at Ariano (Not. Cam., P. Bononia, fol. 136, 1413), the councillor Paolo Barbalunga 50 *starii* at Gaibana (Not. Cam., A. Villa, fol. 43, 1430). Among the many recipients of houses in Ferrara were the foreign nobles Ottaviano Macaruffi (Not. Cam., B. Nigrisoli, fol. 34, 1346), Niccolo Ariosti (Not. Cam., J. Sanvitale, fol. 127, 1369), Francesco and Antonio Visconti (Not. Cam., A. Montani, fol. 59v; Mandati, 1, fol. 51).

[168] ASM, Not. Cam., P. Sardi, A, fols. 4–6; P. Bononia, fol. 136.

in lands, but not in cash.[169] Apart from debts to bankers written off in this way, large numbers of citizens had credits with the *camera*: of salaries as officials, wages as labourers, of debts for the supply of foodstuffs, textiles, wood and so forth. Consequently, it was common practice to accumulate credits at the camera, to be offset in cancellation of tax or rent arrears or in gift of property. Other property, especially in the early 1430s, seems to have been sold specifically to raise money.[170]

Gifts of land were only one of many favours to which service and familiarity with the marquis could give access: tax immunities, of various kinds and for various periods; money gifts and assignments of revenue; loans in money or seed corn; sales and leases of land. And one reward which those closest to the marquis enjoyed was the conversion of their fiefs to allods (or, more rarely, to leases). Few allodialisations are recorded before 1400, although there were some allodial grants of escheated fiefs.[171] From 1400, however, conversion from fief to allod became quite common and some sixty are recorded in the years to 1441. The vast majority of these were to men close to the marquis: among Ferrarese nobles, Uguccione Contrari, Antonio Costabili and Giocolo Giocoli; among foreign nobles, Jacopo Rangoni, Nanne Strozzi, Ricciardo Cancellieri, Bartolomeo Fontana and the Roberti; among officials, Gabriele Pendaglia, Jacopo Giglioli, Bartolomeo della Mella, the Perondoli and many

---

[169] Gift to Novello and Giovanni Novelli of 7,000 vines in the suburb of San Luca and of 398 *starii*, 6,000 vines and 21 *opere* at Copparo in repayment of debts in 1403 (ASM, Leggi e Decreti, B III, fol. 89); to Filippo da Pisa of two houses in Ferrara in part payment of a debt of L.5,000 (arrears of military stipend): Not. Cam., P. Bononia, fols., 53v–4, 1405. The executors of Aliprando Guidizoni, a merchant–supplier of the court, received four houses in Ferrara in 1434 in settlement of outstanding debts of 3,430 ducats: Not. Cam., D. Dulcini, A, fol. 103 and C, fol. 44.

[170] e.g. the sales to Aliprando Guidizoni of property at Bergantino for 8,000 ducats and to Troilo Boncompagni of property at Costa for 1,000 ducats: ASM, Not. Cam., C. Lardi, A, fols. 88 ff. (4 July 1430); AV, Archivio Boncompagni, Prot. 599, no. 7. Troilo had been *podestà* at Ferrara several times since 1425, became a councillor and was knighted by Niccolo III: ibid., Prot. 587, nos. 5 & 6; Prot. 599, no. 6; ASM, Not. Cam., D. Dulcini, C. fol. 27v; Leggi e Decreti, B IV, fol. 116; G. Bertoni, *Guarino da Verona fra letterati e cortigiani a Ferrara 1429–60* (Geneva, 1921), p. 273.

[171] Allodialised fiefs: to Niccolo Roberti in 1365, over 85 *starii* at Villamana (ASM, Not. Cam., J. Sanvitale, fol. 67); and to Niccolo II's physician, Gerardo da Rovigo, 250 *campi* in the Polesine in 1361 (ibid., fols. 22–4). Allodialisations of feudal escheats: to the *referendario*, Francesco Tagliapetri, a piece at Vigarano (Not. Cam., A.Cavaleria, fols., 30v–31v, 1386); to the cameral official Giuliano Gualengo, the fief of the rebel Filippo Montanari, land 'in magna quantitate' at Marrara (ibid., fol. 96v, 1395).

others.[172] Among such men, it was a favour to receive a feudal grant, but it was a greater exercise of favour to release that grant from the restrictions of feudal tenure. Some of these grants were of a single farm, of small fractions of land in the *contado*, or of a house in Ferrara; many however, were of some size, with thirteen over 54 hectares (500 *starii*) and three of those over 110 hectares. The most extraordinary of these is the Contrari grant. In reward for his 'infinite labours and great perils' sustained in the preservation of the marquis' 'status', Uguccione Contrari received the forts at Sariano and Trecenta in the Ferrarese *contado*, and, in the triangle of territory between Stellata, Trecenta and Castelmassa, substantial lands and vineyards, with tithes, pasture and livestock, tax immunities for the inhabitants, civil and limited criminal jurisdiction, the inn, river tolls and control over the retailing of bread, wine and meat.[173] This represents the creation of an aristocratic rural lordship of a type that seems rare in the Ferrarese *contado*: the geographical location of this property is therefore significant – as in the Contrari grant in the Modenese *contado*[174] Niccolo III was making over seigneurial powers in a border area to one of his closest companions and associates.

More representative of the allodial grants of fiefs were those given to Pietro and Francesco Pritati and to Zaccaria Trevisan.[175] The total of feudal land allodialised in the period 1400–41 was well over 2,500 hectares – an extraordinary amount given that the total of Este land under fief in 1394–5 was perhaps only double that figure.[176] Although the recipients sometimes remained vassals of the marquis for other property (occasionally this was a condition),[177] the overall effect of these grants seems quite clear: the removal on a large scale of both lands and vassals from feudal dependence.

There were also, of course, gifts of property to local churches, but

---

[172] For the Giocoli, Roberti, Pendaglia and Giglioli, see below. Antonio Costabili, a regular *podestà* in the territory, received a house in Ferrara and 222 *starii* and 23,000 vines at Viconovo (Not. Cam., F. Libanori, fol. 29, 1426; N. Abbatia, A, fol. 8v, 1405). Nanne Strozzi received 911 *starii* and 13,600 vines at Gambulaga, Cocomaro and Portoverrara (Not. Cam., N. Bonazoli, B, fol. 36, 1400).

[173] ASM, Not. Cam., N. Abbatia, A, fols. 70v–89v (7 Oct. 1409). Though note that the *castalderia Sariani* had earlier been enfeoffed to a leading Este administrator of the mid-fourteenth century (Maio): Not. Cam., M. Benintendi, fols. 112v–14 (7 Mar. 1353).   [174] See below chapter 6.

[175] Together the Pritati received 953 *starii* and 56,500 vines at Cornacervina, while alone Pietro Pritati received 423 *starii* at Porto and Consandolo: ASM, Not. Cam., N. Bonazoli, fols. 59 (21 May 1403), 79 (15 Jan. 1406). Zaccaria Trevisan received 1,567 *starii*, 54,300 vines, 84 *opere* and part of the tithe at Corlo, Ruina and elsewhere (Not. Cam., J. Delaito, fol. 198, 1403).

[176] See below, p. 75.        [177] ASM, Catastri, K, fols. 194–202.

until the second half of the fifteenth century these are not impressively lavish. The reputation of Borso and Ercole as religious patrons so far overshadows that of their predecessors that their liberality seems pinched in contrast. Obizzo d'Este's will of 1292 ordered the construction of a religious house for fifty Franciscan friars near Rovigo and reserved the revenues of his estates at Calaone to fund four priests to celebrate services for his soul continuously in perpetuity.[178] Este patronage of the Franciscans in Ferrara seems to have been limited to laying foundation stones, erecting chapels and ancillary buildings, placing daughters and sisters into Clarissine communities and having tombs in the mendicant churches.[179] Azzo VIII's will of 1308 seems the most generous, with assignments of revenue for the construction of a chapel for six friars to celebrate masses for his soul and for the construction of two hospitals and with cash bequests to the friars and to every chapel in Ferrara.[180] Alberto endowed a chapel in the Servi church with the rents of some property in 1392.[181] Only in the 1430s did the Estensi acquire a major ecclesiastical project of their own: this was S. Maria degli Angeli, built and equipped by Niccolo III and endowed by Leonello in 1444.[182] But Niccolo's own will contains no specific pious bequests at all and is pervaded by the then fashionable concern with simplicity and humility.[183]

The Este patrimony was thus not a fixed collection of estates, but was constantly changing, as properties were acquired and disposed of by inheritance and bequest, purchase and sale, exchange and assignment, escheat and infeudation. Fiscal need might have been one motive for selling land (in 1398, for example, the council was considering the sale of large amounts of property in order to redeem the Polesine from Venice),[184] but this would have been only one of

---

[178] Cipolla, *Documenti*, pp. 370–2. For Borso and Ercole: C. Rosenberg, "'Per il bene di . . . nostra cipta'": Borso d'Este and the Certosa of Ferrara', *Renaissance Quarterly*, 29 (1976); Brown, 'Magnificence', pp. 10–15, 27–31.

[179] P. T. Lombardi, *I Francescani a Ferrara* (4 vols., Bologna, 1974–5), vol. 1, pp. 22–3, 35, 38, 73, 79; vol. 4, pp. 24–7; *cf.* Jones, *Malatesta*, pp. 41, 85, 190.

[180] Gaudenzi, 'Testamento', pp. 108–9.

[181] ASM, Leggi e Decreti, B I, fols. 111–13.

[182] ASM, Leggi e Decreti, B V, fols. 82–v, 165.

[183] ASM, Casa e Stato, b. 324 (fasc. 10/1963), iii. He ordered he be buried in S. Maria, Belfiore, 'in terra nudum omnibus abiectis ambitiosis et superbis funeralibus pompis' and left levels of funeral expenditure and alms for his soul to the judgement of Leonello.

[184] ACF, Deliberazioni, Libro A, fol. 41 (7 Feb. 1399); Cessi, *Venezia e Padova*, pp. 87–8.

many pressures acting on patrimonial management: reward of service, the attraction and maintenance of support, the response to petition, all justify or explain alienations.

## PRIVATE VILLAS AND VILLAGES

Within this constantly changing picture, there were, however, a number of major territorial acquisitions, indicating the deliberate expansion of Este property in selected areas. Chief among these in Niccolo III's reign was the creation of a villa (*delizia*) at Belriguardo, near Voghiera to the south east of the city. As peripatetic lords, interested in the aristocratic pursuits of hunting and hawking, the Estensi had numerous villas in the *contado*. In contrast to their urban and suburban villas (Schifanoia, Paradiso, Belfiore), little is known about these rural *delizie* in the fourteenth and early fifteenth centuries.[185] They were usually associated with demesne farms (*castalderie*) and a reading of Este letters reveals how much time they spent in such places.[186] In addition to the existing villas at Fossadalbero, Quartesana and Copparo, Niccolo III seems to have built two villas, at Consandolo and Belriguardo. Belriguardo, like the others, 'half farm, half palace',[187] was also a major Renaissance construction. Emperor Frederick III, on visiting it, remarked that 'in all the world there is not a villa like this', a remark echoed by Lodovico Sforza later in the century: 'non credo chel mondo abia una simile'.[188] Much of the decoration for which the villa became famous was of the second half of the century, but already in 1452 there were fifty rooms, two loggias and large stables.[189] All this had been created out of nothing. The land itself (over 600 hectares) was bought from a large number of private owners and tenants in 1437–8; and the bishop was persuaded (after some difficulty, it seems) to surrender his rights as direct lord, in exchange for the direct dominion (freehold) of some leases of highly valuable commercial property in and around the main square in Ferrara.[190]

[185] G. Pazzi, *Le 'Delizie Estensi' e l'Ariosto. Fasti e piaceri di Ferrara nella Rinascenza* (Pescara, 1933); U. Malagu, *Ville e 'delizie' del Ferrarese* (Ferrara, 1972).

[186] *Cf.* G. P. Lubkin, 'The Court of Galeazzo Maria Sforza, Duke of Milan (1466–1476)', University of California, Berkeley, Ph.D., 1982, pp. 13–16.

[187] C. M. Ady, *The Bentivoglio of Bologna* (Oxford 1937), pp. 193–5; V. F. Pardo and G. Casali, *I Medici nel contado fiorentino* (Florence, 1978).

[188] Chiappini, *Gli Estensi*, p. 360.

[189] Gundersheimer, *Ferrara*, pp. 254ff; Pazzi, *Delizie*, pp. 143–86.

[190] For the purchases: ASM, Catastri, Appendice; for the exchange with the bishop: ANF, D. Dulcini, pacco 1 (proceedings before the archbishop of Ravenna) and see

More politically important were Niccolo's acquisitions along the northern edge of the Ferrarese *contado* (see Map 6). This area was important for two reasons: first, because the canal that started from Corbola was a major route for river-traffic to and from Venice;[191] secondly, because it was an area traditionally closed to Este influence. In the thirteenth century, the marquises seem to have owned little land there and although they had a fort built at Corbola in the mid-fourteenth century, the area remained dominated by the major landowners: the old noble families, the Giocoli, Turchi and Burzelli; two newer families, the Marocelli and Marinetti; and a Venetian patrician family, the Querini.[192] Of these the Giocoli and Marinetti were prominent at court and in Este service,[193] but the Turchi and Marocelli lived mainly on their estates,[194] while the Querini seem to have been the most privileged and troublesome of Venetian landowners in the Ferrarese *contado*.[195]

Este acquisition here had started in the late fourteenth century, with a renunciation by Albertino Turchi of lands, jurisdiction and tithe that he held of the Archbishop of Ravenna at Cologna and Crespino.[196] This was soon followed by acquisitions, partly by exchange, partly by confiscation, from the Marinetti, Raffeto Marocelli and Bartolomeo della Mella of property at Corbola, Guarda and Crespino.[197] Corbola was gradually absorbed into Este control. Niccolò III promoted reclamation there by tax concessions to owners and share-croppers, having previously secured from the

---

Muratori, *Antichità*, vol. 2, p. 197; G. A. Scalabrini, *Memorie istoriche delle chiese di Ferrara e de' suoi borghi* (Ferrara, 1773), p. 30; Pazzi, *Delizie*, p. 166.

[191] The fifteenth-century 'Statuti della gabella grossa' indicate two transit routes through the Ferrarese: one (for goods from Venice to 'Lombardia') via Stellata (Ficarolo), Bondeno and then towards Modena; another (for goods from 'Lombardia' to Venice and from Venice to Bologna and thence into the Romagna) via 'Corbola de sotto' and various waterways across the Ferrara–Bologna border: ASM, ASE, Cancelleria, Statuti Capitoli Grazie, b. 1.

[192] See below, p. 143.

[193] See below, chapter 5.      [194] See below, chapter 5.

[195] The Querini and their tenants enjoyed immunity from Ferrarese communal taxation and levies. This immunity, confirmed in 1401, was a source of many disputes with the commune in the fifteenth century: Dean, 'Venetian economic hegemony'. Niccolò III was aware of the need for care in handling the Querini, declining to act when the bishop of Ferrara, in combination with the Dominicans and the commune, tried to extend communal taxation to the church at Papozze of which the Querini were patrons: 'perche el non para che nui volgiamo inovare cossa alguna ad quilli da cha quirino che ano a fare li': ACF, Deliberazioni, Libro C, fol. 156v.

[196] ASM, Not. Cam., R. Codegorio, A, fols. 97v–9 (19 Sept. 1381); Tarlazzi, *Appendice*, vol. 2, doc. 195, pp. 364–7.

[197] ASM, Catastri, K, fols. 296, 411; Q, fols 322–6.

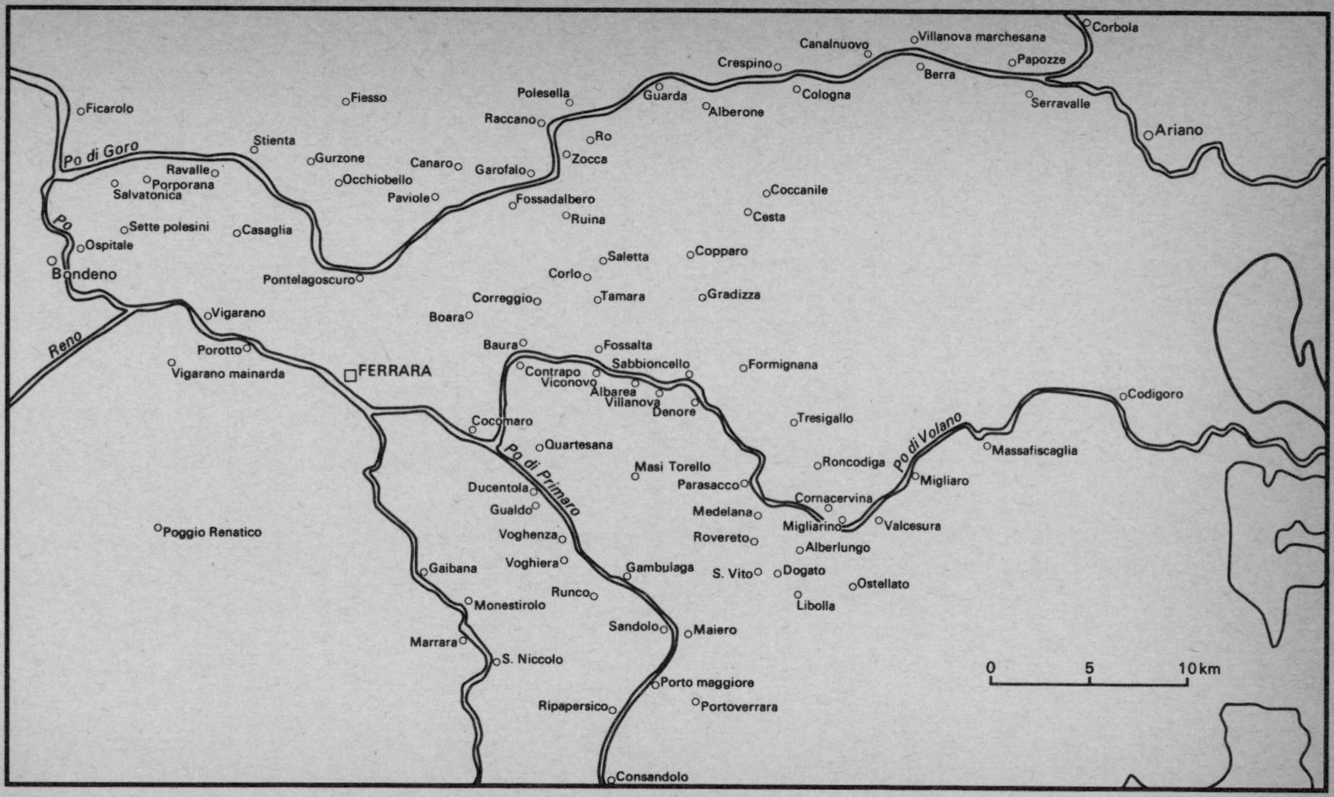

Map 6 The Ferrarese *contado*

Corbola
Ariano
Villanova marchesana
Papozze
Serravalle
Berra
Canalnuovo
Cologna
Crespino
Coccanile
Guarda
Alberone
Casta
Polesella
Ro
Copparo
Zocca
Saletta
Gradizza
Raccano
Fossadalbero
Ruina
Tamara
Formignana
Garofalo
Corlo
Fossalta
Canaro
Correggio
Baura
Fiesso
Boara
Sabbioncello
Contapo
Vicono
Albarea
Denore
Gurzone
Occhiobello
Paviole
FERRARA
Quartesana
Masi Torello
Parasacco
Cocomaro
Stienta
Pontelagoscuro
Coccomaro
Ducentola
Medelana
Rovereto
S. Vito
Ravalle
Porporana
Salvatonica
Sette polesini
Casaglia
Vigarano
Vigarano mainarda
Porotto
Gualdo
Voghenza
Voghiera
Gambulaga
Sandolo
Maiero
Ficarolo
Ospitale
Bondeno
Poggio Renatico
Gaibana
Runco
Monestirolo
Marrara
S. Nicolo
Ripapersico
Porto maggiore
Portoverrara
Codigoro
Massafiscaglia
Migliaro
Valcesura
Roncodiga
Cornacervina
Migliarino
Alberlungo
Dogato
Ostellato
Libolla
Tresigallo
Consandolo

Po di Goro
Po
Reno
Po di Primaro
Po di Volano

0    5    10 km

bishop of Adria the tithe of newly assarted land there.[198] In 1437 local fiscal customs at Corbola were eliminated.[199] Meanwhile, Querini lands at Papozze were bought, partly from the family, partly from their trustees (the *Procuratori di S. Marco*).[200] Arable land at Ariano, given to Aldrovandino Giocoli in 1413 and which the Giocoli had since then let become marsh and wood, was recovered in 1428. Here Niccolo declared his intention of sending in workers to 'dig the dykes and cut down the trees in quick time', in order to bring the land into 'good order and profit'.[201] A few years earlier, Matteo Burzelli had released all his property at Villanova in return for a number of farms at Corbola.[202] This restored to Este control a settlement whose creation they had originally sponsored and which now changed its name from Villanova 'Burzellorum' to Villanova marchesana.[203] Este influence in this area was further advanced through promotion of the landed interests there of Niccolo's secretary, Jacopo Giglioli.[204]

### CASTALDERIE AND LANDED REVENUES

Corbola and Belriguardo were only two estates, of many, where the Estensi retained direct control of their lands. The basic administrative unit of these demesne estates was the *castalderia*, usually comprising the lands in a particular locality (*fundus*) and consisting of demesne and tenant lands, and the revenues from the inn, river crossings and local taxes. The number of these *castalderie* was constantly changing as estates were granted in fief or gift, acquired or recovered.[205] Records do not allow a detailed description of them

---

[198] ASM, Leggi e Decreti, B IV, fol. 114v (1 Mar. 1425); Bocchi, *Sede*, p. 20.
[199] ACF, Deliberazioni, Libro E, fol. 26 (8 Aug. 1437).
[200] ASF, Archivio Tassoni, VI/11 (1418) and VII/3 (1429); ASM, Not. Cam., D. Dulcini, A, fol. 115 (1431); and see R. C. Mueller, 'The Procurators of San Marco in the thirteenth and fourteenth centuries', *Studi Veneziani*, 13 (1971), 199–204.
[201] ASM, Catastri, Q, fols. 604–8.
[202] Niccolo acquired patronage of the church, all property which Matteo held by lease from the monastery of Gavello and from a Veronese citizen, his allods and the direct dominion of over 36 vassals and 15 lessees. In return, Matteo received seven *possessiones* at Corbola (1,007 *starii*, 29,000 vines and 83 *opere*) with tax immunities: ASM, Catastri, Q, fols. 341–60; L, fols. 268–75.
[203] Trombetti, 'Vassalli', p. 195.
[204] See below, chapter 5.
[205] A list of *castalderie* in 1415 comprised, in the Ferrarese: Mellara, Bergantino, Paviole, two at Corbola, Copparo, Fossadalbero, Belfiore, Quartesana, Rovereto, Migliarino, Ostellato, Campolungo, S. Giovanni, Migliaro, Villanova, Papozze, Consandolo and Porto; and in the Polesine: Rovigo, Costa,

until the second half of the fifteenth century,[206] although we know that in the early fifteenth century the *castalderia* at Costa consisted of 124 *campi* (55 hectares) worked by *laboratores* and 230 *campi* held on leases and owing a fraction of the crop.[207] The estate at Casaglia in 1452 had twenty-five *laboratores* (usually *mezzadri*), who produced mainly corn, but also other grains (barley, rye, oats, maize, millet) and other crops (beans, linseed, wine). The bulk of the crop was sent to the marquis' granaries in Ferrara, the rest being remitted or loaned to the sharecroppers for the next year's crop, used to pay wages or sent to other estates.[208] The marquis' *laboratores* were exempt from communal taxation, but were subject to various curial dues, corvées and so on.[209] In addition to these estates, the marquis had large numbers of cattle and other livestock that were leased out separately and to some profit.[210]

Evidence from elsewhere might suggest that aristocratic estate management was dominated by short-term profit-taking,[211] but the free use the Este made of agricultural land for political and recreational purposes would confirm other evidence that the Este did not look to their lands for cash income. Indeed, landed revenue, although of some size, was not large compared to other sources. Arriving at any figures for landed revenue is extremely complex because it was accounted for under many different headings. An account of rents for the year 1414 carried a total of L.4,729 of rents due, but this included sums for river tolls, tithes and urban rents, leaving some L.2,100 due from specifically landed rents. And of the

Villamarzana, Lendinara and Saguedo: ASM, Leggi e Decreti, A 5, fols. 1–2. For the creation of new *castalderie* from confiscated and acquired property: Leggi e Decreti, A 3, fols. 340, 352, 357; A 4, fols. 3, 7.

206 E. Ghidoni, 'Agricoltura nel xv secolo: le castalderie estensi', *AMMo*, s. 11, 4 (1982).

207 AV, Archivio Boncompagni, Prot. 599, no. 7.

208 ASM, Camera ducale, Amministrazione finanziaria dei paesi, Ferrarese, Casaglia, 1452.

209 All those with meadows at Bergantino owed one tenth of all hay to the *curia*: ASM, Not. Cam., M. Conte, fol. 101. Inhabitants at Sariano owed pens for the officials at the castle, straw for the court and osiers for buildings and hedges at Belfiore: Not. Cam., N. Abbatia, A, fol. 88v.

210 A series of leases of livestock in 1393–5 totalled 1,555 cattle, 265 horses and 160 sheep, with a total book value of L.12,493 and a rental yield of L.830: ASM, Not. Cam., F. Capoclo, fols. 1–37. *Cf.* P. J. Jones, 'From manor to mezzadria: a Tuscan case-study in the medieval origins of modern agrarian society', in *Florentine Studies*, ed. N. Rubinstein (London, 1968), p. 221.

211 S. Anselmi, 'Organizzazione aziendale, colture, rese nelle fattorie malatestiane, '1398–1456', *QS*, 39 (1978); M. Mate, 'Profit and productivity on the estates of Isabella de Forz (1260–92)', *EcHR*, s. 2, 33 (1980).

total due in 1414, little more than half had been collected by 1416.[212]
Such figures substantially underestimate landed revenue, however,
since whole *castalderie* were quite often leased out and accounted for
separately: the *castalderia* of Mellara, for example, was rented out for
L.1,350 in 1406.[213] Even so, revenues from land could never reach
the scale of those from the gabelles and *valli*. All the Ferrarese
gabelles were farmed in 1434 for L.39,000 and the most profitable of
the *valli*, those at Comacchio and Fratta, were farmed, together, for
between L.18,000 and L.25,000.[214] Other *valli*, at Adria and in the
Polesine, were leased for smaller sums. In addition to the Ferrarese
revenues, there were also those from the *camarlengherie* of Argenta
(farmed at L.1,200 in 1414), Finale (L.2,930 in 1416) and Modena and
Reggio (the Modenese gabelles were farmed for L.21,000 in
1417).[215] Total receipts in the mid-fifteenth century were about
L.130,000.[216] Especially important in this total were the duties levied
on transit traffic along the Po, a traffic the Estensi were very anxious
to protect.[217] Chroniclers and ambassadors noted the huge revenues
that the commune and later the Este received from this source.[218]
Land, it seems, the source of Este power, was not the source of Este
wealth.

## ESTATE ADMINISTRATION

With the expansion of Este lands and revenues, a special administration came into being to manage them, which gradually absorbed
even administrative control of the public domain, which was thus
transferred from the commune to the *signore*. Although, like other
*signori*, the Este had had, from the first constitution of the *signoria*,
control of communal property and finance, such control was for
many decades exercised through the institutions and officers of the
commune, rather than directly by the *signore*'s own private offi-

---

212 ASM, Feudi Usi Affitti Livelli, 22.
213 ASM, Not. Cam., N. Delaito, B, fol. 107.
214 ASM, Not. Cam., D. Dulcini, C, fols. 6v *et seq.*; B, fol. 64; N. Delaito, B, fols.
81v, 151v.
215 ASM, Not. Cam., P. Sardi, F, fols.76, 136; Leggi e Decreti, A 5, fol. 254.
216 Sitta, 'Saggio', p. 135.
217 When Milanese merchants began to desert the Po route to Venice in the early
1440s, Leonello cut *dazi* rates by one third: ASM, Leggi e Decreti, B v, fol. 117v;
and see Dean, 'Venetian economic hegemony'.
218 *Chron. Parva*, 483; Theiner, *Codex*, vol. 2, p. 538; *Relazioni degli ambasciatori veneti
al senato*, ed. A. Segarizzi, (Bari, 1912), pp. 6–7.

cials.[219] The supplanting of the commune here was a key institutional change in the development of an Este 'state'.

In the first half of the fourteenth century, it seems that Este patrimonial matters were dealt with by *ad hoc* appointments, mainly of curial notaries, but with much still done by the marquis in person.[220] In the 1330s and 1340s, a number of notaries specialised in patrimonial affairs.[221] They tended to do business in an office on the piazza, which from the mid-1340s came to be called the 'chancery' (*cancelleria*), with the notaries called 'chancellors' (*cancellarii*).[222] The 1340s also saw the appearance of the general manager (*fattore generale*), with commission of more general, but still limited, business.[223] By the early 1360s, the *factoria* had separated from the chancery: the latter still had its office on the piazza, the former had moved to another district of the city and had taken over the former office of the communal financial administration (*massaria*).[224] Although the communal *massaro* was still making grants of the city gabelles and receiving their rents in the 1340s, soon afterwards the marquis seems to have taken control of these, along with the commune's urban rents (*terratica comunis*).[225] The *factoria* thus took over not only the revenues and property of the commune, but also the office of its *massaro*. Development continued in the 1360s: the number of cameral and chancery notaries grew, military finance passed to a special official (*officialis super stipendiariis*),[226] and the

---

219 F. Ercole, 'Comuni e signori nel Veneto', *NAV*, 19 (1910), and now in *Dal Comune al Principato*, (Florence, 1929), p. 104; Picotti, *I Caminesi*, pp. 155–7; G. Pardi, 'Dal comune alla signoria in Orvieto', *BU*, 13 (1908), 447; Jones, *Malatesta*, pp. 72, 312–15.

220 For example, purchases and feudal investitures: ASM, Not. Cam., P. Fabro, *passim*.

221 e.g. Maius 'notarius dominorum': ibid., fols. 15v, 16, 41, 106v.

222 ASM, Not. Cam., P.Fabro, *passim*; B. Nigrisoli, fols. 1, 12, 16; Valenti, 'Cancelleria'; *cf*. A. Borgogno, 'Prime indagini sulla cancelleria mantovana al tempo della signoria', *Ricerche medievali*, 1 (1966).

223 Jacopo da Porto, *factor generalis*, was authorised to make feudal investitures *ad voluntatem* only (which allowed revocation by the lord): ASM, Not. Cam., B.Nigrisoli, fol. 43 (1347).

224 ASM, Not. Cam., F. Sale, fols. 65, 87. Though the office of *massaro* continued to have important financial functions, relative to communal taxation: ACF, Deliberazioni, *passim*.

225 ASM, Not. Cam., B. Nigrisoli, *passim*. *Cf*. the transfer of communal revenues to the *signore*'s patrimonial officials at Mantua and Piacenza: G. Coniglio, *Mantova. La Storia. Dalle origini a Gianfrancesco primo marchese* (Mantua, 1958), pp. 390–1; C. Castignoli, 'Il comune di Piacenza nel 1300: organi comunitativi e signorili', in *Studi storici in onore di E. Nasalli Rocca* (Piacenza, 1971), p. 149.

226 ASM, Not. Cam., F. Sale, fol. 87 (1363). Earlier farmed out to Florentine bankers (e.g. ASM, Investiture di Feudi, 11/48), this office gradually became part of the

functions of the *fattori generali*, usually two in number, were expanded. In addition to the wide-ranging business of managing Este estates and properties,[227] the *fattori generali* were coming increasingly to deal with the receipt and disbursement of revenue and this forced a further division of functions, as special *fattori* were appointed to supervise the estates and to make feudal investitures.[228] Meanwhile, from 1380 the chancery had moved into the main Este palace and was followed in 1390 by the camera.[229] This roughly coincided with a further redistribution of responsibilities within the camera: it was now the handling of receipts and issues that was transferred to subordinate officials, while a new *officialis super possessionibus* took control of the estate stewards and of demesne livestock. The *fattori generali*, while continuing to direct the camera's financial business, themselves took on some patrimonial functions (in particular, investitures).[230] This period also saw the absorption by the *factoria* of the *camera rebellium*, previously managed by a separate official.[231]

This was the pattern which then obtained for the rest of our period. From a situation where financial and patrimonial management had depended intimately on the marquis, the camera now had an autonomous structure, with a network of subordinate officials throughout the state (at Modena, Reggio, S. Felice, Finale, Argenta etc.). Although the camera was obviously subject to the marquis' frequent orders (*mandati*), especially as regards payments and purchases, over ordinary business and ordinary procedures, the marquis came to have only limited control, as was made clear in a sharply-worded exchange of letters between the marquis and the *fattori generali* in 1422 over the control of disbursements: 'You are not to

regular administration and its holder an *ex officio* member of the council. *Cf.* the coterminous development of military finance at Florence and Milan: *I Capitoli del Comune di Firenze. Inventario e Regesto*, ed. C. Guasti (2 vols., Florence, 1866 and 1893), vol. 2, pp. 198, 600, 620; C. Santoro, *Gli offici del comune di Milano e del dominio visconteo–sforzesco 1216–1515* (Milan, 1968), pp. 218–19.

227 ASM, Not. Cam., F. Tagliapetri, A, fols. 23–4, 65v, 68, 70v; F. Maroni, *passim*.
228 For the distinct functions of *fattori* and *fattori generali*: ASM, Not. Cam., J. Mizino, fols. 9v, 11v, 14v; R. Codegorio, A, *passim*.
229 ASM, Not. Cam., Z. Coadi, fol. 111v and *passim*; Catastri, Q, *passim*; Valenti, 'Cancelleria', p. 360.
230 ASM, Not. Cam., C. Lardi, fol. 38; A. Villa, fol. 59. A separate *officialis super possessionibus* seems first to appear in 1402 (Catastri, K, fol. 348) and from 1411 the office was held continuously for many years by members of the Sacrati family (see below p. 135).
231 Although the *camera rebellium* long retained documentary separateness: ASM, Catastri, K, fols. 452, 457; S, fol. 212.

make grants of our revenues, nor spend our money, without our permission . . . We shall be the one to make grants and spend our money', Niccolo III fulminated, but the *fattori* replied firmly that this would disrupt the entire ordinary functioning of the camera.[232]

The 1430s and the early years of Leonello's reign (1441–50) saw a number of changes in public administration.[233] Leonello had been given vicegerential powers by his father in 1434 and his control of routine administration is evident from then.[234] In this period, two inquiries were launched into cameral rights. The first in 1431, required all tenants of the marquis to present their charters to the camera.[235] Examination in this way of titles of possession was no innovation at Ferrara: similar exercises are recorded in the thirteenth century and in 1353 and 1394.[236] The second inquiry was an on-the-spot investigation in the Polesine di Rovigo into fiefs granted in the past century.[237] The aim of both inquiries was the resumption of usurped or escheated lands and the updating and reorganising of cameral records.[238] Although feudal registers had existed in some form in the fourteenth and early fifteenth centuries,[239] from 1435 a new series was compiled of deeds of infeudation and lease. These were transcribed from existing notarial registers and started chronologically from the beginning of Niccolo III's reign in 1393. This was a major operation: the *Catastri*, as they were called, were

---

[232] ASM, Mandati, i, fols. 10–11v.

[233] e.g. changes in the communal administration: see my forthcoming study.

[234] ASM, Not. Cam., A. Villa, insert between fols. 63 and 64 (22 May 1434); for Leonello's replies to petitions, see Leggi e Decreti, B IV, *passim*. In his will, Niccolo mentions Leonello: 'omnium rerum suarum ac totius sui status . . . a multis annis citra disponitorem gubernatorem . . . librum elegit . . .': ASM, Casa e Stato, b. 324.

[235] Sitta, 'Saggio', p. 139 n. 4.

[236] For such exercises in 1252, 1262, 1272–3, 1285–6: Trombetti, 'Vassalli', pp. 83–4 and n. 203, p. 132 n. 68; the large number of confirmatory grants in 1353 indicates a general renewal on Aldrovandino's succession: Not. Cam., M. Conte and M. Benintendi, *passim*. For 1394: Catastri, H, *passim*.

[237] ASM, Cam. Duc., Feudi Usi Affitti Livelli, 151. There was also an investigation of rights in the Reggiano in 1436 (ASM, Not. Cam., C. Lardi, A, fols. 74–v; D. Dulcini, C, fol. 151v; BEM, Doc. Campori, Appendice 1313) and from 1435 a special register for fiefs there (ASM, Not. Cam., vol. 68). Also in 1436 an inventory was taken of movables in Este palaces (by Pietro Lardi, the first *Catastri* custodian): ASM, Catastri, S, fol. 498; G. Bertoni and E. P. Vicini, *Il Castello di Ferrara* (1907); G. Pardi, 'La suppellettile dei palazzi estensi in Ferrara nel 1436', *AMF*, 19 (1908).

[238] See below, p. 123.

[239] 'Captastra' are referred to, e.g. in ASM, Catastri, H, fol. 490. Two cameral notaries kept separate registers for fiefs: ASM, Not. Cam., F.Tagliapetri, B, fol. 9; B.Mella, fol. 52.

written, unlike the notarial registers, on parchment, not paper; all repetitious formulae were given in full, without abbreviation; and the whole series kept a group of notaries occupied for several years. This represented a huge input of labour and materials and, following their completion, the *Catastri* were entrusted to a new official, who was clearly expected to use them to maintain a more efficient control of cameral property.[240] The aim of all this work was obviously to simplify administration in the camera: instead of having to search for charters among the rapidly growing numbers of notarial registers, where they were mixed with all varieties of other business, the *fattori* created a chronological record, complete from 1393, for each type of land tenure. The *Catastri* were the 'authorised version' of titles to land, not just for the Estensi, but for all their tenants. Their value as such was recognised by the late fifteenth-century Ferrarese archivist and historian, Pellegrino Prisciani, who placed the *Catastri* at the very beginning of his inventory of the cameral archive.[241]

[240] ASM, Not. Cam., D. Dulcini, D, fols. 33, 44, 94, 135.
[241] On Prisciani, see Trombetti, 'Vassalli', p. 60 n. 149. In 1488 he was appointed 'conservator iurium camere': G. Bertoni, *La biblioteca estense e la cultura ferrarese ai tempi del duca Ercole I* (Turin, 1903), pp. 171–2; G. Campi, 'Cenni storici intorno l'Archivio Segreto Estense ora Diplomatico', *AMMo*, 2 (1864), 336.

# Chapter 3

# THE ESTE VASSALS AND THEIR FIEFS

The Estensi had vassals in Ferrara long before the establishment of their *signoria* in 1264, but it is only from the last decades of the thirteenth century that large numbers of Este feudal grants survive. These are collected in a variety of sources: the 'statements of vassalage' collected from vassals in 1272–3 and 1285–6, individual charters, the registers of cameral notaries from the mid-fourteenth century and the continuous series of *Catastri delle Investiture* from 1393. These provide two means of analysis of Este vassals: the thirteenth-century statements and the first of the *Catastri* offer frozen pictures of the vassals and their fiefs at particular moments, while the charters, registers and remaining *Catastri* provide a continuous chronological picture, complete from 1393. Combined, all these sources enable us to answer a wide range of questions about late medieval feudalism: who the feudatories were, how much land they held, the precise content of the feudal relationship and its connection with the social and political reality of lordship.[1]

## NUMBER OF VASSALS; SIZE OF FIEFS

The first *Catastro* contains almost exclusively renewals of fiefs made in 1394–5 in accordance with a proclamation issued in April 1394 ordering all vassals to present their charters for confirmation and reinvestiture.[2] The total number of reinvestitures made in these two years was 353, but some of these must be deleted (duplications, investitures to heirs), while others must be added.[3] The resulting total is 371 fiefs, with nearly 700 vassals. The first point to note here is that there were more vassals than fiefs: many fiefs were held jointly

---

[1] *Cf.* Trombetti, 'Vassalli', pp. 101–2.
[2] ASM, Not. Cam., J. Delaito, fol. 106.
[3] ASM, Catastri, H, fols. 15, 36, 197, 462, 463, 615, 626; N, fols. 11, 15, 28, 65, 101, 123, 146, 158, 166, 250, 285, 335, 336–7, 417, 440, 442, 482, 523, 629; R, fols. 47, 106,110, 119, 284, 374, 418, 520, 554, 587, 616, 633; S, fol. 535.

by up to a dozen vassals. The second point to note is that this number is substantially lower than the number of vassals recorded in the registers of 1272–3 and 1285–6 (*c.* 500 *groups* of vassals – and some groups could be large).[4] Also substantially reduced since the thirteenth century appears the total infeudated area. Estimating this is not easy, as unmeasured pieces of land are numerous, while vines are given in thousands and meadowland in terms of works (*opere*) due on it.[5] Nevertheless, for the vast majority of 'pieces' (*petie*) constituting each fief, the areas are given and a minimum total can be calculated for Este fiefs in the territories of Ferrara and Adria of over 5,000 hectares and in the Polesine di Rovigo of over 500 hectares. This is considerably below the estimate for the late thirteenth century of a total infeudated area of over 10,000 hectares.[6] Moreover, by 1394 the composition of both the fiefs and the vassals is less varied. As in the thirteenth century, there are fiefs including fortifications,[7] immunities,[8] and seigneurial powers,[9] but these are few and the overwhelming majority of fiefs consist of many, often small pieces of land or of property and rights based on land (houses, mills, tithes, river-crossings).[10] Gone are the money fiefs and fiefs of office[11] and the large numbers of *homines de macinata* (servile dependents) found in the late thirteenth century.[12]

The reduction in numbers of vassals and of total land infeudated might suggest feudalism in decline, but the overall reductions conceal the creation, during the late fourteenth century, of a con-

---

[4] Trombetti, 'Vassalli', p. 103; Laurent, 'Vassals', p. 66.

[5] It seems that about 400–500 vines would be planted on 1 *staio*: ASM, Catastri, S, fols. 44, 338.

[6] Trombetti, 'Vassalli', p. 104.

[7] 'mota et castellarium cum foveis et canalibus' at Salvatonica (ASM, Catastri, H, fol. 235); 'el castello da Sariano', described as a 'pallatium muratum cupatum et solaratum cum foveis circumcirca puteo porte levatorio et curtili in forma castri' (Catastri, N, fol. 209). For other *palatia*: Catastri, N, fols. 309–12, 428–32; R, fols. 92–101, 517. On *motte* see A. Settia, 'Motte e castelli a motta nelle fonti scritte dell'Italia settentrionale', in *Mélanges d'archéologie et d'histoire médiévales en l'honneur du Doyen Michel de Boüard* (Geneva, 1982).

[8] ASM, Catastri, H, fol. 166; R, fols. 243, 562.

[9] Ibid., H, fols. 335–6; N, fol. 524; R, fols. 131–6, 243, 562.

[10] For a mill: ibid., H, fol. 293; for *passus*: H, fols. 175–9, 209; N, fols. 153, 309, 429; R, fols. 231, 342, 477; for tithes: N, fols. 57, 64, 213, 224, 287–8, 295, 336 etc.

[11] Trombetti, 'Vassalli', nos. 196, 198, 202, 206–7, 216, 230, 232, 234, 236, 239.

[12] Over 40 fiefs in the 1270s and 1280s were held by one or more *homines de macinata* (Trombetti, 'Vassalli'), but only one in 1394 (ASM, Catastri, H. fol. 268). The *homo de macinata*, 'sicut servus', was at the complete disposition of the lord ('merum et plenum dominium'): Muratori, *Antiquitates*, vol. 1, 805–6; Trombetti, 'Vassalli', p. 110 n. 17.

siderable number of new large fiefs. Here again, statistical comparison with the thirteenth century yields striking results. In so far as they can be measured, there were only 7 fiefs in the 1270s and 1280s larger than 50 hectares (460 *starii*), while over two-thirds of the fiefs were of between $\frac{1}{2}$ and 20 hectares (5–104 *starii*).[13] This preponderance of very small, 'ignoble' fiefs obtained still in 1394–5 and throughout the first half of the fifteenth century. It was, indeed, characteristic of north-east Italy, as opposed to Lombardy.[14] The majority of fiefs in 1394 (209) were under 100 *starii*, while 8 were of tithe only and 57 of unspecified or unmeasured property. But in addition, there were 21 fiefs of between 500 and 1,000 *starii* (54–109 hectares) and 13 over 1,000, including 3 over 3,000. This meant that the reduction in numbers of vassals conceals a concentration of infeudated land among a very small group: 23 vassals from 9 families held half of the total infeudated area.

It is the identity of these vassals which gives this development a special significance, for they were mainly foreign noblemen, from outside Ferrara. They were often not permanently resident in Ferrara, but were attached to the city and to the Estensi, some by temporary residence and service, others by less direct ties, forming a 'new feudality' of a sort found elsewhere in the period.[15] Of the fiefs over 1,000 *starii*, for example, the three largest were held by two members of the Roberti family from Reggio and by the Ferrarese wife of one of them.[16] These fiefs, situated in twenty-one localities in the *contado*, totalled over 1,300 hectares, with pasture, *valli* and tithes, as well as five houses in Ferrara. No other family, it seems, from the mid-twelfth century to the mid-fifteenth, held lands of such size in fief of the Este in the Ferrarese. The only fief to rival these in size was that granted to Uguccione Contrari in 1401 (see above p. 62). Four other fiefs, although consisting partly of dispersed pieces and properties, added up to considerable landed holdings. Four members of the Pio di Carpi held a tower, 52 hectares and vineyards at Viconovo, with a further 20 hectares at Albarea and Quartesana, while Marco Pio alone held 165 hectares, with meadow and vineyards, at Voghiera and Monestirolo.[17] The Venetian Marco

---

[13] Ibid., p. 103 n. 247.      [14] Magni, *Tramonto*, pp. 108–9.

[15] G. Barni, 'La formazione interna dello stato visconteo', *ASL*, n.s., 6 (1941), 20–3, 26, 30–40; G. Bognetti, 'Per la storia dello stato visconteo', *ASL*, s. 6, 54 (1927), 267–9.

[16] Fiefs of Cabrino: ASM, Catastri, H, fols. 422, 426–7, 431, 442; of Filippo: H, fols. 122, 617; of Margherita Sala: H, fols. 427, 442; of Niccolo: H, fol. 202.

[17] ASM, Catastri, H, fols. 228, 295, 310, 609.

Corner held over 84 hectares mainly at Canaro and Zocca, to the north-east of the city; the Bolognese noble Egano Lambertini over 90 hectares and a river-crossing (*passus*), also to the north-east;[18] and a Milanese nobleman, Otto da Mandello, 142 hectares and vineyards, mainly at Corlo.[19] The remaining large fiefs were held by the Avenante, a Florentine banking family (*valli* on the Ferrara–Bologna border), the Paduan branch of the Rossi from Parma (271 *campi* in the Padovano), two families of officials (the Avogari and the grandsons of a former *fattore generale*, Bonagratia Muratore) and two families from the *contado* (the Moyse from Berra and Tommaso Canonici from Bondeno).[20]

The holders of fiefs of middling size (500–1,000 *starii*) include similar numbers of foreigners and 'new men'. Among them are the foreign nobles Jacopo da Macha (from Mantua), Bartolomeo Malvicini Fontana (Piacenza), Tommaso degli Obizzi (Lucca), Ricciardo Cancellieri (Pistoia), Pietro Morosini and Federico Leon (Venice) and Giordano da Savignano (Modena). Also among this group are foreigners in household service: the cameral notary Jacopo Delaito from Rovigo, the former *fattore generale* Filippo Geri (a Tuscan) and the Mazzoni from Modena, prominent in diplomatic and administrative office.[21]

Such fiefs were not a temporary phenomenon of the late fourteenth century. When some of them reverted to the camera, they were granted out intact to other members of the Este entourage: the Mandello fief to Zaccaria Trevisan, the Savignano fief to Niccolo III's secretary Jacopo Giglioli and the Morosini fief to the Avogari.[22] For others, new groups of property were assembled: over 400 hectares at Consandolo and Bozoleto for the Milanese nobleman Francesco da Lonate in 1418, over 200 for the Paduan Alidosio Forzate in 1400 and so on.[23] With few exceptions it is the *familiares* and military captains, the administrative and diplomatic officers who receive these larger fiefs.

### FOREIGNERS AND 'NEW MEN'

What is clearly new about Este vassals in the 1390s, therefore, is the large number of foreigners not present a century earlier. But who are

---

[18] Ibid., H, fols. 175, 224.      [19] Ibid., H, fol. 254.
[20] Ibid., H, fols. 43, 80, 92–8, 146, 241, 317, 341, 416, 589, 632; N, fols. 28, 146.
[21] Ibid., H, fols. 16, 40, 64, 117, 166, 239, 282, 284, 288, 314, 401, 512, 619; R, fol. 106.
[22] Ibid., N, fols. 176, 290, 546.      [23] Ibid., N, fol. 160; R, fols. 86, 92.

these men? And why were they given land *in fief*? Part of the answer seems to lie in developments in military organisation. The Italian states' military needs, by the later Middle Ages, required the large use of mercenaries and the period from 1350 to 1450 saw the more or less permanent engagement by the major states of large numbers of mercenary captains (*condottieri*) and retainers (*provisionati*).[24] But the maintenance of continuity and loyalty of service was a serious problem. Many *condottieri* came from established families with their own territorial interests and there was considerable movement of such men from state to state. Enfeoffment was one means, among others such as marriage, pensions and political office, by which states sought to attach military commanders permanently to their service.[25] But, as with fee'd retaining in northern Europe, such attachment was not confined to military duties: retainers continued to receive fees in peacetime and were expected to perform political and curial services.[26] Indeed, the recruitment of outsiders could originate from other needs of this sort: lords' territorial ambitions, their sponsorship of exile groups and their refusal to be restricted by local oligarchies. Large use of foreigners was thus a standard feature of the *signorie* and *signori* drew their counsellors, friends and servants from the wider aristocratic world of which they were part and which transcended (and increasingly broke down) the divisions of communal Italy.[27]

Local opposition and resentment naturally developed. At Ferrara it is recorded in the early 1350s, when, at a time of dynastic conflict, several members of old Ferrarese noble families left the city to join forces with the dissident Francesco d'Este. Their revolt was prompted by fear of the power of the Ariosti family from Bologna,

---

[24] P. Pieri, *Il Rinascimento e la crisi militare italiana* (Turin, 1952); M. Mallett, *Mercenaries and their Masters* (London, 1974); C. Capasso, 'I "provvisionati" di Bernabò Visconti', *ASL*, s.4, 15 (1911).

[25] Mallett, *Mercenaries*, pp. 91–4, 216–17; Mallett, 'Venice and its condottieri', pp. 128–9; Bueno de Mesquita, 'Ludovico Sforza', pp. 195–202, 209–10; A. Battistella, *Il conte Carmagnola* (Genoa, 1889), pp. 464–6.

[26] K. B. McFarlane, '"Bastard Feudalism"', *BIHR*, 20 (1943–5); N. B. Lewis, 'The organization of indentured retainers in fourteenth-century England', *TRHS*, 27 (1945); W. H. Dunham, *Lord Hastings' Indentured Retainers 1461–83* (New Haven, 1955).

[27] Sestan, 'Origini', pp. 220–2; Jones, 'City state', p. 89; *idem*, 'Mito', pp. 173–6; *idem, Malatesta*, pp. 298–9, 316–17; A. Vasina, 'La società riminese nel tardo medioevo', in A. Vasina, *Romagna Medievale* (Ravenna, 1970), pp. 267–8, 272–3; B. G. Kohl, 'Government and society in Renaissance Padua', *JMRS*, 2 (1972), 209–11; Galli, 'La dominazione viscontea a Verona', pp. 486–7; Grimaldi, *Signoria*, pp. 95, 102–3.

who had been closely associated with and highly rewarded by Obizzo III. Perhaps reflecting this resentment, at the public 'election' of Obizzo's successor, Aldrovandino, a spokesman 'for the people' entreated him 'in times of extreme danger' to take 'the advice of his citizens, who will never abandon him'.[28] Nevertheless, a number of leading citizens in these years seem to have preferred the opportunities offered elsewhere to the risks of remaining in Ferrara.[29] It was members of the Ferrarese nobility who reacted again in 1398 to domination by a group of outsiders headed by the Roberti and Obizzi: they forced councillors to be removed and their administration to be subjected to close scrutiny.[30] These were, however, isolated incidents, at times of political instability; at other times, the prominence of foreign nobles (and non-nobles) in Este service did not exclude the local nobility, as we shall see. Local families of course there were which are not recorded at court or in office – dormant families such as the Turchi, recorded in these years only in their private affairs – but this was the unsurprising result of inclination, personality, perhaps family tradition, but not of signorial distrust of the local aristocracy (nor of an 'anti-feudal' policy).[31] Ferrarese and non-Ferrarese nobles alike found employment and profit in Este service: the difference between them was that the outsiders lacked properties in Ferrara and its *contado* where they could reside and whose crops and revenues they could draw on. It is for this reason that the enfeoffment of foreign vassals with estates of hitherto unusual size develops. But unlike other states, this new feudality was not exclusively military; on the contrary it embraced various distinct groups and fulfilled diverse functions. It is to these that we shall now turn, examining the Venetian, Bolognese, Reggian and other vassals.

Four Venetian nobles held fiefs of the marquis in 1394–5: Marco di Federico Corner, Pietro di Paolo Morosini, Azolino di Andriolo Molin and Federico di Maffeo Leon. These were later joined by

---

[28] 'in casibus extremis vel periculosis assumeret consilium suorum civium qui nunquam ipsum derelinquent': *Chron Est.*, 469; A. Frizzi, *Memorie storiche della famiglia Ariosti di Ferrara* (Ferrara, 1779), p. 88; A. Frizzi, *Memorie*, vol. 3, p. 320; *cf.* Jones, *Malatesta*, p. 331.

[29] A number of Costabili entered Venetian military service: ASVe, Senato, Miste, reg. 30 fol. 72 (7 May 1362); reg. 32, fol. 23 (9 Nov. 1366); reg. 35, fol. 139v (15 Oct. 1376); Avogaria del Comun, Raspe, 3643, fols. 101–v (1367).

[30] *Ann. Est.*, 931–3; Valenti, 'Consigli', pp. 21–2; ASM, Not. Cam., P. Sardi, A, fols. 98–9, 107v, 113.

[31] J. K. Laurent, 'Feudalismo e signoria', *ASI*, 137 (1979), 163–5; Mallett, *Mercenaries*, p. 91.

Zaccaria Trevisan (1402) and Amoroto Condulmer (1421).[32] For Zaccaria Trevisan, this denoted only a brief attachment to the Este, as he sold his fief to the Contrari within a few years.[33] But the others were more committed in the long term to landholding in the *Terraferma* and to relations with the *signori* there. The Molin were Este vassals from early in the fourteenth century, while the Corner also held property in fief of the bishop of Ferrara and the Morosini held land of the abbey of Pomposa.[34] Venetian landowning in the Ferrarese *contado* often created problems for the Este (as in the case of the Querini), but the marquises' relations with their own vassals were good. Marco Corner was a retainer (*provisionatus*) of the marquis in 1392 and contacts with the Corner were particularly close, in both family affairs and business. Members from each family attended the other's baptisms, marriages and funerals.[35] Federico Corner, the wealthiest Venetian citizen in the late fourteenth century, was Niccolo II's godfather and received him and his entourage in great state ('curia maxima') when they visited Venice in 1370.[36] Niccolo II made a number of loans to Federico and in repayment later Alberto d'Este obtained a house in Venice, in addition to the palace given to the Este by the Venetian state in 1381 (the *Fondaco dei Turchi*).[37] Ties with the Morosini were also close: Paolo was in Alberto d'Este's company on his pilgrimage to Rome in 1391 and his son Pietro is recorded as a retainer and resident in Ferrara in 1394. Other members of the family held office in the Polesine di Rovigo while it was occupied by Venice.[38] This was the sort of external

[32] ASM, Catastri, H, fols. 166, 224, 396, 512; N, fol. 290.

[33] ASF, Archivio Tassoni, V/20 (30 May 1408).

[34] Lazzarini, 'Possessi'. For the Morosini fief of 628 *starii* at Cornacervina and Valcesura, held from the abbey of Pomposa *sine fidelitate*: ASM, Pomposa, b. 3 (1308, 1451).

[35] ASM, Not. Cam., Z. Coadi, fol. 132v. Marco was present at the publication of Alberto's will in 1393 (BEM, Doc. Campori, Appendice 1251, fol. 113) and was the Venetian representative at Niccolo III's marriage in 1397. In 1399 Niccolo d'Este sent an envoy to the baptism of Marco's son: L. Olivi, 'Del matrimonio del M. Niccolo III con Gigliola figlia di Francesco Novello da Carrara', *AMMo*, 5 (1890), docs. 13 & 14.

[36] 'compare e grande amigo del marchexe': Daniele di Chinazzo, *Cronica de la guerra da veniciani a zenovesi*, ed. V. Lazzarini (Venice, 1958), p. 166; Federico was Venetian ambassador in Ferrara for much of 1380: *Dispacci di Pietro Cornaro, ambasciatore a Milano durante la guerra di Chioggia*, ed. V. Lazzarini (Venice, 1939), Appendix *passim; Chron. Est.* 492.

[37] ASM, Casa e Stato, 21/5, 7 & 8; G. Luzzatto, *Storia economica di Venezia dall'XI al XVI secolo* (Venice, 1961), p. 80; F. Lane, *Venice – A Maritime Republic* (Baltimore, 1973), pp. 138, 141–4; Dean, 'Venetian economic hegemony'.

[38] ASM, Leggi e Decreti, A 2, fol. 189; *Chron. Est.* 521; G. Durazzo, *Dei rettori*

influence on its officials that the Venetian state legislated to prevent, but it is found also in the case of Zaccaria Trevisan, whose tenure of an Este fief coincided with his tenure of offices in the *Terraferma* (ambassador to Ferrara in 1400 and 1407, captain of Padua from 1405).[39] Where other Venetians are recorded as companions, Amoroto Condulmer entered continuous administrative service of the Este: for over three decades in the early fifteenth century, he and his brother, Cristoforo, served as chief cameral officials in the major centres of Este, Rovigo, Modena and San Felice.[40] In the 1420s, Amoroto built up feudal holdings in the Polesine di Rovigo to a total of 158 *campi* (70 hectares) and held leases on a further 360 *campi*. Some of this property he obtained by exploiting his position as *camerario* at Rovigo, by refusing to reduce rents to distressed lessees, whose property he then obtained, from the camera.[41] This position of the Condulmer brothers in Este administration might have contributed to the good relations between Niccolo III and the Condulmer Pope, Eugenius IV.[42] What value these contacts might have been to the Estensi in Venice is even harder to assess. Certainly Venice had from the thirteenth century dissuaded its citizens from accepting fiefs and offices from Terraferma *signori*, as part of a general policy of curtailing corrupting influences on internal politics.[43] But contacts flourished despite the prohibitions and at times of conflict between Venice and the mainland *signori* numerous Venetian noblemen were questioned and punished for divulging state secrets to their *Terraferma* masters. Doubtless this 'discovery' of contacts in wartime represented the tip of an iceberg.[44]

*veneziani in Rovigo* (Venice, 1865); ANF, J. Pavesi, 21 July 1400; ASM, Not. Cam., J. Mizino, fol. 11.

[39] P. Gothein, 'Zaccaria Trevisan', *AV*, s. 5, 21 (1937); ASM, Leggi e Decreti, A 3, fol. 262.

[40] Amoroto served as cameral official (*camerario, massaro*) at Este 1406, S. Felice 1407, Rovigo 1419–32 and Modena 1434–5: ASM, Leggi e Decreti, A 4, fols. 59, 159; A 5, fol. 121; Catastri, R, fols. 168, 374, 513, 609; Sitta, 'Saggio', pp. 191–2. Cristoforo served as *camerario* at S. Felice, 1420 and Este from 1424 (Leggi e Decreti, A 5, fol. 181; ASF, ANF, P.Sardi, 28 Jan. 1424; ASM, Casa e Stato, 24/54; Not. Cam., A. Villa, fol. 58).

[41] ASM, Catastri, R, fols. 213, 256, 267, 349; U, fols. 305, 319, 339, 469.

[42] The precise relation between Eugenius IV and Amoroto is unclear: Litta, *Famiglie celebri italiane*, is incorrect in making Amoroto a descendant of Eugenius' brother: L. N. Cittadella, *Documenti ed illustrazioni riguardanti la storia artistica ferrarese* (Ferrara, 1868), pp. 325–7.

[43] Lazzarini, 'Antiche leggi', p. 12; Dean, 'Venetian economic hegemony'.

[44] Dean, 'Venetian economic hegemony'.

With the Bolognese vassals of the marquis, the fiefs served a more clearly defined political purpose. Four Bolognese families held fiefs of Niccolò III – the Gozzadini, Lambertini, Galluzzi and da Panico – while another (the Caccianemici) had close links with the Este and lands in the Ferrarese.[45] Estensi ambitions on Bologna were as old as their *signoria* in Ferrara (see above, chapter 1) and to advance them they needed *amici* in Bologna. Chief among these were the Gozzadini, powerful and ambitious opponents of the incipient *signoria* of the Bentivoglio. The Gozzadini were already members of an Este faction in Bologna at the beginning of the fourteenth century.[46] Contacts continued in the 1320s and 1330s, when both the Estensi and Gozzadini were at odds with the papal legate, but became close and frequent only in the last decades of the century, with the descendants of Gabbione. These included Nanne, one of the major figures in Bolognese politics in the early fifteenth century.[47] Members of this branch are found in Ferrara as courtiers, retainers and officials,[48] and as Bolognese ambassadors.[49] They served the Este as military commanders, both in the field and in city garrisons.[50] They acquired major ecclesiastical benefices in the Este state,[51] had marriage and business contacts with the Ferrarese

---

[45] Links with the Caccianemici go back to the thirteenth century: Dante, *The Divine Comedy, Inferno*, XVIII, 50–66; *Commento alla Divina Commedia d'anonimo fiorentino del secolo XIV*, ed. P. Fanfani (3 vols., Bologna, 1866–74), vol. 1, pp. 406–7; A. Lazzari, 'Il marchese Obizzo II d'Este signore di Ferrara nel poema di Dante e nella storia', *Giornale Dantesco*, 39 (1938). In the fourteenth century, Bruxe Caccianemici married Giovanna di Rinaldo d'Este (ASM, Leggi e Decreti, A 1, fol. 41) and Lambertino served as *camerario* of S. Felice in 1406 (ibid., A 4, fol. 40) and *massaro* of Parma in 1409 (ibid., fol. 277).

[46] Vitale, *Dominio della parte guelfa*, p. 85; Benvenuti de Rambaldis de Imola, *Commentum super Dantis Aldigherii Comoediam*, ed. J. P. Lacaita (5 vols., Florence, 1887), vol. 3, p. 152.

[47] Gozzadini, *Nanne Gozzadini*; Ady, *Bentivoglio*, pp. 8–10.

[48] Simonino di Gabbione was a *familiaris* 1361–86 (ASM, Investiture di Feudi, 12/27, 12/55, 13/40; Not. Cam., A. Cavaleria, fol. 28). His brother Gozzadino was a *provisionatus* and resident in Ferrara 1361–2 (ASM, Not. Cam., J. Sanvitale, fols. 2, 17). Galvanino was *podestà* of Comacchio in 1363 (ASM, Leggi e Decreti, A 1, fol. 2) and his son Giovanni a courtier in the 1390s (ASM, Investiture di Feudi, 14/35; Not. Cam., P. Sardi, A, fol. 46).

[49] *Ann. Est.*, 925; Gozzadini, *Nanne Gozzadini*, p.32.

[50] Gozzadini was commander of the Este siege of Canossa in 1412, captain of Parma 1412–14 and of Reggio 1414–16: A. Cerlini, 'Un assedio a Canossa nel secolo XV', *Studi storici*, 14 (1905), 395.

[51] Battista di Bonifacio was abbot of Nonantola from 1398 and was transferred to Pomposa in 1400, Dalfino di Nanne succeeding him as abbot of Nonantola: Tiraboschi, *Nonantola*, vol. 1, pp. 164–6; Busmanti, *Pomposa*, p. 13.

nobility,[52] and received fiefs in the Ferrarese *contado*.[53] In return, they obtained political and military aid in their frequent conflicts with the papal legate or with the various lords of Bologna. In 1402, for example, Niccolo d'Este ignored the advice of Venice and Padua and gave passage to Giangaleazzo Visconti's army moving to attack Bologna because it was led by the Gozzadini.[54] The following year he allied with Nanne against the papal legate in the face of papal threats and supplied munitions for the defence of Nanne's castles.[55] Following this débâcle, Ferrara served as a refuge for the Gozzadini and it was there that Nanne passed his last years and died.[56]

The Gozzadini stood at the centre of a closely-knit group of Este partisans. Their political associates, the San Giorgio, moved permanently to Ferrara and were employed in Este diplomatic and administrative service.[57] And it is the Gozzadini who seem to stand behind another foreigner in Este service, the Florentine Dante da Castiglione, a leading figure in the financial administration for two decades.[58] Members of both the Galluzzi and Lambertini were often involved in pro-Este plots in Bologna, for example in 1303, 1389 and

---

[52] Simonino married Francesca di Bartolomeo Costabili (Biblioteca comunale, Bologna, Archivio Gozzadini, b. 109, no. 26). Gozzadino married a daughter of Giovanni Sala, who in 1394 provided trading capital of 3,000 ducats for Bonifacio di Gabbione (ibid., 109/46). In 1439, the Sacrati established a bank in Bologna to be run by Nanne's son, Tommaso (ASF, ANF, U. Rossetti, 5 Aug. 1448).

[53] For the fiefs of Giovanni di Galvanino, some 45 hectares at Crespino and of Simonino, some 50 hectares at Ducentola: ASM, Not. Cam., J. Sanvitale, fol. 95; F. Tagliapetri, B. fol. 9; Catastri, H, fols. 87, 100.

[54] *Il Copialettere Marciano della Cancelleria Carrarese 1402–3*, ed. E. Pastorello (Venice, 1915), nos. 249, 267, 516.

[55] Manni, 'Terzi ed Estensi', pp. 127–8; Lünig, *Codex*, vol. 1, 1917–20; Gozzadini, *Nanne Gozzadini*, pp. 299–300.

[56] ASM, Leggi e Decreti, B III, fol. 128. Exiled members of the Gozzadini had also come to Ferrara in 1322: *Chron. Est.*, 384.

[57] G. Gozzadini, *Delle torri gentilizie di Bologna* (Bologna, 1875), p. 474; Gozzadini, *Nanne Gozzadini*, pp. 195–6, 257–8, 272, 460–4; *Copialettere*, no. 624 & n. Antonio da San Giorgio was a *cancelliere* from the 1370s (ASM, Investiture di Feudi, 13/27; Not. Cam., F. Maroni, fol. 90v) and was invested with over 29 hectares in various localities in 1398 (ASM, Catastri, N, fol. 67).

[58] Dante was already working for the Gozzadini in 1399 (ASF, ANF, L. Villa, 3 June 1399) and was involved in 1402 in the negotiation of an accord between Nanne and Giovanni Bentivoglio (*Copialettere*, nos. 188, 202, 209). Dante was Niccolo d'Este's treasurer 1400–1, his envoy in subsequent years and was *fattore generale* from 1410, seconded to Parma from 1412, where he also held Castelnovo di Sotto as an 'adherent' of the marquis: ASF, ANF, J. Pavesi, 7 June 1400; ASM, Not. Cam., P. Sardi, 26 Oct. 1412; Leggi e Decreti, B III, fols. 155, 172; A 5, fol. 264; Not. Cam., J. Pelizari, fol. 49; Catastri, K, fol. 342.

1403.[59] They frequented the Este court, whether as retainers, as in the case of Egano and Aldreghetto Lambertini, or as 'noble of the court', 'tablemate and companion', as in that of Enrico Galluzzi.[60] They formed part of the Este retinue on pilgrimages to Rome and the Holy Land.[61] And among their rewards for such political service and attendance at court were knighthood and fiefs. In 1294, Azzo VIII knighted three members of the Lambertini, having, a few years previously, invested them with former Torelli and Ramberti property on the border between the Ferrarese and Bolognese *contadi*.[62] From 1340, Egano Lambertini and his descendants accumulated a number of fiefs in the Ferrarese *contado*.[63] The Lambertini castle at Poggio Renatico, halfway between Ferrara and Bologna, was an important point in Ferrara's southern border: militarily it was from the south that Ferrara was most vulnerable (as shown in 1333) and the Estensi repeatedly displayed their concern that Poggio should be in friendly hands, both for good defensive reasons and to assist Este designs on Bologna and on the Bolognese town of Cento.[64] In 1291 Azzo d'Este had attempted to make the Lambertini his vassals for Poggio and in the fifteenth century the castle was twice seized by the marquises.[65] While the Lambertini were vassals and courtiers, the Estensi could depend on their support. The Lambertini were involved with other Este partisans in an attempted coup in Bologna in 1389 and Guido was in Alberto d'Este's company which travelled to Rome in 1391. In 1395, Niccolo III specifically rewarded the loyalty of Filippo di Guglielmo Lambertini with a pension of 25 ducats a month, a house in Ferrara and a farm in the *contado* and with provision for the marriage of Filippo's sister.[66] As late as 1402,

---

59 Gozzadini, *Torri*, pp. 255–62; Palmieri, 'La congiura', pp. 174–5, 186ff; *Corpus Chronicorum Bononiensium, RIS*[2], vol. 18, pt 1, vol. 2, p. 451.

60 For the Lambertini: *Chron. Est.*, 520; ASM, Not. Cam., F. Tagliapetri, B, 16 Sept. 1374, 14 Jan. 1376 etc.; B. Mella, fol. 65v; Catastri, H, fol. 586; N, fol. 61. For Enrico Galluzzi: ASM, Not. Cam., N. Abbatia, A, fols. 14, 46; C. Lardi, fol. 28; P. Bononia, fol. 88. Gerardo Galluzzi was one of the foreign nobles drafted in to support the election of Obizzo II in 1264: Muratori, *Antichità*, vol. 2, pp. 25–6.

61 *Chron. Est.*, 520; *Fr. Johannis Ferrariensis ex Annalium Libris Marchionum Estensium Excerpta, RIS*[2],. vol. 20, pt 2, Appendix.

62 *Corpus Chron. Bon.*, 240; ASM, Catastri, A, fols. 32–v.

63 ASM, Not. Cam., P. Fabro, fol. 150 (1340); B. Nigrisoli, fol. 43v (1347); F. Sale, fol. 54 (1356); B. Mella, fol. 85 (1389); A. Florano, fol. 24 (1392); Catastri, H, fol. 175.

64 Gorreta, *La lotta*, p. 27; G. Atti, *Sunto storico della città di Cento* (Cento, 1853), pp. 1–5; and see P. Montanari, 'La formazione del patrimonio di una antica famiglia patrizia bolognese: i Lambertini', *L'Archiginnasio*, 62 (1967).

65 Gozzadini, *Torri*, p. 336.     66 ASM, Leggi e Decreti, B II, fol. 298.

Niccolo was furnishing the Lambertini with gabelle exemptions, but this close association was brought to a dramatic end in 1403, when Niccolo III sacked Poggio Renatico and confiscated the Lambertini fiefs.[67] The precise reasons for this major change in Este political strategy in the Bolognese are not clear, but are probably to be found in Este support of the Gozzadini in the period of confusion following the death of Giangaleazzo Visconti in 1402. Meanwhile, friendship with other Bolognese families continued: Enrico Galluzzi received fiefs at Copparo (1412) and Villanova (1422);[68] and Francesco da Panico, from a family once powerful in the Bolognese Appennines, entered Este service and received land in fief in the Padovano.[69]

This use of fiefs to underpin Este territorial ambitions was not confined to Bolognese families: it also explains the feudal grants to Giovanni Orgogliosi, from an important family of Forlì,[70] and, more significantly, to the Roberti from Reggio. The latter family, who held a castle at San Martino in the eastern Reggiano, played a major part in Este efforts from the mid-fourteenth century to recover Reggio (see below, chapter 6). The Roberti became 'adherents' of Obizzo III in 1346 and although in the following year they submitted to the Gonzaga, then lords of Reggio, already by 1349 Niccolo Roberti is recorded as an Este captain. He and later his son, Filippo, served the Este as ambassadors, counsellors and military retainers.[71] With San Martino covered by Este and papal protection,[72] Niccolo and then Filippo greatly expanded their power

---

[67] *Corpus Chron. Bon.*, 495; Muratori, *Antichità*, vol. 2, p. 168; ASM, Not. Cam., N. Abbatia, B, fol. 176v. Some Lambertini property was later auctioned in Ferrara to Tommasina di Malatesto Lambertini for L.bol. 7,000.

[68] ASM, Catastri, N, fol. 521; R, fol. 248.

[69] Palmieri, 'La congiura', p. 176ff; *idem, La montagna bolognese*, pp. 163–217; Gozzadini, *Torri*, pp. 388–96. Jacopo appears as Niccolo d'Este's *pincerna* in 1399 (ASM, Catastri, N, fols. 96, 109) and as Francesco da Carrara's ambassador to Ferrara in 1402 (*Copialettere*, no. 185). For his fief at Montagnana: ASM, Catastri, R, fol. 145 (1403). Another member of the family served Uguccione Contrari in his Modenese lands: AV, Archivio Boncompagni, Prot. 714, no. 11.

[70] Giovanni Orgogliosi was resident in Ferrara in the 1380s (ASM, Not. Cam., A. Cavaleria, fol. 22; J. Mizino, fol. 8v) and received a small fief at Traghetto (Catastri, H, fol. 158). On Este attempts on Imola and Forlì: Muratori, *Antichità*, vol. 2, p. 51; Albizzi, *Commissioni*, vol. 1, pp. 429, 431.

[71] On Niccolo as retainer and counsellor: *Chron. Est.*, 453; ASM, Not. Cam., J. Sanvitale, fols. 1, 56, 81 and M. Conte, fol. 113. He was an executor of Aldrovandino d'Este's will in 1361 (ASM, Casa e Stato, b. 324) and Este envoy to the Pope in 1363 (*Lettres secrètes et curiales du Pape Urbain V (1362–70) se rapportant à la France*, ed. P. Lecacheux and G. Mollat, no. 701).

[72] ASM, Not. Cam., F. Tagliapetri, A, fols. 50–v, 91; *Lettres Urbain V*, nos. 1727–8, 1731, 1942, 2827.

and landed position at Ferrara, receiving a succession of large and small fiefs from the marquises.[73] In 1388, Alberto d'Este married Cabrino Roberti's daughter, Giovanna, and in 1393 he secured the bishopric of Ferrara for Cabrino's son, Niccolo.[74] Filippo later obtained, 'at great expense', two bishoprics in succession – first Padua, then Adria – for his son, Ugo.[75] When Alberto d'Este died, the power of the Roberti in Ferrara was unchallengeable: both Cabrino and Filippo were permanent members of the regency council (Filippo appeared to more than one observer as 'quasi vice marchese') and Filippo's son, Niccolo, was the Este governor in Modena.[76] And, as we have seen, accompanying this increasingly dominant position in Ferrara were extensive fiefs in the Ferrarese *contado*. From 1400, however, with the rise to influence of Uguccione Contrari, Roberti power in Ferrara went into rapid decline: they were implicated in an obscure intrigue with Marco Pio in 1400, as a result of which Niccolo Roberti was dismissed from the bishopric and Filippo's sons took service with Venice and the papal legate in their joint attack on Ferrara in 1404–5.[77] Though rehabilitated in 1405, their further rebellion later brought a confiscation of all their property.

The Roberti were not the only family from the fringes of the Este state to hold lands in the Ferrarese *contado*. Members of the Pio, Rangone and Savignano, leading Modenese nobles, were also enfeoffed with a number of properties from the middle decades of the fourteenth century.[78] Again, these fiefs reflected their presence in

[73] Niccolo, 1362: 60 *starii* at Villamana (ASM, Not. Cam., J. Sanvitale, fol. 37); Filippo, 1371: 1,912 *starii* and 72,000 vines at Denore, Corlo, Baura, and Correggio (BEM, Doc. Campori, Appendice 1251, fols. 20ff); Cabrino, 1376: 743 *starii* and 16,000 vines at Rovereto, S. Vito, Medelana and Alberlungo (ASM, Not. Cam., F. Tagliapetri, B, fol. 14); Cabrino, 1389: 2,829 *starii* and 42,000 vines at Consandolo, 1,805 *starii* at Margone and Bozoleto and the tithe of Boccaleone (ASM, Not. Cam., B. Mella, fol. 75v); Filippo, 1389: 1,599 *starii* and 67,600 vines at Saletta and Copparo (BEM, Doc. Campori, Appendice 1251, fols. 48v–51); Niccolo di Filippo, 1390: 619 *starii* and 21,200 vines at Copparo and Sabbioncello (ASM, Not. Cam., Z. Coadi, fol. 27).

[74] *Chron. Est.*, 530; Muratori, *Antichità*, vol. 2, p. 153; G. Tiraboschi, *Memorie storiche modenesi* (4 vols, Modena, 1793–5), vol. 3, p. 62.

[75] 'magnis expensis': BEM, Doc. Campori, Appendice 1261; G. Manini Ferranti, *Compendio della storia sacra e politica di Ferrara* (Ferrara, 1808), vol. 3, pp. 5–17.

[76] G. & B. Gatari, *Cronaca Carrarese, RIS*[2], vol. 17, pt 1, vol. i, p. 447; *Ann. Est.*, 919; ASM, Leggi e Decreti, B II, fols. 66, 172.

[77] Gatari, *Cronaca*, p. 531; B. della Pugliola, *Historia miscella bononiensis, RIS*, vol. 18, cols. 584, 587–8, 592, 594; *Libri Commemoriali*, ix, no. 301; Tiraboschi, *Mem. stor. mod.*, vol. 3, p. 75.

[78] For the Pio, see above, p. 76. Jacopino Rangone was first invested with a house in

Ferrara as retainers and counsellors. Lanfranco Rangone was knighted by Obizzo III and served as *podestà* in 1362. Gerardo Rangone was a counsellor in the 1360s. Members of the Pio and Savignano are also found at court.[79]

Fiefs were also used to win the favour and influence of powerful men at the courts of other *signori*.[80] Otto da Mandello, who held a large fief to the east of the city, was the right-hand man of Giangaleazzo Visconti and had played a major part in the coup in which Giangaleazzo had displaced his uncle, Bernabo, as lord of Milan in 1385.[81] Guglielmo Bevilacqua, counsellor and diplomat of the Scaligeri, lords of Verona, and later also of Giangaleazzo Visconti, received Ferrarese citizenship in 1346 and fiefs at Minerba and Montagnana in the Padovano.[82] Francesco da Lonate, a Milanese nobleman who seems to have had the confidence of the Duke of Milan, was much used by Niccolo III and Uguccione Contrari in their tense relations with Milan in the 1410s: through him they tried to contain the Duke's pressure on Parma, which Niccolo III had seized from the Visconti in 1410.[83] Francesco da

Ferrara in 1347 (*Liber Memorialis Familiae Rangoniae*, ed. L. Rangoni Machiavelli (Città di Castello, 1913), p. 141). Jacopo di Lanfranco and Jacopino di Gerardo received land in fief at Peroto (2 pieces) and Stienta (340 *starii*) in 1394 (ASM, Catastri, H, fols. 200, 517, 622). Jacopo's son, a courtier of Niccolo III, received 277 *starii* and 3,000 vines in fief at Crespino in 1408 (Catastri, N, fol. 453). Ginello da Savignano was invested in 1376 with 643 *starii* and 12,000 vines at Consandolo and Margone (ASM, Not. Cam., F. Tagliapetri, B, fol. 26v), which escheated when his son, Alberto, died without male issue in 1413 (Catastri, N, fol. 546).

79 For the Pio: ASM, F. Tagliapetri, B, fols. 11v, 42; Catastri, N, fols. 106, 127, 132, 168; for the Savignano: Not. Cam., J. Sanvitale, fols. 9, 138, 144; for the Rangoni: *Chron. Est.*, 469; L. Rangoni Machiavelli, *Piccolo sunto storico della famiglia Rangone di Modena* (Rome, 1908), p. 23; ASM, Not. Cam., F. Sale, fol. 86; F. Tagliapetri, A, fols. 1, 73, 91; J. Sanvitale, fols. 64, 120.

80 *Cf.* B. D. Lyon, 'The money fief under the English kings 1066–1485', *EHR*, 66 (1951), 175–7; McFarlane, '"Bastard Feudalism"', p. 168; Lewis, 'Decayed and non-feudalism', p. 172.

81 For Otto's fief of some 150 hectares at Corlo, Correggio, Ruina and Tamara, held from 1390 to 1402: ASM, Not. Cam., A. Florano, fol. 5; Catastri, H, fol. 256 and N, fol. 290. Otto received a loan of 2,000 florins from Niccolo II in 1385: Not. Cam., N. Camarlengo, fol. 88v. On Otto: Gatari, *Cronaca*, p. 233 n. 5; E. Cordani, 'La famiglia dei da Mandello di Caorso (secc XIII–XV)', Tesi di Laurea all' Università di Milano, 1978–9, pp. 46–64 and Appendix, pp. 28–90.

82 Fiefs of over 76 *campi* at Minerba, later exchanged for 75 *campi* at Montagnana: ASM, Not. Cam., B. Nigrisoli, fol. 8; M. Conte, fol. 136; Catastri, N, fol. 166. On Guglielmo: A. Frizzi, *Memorie storiche della nobile famiglia Bevilacqua* (Parma, 1779), pp. 24–39; G. Sandri, 'I Bevilacqua e il commercio del legname tra la val di Fiemme e Verona nel sec. XIV', *AV*, s. 5, 26 (1940), 174.

83 ASM, Not. Cam., J. Pelizari, fol. 58v; Cancelleria, Estero, Ambasciatori, Venezia, 1, 2, fol. 3; BEM, Documenti Campori, Appendice 1321; *Lucca Regesti*, vol. 3, pt ii, no. 337.

Lonate is recorded as a *provisionato* of the marquis in 1417 and in the following year he was invested with a large fief at Consandolo and Bozoleto and with a house in Ferrara.[84]

The Este court entourage was thus drawn not only from their own state, but also from many other cities of north and central Italy. Some of these families remained attached to the Estensi over several generations, for example the Cancellieri from Pistoia. Ricciardo Cancellieri had moved into Este service in the 1350s and became a counsellor of Niccolò II, *podestà* of Ferrara and then captain of Modena, before his death in Ferrara in 1378. He was invested in 1371 with a house in the city and with land (500 *starii*) at Cesta and Coccanile.[85] Of his sons, Antonio and Bartolomeo remained in Este service: Bartolomeo was a military commander and counsellor; Antonio's son, Ricciardo, served as *podestà* of Modena in 1395.[86] Other foreigners who made whole careers in Este service would include members of the Confalonieri from Brescia[87] and Dondacio Malvicini Fontana from Piacenza. Some, though, while retaining their fiefs in the Ferrarese, moved into the service of other lords, for example Leonardo Malaspina, a retainer of Alberto d'Este, but later the governor of Bologna for the Visconti,[88] or the military captain, Filippo da Pisa, who took service with several lords before finally settling at Ferrara.[89] But such periods of mobility did not last long: Filippo da Pisa settled his family in Ferrara (the Tibertelli), as did Alidosio Forzate, from an important Paduan family. Alidosio had

[84] 4,335 *starii*, 27,600 vines and 138 *opere*: ASM, Catastri, R, fol. 92.

[85] S. Ammirato, *Delle famiglie nobili fiorentine* (Florence, 1615), pp. 58–9; ASM, Not. Cam., F. Tagliapetri, A, fols. 30, 125; B, fol. 43; J. Sanvitale, fols. 115, 127 etc.; M. Conte, fol. 126; Leggi e Decreti, A 1, fol. 161.

[86] Ammirato, *Famiglie*, p. 60; ASM, Leggi e Decreti, A 1, fols. 161–2; Not. Cam., R. Codegorio, A, fol. 51; A. Cavaleria, fol. 5; F. Tagliapetri, B, fol. 43; Catastri, H, fol. 401; Vicini, 'Podestà', pp. 198–9.

[87] Gerardo Confalonieri was a *iudex curie* and diplomatic envoy in the 1380s, Niccolò II's vicar-general in Faenza in 1371 and *Giudice dei Savi* in Ferrara 1392–6 (ASM, Not. Cam., R. Codegorio, A, fols. 23v, 82; B. Mella, fol. 35v; A. Cavaleria, fol. 22; J. Mizino, fol. 7v; Leggi e Decreti, A 1, fol. 350; ACF, Deliberazioni, Libro A). Giovanni is recorded in Ferrara in the 1360s and in 1373 was *podestà* of Modena (ASM, Not. Cam., J. Sanvitale, fol. 91; Leggi e Decreti, A 1, fols. 4v, 199; *Chron. Est.*, 517). For Giovanni's fief of 1362, held by his son in 1394: Not. Cam., J. Sanvitale, fol. 47; Catastri, H, fol. 308.

[88] ASM, Not. Cam., B. Mella, fol. 112; Leggi e Decreti, B III, fol. 87; E. Branchi, *Storia della Lunigiana feudale*, vol. 3 (Pistoia, 1898), pp. 669–73; *Chron. Est.*, 521. His fief was confirmed to his sons in 1405 and 1440: ASM, Catastri, H, fol. 554; N, fol. 339; BC, fol. 85.

[89] *Ann. Est.*, 911, 935, 955; Gatari, *Cronaca*, pp. 507, 534, 548. He was enfeoffed in 1407 with a *palatium* and over 100 hectares, mainly at Cornacervina: ASM, Catastri, N, fol. 427; R. fol. 50.

close ties with Francesco II da Carrara and probably as a result of these found service with Niccolo from 1403, having received a fief of over 200 hectares at Maiero in 1400. Alidosio became captain of Modena in 1409, but died the same year from wounds received at the assassination of Ottobuono Terzi (see above, p. 25). His son married a daughter of Uguccione Contrari and was captain first of Modena, then of Parma.[90] In these and in other cases, military service and attendance at court hardened into permanent settlement at Ferrara (see below, pp. 97–8). Fiefs to this group rewarded, but did not specifically remunerate service; and service, as we have seen, could vary from the military and diplomatic to the administrative and purely honorific. The character of this group of vassals was thus very varied. A large part was made up of *provisionati*, military retainers, who participated in recorded Este military actions in these years. But their fiefs had no military function: they were not bases for recruitment or quartering, still less part of a system of military obligation.[91] Armies were recruited and maintained by short-term contract (*condotta*), not by feudal obligation. Fiefs were, however, a way of supplementing contractual obligations and rewards with attachments of a more stable and general kind. When comprising both lands in the *contado* and a house in the city, fiefs were a means of providing for the members of a retinue who were expected to be resident at Ferrara. Even where retainers did not become vassals of the Este, they were provided with lands in the *contado* which they retained for as long as they were in Este service, as the case of Guido Torelli illustrates. Guido became an Este captain after the defeat of the Terzi in 1409 and acquired some 150 hectares of allodial lands at Porto in 1414 from the courtier Pietro Pritati.[92] However, Guido's own territorial interests between Reggio and Parma led to his defection to Filippo Maria Visconti as Visconti pressure on Parma intensified and he surrendered his lands at Porto in 1422.[93] Torelli is an example of what happened when territorial interests and service loyalties diverged; in many more cases the Este were able to bring them together. For many of the Este military and political support-

[90] Gatari, *Cronaca*, pp. 438; 472; *Copialettere*, no. 47 and n.; ASM, Catastri, N, fol. 160; R, fol. 86.

[91] Mallett, *Mercenaries*, p. 92; but *cf.* Milan where F. M. Visconti ordered *condottieri* to use their fiefs to quarter their companies: Bognetti, 'Stato visconteo', pp. 304–5.

[92] ASM, Not. Cam., P. Bononia, fol. 153v.

[93] ASM, Leggi e Decreti, B IV, insert fols. 63v–4; on the Torelli and their *signoria* at Guastalla; *Ann. Est.*, 1070; I. Affo, *Istoria della città e ducato di Guastalla* (4 vols., Guastalla, 1785–7), vol. 1, pp. 287–93; vol. 2, pp. 1–17.

ers came from the provincial nobility of their state, whom the Este sought to attract to Ferrara. Fiefs often included, or comprised only, a house in Ferrara (e.g. the fiefs of the Pio, Roberti, Rangoni and Boiardi).[94] These nobles' inclusion in the feudal entourage was thus part of the *signore*'s effort to extend his authority over his more distant territories and in drawing the territorial nobility to court and into service, the Este seem to have had far greater success than other lords, for example the Visconti.[95] Part of their success seems to have lain in their conspicuous and deliberate promotion of these nobles' landed interests in the Ferrarese *contado*: some received large fiefs, others gifts or favourable exchanges;[96] leases were added to fiefs;[97] and fiefs were allodialised.[98]

At the level of the newer and larger fiefs, the Este vassals thus coincided with the Este retinue or entourage: the service of outsiders and reward in fief went together. The value to the *signore* of having a court populated with nobles from many parts of Italy are fairly obvious: the display of self-importance, the useful political contacts made available and the possible political advantages to be gained from the sponsorship of exiles. To these would be added important internal political benefits: the attraction to Ferrara of nobles from the periphery of Este possessions, and the reinforcement of Este power in Ferrara through the resources and talents of men drawn from outside. The danger of alienating the local aristocracy, though present, need not be stressed (*cf.* Rimini):[99] as we have seen, contacts could be close between newcomers and old Ferrarese families and there are no indications that Este service was ever closed to Ferrarese noblemen. There was no policy of deploying against the old nobility a new nobility created by and therefore dependent on the *signore*. It is, however, the case that immigration via the court served to restock the Ferrarese aristocracy. Evidence from elsewhere suggests that

---

[94] For Salvatico Boiardi and Dondacio Fontana: ASM, Not. Cam., F. Tagliapetri, A, fols. 3, 109.

[95] Chittolini, 'Particolarismo', pp. 269–70.

[96] For the examples of Giovanni da Marano (1396), Marco and Alberto Pio (1402), Enrico Galluzzi (1434) and Alessandro Sforza (1437): ASM, Not. Cam., N. Magnani, C, fol. 77; D. Dulcini, C, fol. 21; C. Lardi, A, fol. 77v; Catastri, Q, fols. 121–36.

[97] Feltrino Boiardi held leases of land at Quartesana and of all Niccolo III's property at Ostellato: ASM, Catastri, U, fol. 518.

[98] For Aldreghetto Lambertini, the Roberti and Ricciardo Cancellieri: ASM, Not. Cam., P. Sardi, A, fols. 47, 124; N. Bonazoli, B, fols. 43v, 49.

[99] Jones, *Malatesta*, p. 331 and n. 7.

aristocratic extinction rates were often high.[100] Among the Italian states it was easier for some replacement to come from immigration; what is perhaps unusual in Ferrara is the centrality of the court in that process, but in a city where a mercantile aristocracy had failed to emerge, the only means of social advance would seem to be finance or signorial service (and often finance *in* signorial service), as we shall see (below, chapter 5).

OFFICIALS AND HOUSEHOLD STAFF

In one sense, the infeudation of land to foreign nobles was nothing new, but rather a continuation of a practice by which servants and supporters, from the humblest household menials to powerful nobles, were rewarded or attracted by grants of land in fief.[101] The number of such fiefs in reward of service was very high and the preambles to a number of grants make eloquent testimony to the 'unbroken fidelity' of recipients, their 'virtues and merits', the 'great services, loyalty and obedience' 'unceasingly' given, the dangers faced and the missions promptly performed at the marquis' command.[102] Though such sentiments were not always expressed, the number of such fiefs explicitly or implicitly in reward of service was very large. Almost all courtiers and administrators were included: most of the *fattori generali*;[103] a number of lesser cameral officials at Modena, Rovigo, Este and Lendinara; estate stewards and cameral notaries; the secretaries and *referendari*;[104] many of the *cancellieri* and local officials (*podestà, visconti*) of the Ferrarese *contado* and other subject provinces; household officials and servants in large numbers: *familiares* and *camerarii*, pipers, doctors, falconers, domestics and so

---

[100] K. B. McFarlane, *The Nobility of Later Medieval England* (Oxford, 1973), pp. 142–67; A. Grant, 'Extinction of direct male lines among the Scottish noble families in the fourteenth and fifteenth centuries', in *Essays on the Nobility of Medieval Scotland*, ed. K. J. Stringer (Edinburgh, 1985).

[101] Chittolini, 'Infeudazioni', pp. 49, 65–6.

[102] e.g. ASM, Catastri, H, fols. 13, 64, 194, 202, 477, 616, 637.

[103] Filippo Geri, 1363 and 1378: ASM, Not. Cam., M. Conte, fol. 64; M. Benintendi, fol. 171v; Bonagratia Muratore, 1369: F. Tagliapetri, A, fol. 94; Jacopo da Porto, 1353: M. Conte, fol. 32; Andrea Perondoli, 1377 and 1389: F. Tagliapetri, B, fol. 14; B. Mella, fol. 109; Bartolomeo Mella, 1390s: Catastri, H, fol. 620; N, fols. 59, 72–3, 82, 125; Novello Novelli, 1401–8: Catastri, N, fols. 228, 314, 328, 438, 456; Gabriele Pendaglia, 1416–18: Catastri, R, fols, 45, 81; Giovanni Bianchini, 1431: Catastri, R, fol. 456; and for Matteo Mazzoni and Delaito Delaiti, see below, p. 92.

[104] For Jacopo Giglioli and Niccolo dell'Abbadia: ASM, Catastri, N, fol. 546; R, fols. 49, 202, 208, 212, 263, 294, 560.

on.[105] Some of these fiefs were large, or became so by accumulation: those of the Boioni brothers, for example. Avogario Boioni was a *familiaris* of the Este in the 1360s and 1370s and was invested with some modest property in 1376. Two of his sons are also recorded as familiars, while a third, Galeotto, reached a position of some prominence: major-domo (*magister camerarius*) from 1405, lieutenant of the marquis in Ferrara in 1409 and councillor from 1410. In 1394 the brothers held over 1,000 *starii* (109 hectares) in fief in six localities and these holdings were almost doubled in the following years.[106] Other examples could be the Mazzoni and Niccolo dell'Abbadia: Ricobono Mazzoni (*cancelliere* 1349–76) received six feudal grants which were added to by his sons, Matteo (*fattore generale*) and Antonio (a counsellor); Niccolo dell'Abbadia, *cancelliere*, ambassador and then secretary of Niccolo III, received over 225 *campi* in fief in the Polesine di Rovigo (1434).[107] These examples, merely illustrative, could be multiplied: the careers and fiefs of the judicial official and *Giudice dei Savi* Antonio Banchi, the secretary Jacopo Giglioli, the cameral notaries Giuliano Gualengo and Paolo Sardi, and so on.

Many of the fiefs of these civil and household servants were, however, of modest size: a more or less compact farm of two or three hundred *starii* (22–33 hectares) and a few thousand vines, with a dependent worker or lessee. Such were the fiefs of the cameral official Delaito di Nascimbene Delaito, of the seneschal Pietro da Roma, of the provincial official Niccolo Nigrisoli and of Niccolo d'Este's cook.[108] Some fiefs were of isolated or widely dispersed

---

[105] ASM, Catastri, N, fols. 236, 251, 296; R, fols. 378, 411 etc.

[106] On Avogario and his sons: ASM, Not. Cam., F. Sale, fol. 82; J. Sanvitale, fol. 149; A. Cavaleria, fol. 35; Z. Coadi, fol. 159; P. Bononia, fol. 57v; J. Pelizari, fol. 69v; Catastri, N, fols. 56, 62, 459, 473. On their fiefs: ASM, Not. Cam., J. Sanvitale, fol. 59v; F. Tagliapetri, B, fol. 23; Catastri, H, fols. 416, 589; N, fols. 84, 176, 201, 216, 369; R. fols. 484–5, 564–5, 636.

[107] For the Mazzoni: ASM, Investiture di Feudi, 13/16; Not. Cam., R. Codegorio, A, fols. 57, 94; J. Delaito, fol. 145v; Casa e Stato, 21/3; and for their fiefs: Not. Cam., M. Benintendi, fol. 84; J. Sanvitale, fols. 1–3, 70, 96; F. Tagliapetri, B, fol. 37v; R. Codegorio, A, fol. 94; Z. Coadi, fol. 36; Catastri, H, fols. 282, 284, 288; N, fols. 100, 134. For Abbadia and his fief: Catastri, N, fol. 360; R, fol. 560; Mandati, vol. 1, fols. 4v, 9, 35v, 37v, 40v, 58v, 62v, 83, 92, 98v, 107, 117, 127, 133, 171v, 181v.

[108] Delaito was a cameral official from 1394, *fattore generale* from 1398 and *massaro* of Modena from 1407 (ASM, Not. Cam., Z. Coadi, fols. 119v, 154; J. Delaito, fol. 145; N. Delaito, B, fol. 53; Leggi e Decreti, A 4, fol. 163). Niccolo Nigrisoli was *podestà* at Badia and Montevecchio (Modena) in the 1370s and a member of the regency council in 1394 (ASM, Leggi e Decreti, A 1, fol. 390; Investiture di Feudi, 13/9; ACF, Deliberazioni, Libro A, fol. 10). For their fiefs and those of Pietro da Roma and Stefano Cumi: ASM, Catastri, H, fol. 337; N, fols. 174, 193, 243, 269.

pieces.[109] Many were of small urban or rural property: the court paymaster, Princivalle Ariosti, held a little meadow at Corlo; Antonio Montecatini, *iudex curie* and councillor, held a house in Ferrara and the tithe of the suburb of San Luca.[110]

### THE FERRARESE NOBILITY, OLD AND NEW

In contrast to the nobles of the Este entourage, the surviving old nobility, the families which had created and run the commune of Ferrara in the twelfth century, held little land in fief of the Este by 1394. Of the thirty-three families described by the chronicler Riccobaldo as noble in the twelfth century, twelve survived into the late fourteenth (though to these should be added the Turchi, omitted by Riccobaldo).[111] All of these families were Este vassals in the mid-thirteenth century, some with fiefs of considerable size.[112] In 1272, for example, six groups of the Contrari held over 430 hectares and a castle ('castrum vetus') at Gurzone.[133] The Turchi held part of the tithes of Voghiera and Ducentola, subvassals at Ciniselli and a house in Ferrara.[114] But between the mid-thirteenth and late fourteenth centuries, a number of these families ceased to be Este vassals (the Pagani, Signorelli and Bocchimpani).[115] The fiefs of other families were considerably reduced in size. The feudal holdings and number of vassals of the Costabili family were much reduced by escheats and renunciations in the second half of the fourteenth century.[116] The Giocoli fief contracted from one of the largest to merely a house in Ferrara.[117] And the thirteenth-century fief of the Mainardi, 'once all-

109 ASM, Catastri, N, fols., 137, 373.
110 ASM, Catastri, H, fols. 504, 617.
111 *Chron. Parva*, 480; Laurent, 'Vassals', p. 45.
112 Trombetti, 'Vassalli', nos. 7, 16, 65, 79, 85, 99 and pp. 198, 200–5.
113 Ibid., no. 99.                     114 Ibid., no. 65.
115 The Pagani had become vassals of the Adelardi in 1162 and later of the Estensi (Castagnetti, 'Enti'; Trombetti, 'Vassalli', p. 200; Laurent, 'Vassals', pp. 82–3), but lost their fiefs in the fourteenth century through escheat, renunciation and the revocation of a *feudum ad voluntatem* (following the rebellion of Filippo Pagani): ASM, Not. Cam., F. Sale, fols. 54, 70; J. Sanvitale, fol. 129. There were Bocchimpani vassals in mid-fourteenth century, but not by 1394 (Not. Cam., M. Benintendi, fol. 117; F. Sale, fol. 68v).
116 The thirteenth-century fief of the Costabili is not recorded (Trombetti, 'Vassalli', pp. 204–5), but 26 feudal grants to 23 members of the family from 1344 to 1364 totalled over 1,603 *starii* and 12,000 vines, with 3 houses in Ferrara (Not. Cam., M. Benintendi, fols. 33, 34v, 36–9, 53–4, 85, 90, 106–8, 115v, 121v–2v; B. Nigrisoli, fol. 19v; F. Sale, 95). 14 vassals held 392 *starii*, 25,400 vines and the houses in 1394 (ASM, Catastri, H, fols, 26, 360–5, 562).
117 See below, pp. 95–6.

powerful' (Riccobaldo), was slowly reduced in the fourteenth century and by 1394 only Mainardo Mainardi held any land in fief of the Este, smallholdings at Tamara, Copparo and Saletta. And these he sold to Vitaliano Trotti early in the fifteenth century.[118] Although some of these families acquired new Este fiefs in the first half of the fifteenth century (the Trotti, Turchi and Signorelli),[119] the overall trend was clearly towards the reduction of fiefholding among the older Ferrarese noble families.

The means varied by which these fiefs were reduced or eliminated. In some cases it coincided with a decline in political position and landed wealth. The Guidoberti and Mainardi, as former Torelli partisans, disappeared from public life with the establishment of the Este *signoria*, reappearing in minor positions only much later.[120] Some of the Mainardi moved permanently to Bologna, their fiefs forfeit, leaving in Ferrara a rump whose members were by 1400 beginning to appear as minor officials of the commune and of the *signore*.[121] But indicative of their decline was the removal of the Mainardi family tomb in the church of S. Domenico in 1406 to make way for the chapel of the rising Lavezoli family.[122] Other evidence suggests impoverishment among these families. When Jacopo di Vitaliano Pagani sold his cousin's inheritance to Niccolo II d'Este in 1387, Niccolo gave part of it back to him 'considering his reduced means and imminent poverty'.[123] The Visdomini family, already 'of little wealth' according to Riccobaldo, contained by the early fifteenth century a pair of unsuccessful spice-traders who were forced out of business by high rents and poor trade.[124]

---

[118] In the early thirteenth century, the Mainardi had owned the territory around Vigarano Mainarda (to the west of the city) and held land, mainly around Saletta (near Copparo) of the bishops of Ferrara and Ravenna and of the Este (Bocchi, 'Patti e rappresaglie', pp. 54–5; *Reg. Ch. Rav.*, vol. 2, no. 555; Trombetti, 'Vassalli', no. 85). For Mainardo's smallholdings: ASM, Catastri, H, fol. 607; N, fol. 496; R, fol. 137.

[119] ASM, Catastri, H, fol. 637; N, fols. 64, 90, 330, 496; R, fols. 137, 156, 233; BC, fol. 18.

[120] Laurent, 'Vassals', pp. 80–1, 83. Ubertino Guidoberti served as captain of Lugo (1375) and Nonantola (1377), as *massaro* of Modena and temporary member of the regency council in the early 1390s (*Chron. Est.*, 499; *Ann. Est.*, 909; ASM, Leggi e Decreti, A 1, fol. 326; A 2, fol. 39).

[121] ASF, Archivio Tassoni, V/14; ASM, Leggi e Decreti, A 2, fol. 217; A 4, fol. 135; Not. Cam., F. Libanori, fol. 75.

[122] ASF, ANF, J. Pavesi, 27 Aug. 1406.

[123] 'considerans . . . extenuatas dicti Jacopi . . . facultates et suspectum eius eventum inopie': ASM, Not. Cam., P. Arquada, fols. 5v–8v; Catastri, K, fol. 64.

[124] *Chron. Parva*, 480; ASM, Mandati, 1, fol. 29v.

## The Este vassals and their fiefs

However, this correspondence of reduced feudal holdings with reduced social and political importance is not to be found in the histories of other families: the Giocoli, Contrari or Costabili. Members of these families are found throughout the period in all types of civil and military service. Of the Costabili, Albertino di Elia, 'one of the nobles of the court', held the captaincies of Parma, Modena and Reggio several times between 1419 and 1440, had earlier been *visconte* at Rovigo and was the Este *commissario* in the 1427 campaign against the Fogliani.[125] Nine other members of the Costabili between 1340 and 1440 are recorded as holding captaincies, *podesterie* and estate-stewardships.[126] Of the Giocoli, Giocolo was a councillor of Niccolò III, an ambassador and lieutenant in Ferrara during Niccolò's absence in 1401. Aldrovandino Giocoli was lieutenant in Modena in 1402 and in Rovigo in 1404–5 and at various times envoy to Bologna, Venice and Forlì. Obizzo (the name itself signifying attachment to the Estensi) was a familiar of Niccolò III's wife and *podestà* of Cornacervina in the *contado* in 1395.[127] Such examples could be multiplied. In two of these families dispersion by feudal inheritance law explains the reduction in the size of their fiefs, but this was far from typical, and the same families can be used to illustrate the reverse process: concentration of property, not dispersion or fragmentation (see also below, p. 112). The Giocoli offer the simplest example. Throughout the period from the mid-thirteenth century, their fiefs consisted of land at and around Guarda, along the Po to the north-east of the city, with tithes in an area to the north-

---

125 ASM, Not. Cam., C. Lardi, A, fol. 49; Leggi e Decreti, B III, fol. 169; B IV, fols. 164, 175; Vicini, 'Podestà', pp. 247–8.
126 Elia, captain of Cotignola, 1393–4 (ASM, Leggi e Decreti, B II, fol. 14; Investiture di Feudi, 14/44); Aldrovandino, captain of Campogalliano, 1340 (Not. Cam., P. Fabro, fol. 151); Albertino, captain of Scandiano, *podestà* of Montevecchio, 1378, *visconte* of Argenta, 1393 (Leggi e Decreti, A 1, fols. 376, 381; B II, fol. 27; Vicini, 'Podestà', pp. 247–8); Brandelisio, *podestà* of San Felice and of the Frignano, 1430 (P. Costa Giani, *Memorie storiche di San Felice sul Panaro* (Modena, 1890), p. 274; ASF, ANF, S. Todeschi); Antonio, *podestà* of Codegoro, of Massa and of Finale, 1419 and 1429 (ASM, Mandati, 1, fol. 14v; ACF, Deliberazioni, C, fol. 96; Vicini, 'Podestà', pp. 247–8); Conte, *podestà* at Migliaro and Fellina (ASM, Leggi e Decreti, A 4, fol. 137; *Lucca Regesti*, vol. 3, pt. i, p. 131); Giovanni, *podestà* of Bondeno, 1393 (Vicini, 'Podestà'); Jacopo, captain of Conselice (ASM, Leggi e Decreti, A 5, fol. 223).
127 ASM, Not. Cam., J. Delaito, fol. 165v; J. Pelizari, fol. 33; J. Gualengo, fol. 17; Mandati, 1, fols. 40v, 101; Leggi e Decreti, A 5, fols. 287, 297; B II, fol. 308; Catastri, N, fol. 123; Cancelleria, Carteggio di Referendari Consiglieri etc., b. 1; Vicini, 'Podestà', pp. 204–5; Manni, 'Terzi', doc. 20; *Annales Forolivienses, RIS²*, vol. 22, pt 2, p. 86.

west.[128] From 1387 one member of the family began to concentrate these fiefs in his own hands and in 1391 they were redistributed among the three remaining Giocoli vassals, Albertino, Obizzo and Niccolo.[129] The fief of Albertino passed to his son, Giocolo, and was then converted to an allod for him in 1400.[130] Part of Obizzo's fief was used to provide a dowry for his daughter Taddea in her marriage to Matteo Gozzadini in 1423 and the rest passed to Giocolo's son, Aldrovandino, when Obizzo died without male issue.[131] What happened to Niccolo's fief is not clear. But Giocolo's sons all died without male issue and all Giocolo's fiefs were claimed as escheats by the camera and thus left the family (1430).[132] Aldrovandino did, however, have a brother (perhaps illegitimate) who inherited the rest of his property and who now became the sole vassal of the Este among the Giocoli, but his fief consisted only of a house in Ferrara.[133] By a combination of tight cameral discipline (in claiming the escheat) and signorial liberality (in giving one fief to the Giocoli and allowing them to alienate part of another) the Giocoli thus almost ceased to hold property in fief by 1440. In similar case were the Cattanei da Lusia, who held large property of the Este at Lusia and Rasa near Lendinara: again, the fiefs were concentrated in the hands of one member of the family through the failure of other lines, but this one member (Simone di Berto) proved to be the last of the family and the whole property escheated (1435).[134]

Among this group of old noble families there was thus little correspondence between Este service and the granting of fiefs. Fiefs were reduced across the board, among both the Giocoli, Trotti, Costabili and Contrari, who were prominent in Este service and among the Turchi, Pagani and Bocchimpani, who were not.[135] Yet

[128] Trombetti, 'Vassalli', no. 16; for the fiefs in the mid-fourteenth century, consisting of unspecified land at Zocca, Ro and Bozoleto, three-twelfths of Guardazolla and tithe: ASM, Investiture di Feudi, 11/9, 14, 15, 19; Not. Cam., M. Benintendi, fol. 43.

[129] ASM, Not. Cam., B. Mella, fol. 39; A. Florano, fol. 15; Catastri, H, fols. 92–100.

[130] ASM, Catastri, H, fol. 632; Not. Cam., P. Sardi, A, fol. 130.

[131] ASM, Catastri, R, fols. 259, 283.

[132] ASM, Catastri, N, fols. 62, 95, 263; R, fols. 254, 420.

[133] ASM, Catastri, N, fol. 448; Not. Cam., P. Lardi, fol. 88v.

[134] The Cattanei are mistakenly referred to as extinct by Riccobaldo (*Chron. Parva*, 480). For their fiefs: ASM, Not. Cam., M. Conte, fol. 54; R. Codegorio, A, fol. 74v; B. Mella, fol. 9v; A. Villa, fol. 73v; Catastri, H. fol. 43; R, fol. 597.

[135] For the Signorelli: ASM, Investiture di Feudi, 12/27, 13/1; Not. Cam., F. Tagliapetri, A, fol. 111; B, fol. 48; P. Fabro, fol. 142; R. Codegorio, A, fols. 49–50v; Leggi e Decreti, B II, fol. 26; A 4, fol. 265; Mandati, 1, fol. 89. For the Trotti: ASM, Not. Cam., D. Dulcini, D, fol. 134; Leggi e Decreti, A 1, fols. 181, 326,

the Costabili, Contrari, Giocoli and Turchi remained powerful families throughout the fourteenth and fifteenth centuries. With, as will be seen (below, chapter 5), landed wealth that owed little to feudal holdings, with political and administrative office (especially in the *contado*), military commands and court favour, these families were neither distrusted by the *signore*, nor subjected to control by means of feudal grants.[136]

Of the old noble families of the twelfth century, as we have seen, few survived into the fifteenth. As a class, however, the nobility showed no sign of decline. Old families were replaced, partly by local families, partly by immigrant nobles, drawn to Ferrara through friendship with the Este, marriage ties or exile. Some of these families came from the group of foreign nobles in Este service, settling permanently at Ferrara and becoming identified by residence, landed interests and marriage more with Ferrara than with their city of origin. Not that links between branches of a single family in various cities were ever reduced to insignificance, as the Ferrarese Strozzi, exiled from Florence in the late fourteenth century, showed by their continuing contacts with their Florentine cousins.[137] The Strozzi are, nevertheless, a good example of an exile family settling permanently at Ferrara. Nanne's father, Carlo, had come to Ferrara in 1382 and died there in 1385. Nanne is recorded as a courtier and retainer of the marquis from 1399 and was invested with a house in the city and lands in the *contado*. He was captain of Parma for Niccolo III from 1409 and of Modena in 1415 and died fighting in Este service.[138] Another family on the move were the Ariosti from Bologna, who had settled in Ferrara in the 1340s, from when they were prominent at court and in office.[139] Colo was a courtier in the 1360s and 1370s, his brother Francesco a retainer and counsellor of

381; Rettori dello Stato, b. 32; Sitta, 'Saggio', pp. 191–2; Frassoni, *Finale*, p. 43; 'Statuti di Massafiscaglia', pp. 275, 277; Ferraresi, *Bondeno*, p. 275. For the Turchi, Bocchimpani and Pagani: Laurent, 'Vassals', pp. 69, 77–8; ASF, ANF, S. Todeschi, *passim*.

136  *Cf*. Laurent, 'Feudalismo', p. 165; who perceives 'un nuovo sistema di controllo autoritario', 'un nuovo modo di governare'.

137  *Albizzi Commissioni*, vol. 2, pp. 3–18, 51, 55, 569; ASM, Mandati, 1, fols. 40v, 108v, 148v; 'Diario di Palla di Nofri Strozzi', *ASI*, s. 4, 13 (1884), 156, 164–5 and 14 (1884), 3; F. W. Kent, '"Più superba de quella de Lorenzo": Courtly and family interest in the building of Filippo Strozzi's palace', *Renaissance Quarterly*, 30 (1977).

138  G. Brucker, *The Civic World of Early Renaissance Florence* (Princeton, 1977), p. 274; ASM, Not. Cam., N. Abbatia, A, fol. 130; Leggi e Decreti, A 5, fol. 280; Pezzana, *Parma*, vol. 2, p. 125. For Nanne's fief: ASM, Catastri, N, fol. 97.

139  Frizzi, *Ariosti*, pp. 87–92.

the 1370s and 1380s and sometime captain of Modena.[140] Aldrovandino di Francesco was captain-general of the Polesine di Rovigo, captain of Modena (1386–8) and *podestà* of Parma (1411).[141] Princivalle was a cameral official and Niccolo was several times *podestà* of Modena and Reggio and *Giudice dei Savi* in Ferrara from 1418 to 1421.[142] From the late fourteenth century, the Ariosti were showered with Este fiefs of various sizes and conditions: Francesco's fief was large, Bonifacio's and Aldrovandino's were more modest and those of Princivalle and Niccolo were mere fragments.[143] Other immigrant families in Este service, who put down roots in Ferrara, were also invested with large fiefs: the Pritati and Novara, for example.[144]

Of equal or greater importance in the process of aristocratic replacement were the local families, though as yet we know little about these. Among families later described as noble who first rise to prominence in the late fourteenth and early fifteenth centuries are the Sala and Sacrati, the Marinetti, Boioni (Avogari), Bonlei, Gualengo and Novelli. All of these families held Este fiefs. Giovanni Sala, for example, was enfeoffed with substantial property in the early years of Niccolo III, to add to the fief he inherited from his father, Giberto.[145] Giuliano Gualengo received a number of large grants at Finale and in the Ferrarese *contado* in the 1390s and early fifteenth century.[146] Apart from the Novelli, who seem to have picked up feudal properties mortgaged to them in return for loans,[147] most of these families probably acquired their fiefs as a result of service to the

---

140  Ibid., pp. 89–90; ASM, Not. Cam., J. Sanvitale, fols. 81, 90; B. Nigrisoli, fol. 74; R. Codegorio, A, fol. 82v; Leggi e Decreti, A 1, fol. 45; Investiture di Feudi, 13/36.

141  ASM, Leggi e Decreti, A 1, fol. 369; Nicolio, *Rovigo*, p. 146; Vicini, 'Podestà', pp. 225–6; Pezzana, *Parma*, vol. 2, p. 109.

142  ASM, Leggi e Decreti, B III, fol. 358; ACF, Deliberazioni, Libri C & F, *passim*; Vicini, 'Podestà', pp. 224–5.

143  ASM, Not. Cam., F. Tagliapetri, B, fol. 33; R. Codegorio, B, fol. 50v; Z. Coadi, fol. 50v; M. Benintendi, fol. 19; M. Conte, fols. 95, 97, 102; N. Delaito, B, fol. 188; Catastri, H, fols, 504, 615; N, fols. 278, 295; R, fol. 104.

144  The da Novara held over 160 hectares from 1389: ASM, Not. Cam., Z. Coadi, fol. 11; Catastri, H, fol. 410; N, fol. 475. For the Pritati, see above, p. 62; Pietro was invested with further land and a *palatium* at Migliaro (378 *starii*, 43,100 vines) in 1430 and 1441: Catastri, R, fol. 440; BC, fol. 112.

145  ASM, Not. Cam., M. Benintendi, fol. 160v; F. Tagliapetri, A, fol. 83; Catastri, H, fols. 16, 621, 624. At his death, Giovanni's fief comprised 1,475 *starii* and 23,000 vines at Bozoleto, Alberlungo, Migliarino and Medelana, with parts of the tithes of Albarea, Viconovo, Settepolesini and Senetica: Catastri, N, fol. 119.

146  ASM, Catastri, H, fol. 62; N, fols. 29, 54, 79, 114, 463, 506, 539.

147  Ibid., N, fols. 328, 438, 456.

Este (which also seems largely to explain their rise to prominence: see below, chapter 5).

## CITIZENS AND 'CONTADINI'

Este feudality included not only much of the nobility and of officialdom, but also large numbers of ordinary, inconspicuous citizens and peasants, 'coqs de village' and sharecroppers. Among the citizens or inhabitants of Ferrara, there were, excluding those minor Este servants and officials who can be identified, 62 groups of vassals in 1394–5 and an equal number among new vassals in subsequent years to 1441. Their occupations, where recorded, were various: a good number of notaries, but also cobblers, spice-traders, smiths, butchers, barbers, doctors and so on. None of these fiefs was large: they consisted usually of a single farm, or of pieces scattered in several localities, or of houses and plots in Ferrara and vines in the suburbs. Unless they were inherited from former Este servants, it is difficult to see any political significance in these fiefs, which probably reflect only the ubiquity of feudal property: since fiefs were bought and sold, many citizens could become Este vassals by chance, by the mere circumstance that property that they bought was feudal.

The fiefs held by *contadini* are not, as a group, easily definable. It is not clear how many of the lesser inhabitants of the city worked land in the *contado*, nor how many of those here defined as *contadini* lived in the city and leased out land. At this level of society, at which it is possible to discover the social position of families and individuals only with great difficulty, if at all, the two groups are hardly distinguishable. There is nevertheless a group of fiefs which can be treated separately: those of families and individuals not described as citizens or inhabitants of Ferrara, nor given any occupational title or description, with small feudal holdings in the village of their origin. In 1394–5 there were 98 groups of such vassals (240 vassals in all). This contrasts with the 380 groups of *contado* vassals recorded in the late thirteenth century.[148] Some of these families had local importance: the Vaccari at Porto, for example, or the Spinelli at Vallicello, who held a river-crossing (*passus*) in fief.[149] Some are recorded as estate stewards or toll collectors, but of the majority, little is known.

---

[148] Trombetti, 'Vassalli', pp. 104, 142ff.
[149] Both the Vaccari and Spinelli were vassals in the thirteenth century: ibid., pp. 158, 165. On their local importance: *Ann., Est.*, 923; ASM, Rettori dello Stato, Ferrara, b. 56 (Porto), letters of 8 Apr., 24 Apr., 16 June and 20 June 1454.

Some of these fiefs were of medium size, farms apparently worked by the tenant family: for example, the holdings of the Alessi at Canaro or of the Mantoani at Salvatonica and Ravalle.[150] But very few of the fiefs were larger than 100 *starii* (11 hectares), while the majority (73) were under 50. Over half of the fiefs (61) and of the vassals (151) were concentrated at four localities to the north-east of Ferrara along the Po: at Crespino (20 groups), Corbola (17), Villanova marchesana (12) and Garofalo (12).

Many of these fiefs had been created by the Estensi or other lords in the course of the thirteenth and fourteenth centuries to settle and reclaim lands on either side of the Po. In the mid-thirteenth, Azzo d'Este, in association with the Burzelli family, had established the village known until the fifteenth century as 'Villanova burzellorum'.[151] As we have seen, Burzelli interests were bought out by Niccolo III in 1418, who acquired from Matteo Burzelli his 37 vassals and 15 lessees, to add to his own 47 vassals there.[152] Este interest in the area was evident from the mid-fourteenth century – the building of a fortification (*stellata*) at Corbola in 1334, some new settlement at Canalnuovo in the 1350s – but especially from the 1380s, with the acquisition of land and rights from local landowners. Almost all the marquis' fiefs at Crespino in 1394 derived from recent acquisitions from the Marocelli and from the *referendario*, Bartolomeo Mella. Mella seems to have used his influence on the council to make a very favourable exchange of his property at Crespino for some farms that the marquis held in the Bolognese and for three houses in Bologna.[153] Along with property acquired from the Marocelli, all these fiefs seem originally to have been held of the Turchi family, who had dominated this area in the thirteenth century.[154]

More clearly revealing very recent settlement and distribution in fief are the possessions at Corbola which the Este acquired from the Marinetti. Of the 17 Corbola fiefs, 10 were of only 6 *starii* and none

---

[150] ASM, Catastri, H, fols. 206–7, 473.
[151] Trombetti, 'Vassalli', p. 195 n. 170.
[152] For the acquisition from the Burzelli, see above, p. 67. For Niccolo d'Este's own vassals: ASM, Catastri, H, fols. 325, 511, 532, 545, 548–9, 551, 564, 582–3, 585; N, fol. 285. For the Burzelli fief of 'tota villa villenove': ASM, Not. Cam., M. Conte, fols. 46, 86 (1353); A. Cavaleria, fol. 18v (1383); Catastri, H, fol. 282.
[153] Mella exchanged 690 *starii* and 7,800 vines (over 75 hectares) for 1,143 *tornature* (238 hectares) and 3 houses in Bologna: ASM, Casa e Stato, 21/52 (1 Jan. 1394).
[154] Trombetti, 'Vassalli', pp. 210–1; ASM, Catastri, H, fols. 395, 496–8, 500–1, 535–6, 580, 593–603; R, fol. 119.

was larger than 40 *starii*.[155] These fiefs were distinguished not only by their uniform small size, but also by the type of obligations that were owed to the lord. They in fact formed rustic, 'unaristocratised' fiefs: peasant tenures owing rents and services.[156] Fiefs of this kind are found in the Ferrarese only at Corbola and Crespino. Originally all held of the Turchi, 'secundum consuetudinem domus de Turchis',[157] some had passed, via Bartolomeo Mella, to the Este, others to the Marocelli.[158] Nearly all the Este fiefs at Corbola carried the same obligations. All owed annually a 7lb shoulder of pork (a common token render) and were obliged to keep a shield bearing the Este arms and a dog and hunting equipment to hunt at the request of the marquis or of his officials.[159] Some were liable to provide hospitality (*albergaria*).[160] The agricultural services due varied: some were required to assist other dependent agricultural workers ('bobulcis vassallis') at Corbola in working the land,[161] some to keep a plough with oxen for ploughing the marquis' lands and to plant and harvest the crops, which were to be deposited at the marquis' granary,[162] or to assist every year in threshing.[163] Este fiefs at Crespino show a similar pattern.[164] The remaining Turchi and Marocelli fiefs there show a greater variety: some dues in kind or cash mixed with agricultural services or *albergaria*; the obligation to keep shields with the arms of the granting family (a common sign of dependence).[165] It is not clear, however, that these services and dues were exacted. A register of 1410 recording the payment of token renders lists as paid only 13 of the 46 shoulders of pork due (7

---

[155] Catastri, H, fols. 303–7, 329, 333–4, 375–84, 530, 566.

[156] *Cf.* C. Cipolla, 'Per la storia della crisi del sistema curtense in Italia. Lo sfaldamento del manso nell'Appennino bobbiese', *BISI*, 62 (1950), 298–300; Jones, 'From manor to mezzadria', pp. 214–15.

[157] ASF, Archivio Tassoni, VII/20.

[158] On the Marocelli, see below, chapter 5.

[159] 'tenere unum scutum pictum ad armam ipsius domini Marchionis', 'tenere continue preparatos in domo sua unum canem et unum spitum a Cenglariis pro venando cum eis ad omnen requisitionem dicti domini vel eius officialis': ASM, Catastri, H, fols. 303–7, 333–4, 375–8, 380, 531.

[160] 'tenere continue preparatos in domo sua pro omni necessitate dicti domini et casu opportuno unum lectum accoredatum': Catastri, H, fols. 329, 379–84.

[161] 'prestare auxilium et favorem bobulcis vassallis dicti domini laborantibus de terris ipsius in Corbula existentibus in onerando, exonerando et stasonando blada et fructus': above, n. 159.

[162] ASM, Catastri, H, fols. 329, 379–84.

[163] 'dare omni anno . . . unam operam a tiblis': Catastri, H, fol. 566.

[164] Ibid., fols. 395, 496, 501, 535, 580, 593–9, 600–3.

[165] ASF, ANF, S. Todeschi, 23 & 26 Sept. 1407, 14 July & 8 Aug. 1415, 14 & 19 Sept. 1417 etc.; *cf.* Heers, *Clan*, pp. 110–11.

delivered direct to the court, 6 paid at a cash value of 7s. to the camera) and only one of the 11 agricultural works.[166] On the other hand, in 1431 the Corbola vassals complained of new works which they had to perform for the marquis which had been imposed since the estates at Corbola had passed to the Estensi from the Marinetti.[167] This complaint, when considered along with the uniformity of Este fiefs, in contrast to those of other lords in the area, would suggest that the Este were more insistent in demanding services of their rustic vassals than were other aristocratic lords.

Such rustic fiefs are usually dismissed as no more than perpetual leases, 'pseudo-feudi'.[168] In other parts of Emilia, the fusion of fief and lease is clear enough – in the Reggiano, for example,[169] – but the fiefs at Corbola and Crespino were considered distinct from lease-holds[170] and the range of obligations and services due from them is not found on Este leases there. Some leases at Corbola owed only money rents, others mixed rents and agricultural services.[171] But only some of the agricultural works required were similar to those due from fiefs: two sharecropping grants of 1410 included an obligation to work on the lord's possessions as required by the lord's steward;[172] a number of leases bound the tenants to work one of the lord's farms and to harvest part of its crops every year.[173] On the whole, among Este grants, fiefs and leases were distinguishable. Again, however, this was not the case on other estates: the older Turchi leases show a greater similarity to fiefs, owing mixed rents in cash and kind, threshing works and corvées according to local custom.[174] Marocelli vassals owed rents (*pensiones*).[175] It seems almost as if contact with the more rigorous legal concepts and categories of the Este administration enforced a practical differenti-

[166] ASM, Feudi Usi Affitti: Livelli, 152, fols. 56–62.
[167] ASM, Leggi e Decreti, B IV, fol. 214v.
[168] C. G. Mor, 'Conte di Savoia, feudali e comunità in Valle d'Aosta nei sec XI–XV', in *XXXI Congresso Storico Subalpino*, 1956 (1959), pp. 242, 270–1, 294.
[169] e.g. some 'feudal' investitures by the abbot of Marola 1448–68, in which the property is regarded as feudal, but the grants are referred to as 'locationes' and the investitures had feudal forms ('genibus flexis', to male descendants in perpetuity, with the swearing of fealty) but the tenant owed a cash rent and promised to be 'fidelem afficuarium et feudatarium': ASM, Feudi Usi Affitti Livelli, 117; and see below, chapter 4.
[170] ASM, Catastri, L, fols. 269–75; Q, fol. 352.
[171] ASM, Catastri, L, fols. 234, 238, 247.
[172] Ibid., fols. 184–5.
[173] Ibid., fols. 215, 232.
[174] ASF, ANF, S. Todeschi, 14 Sept. 1417.
[175] ASF, Archivio Tassoni, VI/14 (12 May 1419).

ation between fiefs and leases among these otherwise confused tenancies.[176]

To complete this survey of Este vassals, we must briefly consider three further areas: Adria (between Ferrara and the coast), the Polesine di Rovigo and the Padovano. In the district of Adria in 1394 there were 13 Este fiefs held by 20 vassals. The fiefs were mainly at Serravalle (near Corbola and Papozze) and ranged from a single farmhouse to 24 hectares.[177] Among the fiefholders was the commune of Adria itself, which had held some jurisdiction and part of the local woodland in fief since 1198.[178] New fiefs created in this area between 1396 and 1441 included the *ripata de Mesola*, a large wooded area near the mouth of the Po di Goro.[179] In the Adriano, as in the Ferrarese, those close to the marquis were rewarded with land: Niccolo III's paymaster-general (*expensor generalis*), Pandasio Munari, who came from a local Adrian family, greatly expanded his holdings at Adria and Ariano, partly by fief and partly by lease.[180]

In the Polesine di Rovigo in 1394–5, there were 57 groups of vassals, whose combined fiefs exceeded 523 hectares (1,171 *campi*). Only four of these fiefs were larger than 125 *campi* (56 hectares): those of the Cattanei da Lusia, a major local family, of the Venetian Federico Leon, of the cameral official and chronicler Jacopo Delaito and of Filippo Geri, a former *fattore generale*.[181] Of the rest, 40 fiefs were under 60 *campi* (27 hectares). Among these vassals were the Manfredini, who were apparently lords of Concadirame and distant kinsmen of the Ferrarese Turchi. Since the early thirteenth century, they were invested by the Este with fiefs in the Polesine and Padovano.[182] Investitures to them in 1294 and 1352 included land at

---

[176] For the confusion: ibid., IV/13, VII/20; ANF, S. Todeschi, s.d.
[177] ASM, Catastri, H, fols. 54, 57–8, 252, 264, 266–7, 277, 552, 557–8, 575.
[178] Ibid., H, fol. 54; and see above, p. 40.
[179] ASM, Catastri, N, fols. 210, 576; R, fols. 65, 344; BC, fol. 91.
[180] Ibid., H, fol. 575; R, fols. 65, 344; U, fols. 19, 46, 108, 220, 223, 246, 301, 379, 398, 404, 412.
[181] Federico Leon: 178 *campi* and 10 pieces at Buso, Grompo and Villadose (Catastri, H, fol. 166); Jacopo Delaito: 125 *campi*, 2 *valli* and a mill at S. Apolinare, Borsea and Contre and a house in Rovigo (ibid., fol. 16); the Geri: 102 *campi*, 10,000 vines and a piece at Fratta and 'Codognano' (ibid., fol. 40); for the Cattanei, who held in fief half of the village of Lusia and its surrounding area, see above, p. 96.
[182] A. Lazzari, 'Il padre dell'Ariosto', *AMF*, s. 1, 30 (1936), 4–5. The Turchi also had property in the Polesine: ASF, Archivio Tassoni, III/15, VI/8.

Grompo, Rovigo, Concadirame and in the Padovano, as well as some riverine jurisdiction in the Polesine.[183] During the reign of Niccolo III, members of this family served as Este officials on the Paduan estates and Cristoforo became Niccolo's physician and was employed by Niccolo in negotiations with Azzo d'Este.[184] He was invested with land at Este in 1407, with the tithe of Mardimago in 1418 and was created a count palatine in 1414.[185] The Manfredini are only one example of a general tendency for the local élite of the Polesine to take service with the Este. The Silvestri served as estate managers in the first half of the fourteenth century and appear at Ferrara as *camarlenghi* and *familiares* from the 1360s.[186] They were invested with lands and tithes in the Polesine.[187] Another of this group, Boetio di Benastruto Ipocrati, major-domo in the late 1420s, was enfeoffed with property at Quartesana in the Ferrarese *contado* (the site of an Este villa): first land and a tower, later the inn and tithe.[188] Other individuals and families from these areas in Este service and receiving fiefs include the Delaiti, Catti and Menegatti.[189]

## VASSALS IN THE PADOVANO

The last group of fiefs to be considered are those in the southern Padovano. At the end of the thirteenth century, over half of the marquises' property there was infeudated, with over 4,000 *campi* (1,545 hectares) distributed among 169 vassals.[190] The identity of these vassals is not given systematically in the late thirteenth-century surveys of Este lands (see above, p. 48), but is partly revealed in a series of 46 reinvestitures made to 115 vassals by Francesco and Azzo d'Este in 1294.[191] Only three of these vassals are described as 'of Padua' and 23 fiefs were held by 70 vassals at Calaone, all rustic fiefs,

183 ASM, Investiture di Feudi, 7/25; Not. Cam., M. Benintendi, fols. 64, 75.
184 ASM, Leggi e Decreti, A 3, fol. 128; A 4, fol. 25; A 5, insert fols. 342–3.
185 ASM, Catastri, N, fol. 391; R, fol. 75.
186 ASM, Investiture di Feudi, 9/32; Not. Cam., J. Sanvitale, fols. 25–6; F. Tagliapetri, B, fol. 48; Catastri, H, fols. 186, 218, 635; R, fol. 509; Nicolio, *Rovigo*, p. 135.
187 ASM, J. Sanvitale, fols. 23, 65; Catastri, N, fols. 57, 541; H, fol. 528.
188 Ibid., N, fols. 80, 565, 599; R, fol. 297; U, fol. 289; Not. Cam., P. Lardi, fols. 38, 91; ASE, Giurisdizione sovrana, 250, fol. 100.
189 Nicolio, *Rovigo*, pp. 105–6, 149, 152; ASM, Leggi e Decreti, A 3, fol. 358; Not. Cam., N. Delaito, B, fol. 155v; Catastri, N, fols. 89, 185, 218.
190 Trombetti, 'Beni Estensi', pp. 196–8.
191 ASM, Not. Cam., F. d'Este.

paying a fraction of the crop or a rent, according to local custom. There was, however, vestigial evidence of military service in the number of vassals who owed horse-service.[192]

In 1394–5 few of the Paduan vassals secured reinvestiture – as will be seen, there were recurrent difficulties in securing recognition of vassalage from vassals outside Este dominions. But extrapolating from later confirmations of fiefs, we can see that both the number of vassals and the total of land held by fief appear much reduced in the century since 1294. The number of fiefs around 1394 would seem to be 18, totalling little more than 1,130 *campi*, and the number of vassals about 32. Only one fief was certainly larger than 250 *campi* (96 hectares), that of the Rossi, though the Cumani fief, too, was probably large.[193] Conversely, all the small, rustic fiefs are no longer recorded. The feudatories now include a number of Paduan noble families with clear links with the Estensi. Naimerio Conti, a major figure in Carrara financial administration, held land in fief from the mid-fourteenth century (another case of influential officials of other *signori* receiving fiefs from the Este). His son, Antonio, married a daughter of the Este vassal Jacopo Cumani and another member of the family, Prosdocimo Conti, was tutor to Niccolo III's son, Meliaduse.[194] Members of two leading families of Parma, the Lupi and Rossi, settled at Padua and entered the service of the Carrara and the Este.[195] Ugolino Lupi was invested with 200 *campi* at Montagnana in 1390 and Francesco Rossi with 271 *campi* in 1372.[196] However, as with Guido Torelli (above, p. 89), this property was disposed of when the Rossi moved away: Francesco's son, having returned to Parma, sold the fief in 1422 'as the property is of great inconvenience to him, because much of it remains uncultivated and

---

[192] 'Nomina illorum qui solvunt pheuda equorum' at Montagnana (16 individual entries of amounts varying from 6s to L.12 10s and totalling L.46 10s 2d): ASVe, Provveditori sopra camere, A 1, 2, fols. 60–v. For a similar list of tenants at Este: ASM, Camera Ducale, Affitti di Este 1296, fol. 6v.

[193] ASM, Catastri, H, fols. 155, 241, 249, 477, 613, 638; N. fols. 123, 166, 417, 440; R, fols. 47, 110, 284, 374, 418, 520, 633. Between 1396 and 1441, there were 25 new grants to 32 Paduan vassals and covering 272 *campi*: Catastri, H, fol. 613; N, fols. 110, 172, 387, 417–18, 557–8; R, fols. 145, 225, 240, 251, 298, 418, 548.

[194] ASM, Not. Cam., M. Benintendi, fol. 103; F. Tagliapetri, A, fol. 22; Gatari, *Cronaca*, pp. 331 n. 2, 355, 403, 438, 500 n. 5, 574; A. Gloria, *Monumenti della Università di Padova* (2 vols., Padua 1888), vol. 1, pp. 206–7; vol. 2, p. 271; Hyde, *Padua*, pp. 70–2.

[195] Antonio Lupi was a *provisionatus* in 1364 and 1376, while Bonifacio served as *visconte* at Mellara in 1411: ASM, Not. Cam., F. Tagliapetri, B, fol. 11v; J. Sanvitale, fol. 60; Leggi e Decreti, A 4, fol. 236; Gatari, *Cronaca*, pp. 729–30.

[196] ASM, Not. Cam., F. Tagliapetri, A, fol. 137.

because of the tedium of the journey, the great distance and the shortage of workers'.[197]

The most important of these families were the Cumani, from Monselice (see Map 5), major supporters of Este political influence in the Padovano. With claims of descent from the counts of Monselice, the family were vassals of the Estensi from at least the late thirteenth century.[198] The first to be recorded at Ferrara and in Este service is Belloto, *visconte* of Rovigo in 1335. Jacopo lived in Ferrara from 1352 and his son Azzo was a courtier (*domicello*) of the marquis in the late 1350s. Rinaldo Cumani was *podestà* of Lendinara in 1368 and *visconte* of Argenta in 1364.[199] The family seems to have been divided into two main groups: one, the more numerous, at Monselice, the other at Padua. Members of both were attracted to Ferrara. The Cumani fief first becomes visible in 1333 when nine members of the family were invested with all the property and tithes at Solesino ('in tota curia et plebatus Solesini') that their ancestors had held.[200] The following century saw the gradual concentration of this property, largely it seems through regranted escheats, among the descendants of one of the nine (Jacopo di Guglielmo) and eventually into the hands of only one individual (Jacopo's grandson).[201] As might be expected, the family also had a number of Este fiefs in the Ferrarese *contado*.[202]

Finally, we shall consider here fiefs held of the Este *signori* by minor members of their own family. Some of these are not recorded in the genealogies of the family, for example, Niccolo di Francesco, of an illegitimate branch which held lands in fief in both the Padovano and the Ferrarese.[203] Niccolo's son, Francesco, received further land in fief in 1380.[204] These passed in turn to Francesco's son, Tommaso, who died without male issue in 1430, when the escheat was granted to another obscure member of the family,

[197] ASM, Catastri, R, fol. 240.
[198] Hyde, *Padua*, pp. 76–7.
[199] ASM, Not. Cam., P. Fabro, fol. 56v; M. Conte, fol. 96; J. Sanvitale, fol. 21; Leggi e Decreti, A 1, fol. 69; D. Bandi, *Memorie storico-cronologiche di Argenta* (Argenta, 1868), p. 26.
[200] ASM, Not. Cam., P. Fabro, fol. 11.
[201] ASM, Not. Cam., F. Sale, fol. 101v; J. Sanvitale, fols. 40, 115, 130, 153, 158; Catastri, H, fol. 241; R, fol. 229; BC, fol. 110; and *cf.* above, the Giocoli, p. 96.
[202] ASM, Not. Cam., J. Sanvitale, fols. 40, 115, 130; M. Conte, fol. 96; F. Sale, fol. 83v; Catastri, H, fol. 241. And for land held of the bishop: ASE, Giurisdizione sovrana, 250, fols. 60, 79, 91v.
[203] ASM, Not. Cam., F. Tagliapetri, B, fol. 45; J. Sanvitale, fol. 140.
[204] Ibid., F. Tagliapetri, B, fol. 59.

Gerardo (son of Obizzo di Aldrovandino: see genealogy, above, p. 52).[205] The preamble to one grant commended Gerardo's 'outstanding displays of devotion' ('praeclara devotionis obsequia'), but we remain in the dark as to what these might have been. Another member of the family, Azzo di Rinaldo, was invested by his uncle Obizzo III in 1351 with a house in Ferrara and land at Voghiera, but there is no further record of this fief.[206] In the Padovano, Taddeo and Francesco di Azzo, of the Este branch, held in fief a number of *valli* at Este.[207] These grants do not conflict with the Este policy, analysed above, of depriving lesser kinsmen of rights in the patrimony; rather, they were another means of providing for them within a relationship of dependence. One may assume that Gerardo's 'displays of devotion' were exactly what was wanted.

There were clearly various levels of fiefholding in late medieval Ferrara: many fiefs were small, owing only agricultural services; others bore witness only to the ubiquity of feudal property and were little different from leases beyond the performance of certain antiquated ceremonies and the payment of an unusual form of rent; but in addition to these, there was a further group, of fiefs granted in reward of service to members of the Este entourage and retinue. Feudal grants remained still an appropriate form for expressing relations of service and dependence within this group. These many levels make it difficult to speak of the vassals as a single group. Indeed, given that fiefs could be bought and sold or combined with allodial and leasehold properties, it might be wondered whether it is valid to pick out fiefholding as the distinguishing feature of these groups at all. And of course, the number of vassals in proportion to the total population of Ferrara was tiny; and numerically, the feudality was made up preponderantly of peasants and relatively unimportant citizens. But looked at more closely, the common characteristic of many of these vassals emerges: they were intimately involved in the working of the Este lordship, whether as retainers, courtiers, household servants, officials of the camera or chancery, estates stewards or dependent peasant farmers. When such men acquired fiefs, not through the accidents of the land market, but

---

[205] For Tommaso: ASM, Catastri, H, fols. 388, 390; for Gerardo's accumulated feudal property, totalling 1,452 *starii*, 26,900 vines, numerous smallholdings and a house in Ferrara: ibid., N, fol. 590; R, fols. 38, 242, 325, 415, 583.
[206] ASM, Not. Cam., M. Benintendi, fols. 48–9.
[207] ASM, Catastri, R, fols. 288, 355, 418.

through a specific grant which praised their services and loyalty, we are led to conclude that there was something about the specific content of the fief which recommended itself to the Este for this purpose. What that specific content was is the subject of the next chapter.

The drawing into the Este feudal entourage of the mass of foreign nobles who took Este service and frequented the Este court created a 'new feudality' only in so far as it added a new element to an existing group, extending or re-employing forms of reward and maintenance already widely used. With the Este *signoria*, 'the organisation of client-relationships on the basis of feudal grants becomes the norm.'[208] But this political use of fiefs was nothing new in Ferrara. The granting of fiefs after 1240 to families not previously among the Este vassals (for example, the Mainardi) and the large size of some late thirteenth-century fiefs certainly emphasise the feudal basis of the early *signoria*; but already in the early thirteenth century, fiefs bound together both of the factions, Estensi and Torelli, seeking to take over the public domain.[209] In the constitution of a feudal *signoria* at Ferrara by the Estensi, it was the *signoria*, not the use of fiefs that was new.[210] During the fourteenth century, some Ferrarese families ceased to be Este vassals, and the reduction in the size of others' fiefs indicates the new direction taken by Este feudal grants. Those brought into Este feudality from the late fourteenth century, those who figured most prominently in it, were the foreign nobles and the socially ambitious (e.g. the Giglioli and Boioni) promoted by the Este. Not that these formed a 'new feudality' to be set against the old, for territorial, marital and political links bound old and new together into groups, at least, *within* the political community.

[208] Castagnetti, *Società e politica a Ferrara*, p. 234.
[209] Montorsi, 'Considerazioni', p. 39.
[210] *Cf.* Laurent, 'Feudalismo', p. 165; Laurent, 'Vassals', pp. 80–1.

# Chapter 4

# FEUDAL TENURE AT FERRARA

### WHAT IS A FIEF?

This is the question with which feudal lawyers usually began their treatises on fiefs. The answer provided by one of them (Hugolinus) and copied by another (Baldus) may serve as our starting point. 'A fief is a benefice (*beneficium*), which, by the goodwill of one man is granted to another in such a way that the ownership of some immovable property remains with the grantor, while the usufruct passes to the recipient and belongs to him and his male heirs (and female heirs if they are specifically mentioned) in perpetuity, with the intention that he and his heirs should faithfully serve the lord, whether that service is specified by the lord or is only indeterminately promised'.[1] This definition centres on three points: the distinction between ownership (*directum dominium* in legal terminology) and usufruct or possession (*utile dominium*); the limitation to male heirs; and the requirement of service. These three elements are sufficient to explain many of the peculiar characteristics of feudal law. The distinction between ownership and possession meant that the lord had continuing rights in the property which the vassal had to respect: 'the *utile dominium* is not free', as Baldus explained, 'but subject to servitude and loyalty to the lord'.[2] In other words, the lord's 'goodwill', his acceptance of the vassal, had to be retained. So, when the vassal died, his heirs had to petition for reinvestiture, for acceptance, at the risk of forfeiting the fief. Similarly, the fief could not be disposed of by the vassal outside the normal line of succession without the lord's permission; and if the fief was sold, the lord had a right to a share of the proceeds, as well as

---

[1] 'Hugolini Summa super usibus feudorum', ed. J. B. Palmieri, in *Bibliotheca iuridica medii aevi*, vol. 2 (Bologna, 1892), p. 183; Baldus de Ubaldis, *Opus aureum . . . super feudis* (Venice, 1500), fol. 2v. See also, for the *Libri Feudorum*, K. Lehmann, *Das Langobardische Lehnrecht* (Göttingen, 1896).

[2] 'utile dominium non est francum, sed suppositum servituti et obsequio domini': Baldus, *Opus aurem*, fol. 36v.

to a payment for his 'goodwill' from the purchaser. Secondly, the limitation to male heirs meant, obviously, the exclusion of women, but also generated debate as to the definition of 'male heirs': were brothers and nephews male heirs? were fathers and uncles? or more distant (collateral) male kinsmen? or illegitimate sons? By the later Middle Ages, there were clear legal rules on these points, which involved a further distinction between newly acquired and inherited fiefs: new fiefs could be inherited only by the sons of the recipient and reverted to the lord if there were none; old fiefs could be inherited by other male kinsmen (the *agnati*), in the absence of sons of the latest vassal. For old fiefs, legitimate birth was a further necessary condition for inheritance. Finally the fief was granted to enable the vassal to serve the lord and this imposed severe limitations on the vassal's freedom of action, both in relation to his lord and in relation to the fief. In the first place, service had to be performed within the terms of feudal fealty (the very word *feudum* was, after all, according to the lawyers, derived from the word *fidelitas*). This would require the vassal, in general terms, to assist the lord and protect his interests at all times and against all other persons and might specify certain forms of service to be performed (for example, military service). It also meant that there were fixed circumstances in which fiefs could be confiscated for disloyalty, failure to serve or offence against the lord. Secondly, the vassal could not do with the fief as he wished, as it was tied to his obligation to serve the lord. Vassals could not dispose of fiefs for their own ends, as opposed to those of their lord: fiefs could not be used to repay a vassal's debts nor to provide a dowry for a vassal's daughter. Fiefs could not be demised by will: succession was regulated by feudal law and was not open to the vassal's choice. Indeed, the fixing of succession by feudal law had two further consequences affecting the freedom of the vassal and of the lord. First, because a vassal might die without sons, all a vassal's male kinsmen had potential rights in the fief, which the vassal could not prejudice (by, for example, selling the fief) without their consent. Secondly, these *agnati* also had a prior claim on fiefs forfeit for defaults of service or for offence against the lord: as Baldus wrote, 'the will of the lord does not prejudice the *agnati*'.[3]

This is obviously a lawyer's picture: there is little in it of the realities of lordship and of lord–man relations. This does not mean that it is a legal fiction. Most social reality can be transmuted by the

---

[3] 'voluntas domini non preiudicat agnatis', ibid., fol. 63.

application of legal learning. In this case, the legal learning does itself point towards the social context: every statement of a rule contained a clause allowing the waiving of the rule by prior agreement of lord and vassal. Since, as Baldus argued, 'the contract of a fief is personal', lord and vassal could establish whatever terms they liked for the tenure of the fief: succession could include women or could be diverted to include illegitimates and remoter kinsmen; fealty could be waived (*feudum sine fidelitate*), as could service; fiefs could be granted for finite periods and so on. From the lawyers' point of view, such fiefs lost the 'true nature of a fief' (the *propria natura feudi*), but they demonstrate that feudal law could take account of individual relationships between lords and men. It was *because* they had to consider all possible contingencies that the feudal lawyers speculated at such great length. But we can tell how far feudal law was merely an academic legal exercise only by investigating a particular society: and that is the object of this chapter.

### FEUDAL LAW AND THE NOBILITY

Despite the 'return to the land' in Italian medieval studies, historical treatment of the technical aspects of north Italian (Lombard) feudalism has remained frozen into a chronology that is now abandoned: the chronology of rising communes and declining feudality. To explain the submission of nobles to the communes in the twelfth century, historians used to suggest a 'crisis' of the nobility, and one element in this crisis was the alleged operation of feudal inheritance laws. These laws were simplified in order to support a general theory of a weakened feudal nobility.[4] Differences between Lombard and French feudalism were presented as robbing the former of much of its force: homage allegedly disappeared, the real element (the grant of land) was said to have prevailed over the personal (the performance of service) and the fief was represented as alienable, partible (that is, divided equally among all male heirs) and transmissible to women.[5] As a result, it has been assumed that, by constant subdivi-

---

[4] Zorzi, *Territorio padovano*, pp. 119, 181; G. Curis, 'Feudo', in *Nuovo Digesto Italiano*, vol. 5 (Turin, 1938), pp. 1094–5; Luzzatto, 'Tramonto', p. 403; E. Sestan, 'I conti Guidi e il Casentino', in *idem, Italia medievale* (Naples, 1966), pp. 360–71; Cherubini, *Comunità*, pp. 155–6; Evergates, *Feudal Society*, pp. 147, 149; Laurent, 'Vassals', pp. 71, 75, 155; Bertelli, *Potere*, p. 21.

[5] P. S. Leicht, *Studi sulla proprietà fondiaria nel medio evo* (Milan, 1964), pp. 113–17; P. S. Leicht, *Storia del diritto italiano. Il diritto pubblico* (Milan, 1940), p. 186; Laurent, 'Vassals', pp. 64–5; G. Cahen, *Le régime féodal de l'Italie normande* (Paris, 1940), p. 49.

sion and the operation of these rules, patrimonies were fragmented or pulverised, that fiefs were dispersed and services rendered unobtainable, such that the feudal nobility became structurally weak and increasingly debilitated, an easy target for communal attack. Families' attempts to preserve their patrimonies through forms of collective ownership (indivision, *consorzi*) are dismissed as exceptional: the norm was division of the inheritance and division made the feudal nobility vulnerable.[6]

That collective ownership was the exception is far from clear,[7] and in other respects the claimed operation of feudal inheritance laws does not support the notion of noble 'crisis'. Subdivision of property did not necessarily prevent a strong sense of family unity being expressed in other forms and the equal succession of all heirs arguably strengthened, rather than weakened, feudality through binding whole families to a lord and not only individuals.[8] But most importantly, feudal succession customs have been over-simplified, for through the progressive protection of inherited fiefs and of the reversionary rights of *agnati*, they could operate just as effectively in the opposite direction: to the concentration, rather than the dispersion, of feudal patrimonies.[9] Biology was as important as law here. And family fortunes were in any case not determined by the rigorous application of allegedly rigid inheritance laws: concentration on property divisions and property losses through dowries and pious donations has, throughout medieval Europe, brought historians to see nobility in crisis, while ignoring the many other factors that, in their interplay, affected the power of noble families (incoming dowries, inheritances, purchases, territorial gains through other means, legal or illegal).[10]

Moreover, the distinction between Lombard and French fiefs, however valid in the twelfth century, was increasingly broken down. A major element in that distinction was the fact that in the Lombard fief investiture preceded the swearing of fealty by the

---

[6] Leicht, *Studi*, pp. 128–30; P. Cammarosano, 'Aspetti delle strutture familiari nelle città dell'Italia comunale (secoli XII–XIV)', *SM*, 16 (1975), 431–2.

[7] Heers, *Clan*, pp. 39, 221–3; P. Torelli, *Un comune cittadino in territorio ad economia agricola* (Mantua, 1930), pp. 71–2; Mor, 'Conte di Savoia', p. 269; *cf.* Duby, *Société*, p. 279.

[8] Leicht, *Diritto pubblico*, p. 182; M. Berengo, 'Patriziato e nobiltà: il caso veronese', *RSI*, 87 (1975), 512, 514–15; but *cf.* Leyser, 'German aristocracy', pp. 36–8.

[9] *L.Feud.*, Vulg. 1, 1, 3; 1, 4, 2; 1, 11; 1, 18. And see above, pp. 95–6, for the examples of the Giocoli and Cattanei.

[10] Berengo, 'Patriziato', pp. 512, 514–15; Tangheroni, *Politica, commercio, agricoltura*, pp. 8–14; Torelli, *Comune cittadino*, pp. 71–2.

vassal, implying the dependence of the personal element on the real. Baldus' explanation of this precedence, however, was simply that the principal party in a contract (here the lord) should act first.[11] It is hard to see why a mere formulaic arrangement should be allowed to determine the whole nature of Lombard feudalism. Moreover, homage, as we shall see, did not disappear. And by the thirteenth century, French fiefs too were both alienable and transmissible to women.[12] More generally, the progressive 'materialisation' (*réalisation, patrimonialità*) of the fief – the shift of emphasis from service to inherited rights in land – was not peculiar to Italy, but common to the whole of feudal Europe. Almost the whole history of feudalism was one of the increasing protection of tenant right: the definition (followed by commutation) of previously unconditional services; the increasingly contractual nature of the fief; the ubiquitous fraudulent contracts which deprived lords of their services or 'incidents'; above all, the early establishment of heritability and the continuing efforts of vassals to increase their freedom to dispose of feudal property as they wished.[13] In France already by the twelfth century, fealty and service were due by reason of a grant of land, where earlier service had been due by reason of fealty, and in England by the early thirteenth century, feudalism was becoming essentially a fiscal system, a means of raising revenue, not service.[14]

Nevertheless, the full materialisation of fiefs was a slow process (witness distraint of knighthood in England),[15] and the early materialisation of the Lombard fief has been exaggerated.[16] That feudality declined as the communes rose is a highly contrived interpretation. For Baldus, writing at the end of the fourteenth century, fealty and service remained the most important elements of

---

[11] Baldus, *Opus aureum*, fol. 34v.

[12] Boutruche, *Seigneurie*, vol. 2, pp. 228–9; Evergates, *Feudal Society*, p. 130.

[13] Leicht, *Diritto pubblico*, p. 175; Torelli, *Comune cittadino*, pp. 219–20; Magni, *Tramonto*, pp. 16–19, 133–5; G. Rippe, 'L'évêque de Padoue et son réseau de clientèles en ville et dans le contado (xe siècle–1237)', in *Structures féodales*, pp. 424–5; Jones, 'Mito', pp. 121–2; D. Herlihy, *The History of Feudalism* (New York, 1970), p. 77; Duby, *Société*, p. 481; J. M. W. Bean, *The Decline of English Feudalism* (Manchester, 1968), pp. 29–48, 66–79.

[14] A. Dumas, 'Encore la question: "Fidèles ou vassaux?"', *NRHD*, 44 (1920) 221–5; Bean, *Feudalism*, pp. 5–6.

[15] See, *inter alia*: M. R. Powicke, 'Distraint of knighthood and military obligation under Henry III', *Speculum*, 25 (1950).

[16] Lombard fiefs as 'plus proches de possessions privées' (Cahen, *Régime féodal*, pp. 49, 82) or 'come una proprietà assoluta del vassallo' (Leicht, *Studi*, p. 134). Also: Torelli, *Comune cittadino*, p. 225ff; G. Arnaldi, 'Il feudalesimo e le "uniformità" nella storia', *SM*, s. 3, 4 (1963), 320.

the fief.[17] Similarly, the confusion of fief and lease, the reduction of fiefs to 'mere' leaseholds, has been overemphasised.[18] Confusion in many areas there certainly was, even from as early as the twelfth century, with fiefs granted for three lives or twenty-nine years and obliged to annual rents or 'service' in cash: *feuda censualia*, as the lawyers would call them, in which fealty had little more than a negative content.[19] But Ferrara was presumably not unique in preserving feudal forms which carried none of these elements of leasehold tenure. Notions of the inalienability of fiefs (a large part of the *propria natura feudi*) long persisted at Ferrara.[20] And to contemporary lawyers fiefs and leases were simply not comparable: Baldus unequivocally rejected the idea that feudal tenure (the *utile dominium*) was only a 'chymera', indistinguishable from a 'perpetual and transmissible usufruct'.[21]

### THE PROGRESS OF TENANT RIGHT

As in the rest of Europe, the extension of vassals' rights began early in Italy. The *Edictum de beneficiis* of Emperor Conrad II in 1037 created real rights to infeudated property by limiting the lords' powers to revoke and transfer fiefs and began the process, complete by perhaps the mid-twelfth century, by which the fief assumed the legal character of a *ius in re aliena* (a legal right in someone else's property). From the early twelfth century, in fact, the fief no longer denoted only a stipend, but a real and hereditary patrimonial

---

[17] See the views of Baldus on female and clerical vassals, on substitution and alienation: *Opus aureum*, fols. 8, 18, 18v, 36v–7v, 41v, 48, 61v.

[18] S. Pivano, *Contratti agrari in Italia nell'alto medio evo* (Turin, 1904), pp. 278–9; F. Ciccaglioni, 'Feudalità', in *Enciclopedia giuridica italiana* (Naples and Rome, 1881–), vol. 6, p. 445; Borsari, *Contratto d'enfiteusi*, pp. 35–40, 784, 800; Torelli, *Comune cittadino*, p. 224 n. 3, 227–30; C. d'Arco, *Studi intorno al municipio di Mantova*, vol. 1 (Mantua, 1871), pp. 109–17; Magni, *Tramonto*, pp. 12–13, 109.

[19] Toubert, 'Latium', pp. 1162–8, 1171, 1179–80; Rippe, 'L'évêque', p. 423; Cahen, *Régime féodal*, pp. 79, 82; F. Menant, 'Les écuyers ("scutiferi") vassaux paysans d'Italie du nord au XIIe siècle', in *Structures féodales*, p. 296; L. Dillay, 'Le service annuel en deniers des fiefs de la région angevine', in *Mélanges P.Fournier* (Paris, 1929). For examples in Italy, limited to ecclesiastical fiefs: Cipolla, *Documenti*, pp. 147–50, 198–9, 203–4; F. Milani, *Viano e il Querciolese nella storia* (Castelnovo ne' Monti, s.d.), p. 53; and see above, p. 102 n.

[20] In 1280 a grant was made specifically in fief 'ut nemini eam [rem] vendere possit nec aliquo modo alienare': Trombetti, 'Vassalli', p. 189, no. 158. In 1432 the marquis converted a fief to a lease, so that the vassal could sell, 'quia si esset iure feudi illam minime vendere possit': ASM, Catastri, U, fol. 480.

[21] Baldus, *Opus aureum*, fol. 3.

right.[22] In the following century, the vassal's real rights hardened and alienations of fiefs by vassals became common, although expressly forbidden by two imperial edicts (of 1137 and 1154).[23] By then the distinction between ownership (*proprietas*) and tenure (*usufructus*) was already formulated and was joined in the thirteenth century by the distinction between *directum* and *utile dominium*, which defined the respective rights of lord and vassal in the same property.[24]

Further advances in tenant right were by local means – by city statutes and by locally negotiated settlements between lords and their vassals. From the mid-thirteenth century, if not earlier, lords came under pressure from their vassals to grant them concessions allowing some freedom to alienate fiefs.[25] In the cities, this process was assisted by 'anti-feudal' legislation, which, in general terms, sought to impede the creation, effectiveness and advertisement of feudal ties.[26] In places the attack on lords' rights was extensive, in intent at least. At Modena, for example, statutes in 1221 established full freedom to alienate fiefs and further removed them from lords' control by ending the obligation to secure reinvestiture within a year of succession. The statute also declared all buildings in the city and suburbs and all land within ten miles of Modena allodial and free of feudal ties.[27] A similar statute at Mantua in 1299 permitted all types of alienation of fiefs (though only between Mantuan citizens), while at Verona the statutes of 1276 set out conditions under which fiefs could be sold and the rates of compensation for lords.[28]

[22] P. Brancoli Busdraghi, 'La formazione storica del feudo lombardo come diritto reale', *Quaderni di 'Studi senesi'*, 11 (1965), 52–60, 62, 72, 127–9.
[23] *MGH*, Leg. sect., iv, tom. i, pp. 175–6, 247; *L.Feud.*, Vulg. 1, 5; 1, 12; 11, 9; A. Pertile, *Storia del diritto italiano*, vol. 4 (Rome, 1893), pp. 381–4.
[24] Busdraghi, 'Formazione', p. 131.
[25] Toubert, 'Latium', pp. 1167–8; G. Luzzatto, 'Le sottomissioni dei feudatari e le classi sociali in alcuni comuni marchigiani (secoli XII e XIII)', in G. Luzzatto, *Dai servi della gleba agli albori del capitalismo* (Bari, 1966), pp. 358–9, 384, d'Arco, *Studi*, vol. 1, p. 116; Cherubini, *Comunità*, pp. 96–101; A. Sisto, *Banchieri-feudatari subalpini nei secoli XII—XIV* (Turin, 1963), pp. 58–60, 81; G. Cherubini, 'La signoria degli Ubertini sui comuni rurali casentinesi di Chitignano, Rosina e Taena all'inizio del Quattrocento', in G. Cherubini, *Signori, contadini, borghesi* (Florence, 1974), pp. 204–5.
[26] Fasoli, 'Legislazione antimagnatizia'.
[27] *Statuta Civitatis Mutine*, ed. C. Campori (Modena, 1864), pp. 332–41.
[28] d'Arco, *Studi*, vol. 3, pp. 247–9; vol. 4, p. 107; *Gli statuti veronesi del 1276*, ed. G. Sandri (Venice, 1940) p. 365.

## THE CASE OF FERRARA

At Ferrara, however, now a fief-based *signoria*, statutes issued in the years after 1264 were aimed not at weakening feudalism, but at controlling it in the interests of the *signore*. Elsewhere, statutes forbade the introduction of vassals into the city at times of disorder, but Este infeudations insisted that vassals come into Ferrara at such times and take up the cause of the marquises.[29] And to ensure that at such times Este vassals were not bound to other lords, multiple lordship was forbidden, both generally[30] and in particular regard to the marquises' own vassals[31] and to the inhabitants of the strategic villages of Bondeno and Bergantino.[32] Here, as we have seen, the Este were appropriating the manpower resources of the bishop of Ferrara (above, chapter 2); at Massafiscaglia, where a similar prohibiting order was issued, it was the resources of the commune that were appropriated, for Massafiscaglia had been founded as a military colony by the commune in 1219.[33] More clearly directed against rival nobles were the suppression of Easter and Christmas feudal courts (*curie*),[34] and the freeing of some vassals (townsmen) from the obligation to pay tribute (*collecta*) to their lords (though gifts to lords getting married or knighted were allowed).[35] But it was accepted that lords might require their vassals to reside in Ferrara or in the *contado* (the fourteenth-century statutes of Rovigo, in fact, required

---

[29] See below, p. 130.

[30] 'Quod quilibet . . . teneatur habere unum solum dominum laicum': *Stat. Fe.* 1287, II, 125; cf. Verona, where multiple lordship was an accepted fact: *Statuti veronesi*, p. 365.

[31] 'Quod nullus laicus recipere debeat aliquem vassallum domini Marchionis vel filium vassalli nec nepotem . . . in vassallum': *Stat. Fe.* 1287, I, 14.

[32] 'Quod aliquis terrenis vel habitator Bondeni vel Bragantini non audeat . . . fieri vassallus cum feudo vel sine feudo alicuius militis vel civis ferrariensis': ibid., II, 68. Other statutes insisted that all inhabitants wear only the marquis' 'insignia' and allowed no foreigners to reside there without licence: ibid., II, 66–7; Ferraresi, *Bondeno*, pp. 432–4.

[33] In 1219 a syndicate of original settlers undertook to bring to Massafiscaglia 700 men, with specified military equipment, who were to swear fealty to the commune and were not to become vassals of any Ferrarese lord on pain of expulsion from the settlement: *Stat. Fe.* 1287, pp. 223–7. For the fourteenth century: 'Statuti di Massafiscaglia', 218.

[34] 'Quod vassalli non teneantur facere curiam dominis suis in pascate et nativitate': *Stat. Fe.*, 1287, II, 126. Presumably in compensation for their loss of Christmas and Easter gifts, the Este were to receive L. 300 from the commune: ibid., II, 102–3.

[35] 'Quod vassalli qui sunt in civitate cives Ferrarie non teneantur dare collectam domino suo': ibid., II, 102–3, 128. This was not an exemption from communal taxation, as has been claimed by Laurent, 'Vassals', p. 94; Franceschini, *Frammenti*, p. 32.

Este vassals there to reside in that town).[36] All this confirms the analysis in the last chapter of Este vassals in the thirteenth century. The Este *signoria* was feudal and the *signore* openly used his newly acquired legislative power to protect his own feudal resources, in terms of manpower, allegiance and service, at the expense of other lords, whose rights were invaded and abrogated. Public enactments were used to ensure that the marquis could freely mobilise and deploy his own vassals whenever necessary, while at the same time undermining the bonds between other lords and their vassals.

By the time that the Ferrarese statutes were revised in 1456 (earlier revisions do not survive), a number of these statutes were no longer necessary: those on multiple lordship, on residence and on *collecta* no longer appear. Their disappearance indicates how, in the period since the mid-thirteenth century, fiefs had lost much of their importance in the internal power structure of the *signoria*. The other statutes on fiefs were, however, confirmed, with minor modifications and three new statutes appeared.[37] One assigned all feudal disputes to the *podestà*, in contrast to the 1287 statutes which preserved the jurisdiction of lords and peers and suggesting that feudal jurisdiction had, between these dates, broken down.[38] The second statute exempted minors from the obligation to secure reinvestiture within thirteen months of succession. Elsewhere, this seems to have been customary anyway, and its enactment as statute should not have been necessary unless lords were exploiting minorities to seize fiefs from young heirs. Such an enactment would, of course, also be needed if feudal jurisdiction had, as it seems, broken down. The third statute reversed the rule which transferred succession to a fief from the lineal descendants to the *agnati* in certain cases of crime committed by the vassal. This statute also protected the lord's rights in the case of crimes for which the vassal's property was forfeited to the commune: in such cases, feudal property was exempted from confiscation and was to revert to the lord.[39] These were abstruse points of feudal law, but it is easy to see the possible political realities

---

[36] *Stat. Fe. 1287*, II, 136; BCF, Cl. I, 126, Statuta Rhodigii, fol. 42; repeated in revised Rovigo statutes of 1440: ASVe, Provveditori sopra camere, A I, 18, cap. 141. Other statutes in 1287 repeated standard rules of feudal tenure: *Stat. Fe. 1287*, II, 127–135. See also Trombetti, 'Vassalli', pp. 87–91.

[37] *Statuta civitatis Ferrariae* (Ferrara, 1476), fols. 56v–7v.

[38] *Stat. Fe. 1287*, II, 178. *Cf.* S. F. C. Milsom, *The Legal Framework of English Feudalism* (Cambridge, 1976), ch. I.

[39] *Cf.* England, where entails were excluded from forfeitures for treason: McFarlane, *Nobility*, pp. 76–7.

behind them: relations between lords and vassals and between feudal lords and the Este were still a source of dispute. Indeed, the last of the three statutes was issued specifically 'to settle a question long debated'.[40] Jurisdiction over vassals and the correct application of feudal rules of inheritance were still matters requiring political decision.

Nevertheless, the trend was towards relaxation of feudal law in favour of feudal tenants. We have already seen this in operation in ecclesiastical tenancies in 1391 (above, p. 45). Exactly a century later, Ercole d'Este, now Duke of Ferrara, in response to pressure from Ferrarese citizens, further relaxed the rules affecting secular feudal tenure.[41] His decree noted the frequent complaints of his subjects on three heads: that old fiefs could not be alienated, even with ducal licence, without the consent of the *agnati*, who, understandably, refused to surrender their reversionary rights;[42] that, because fathers could not by law give feudal property as dowry, unmarried daughters, on their father's death, 'are forced to go begging'; and that, in family divisions in which one party was given allodial property and the other feudal property, the former had freedom to dispose of his share, which was denied to the latter.[43] In response to this pressure, the Duke granted limited freedom to dispose of fiefs (alienation by will remaining forbidden), thus abrogating the rights of both lineal descendants and *agnati*.

This progressive relaxation of feudal inheritance law at Ferrara contrasts with the trend towards the reintroduction or strengthening of such laws in Milan. There was legislation to re-establish the obligation to obtain reinvestiture within a year, insistence on legitimate male succession, a ban on alienations and consolidation of the custom of payment of annates in substitution of military service.[44] This process can be seen too in Baldus' *Opus aureum . . . super feudis*, written for the Duke of Milan at the end of the fourteenth century: Baldus is hostile to alienations and bequests of feudal property, and to money fiefs and succession by illegitimate (and even

---

40 'ad sedandum questionis materiam diutius agitate'; *cf. L.Feud.*, Vulg. II, 26, 18; II, 31; Baldus, *Opus aureum*, fols. 45–v.

41 ASV, Arm. xlviii, vol. 14, fols. 73–v.

42 For an example of such a difficulty in 1420: ASM, Leggi e Decreti, A 5, fol. 330.

43 The practice was, in fact, common, in family divisions of placing all the feudal property in one portion: ASM, Catastri, N, fols. 111 (Conte), 502 (Guidoberti); R, fols. 56 (Mella), 224 (Specia), 331 (Griffi), 368 (Gualengo); BC, fol. 102 (Costabili). See also *L.Feud.* Vulg. II, 26, 8; II, 50.

44 Chittolini, 'Infeudazioni', pp. 68, 72.

legitimated) sons. The chronology at Ferrara would seem to be very different from that at Milan: instead of decay followed by revival, a long period of continued observance followed by gradual relaxation. And one reason for the prolonged observance of feudal law must be the discipline created by the Este camera.

## CAMERAL CONTROL

Cameral control of Este fiefs was certainly far from complete: it was often only through sharp-eyed petitioners that the camera learned that it could claim certain fiefs as escheats;[45] investitures were often secured on the petitioners' mere assertion that they had succeeded to the property;[46] and usurpations were a constant problem, especially in the remoter areas, for example the Padovano, where members of the Este themselves and the Cumani were particularly guilty.[47] On the other hand, escheats were often claimed by the camera for failure to obtain investiture, for alienating feudal property without a licence or, more frequently, for default of male heirs (in apparent contrast to northern Europe, where such 'natural' escheats were restricted by concessions to family claims).[48] In addition, the *fattori generali* could be obstructive to those petitioning for investiture. At times detailed investigations were carried out into claims to succeed to fiefs, sums were demanded for legitimate succession and investitures were refused without a written mandate from the marquis.[49]

The result of this uneven control, combined with interventions by the marquis, was that at times there appeared to be little consistency in cameral decisions. This is well illustrated in the treatment of three irregular claims to succession through women. In the first case in 1432, Amoroto Condulmer and Giovanni Caleffini (both cameral

---

45 ASM, Catastri, N, fols. 344–9, 539; R, fol. 302.
46 e.g. ibid., N, fols. 324ff.
47 Tommaso d'Este sold as allodial some property he held in fief of Niccolò III: ibid., R, fols. 548, 594. In 1466, the *camerario* of Este, investigating usurpations by Bertoldo di Taddeo, remarked 'ogni di ne trovo de novo': ASM, Amministrazione finanziaria dei paesi, Ferrara (Camarlengheria di Este), letter of 31 Mar. 1466.
48 Escheats for failure to obtain investiture: Catastri, N, fols. 298, 419, 546–9 etc.; for alienation without licence: ibid., N, fols. 72, 239, 467 etc.; for default of male heirs: ibid., H, fols. 17, 32, 247; N, fols. 56, 62, 64–5, 89, 97, 106, 108–9 etc. *Cf.* J. Green, 'William Rufus, Henry I and the royal demesne', *History*, 64 (1979), 342; K. B. McFarlane, 'Had Edward I a "policy" towards the earls?', *History*, 50 (1965); Arnold, *Knighthood*, pp. 84–5, 88.
49 ASM, Catastri, N, fol. 344; R, fols. 84, 143, 156, 163, 477, 533, 568, 573; BC, fol. 18 etc.

officials) were allowed to succeed to a fief previously held by their wives, who were sisters. The sisters were not, in fact, regular tenants, as they had had only informal possession for a number of years of land infeudated not to them, but to their father and his brother.[50] There is little doubt (especially given Amoroto Condulmer's other dubious activities, above, p. 81) that these irregularities were overlooked because of the identity of the persons involved. Other petitioners were less fortunate. One, a poor eighty-year-old, was denied any claim by succession to land which his wife had inherited from her father: when the *camerario* of Rovigo (the same Amoroto Condulmer) discovered that this property was feudal, he claimed it as an escheat, declaring roundly that 'feudal property does not pass to women'.[51] In the third case, the marquis had promised some land in fief to Agneta Curioni, but she asked to hold it in lease, rather than in fief, 'considering that if I am invested in fief, my only child, a daughter, will not be able to inherit the property after my death'. The *fattori generali* refused.[52] As in other feudal lordships and at other times, personal and political considerations could have more effect than law in determining feudal succession.[53] This is what the personal nature of the fief meant in practice. What is clear is that warranty – the dependence of tenure on the lord's acceptance of the vassal – was in some sense still a reality in late medieval Ferrara. It can be seen in the numbers of substitutions effected only after obtaining the marquis' approval and in the marquis' occasionally conditional reply to proposed substitutions where the new vassal was not specifically named: 'provided he gives us a good vassal'.[54] It can also be seen in the rearrangements, with the lord's permission, of titles to fiefs in order to allow bastards or brothers or nephews to succeed where there was no legitimate male offspring.[55] And it can be seen in the marquis' interventions, often against the advice of the *fattori*, to relax strict application of feudal law for petitioners who, through court position or office, had his favour. Escheats from one member of a family, for example, would be granted 'by favour' (*de gratia*) to

---

[50] Ibid., R, fols. 515–16. In such cases the husband's title was liable to be challenged by the *agnati*: *L.Feud.*, Vulg. II, 15; Antiq. IX, c. 4.
[51] ASM, Catastri, R, fols. 396–7.
[52] 'considerato maxime quod si ipsa foret investita iure feudi unica eius filia quam ipse supplicans habet, post eius mortem, non succederet in dicta re': ibid., R, fol. 357.
[53] McFarlane, 'Edward I'.
[54] 'pure che ello ce daga uno bono vassallo': ASM, Catastri, N, fol. 563 (1413); 'dummodo [emptor] sit idoneus ad vassaliticum': R, fol. 359.
[55] *Cf.* Milsom, *Legal Framework*, pp. 109–10.

other members of the same family, even in the case of new fiefs, to which the *agnati* had no legal claim.[56] New investitures were made allowing succession by *agnati*.[57] Fiefs were allowed to pass to illegitimate and female issue.[58] But all this had to be done with the camera's consent. The marquis was not unmoved in such cases by the argument, used by one citizen petitioning for his deceased brother's fief, that 'it is right that he should have it, rather than any outsider'.[59] It was this sort of 'right' that led, of course, to pressure for the eventual relaxation of feudal inheritance laws. But the camera was, in any case, not as hard-faced as it endeavoured to appear: in 1431 it had ordered all vassals to present their charters for confirmation and proclaimed strict deadlines within which this was to be done; but as late as 1433 the *fattori* were prepared to allow a reinvestiture on the grounds that 'the proclamation was issued so that cameral rights should come to light, and rather to instil fear than to impose penalties'.[60]

As some of the examples above show, irregular possession, always excused once discovered by a plea of ignorance, could escape cameral control for years, sometimes decades. It is possible that the camera had little control over real possession at all, though this is not suggested by the way such cases came to light and were dealt with. Even a former *fattore generale*, Baldino Baldini, was found after his death to have held and sold, as his own, property that belonged to the marquis, 'not with any deceit, but out of ignorance'.[61]

Yet it is the reverse that is really striking in the evidence: the extent of awareness among vassals of the terms of feudal tenure and the high degree of control maintained by the camera. Restrictions on alienability remained in force. Licence was required for all alienations, which were effected by renunciation by the vendor and investiture of the purchaser, and for the subleasing of feudal property.[62] The considerable number of such acts recorded indicates that

[56] ASM, Catastri, N, fols. 344–50; R, fols. 481, 529, 557, 602.
[57] Ibid., N, fols. 213, 304, 550; R, fols. 368, 611.
[58] Ibid., N, fols. 367, 426, 550; R, fols. 235, 238.
[59] 'iustum est quod ipse habet quam extranei': ibid., R. fol. 557; R, fols. 258, 271.
[60] 'illud proclama emanasse ut iura camere venirent in lucem et potius ad terrorem quam ad penam imponendam': ibid., R, fol. 534.
[61] 'non dolo aliquo nec fraude sed potius ex ignorantia': ASM, Not. Cam., D. Dulcini, D, fol. 21 (1437).
[62] ASM, Catastri, H, fols. 155, 194; Leggi e Decreti, B III, fols. 65, 75, 268; Not. Cam., P. Fabro, fol. 49; F. Sale, fol. 109v; F. Tagliapetri, B, fol. 50; J. Sanvitale, fol. 119. Subinfeudation had been common in the thirteenth century (Trombetti, 'Vassalli', nos. 2, 4, 7, 9, 13, 34, 52, 65, 79, 92, 135, 180, 271, 354, 356; Laurent,

a large proportion of alienations were declared to the camera (although this was doubtless in part a fiscal formality). Substitutions were common and these might, of course, have concealed any sort of transfer.[63] But the camera doubted the legality of using feudal property to repay debts[64] and alienation by dowry and will remained forbidden, except in rare cases.[65] As a result, the number of women holding fiefs was very small, as was the number with explicit female succession in default of males.[66] Moreover, during the fourteenth century, there is evidence that the Este gave especial concern to the preservation of their feudal rights. The terms on which Rinaldo di Niccolo recovered his share of the Este patrimony, retained for many years by his uncles (above, p. 53), included the condition that he should ratify all feudal grants made by them out of that property.[67] Also, the marquises seem to have been almost reluctant to empower the *fattori generali* to make feudal investitures, as if they considered their own personal involvement to be essential.[68] But the most striking evidence of this concern to control the fiefs, to know who the vassals were and to ensure that they were in regular possession, were the repeated demands for the inspection and confirmation of charters. As we have seen, (above, p. 72) such inspections were made at irregular intervals throughout the later

'Vassals', p. 76), but by the early fifteenth the only families with subvassals seem to be the Cattanei, Burzelli and Visdomini (ASM, Catastri, H, fol. 49ff; Q, fols. 347–60; ASF, ANF, L. Villa, 28 Dec. 1404). This was possibly as a result of Este policy: in two cases of escheat, the subvassals became direct vassals and were excluded from subsequent grant of the fief (ASM, Catastri, R, fol. 597; Not. Cam., F. d'Este). *Cf.* Scotland, where substitution was more common that subinfeudation: A. Grant, 'The Higher Nobility in Scotland and their Estates, 1371–1424', Oxford D.Phil. thesis, 1975, pp. 197–9.

[63] C. G. Mor, 'I "feudi di abitanza" in Friuli', *Memorie storiche forogiuliesi*, 54 (1974), 88–9; *cf.* Milsom, *Legal Framework*, pp. 104–10.

[64] ASM, Catastri, N, fol. 456; Leggi e Decreti, B v, fol. 230; and see 'Hugolini Summa', pp. 184–5.

[65] The Giocoli, admitting that 'feuda in feminas transire non possunt', nevertheless persuaded the marquis to allow them to alienate some feudal property in dower by substitution: ASM, Catastri, R, fol. 259. For the customary prohibitions: *L.Feud.*, Vulg. II, 9.

[66] ASM, Catastri, H, fols. 143, 157, 166, 442; N, fols. 124, 553, 561, 578, 580; R, fols. 137–8, 547, 617, 656.

[67] ASM, Casa e Stato, 18/1; Not. Cam., M. Benintendi, fol. 57.

[68] The *fattori generali* were empowered at first to make investitures only *ad voluntatem* (ibid., B. Nigrisoli, fol. 43), then from 1390 also to successors to old fiefs (ibid., J. Mizino, fol. 11v) and for all fiefs only from the early fifteenth century (ibid., C. Lardi, fol. 38). *Cf.* Baldus: 'vetus investitura potest . . . a quocumque fieri . . . nova investitura non potest fieri ab aliquo quam eo qui habet legitimam bonorum administrationem': *Opus aureum*, fol. 33v.

Middle Ages: in 1252, 1262, 1272–3, 1285–6, 1353, 1365 (the Padovano), 1394, 1431, 1436 (the Polesine). These suggest an extraordinary degree of cameral discipline: in England, by contrast, such demands by the Crown would have been unthinkable after the twelfth century (*Quo Warranto* was something different).

One inquiry which reveals the tenacity with which rights were pursued, but also the extent of 'lost' fiefs, was that of 1435 into tenures in the Polesine di Rovigo (and the Padovano).[69] This inquiry was divided into two parts: bald notes were excerpted from cameral registers and divided into two groups, investitures made since 1393 and those made before 1393 (but with few made before 1352). A cameral agent was then despatched to the Polesine to investigate these fiefs. He made notes against each entry indicating who the current holders were, how they had acquired their title and, if necessary, what further inquiry or action was required (as, for example, in resuming usurped property). Perhaps as an after-thought, coverage was extended to the Padovano, but against many of the Paduan entries no notes were made.[70] For the period since 1393, there were 175 entries. Of these, 25 were still held by the original vassals, while 44 had passed to the sons of the original vassals. 23 had passed to third parties, 6 had escheated and another 9 escheats were due. A small number had been converted by the marquis to other tenures: 9 to leasehold, 11 to allods. No notes were made against 45 entries, but most of these (39) were in the Padovano. The number of irregularities here was very small: only five aliena-tions had been made without licence and there were only four cases of illegal occupation of fiefs. With the 165 investitures from before 1393, the camera faced greater difficulties. Of these, 25 had passed to sons and 32 to third parties; 2 had reverted to the camera, 7 had been converted to leases and 4 to allods. But 57 carried no annotation and in a further 26 cases the official noted, despairingly, that 'this is a hopeless task', 'nothing can be found' or 'there is no one who knows'. These figures suggest that, over a period of nearly a hundred years, the camera retained control of only about half the infeudations made during that time. This seems to be a very high loss-rate and is probably not typical of Este fiefs overall: it was doubtless awareness of high losses that prompted the inquiry anyway, especially as the

[69] ASM, Camera ducale, Feudi Usi Affitti Livelli, 151. I have excluded from consideration a small number of difficult cases.
[70] The last inquiry in the Padovano had been in 1365: ASM, Leggi e Decreti, A 1, fol. 37.

Polesine had been governed by Venice for forty years, during which time there had been repeated difficulties with Venetian officials refusing to respect the Este administration or its practices.[71] It was, of course, only through regular inquiries and well-organized records that control could be maintained over several hundred vassals; and here the 1430s do seem to witness a striving for greater administrative competence. The compilation of the *Catastri*, clear and ordered records, was a sign of tightening control. As the *camerario* of Este complained in 1466 when having trouble in obtaining transcripts from the *Catastri*, without them he simply could not control usurpations nor repudiate feudatories' claims to owe nothing to the camera.[72]

### 'THE CUSTOM OF THE HOUSE OF ESTE'

Despite broad consistency with feudalism throughout northern Italy, Este fiefs were granted 'according to the custom of the house of Este'. Apart from the highly local practices that we have seen on some rustic fiefs, there were specific customs in terminology, types of fief, token renders, homage and fealty.

A major peculiarity was in terminology, in the categories of fiefs granted. Most fiefs were held *iure feudi ad usum regni* (that is, according to the usage of the old *regno italico*). Grants *extra usum regni*, found in the thirteenth century for enfeoffments to women, are not found in later centuries.[73] A small number of fiefs were qualified as 'with honour' (*cum honore*), others as 'noble' (*nobile*) or 'at pleasure' (*ad voluntatem*). Both the *feudum cum honore* and the *feudum ad voluntatem* were standard forms, though with precisely opposite effects: the former was irrevocable, the latter revocable. The *feudum ad voluntatem* abrogated the vassal's heritable right in the fief and preserved the lord's power to revoke it at will. As Baldus explained: 'Long ago lords had the power to take fiefs back whenever they wanted, but this is not so today unless the fief is granted at will.'[74] At

---

[71] Ibid., A 3, fols. 13, 20; A 4, fols. 236 and insert 320–1.

[72] ASM, Amministrazione finanziaria dei paesi, Ferrara (Camarlengheria di Este), letter of 31 Mar. 1466.

[73] Trombetti, 'Vassalli', p. 110 n. 15; Castagnetti, *Società e politica*, pp. 228–9.

[74] 'Nota quod antiquissimo tempore erat in potestate dominorum quando vellent feudum auferre, sed hodie non est ita nisi feudum concederetur ad beneplacitum': Baldus, *Opus aureum*, fol. 7; see also 'Hugolini Summa', p. 185; H. Richardot, 'Le fief roturier à Toulouse aux XIIe et XIIIe siècles', *RHDF*, s. 4., 14 (1935), 333–4. There were also life-fiefs at Ferrara: ASM, Catastri, H, fol. 403; R, fols. 304, 583.

Ferrara in the thirteenth century, this type of fief was used especially in grants of land to which the marquis' title was, or might later become, doubtful – for example, lands taken from rebels, which the Este might in future wish to restore.[75] This fief was also used to preserve the Este patrimony: in 1293, the marquises agreed not to alienate any of the inheritance of their father, Obizzo II, and to enfeoff only *ad voluntatem*, thus making no permanent reduction in the patrimony.[76] As a direct result of this decision, it seems, such fiefs were common in the early fourteenth century, though by 1400 such fiefs were allowed to pass to the heirs in the normal way and new enfeoffments *ad voluntatem* were not common.[77]

The most idiosyncratic of the Ferrarese fiefs, although not very common, was the *feudum nobile*. The lawyers' definition of this fief was that it ennobled the recipient.[78] But at Ferrara nobles did not hold 'noble fiefs', nor were those holding them ennobled.[79] The only evident effect of holding a 'noble fief' was exemption from the payment of annual dues to which all other fiefs were subject. The Ferrarese *feudum nobile* is thus the *franc fief*, the *feudum francum*, the essential characteristic of which was its freedom from services, in France even from homage and relief.[80] At Ferrara it was from payment, not service that the 'noble fief' exempted the vassal. But these fiefs are found there only from the 1430s: elsewhere, for example in the Mantovano and Reggiano, fiefs of the same kind are found much earlier.[81] A similar type of fief, the *feudum sine fidelitate*,

---

For fiefs *cum honore*: ibid., H, fols. 70, 335, 347; N, fols. 99, 114, 314, 418; Investiture di Feudi, 11/7, 11/42.

[75] Trombetti, 'Vassalli', pp. 61 n. 151, 111 n. 20, 140 n. 84, 168 no. 270.

[76] Muratori, *Antichità*, vol. 2, p. 49; Trombetti, 'Beni estensi', pp. 199–200.

[77] Catastro H contains 26 *feuda ad voluntatem*, mainly at Villanova, Serravalle and in the Polesine; Catastro N contains 11, mainly renewals. For rare revocation: Catastri, N, fol. 248; Not. Cam., F. Sale, fol. 54.

[78] Baldus, *Opus aureum*, fol. 4v.

[79] ASM, Catastri, R, fols. 531, 533, 537, 597, 610, 625, 636.

[80] Baldus, *Opus aureum*, fols. 4v, 70; H. Richardot, 'Francs-fiefs', *RHDF*, s. 4, 27 (1949), 30, 40ff, 259–64; Torelli, *Comune cittadino*, pp. 217–19; Boutruche, *Seigneurie*, vol. 2, pp. 203–4; E. Chenon, *Etude sur l'histoire des alleux en France* (Paris, 1888), pp. 88–93; F. Carreri, 'Del feudo onorifico rispetto alla nobiltà', *Rivista araldica*, 11 (1913); G. Giordanengo, 'Vocabulaire et formulaires féodaux en Provence et en Dauphiné (XIIe-XIIIe siècles)', in *Structures féodales*, pp. 101–2.

[81] For examples in the Reggiano in the 1370s: ASM, Investiture di Feudi, 13/23. At Mantua in 1388 a due was imposed on a *feudum nobile*, which was still to be treated as *nobile*, not *censuale*: ASMn, Archivio Gonzaga, b. 242, no. 478. At Ferrara there was doubt whether a *recognitio* could be imposed on a noble fief without derogating from the *propria natura feudi*: ASM, Catastri, BC, fol 58 (1446). See also A. Battistella, *Il conte Carmagnola* (Genoa, 1889), p. 464.

exempt from homage, loyalty and service, although found in Ferrara in the twelfth and thirteenth centuries, then largely disappeared: there are none among Este fiefs in the period from 1340 to 1440.[82] It thus seems that fiefs at Ferrara with exemptions from tenurial obligations were neither common nor of any social value.[83]

### TOKEN RENDERS

The appearance of 'noble fiefs' is in fact closely connected with the imposition in the late fourteenth century of annual recognitory dues (*recognitiones*) or token renders, on most Este fiefs. Elsewhere, from as early as the twelfth century, we find fiefs charged with such dues, even with rent (*census*), and many historians have interpreted this as 'the deep, indeed final deformation of the [feudal] system'.[84] At Ferrara, however, there is no record of such dues before the mid-fourteenth century. Between 1340 and 1380 they are found on a very small number of fiefs, mainly held by 'foreign' vassals, whose absence from Ferrara presumably increased the need for a regular recognition that the land they held was feudal, not allodial.[85] Then from 1380 the practice was generalised to most Ferrarese fiefs, though not to those in the Polesine.[86] Henceforth, all vassals, on an appointed feast-day each year, had to deliver certain objects or commodities to the marquis. The objects required varied greatly: birds and fishes (partridges, pheasants, hawks; pike, tench,

---

[82] On *feuda sine fidelitate*: G. Rippe, 'Feudum sine fidelitate. Formes féodales et structures sociales dans la région de Padoue à l'époque de la première commune (1131–1236)', in *MEFR*, 87 (1975); *Stat. Mo. 1327*, p. 338. For such fiefs in the Ferrarese: Trombetti, 'Vassalli', pp. 29–32 (1077); Alessi, *Este*, vol. 1, p. 524 (1142); Muratori, *Antichità*, vol. 1, pp. 348 (1178), 368 (1196); Trombetti, 'Vassalli', pp. 50 n. 121 (1197), 152 n. 120 (1214), 127 n. 59 (1228), 133 no. 92 (1262); Lazzarini, 'Possessi', p. 228 (1271); Castagnetti, *Società e politica*, p. 230.

[83] *Cf.* Jones, *Storia d'Italia*, p. 1793; Jones, 'Mito', pp. 69–70; Petronio, 'Giurisdizioni', pp. 399, 401; Boutruche, *Seigneurie*, vol. 2, pp. 288–9; Duby, *Société*, pp. 632–3; Evergates, *Feudal Society*, pp. 127, 135; Sisto, *Banchieri*, pp. 32, 61–2; Fiumi, 'Fioritura', pp. 401ff. On the dictum 'feudum antiquum nobilitat': Baldus, *Opus aureum*, fol. 38; Giordanengo, 'Vocabulaire', p. 105.

[84] 'la deformazione gravissima anzi definitiva dell'istituto': Chittolini, 'Cremona', p. 228; Torelli, *Comune cittadino*, pp. 227–8; P. J. Jones, 'An Italian estate, 900–1200', *EcHR*, s. 2, 7 (1954), 23; Duby, *Société*, p. 184. For recognitory dues on Mantuan fiefs from at least the early fourteenth century: ASMn, Archivio Gonzaga, b. 242.

[85] For the Lambertini, Bevilacqua, Conte, Piscatori and Marinetti: ASM, Not. Cam., P. Fabro, fol. 150; M. Conte, fols. 13, 100; F. Sale, fol. 72v; F. Tagliapetri, A, fol. 22; R. Codegorio, A, fol. 13.

[86] ASM, Camera ducale, Feudi Usi Affitti Livelli, 151.

sturgeon); hats and gloves; foodstuffs (pepper, cherries, wine, shoulders of pork); and, mainly due from nobles, hunting and jousting equipment (horses, spurs, weapons such as lances and crossbows etc.). There was clearly some effort to appoint objects appropriate to the status of the vassals: household servants might owe objects related to their daily tasks.[87] The symbolic value of these renders should not in fact be overlooked.[88] Hunting and jousting were two activities by which the aristocracy most displayed their status and the expectation that vassals should contribute to these pursuits was a real reflection of the lord's power. Indeed, in other states, the delivery of token renders was itself made into a semi-religious act of collective homage, as the renders were offered at a church on a saint's day significant in the local calendar.[89] The imposition of recognitory dues would thus form part of the increasingly ceremonial and ritual nature of political relationships in the fifteenth century, as perceived by some historians. In this process, 'ritual gift-giving' has assumed an important place, along with theories of magnificence and the manipulation of festivals.[90]

We have been warned not to take the apparent solemnity of medieval ceremony too seriously,[91] but there are cases where the message is clear and unequivocal that fiefs and feudal ceremony were used to express relations of affection and dependence. In 1449, for example, Leonello d'Este granted to his sister Isotta, recently married to Stefano Frangipani, count of Segna, a house in Ferrara in fief 'such that our sister . . . should know and such that it should not escape her husband either, with what sincerity of heart and purity of faith we have loved our sister and that she should see that, although physically absent, she is not absent from our thoughts'.[92] Or take the investiture in 1453 of Cesare Montecuccoli with some Modenese castles in a formal ceremony in the cathedral: Borso d'Este, seated on a raised *cathedra* in front of the main altar and dressed in his new ducal

---

[87] For example, a barber's basin, razor and comb due from a barber: ASM, Catastri, R, fol. 83.

[88] *Cf.* J. Le Goff, 'Le rituel symbolique de la vassalité', *Pour un autre moyen âge* (Paris, 1977), pp. 360–2.

[89] Pansini, 'Feudalesimo nel Granducato', p. 164.

[90] Brown, 'Magnificence', pp. 25–6, 352–91, 435–552; Lubkin, 'Galeazzo Maria Sforza', pp. 58–61, 67, 109, 132–5, 142–4, 291–5, 331–5, 356–70.

[91] Wormald, *Bonds of Manrent*, pp. 22–3.

[92] 'ut intelligat . . . soror nostra . . . idque non fugiat . . . eius virum quam sincero corde quam purissima fede ipsam sororem nostram dilexerimus videatque ipse soror nostra se etiam absentem nostra memoria non excludi': ASM, Leggi e Decreti, B vi, fol. 105.

attire, invested Cesare, who was kneeling before him, by delivery of his ducal sword and then received Cesare's oath of fealty.[93] That fiefs could express such relations of dependence and affection was, of course, formulaic,[94] but these examples remind us that the formulae were not empty.

Recognitory dues were not, therefore, rents. Although the camera, for accounting purposes, treated them similarly, in general the distinction was maintained between rents and renders. In 1421 a cameral official was disturbed to discover that some vassals were paying a rent (*terraticum*) of L.9 and had it cancelled.[95] On the other hand, the payment of recognitory dues began to displace other vassalic obligations, such as that to obtain reinvestiture. Legal counsel in 1417 approved the relaxation of this requirement, such that, if a new vassal failed to obtain investiture within a year, but continued to pay the *recognitio*, the marquis lost his claim to reversion of the fief. The recognitory function of investiture was obviously seen as unnecessary in addition to the payment of the render.[96] Previously, there had been numerous escheats for failure to obtain investiture: now the camera, which seems to have sought to restrict application of the new ruling, was strict in its exaction of *recognitiones* and their arrears.[97]

Fiefs were not of great financial value to the marquis, although one vassal, seeking to divide up and sell his fief, did argue to the camera the case for the marquis having more vassals, as they would bring increased *census* and entry-fines.[98] Recognitory dues did not generate much income: some were delivered direct to the court, others were paid, in cash equivalents, to the camera, but the estimable money value of these was only around L.500. And in practice under half of

[93] ASM, Archivio Montecuccoli, b. A, 23. *Cf.* the ceremonial investiture of the count of Gorizia by the Doge of Venice in 1424: *Libri commemoriali*, xi, p. 59, no. 170.

[94] e.g. the formulary of Orlandinus: *Orlandini Rodulphini bononiensis doctoris in utroque iure consumatissimi in artem notariae ordinatissime summule* (Venice, 1565), fol. 13v.

[95] ASM, Catastri, R, fol. 213.

[96] For the ruling of the marquis' vicar-general, Bartolomeo Caroli: ASM, Leggi e Decreti, A 5, fols. 255–6. For cases in which the ruling was invoked: Catastri, R, fols. 106, 114 (1418); Not. Cam., C. Lardi, A, fols. 83v–4 (1433). Similar provision is found much earlier elsewhere: *Stat. Mo. 1327*, p. 335; Muratori, *Antiquitates*, vol. 4, 437–8; Torelli, *Comune cittadino*, p. 234 n. For the *prescriptio annalis* in feudal law: *L.Feud.*, Vulg. ii, 33; Baldus, *Opus aureum*, fols. 10v, 21, 37v, 42, 49–v, 58.

[97] ASM, Catastri, N, fols. 72, 166; R, fol. 427. In one case the *fattori* claimed a fief as an escheat for the arrears: Catastri, R, fol. 404.

[98] Ibid., R, fol. 165.

such dues were paid.[99] More lucrative were the entry-fines (*caposolda*) of one third of the purchase price claimed on all sales of fiefs.[100] Although entry-fines varied from place to place, they were rarely as high as one third[101] and even at Ferrara the rates were lower for other tenures: one twentieth on Este leases, one sixth on ecclesiastical fiefs.[102] The revenue accruing from entry-fines was a major source of income for many ecclesiastical lords,[103] but for the Este landed revenues were less important and entry-fines were sometimes reduced or remitted. Indeed, as one vassal claimed in 1434, 'it is not and never has been the practice of your lordship and your predecessors to care about amounts of feudal payments, but rather about fealty and the oath of vassals'.[104] It is important, therefore, to look next at what these involved.

### HOMAGE AND FEALTY

Homage, the act of the vassal, on investiture, placing his hands between those of his lord, was a powerful symbol of the vassal's commitment and dependence. Both the act and the word, however, seem to have disappeared from Lombard feudalism in the tenth century, although they reappeared in some areas in the twelfth and thirteenth.[105] But homage was, in any case, partly replaced by the 'new formula for fealty' (the *nova forma fidelitatis*), common to all Europe, and which bound the vassal closely to the lord by obliging him to swear to defend the lord 'against all men' (*contra omnem*

[99] ASM, Camera ducale, Feudi Usi Affitti Livelli, 23; *cf.* Pansini, 'Feudalesimo nel Granducato', pp. 170–1.

[100] e.g. ASM, Catastri, S, fol. 46; H, fol. 610.

[101] *Cf.* Cremona, Mantua and the Appennines: Chittolini, 'Cremona', p. 251; Torelli, *Comune cittadino*, p. 221; Cherubini, *Comunità*, pp. 103–4. In general, see P. J. Jones, 'Italy', in *Cambridge Economic History of Europe*, vol. 1, 2nd edn (1966), p. 408.

[102] ACF, Deliberazioni, Libro D, 16 Apr. 1434.

[103] Torelli, *Comune cittadino*, pp. 221–2; Cherubini, *Comunità*, pp. 84–6, 103–4.

[104] 'scientes quod dominorum . . . predecessorum vestrorum et vestri dominationis moris non est nec unquam fuit attendere quantitates solutionum feudalium sed fidelitatem et iuramentum vassallorum': Catastri, R, fol. 574.

[105] P. S. Leicht, 'L'omaggio feudale in Italia', *RSDI*, 26–7 (1953–4); Busdraghi, *Formazione*, pp. 118–19; Toubert, 'Latium', p. 1140. The disappearance of homage has provoked from French historians dismissive remarks on Italian feudalism: Boutruche, *Seigneurie*, vol. 1, p. 227; G. Fourquin, *Seigneurie et féodalité* (Paris, 1970), pp. 69–70. Homage is found in Piedmont, Liguria, Lazio, Lunigiana and Veneto in the twelfth century: Busdraghi, *Formazione*, p. 118 n.; and see Picotti, *Caminesi*, doc. 4, p. 249.

*hominem*).[106] In some areas, this was reinforced by the concept of liegeance: where vassals had many lords, priority was given to one lord (for example, a king). At Ferrara, homage was absent in the thirteenth and early fourteenth centuries, but reappears in the course of the fourteenth, becoming common by 1400.[107] Este fiefs also became liege (although the term *ligium* never appears) through the disappearance of reservations of prior fealty to other lords, such as the Emperor or Pope. Reservations had been present in Ferrarese fiefs in the thirteenth century and their disappearance probably reflects Este legislation against multiple lordship and the increasingly sovereign powers of the princely rulers of Italy.[108]

The Este oath of fealty was also peculiar. Although basically identical with the *nova forma fidelitatis* laid down in the *Libri Feudorum*, it contained an additional clause, absent from infeudations by other Ferrarese nobles, which transformed the 'fundamentally negative' character of fealty into a positive instrument in the creation and maintenance of political support.[109] This clause obliged the vassal, 'at times of any disturbance or disorder in the city', to rally to the marquises, 'with or without weapons', but in any case 'without a specific summons'. The implications of this are obvious: vassals were expected automatically to take part in street-fighting to maintain the Este *signoria*.[110]

Occasionally, vassals were obliged to more specific service. A handful of fiefs from 1316 to 1381 demanded military service, the vassal being required to 'serve the marquises with arms . . . at their expense whenever requested' or to send in his place 'one well-armed man'.[111] On the whole, however, Este fiefs were obliged to no

---

[106] *L.Feud.*, Vulg. II, 6–7; Leicht, 'Omaggio'; Dumas, 'Encore la question', pp. 198, 215–16; Boutruche, *Seigneurie*, vol. 2, pp. 165–8.

[107] Laurent, 'Vassals', p. 62; ASM, Catastri, H & N, *passim*.

[108] For the thirteenth century: Muratori, *Antiquitates*, vol. 1, 803–4; Trombetti, 'Vassalli', pp. 94, 147; Cahen, *Régime féodal*, p. 46; Toubert, 'Latium', pp. 1153–6. Reservations remained on fiefs held of other Ferrarese nobles: ASF, Archivio Tassoni, IV/13, VI/2 & 14; ANF, S. Todeschi.

[109] Rippe, 'L'évêque', p. 423; *cf.* Toubert, 'Latium', pp. 1143–4. The clause replaced two, more limited clauses in the *nova forma fidelitatis: L.Feud.*, Vulg. II, 7.

[110] 'Et si contingat . . . quod rumor aliquis sonuerit in civitate Ferrarie vel districtu occasione alicuius rixe mote vel etiam movende vel aliqua rixa fuerit in civitate Ferrarie vel districtu, ad dictum dominum Marchionem traham cum armis nulla expectata requisitione et ad voluntatem dicti domini Marchionis vel sui nuncii ibo et stabo cum armis et sine armis nec ad aliquem partem traham cum armis vel sine armis absque licentia et voluntate domini Marchionis': ASM, Catastri, G, fols. 12–v; Not. Cam., F. Tagliapetri, B, fol. 9; Trombetti, 'Vassalli', p. 96. And see Castagnetti, *Società e politica*, pp. 232–3.

[111] 'servire cum armis dictis dominis Marchionibus . . . et sequi cum armis expensis

specific service (what the lawyers called *feuda recta*: correct fiefs).[112] This was a major distinction between Lombard and French (especially Norman) feudalism and a major limitation in assessing the efficacy of feudal service.[113] Where service was not commuted into a cash sum, nor demanded by reason of quotas, it is difficult to see what obligations fiefholding still carried in the later Middle Ages. That unspecified service meant no service, however, is an unwarranted conclusion. For Baldus, the essence of the fief remained fealty and the lord could resume fiefs for failure to serve (or to make payments in lieu).[114] At Milan in the later fifteenth century, a variety of service was demanded by the Duke from his feudatories, from military service and attendance at court to marriage gifts and loans.[115] Galeazzo Maria Sforza summarily called on feudatories for escort duties and similar services and revived the practice of holding annual courts (at Christmas, Easter and the anniversary of his accession) which feudatories were expected to attend.[116] As noted above, however, Milan and Ferrara did not follow the same feudal pattern and there is less evidence for direct calls on vassals for service. The only example, in fact, is a feudal marriage aid levied from vassals on the occasion of Niccolo III's marriage to Gigliola da Carrara in 1397.[117] It is, of course, possible that recognitory dues replaced all service, as for example in late medieval Scotland.[118] But there is indirect evidence that some forms of indeterminate service or, more evidently in the sources, personal dependence were still implicit in feudal tenure. In 1417, for example, the *condottiere* Sforza degli Attendoli was described as 'the marquis' man . . . ready to do and

dominorum quandocumque et totienscumque requisitus fuerit': ASM, Investiture di Feudi, 9/18 (1316), 9/22 (1317); Not. Cam., M. Benintendi, fol. 120v (1353); M. Conte, fol. 114v (1364); R. Codegorio, A, fol. 70 (1381).

[112] 'feudum non dicitur rectum ubi est certum servitium limitatum': Baldus, *Opus aureum*, fol. 3. The strict definition of service (as in Norman feudalism) is, in this sense, 'improper', as perceived, too, by feudal lawyers in early modern Scotland: Wormald, *Bonds of Manrent*, p. 12.

[113] Rippe, 'Feudum sine fidelitate', p. 201; Cristiani, *Nobiltà e popolo*, p. 154 n. 229; Torelli, *Comune cittadino*, p. 226; Menant, 'Ecuyers paysans', p. 295; Toubert, 'Latium', p. 1144; Duby, *Société*, pp. 185, 565.

[114] Baldus, *Opus aureum*, fols. 2v, 3v, 34, 54v, 64, 75v, 79.

[115] Bueno de Mesquita, 'Ludovico Sforza', pp. 207–8; *cf.* detailed services on Roman and Umbrian fiefs: D. Waley, 'La féodalité dans la région romaine dans la 2e moitié du XIIIe siècle et au début du XIVe', in *Structures féodales*, pp. 517–18; M. Antonelli, 'Di alcune infeodazioni nell'Umbria nella seconda metà del secolo XIV', *BU*, 13 (1907).

[116] Lubkin, 'Galeazzo Maria Sforza', pp. 284–5, 328, 356–7.

[117] ASM, Catastri, N, fols. 298–9.

[118] Grant, 'Nobility', p. 189.

follow his will' and it is therefore hardly surprising to find that Sforza had been Niccolò III's vassal since 1411 (for territory in the Parmense and some houses in Ferrara).[119] In 1420, Niccolò III and Uguccione Contrari were negotiating the restoration of Parma and its *contado* to Filippo Maria Visconti and were trying to persuade him to allow Contrari to retain some castles there: Contrari offered to hold them in fief of the Visconti, but 'without being personally bound', as Niccolò wished him to remain in 'freedom for the lands in the Parmense'.[120] Here, clearly, the fief was regarded as involving personal dependence. Similarly, in 1428 Rinaldo Cumani, petitioning for licence to move from Ferrara to Padua (itself significant here), undertook as a vassal to be 'always obedient to the marquis' orders in my person and possessions'.[121] Enfeoffments to Este administrators and diplomats, as we have seen, often recall the services and loyalty given. Licences to alienate were sometimes conditional on the purchaser being 'suitable for vassalage'. And fiefs were confiscated for disloyalty and rebellion[122] or recovered when individuals ceased to serve the Este (above, p. 85). This vague and implicit expectation of service, dependence and loyalty was not, of course peculiar to Ferrara. Elsewhere in the Este state, control of vassals was important in territorial disputes between nobles;[123] and elsewhere in north Italy, enfeoffment was used to create and express political dependence.[124]

The general picture that emerges of Ferrarese feudalism is not a simple one. Este feudality was an elastic entity, in terms both of

[119] 'homo del marchese . . . prompto a fare e seguire la volonta de messer lo marchese': ASM, Cancelleria, Ambasciatori, Venezia, 1, 2, fol. 5; Catastri, N, fol. 489.

[120] 'non essendo mi per la persona obligata': BEM, Documenti Campori, Appendice 1321.

[121] 'semper cum personis et ere ad ipsius dominationis mandata dispositus obediens': ASM, Leggi e Decreti, B IV, fol. 177. Some vassals petitioning for their fief to be converted to an allod in 1422 declared: 'cum per hoc non restat quin vester dominatio supplicantes predictos pro vassalibus familiaribus et subditis in ere anima et corpore continue et perundique ad mandata sua possit et valeat habere': Catastri, S, fol. 45.

[122] ASM, Catastri, H, fols. 197, 199, 538, 624; N, fol. 541; R, fol. 281; Not. Cam., J. Sanvitale, fol. 70.

[123] Ibid., B. Nigrisoli, fols. 40–2; Investiture di Feudi, 13/18; Leggi e Decreti, B IV, fols. 175–v.

[124] The Gonzaga held Reggio in fief of the Visconti (Waller, 'Diplomatic relations', pp. 14, 228–9, 233), as the Manfredi held Faenza of the Este (Muratori, *Antichità*, vol. 2, pp. 150–1).

personnel and of the precise conditions of feudal tenure. There were differences between Este feudal custom and that of other noble families and variations between the Ferrarese and the Polesine and between different social groups in the Ferrarese. Feudalism was not a rigid 'system'. Moreover, the political role of feudalism changed in the course of the first two centuries of the Este *signoria* (1240–1440): it was used first to demonstrate and make effective Este power and later to advance territorial ambitions and to reward the growing numbers of courtiers and administrators. Internally, efforts by legislation to maintain uncompromised Este control over vassals argues the importance to the marquises of feudal bonds in preserving their supremacy. As a result, it seems, feudal tenure in the thirteenth and fourteenth centuries did not decay, but rather retained its distinctiveness as a tenure, and with it, notions of service and fealty, of personal dependence. However, by the late fourteenth century, two new, contrary trends were at work: the large infeudations to foreign nobles; and the reduction in numbers of vassals, the frequent sales of fiefs and the progressive relaxation of feudal inheritance law. At the same time, it seems, as the Este camera was tightening its control over vassals and as new roles for fiefs in territorial government were being worked out at Milan, the distinctive elements of feudal tenure at Ferrara were disintegrating. How these conflicting trends combined in the later fifteenth and early sixteenth centuries is unfortunately beyond the scope of this study.

*Chapter 5*

# NOBLE SOCIETY AT THE CENTRE

Only in very few cases did the fiefs held by Ferrarese nobles of the Este form a major part of noble patrimonies. The pattern of noble landowning was extremely varied and Este fiefs were only one part of a complex structure of landownership. As we have seen, the chief churches of the city held extensive possessions in the *contado* which were in large part distributed among the nobility and citizens, to say nothing of the property of lesser monasteries and churches, which often fell into the control of important local families. The Este patrimony itself, as we have seen, was largely made up of church land. It is the purpose of this chapter to investigate the relationship between Este grants and families' other sources of wealth and social prestige.

### THE ELEVATION OF NEW FAMILIES

It might be expected that Este grants would form a greater proportion of the landed possessions of 'new' and immigrant families than of the ancestral lands of the old nobility. In some families this was so, most conspicuously in the case of the Roberti, for whom there exists complete documentation of their acquisitions, in the form of a cartulary compiled in 1398–9 of documents running from 1363.[1] This reveals that in the period from 1363 to 1392 the bulk of Roberti lands in the Ferrarese were held in fief of the marquises and that purchases of allodial land added only slightly to them. The same combination of Este grants and political prominence that advanced Roberti power is also seen in other new families. Some received lands and jurisdiction in the *contadi* of Modena and Reggio, for example the Sala and Sacrati. Alberto di Giovanni Sala and his brothers were given outright possession in 1413 of the former

---

[1] BEM, Documenti Campori, Appendice 1251. On the Roberti, see above, pp. 85–6.

Fogliani castles of Dinazzano, Salvaterra and Casalgrande and made further acquisitions there in the following years (see below, chapter 6). The Sacrati received in fief two former Boiardi 'palaces' in Rubiera, to add to other Boiardi property which Francesco Sacrati bought from the camera.[2] Francesco also acquired Fusignano in the Romagna in 1441, which he surrendered four years later to Leonello d'Este in return for further lands in the Reggiano.[3]

The position of these new families was, however, often based at first not on land, but on office and the political power and wealth that it brought. Jacopo Giglioli, for example, entered Este service as a notary in the early fifteenth century, becoming a close associate of the *referendario*, Bartolomeo della Mella.[4] On Mella's death in 1418, Jacopo succeeded to his office and held growing power through his control of access to the marquis. According to complaints after his downfall in 1434, there was little that could be done without Jacopo's knowledge and he used his position to stifle protest at his abuses of power.[5] His rise, from notary to provincial governor and count in under thirty years, revealed how far Este sponsorship could take a man. The history of the Sacrati and Sala is similar. The Sacrati colonised the office of supervising Este estates (the *officium super possessionibus*): Jacopo di Salamone held it from 1411 to the late 1420s, Francesco di Francesco from 1429 to 1436 and Jacopo's son Paride from 1437.[6] The basis of Giovanni Sala's landed and political power was his close support of the Roberti and his membership of the regency council of Niccolo III's minority.[7] The regency councillors lost little time in awarding themselves considerable quantities of Este property and Giovanni is found building up lands right across the south-eastern Ferrarese, from Consandolo to Migliarino, mainly by Este gift and fief, during these years.[8]

The origins of these new families were often quite modest. The first member of the Gualengo found in Ferrara, for example, was a military tailor (*ziponarius*), although the family was probably related to the Bolognese noble family of the same name, which disappears

---

[2] ASM, Catastri, R, fol. 543 (1433); Not. Cam., D. Dulcini, B, fol. 103; C, fol. 6.
[3] G. A. Soriani, *Notizie storiche di Fusignano* (Lugo, 1819), pp. 19–20; Tiraboschi, *Dizionario*, vol. 2, p. 385.
[4] ASM, Not. Cam., C. Lardi, A, fol. 60v.
[5] ASM, Catastri, R, fols. 641–2; BC, fol. 99.
[6] ASM, Leggi e Decreti, A 4, fol. 226; B iv, fol. 175v; Not. Cam., P. Bononia, fol. 171v; C. Lardi, A, fols. 57v, 72v, 88.
[7] *Ann. Est.*, 907, 911.
[8] Giovanni was given 821 *starii* and 26,000 vines at Marrara, Fossalta and Tamara (Not. Cam., J. Delaito, fols. 150–4) to add to his fief, for which see above, p. 98.

from Bologna at the same time as it appears in Ferrara.[9] Jacopo Giglioli's father, Bartolomeo, was a spice-trader, who owned a number of houses in Ferrara and some smallholdings in the *contado*.[10] The Sala were a family of notaries employed by the Este.[11] In some cases, the initial impetus to their rise seems to have come from profits made in the management of government revenues. Salamone Sacrati was *massaro* of the commune for a number of years from 1369 and was described as a 'rich citizen' in 1375.[12] The Pendaglia held numerous offices and farms from which they might be expected to have drawn financial reward: Gabriele first appears as a cameral notary, then as court paymaster and *fattore generale*, a post he held from 1410 until his death at Christmas 1429; his son, Bartolomeo, held farms of the *valli* in the 1420s and 1430s and was *fattore generale* from 1434.[13] According to a sixteenth-century poem celebrating the family's achievements, Gabriele, as farmer of the *valli* of Comacchio, 'made untold gains, with which he bought many lands in the Ferrarese'.[14] Another new family active in financial administration were the Marinetti, several of whom appear as gabelle farmers, Este treasurers and *massari* of the commune.[15] Obviously, financial service did not bring rewards to all who entered it: to many it brought ruin as they were saddled with bad debts and unpaid assignments or obliged to use their own money to meet their commitments. But for the lucky few who prospered, the gains could be immense – and it was doubtless in order to hold on to them that dynasties of rich and powerful financiers began to emerge (the Sacrati and Pendaglia, as we have seen), especially as the marquis could suddenly confiscate the profits he had allowed them to take (as happened, for example, with Dante Castiglione and Jacopo Giglioli).[16]

9  ASF, ANF, F. Santi, 2 July & 29 Sept. 1363; Gozzadini, *Torri*, p. 318.
10  ASF, ANF, J. Pavesi, 2 Aug. 1400, 14 Mar. 1401, May 1402.
11  ASM, Not. Cam., J. Sale (1331–5) and F. Sale (1341–73).
12  *Chron. Est.*, 498; Not. Cam., Diversorum, fol. 20 (1369): Rettori dello Stato, Ferrara, b. 6; Not. Cam., B. Nigrisoli, fol. 51v; F. Tagliapetri, B, fol. 11v.
13  ASM, Not. Cam., N. Delaito, A, fols. 62–87; J. Pelizari, fol. 49; D. Dulcini, A, fol. 30v, B, fol. 64; Rettori dello Stato, Adriano; Catastri, R, fol. 556.
14  'fece un guadagno smisurato del quale ne comprò molti terreni nel Ferrarese': *Quattro canti del Magnifico Sgr Bartolomeo Pendaglia* (Ferrara, 1563), pp. 9–10.
15  ASM, Not. Cam., B. Nigrisoli, fols. 13v, 23–4, 35v; F. Maroni, fols. 11v, 15v, 68; J. Pelizari, fol. 7; R. Codegorio, A, fol. 23; Investiture di Feudi, 11/27, 13/30, 13/46; BEM, Documenti Campori, Appendice 1251, fol. 35.
16  ASM, Leggi e Decreti, B IV, fol. 53; *Diario Ferrarese*, p. 20; A. Tissoni Benvenuti, 'La *Comediola Michaelida* di Ziliolo Zilioli e il *Lamento* di Giovan Peregrino da Ferrara', *Romanistisches Jahrbuch*, 29 (1978).

Some of these profits were invested in government stocks and spent on luxury goods. Alberto Sala had cash deposits at Venice and on the Florentine *Monte*.[17] According to the chroniclers, Jacopo Giglioli's movable wealth on his downfall had a value of 200,000 ducats and took two weeks to remove to the Este court.[18] But much was used, it seems, to purchase and improve land. Some of these families apparently concentrated their landed property in certain areas: the Sacrati at Contrapo, the Giglioli at Serravalle and Consandolo, the Marinetti at Guarda and Coccanile.[19] But some spread their property interests all over, and outside, the Este state. Giberto Sala was described in 1365 as having 'many farms' ('multas possessiones') at Parasacco and Medelana and his descendants acquired lands also at Finale and in the *contadi* of Bologna and Parma.[20] The Gualengo too had lands in the Bolognese: eleven farms totalling 350 hectares (1,665 *tornature*) which they sold to Annibale Bentivoglio in 1445. This was a major acquisition for the Bentivoglio, as it quadrupled the size of their landed patrimony, but that a rising family of Ferrara should own more land in the Bolognese than Bologna's own emerging *signori* seems remarkable.[21] Gualengo acquisitions are in fact documented in some detail. Giuliano Gualengo, a notary with a large clientele among the nobility, began from the late fourteenth century to acquire land in two separate areas: to the east of Ferrara, around Formignana and Sabbioncello, and at Finale, between Ferrara and Modena.[22] Sales of allodial land by the Este camera greatly expanded these possessions: one in 1395 of land 'in great quantity' at Marrara, the other in 1400 of 269 *biolche* (perhaps 75 hectares) at Finale.[23] By the 1440s, the Gualengo had over a thousand *biolche* of woodland at Finale, which they were

[17] ASV, RV, 385, fols. 129–31v; M. del Piazzo, *Il carteggio Medici–Este dal sec XV al 1531*, Quaderni della Rassegna degli Archivi di Stato (1964), no. 639.

[18] *Diario Ferrarese*, p. 20; G. Bertoni, *Guarino da Verona fra letterati e cortigiani a Ferrara 1429–60* (Geneva, 1921), p. 28.

[19] ASM, Not. Cam., D. Dulcini, A, fol. 94; Diversorum, 28 Feb. 1420; Leggi e Decreti, B IV, fols. 61v–3; Catastri, K, fol. 411; ASF, Archivio Tassoni, III/40, VII/45; ANF, J. Pavesi, 23 Dec. 1401, 16 Mar. 1402.

[20] ASV, RV, 254, fol. 91v; ASM, Not. Cam., A. Cavaleria, fols. 126–7; ASF, ANF, R. Jacobelli, 17 Nov. 1407 etc.; *I registri viscontei*, ed. C. Manaresi (Milan, 1915), p. 72.

[21] F. Bocchi, *Il patrimonio bentivolesco alla metà del Quattrocento* (Bologna, 1970), pp. 38ff.

[22] ASM, Not. Cam., A. Cavaleria, fol. 126; ASE, Cancelleria, Giurisdizione sovrana, 250, fols. 86v, 90v, 91v; ASF, Archivio Tassoni, IV/22.

[23] ASM, Not. Cam., A. Cavaleria, fol. 96v; BCF, Antonelli, 966 (Canani); Frassoni, *Finale*, p. 33.

intending to bring into cultivation.[24] Further large acquisitions were made by Giuliano's sons: tithes from the bishop of Ferrara, nearly 400 hectares from Brandelisio Boccamaiori and the confiscated town house of Jacopo Giglioli from the camera.[25]

These new families, like the old, often extended their lands at the expense of the church. Short-term mesne tenancies were common: Alberto Sala obtained a lease of all the property of the church of San Giorgio in 1407; Giovanni Bertazzi took a lease in 1413 of all the property in the Ferrarese of the archbishop of Ravenna; and the Gualengo seem to have had control of the two churches at Sabbioncello, one of which they let fall into ruin.[26] And control of ecclesiastical land went hand in hand with control of ecclesiastical office: as we have seen, Baldassare Sala became commendatory abbot of Pomposa and two of the Novelli became abbots of Cella Volana (above, chapter 2).

Este grants and fiefs certainly played a part in these families' rise, though that part was not as large as in the case of the Roberti. The Pendaglia received large estates at Villanova (1412), at Consandolo (1435) and at Mellara (1437); the Perondoli received lands at Porto (above, p. 62). But none of the Sacrati fiefs was very large: they held small pieces of land at Formignana, Bondeno and Adria, the tithe of Quartesana, the *Po morto* at Raccano and the river-crossing and inn at Canaro.[27] And other new families built up landholdings independently of the Este, the Brancaleoni and Marocelli, for example. Bandino Brancaleone, of a branch of a powerful family from the Montefeltro, moved to Ferrara in the 1390s and soon began acquiring land around Bondeno.[28] Members of the Marocelli, a Genoese noble family, are found at Ferrara from the early fourteenth century and seem to have built up their possessions in the north-east Ferrarese and in the Polesine di Rovigo through marriage and other ties with the Turchi.[29] In 1349 they were invested by the bishop of

24 Frizzi, *Memorie*, vol. 1, p. 51.
25 ASM, Not. Cam., P. Lardi, fols. 9–v, 19v; ASF, Archivio Tassoni, vi/31; *Diario Ferrarese*, p. 20.
26 ASF, ANF, R. Jacobelli, 15 Nov. & 12 Apr. 1407; ASM, Not. Cam., P. Sardi, F, fol. 56; Ferraresi, *Giovanni Tavelli*, p. 338.
27 ASM, Catastri, H, fols. 475, 484; N, fols. 135, 232, 373; R, fols. 122, 158, 301; 'tantum de pado mortuo . . . posito in districtu Ferrarie et in potestaria Rechani quem ipse dominus Marchio tenere solebat', with the 'passu et taberna Canarii' and 'potestate . . . exigendi datium et affictum . . . dicti padi, passus et taberne': Catastri, N, fol. 153.
28 ASF, ANF, N. Sansilvestri, 5 June 1403, 22 Feb. 1406; BCF, Antonelli, 966, b. 5.
29 Dalida di Marocello Marocelli married Morbassano Turchi (ASF, ANF, S. Todeschi, 15 May 1408) and Marocello later acted as guardian of Morbassano's

Adria with the village of Alberone and with land at Guarda, and there are also scattered references to their property in the Polesine.[30] The family had vassals at Crespino (probably acquired from the Turchi) and seem to have adopted the Turchi preference for living mostly on their estates, though they are also recorded in Este service, especially as governors of the more distant territories.[31]

The impression that remains is that the chief source of social advance in Ferrara was Este service, whether political, administrative or financial. The list of administrative and banking families of the late fourteenth and early fifteenth centuries who were considered noble by the second half of the fifteenth century is a long one: among civil servants, the Sacrati, Gualengo, Bonlei, Montecatini, Tassini, Mazzoni, Bendedeo and Pasini; among bankers, the Marinetti, Perondoli, Bonacossi, Bertazzi and Avenante.[32] It was the early fifteenth century, in fact, which saw the emergence in Ferrara of a native financial élite: earlier, the Este had relied on foreigners, mainly Tuscans, to provide the financial services necessary for government. This was part of the movement among the smaller cities of Renaissance Italy towards greater economic autonomy. At Ferrara, cloth manufacture seems to have expanded enormously in the first half of the century, while the bankers' guild makes its first appearance in 1426.[33] The number of registered bankers in that year was forty-four. These included members of both old and new noble families: Antonio Costabili, Esau Trotti, Jacopo Sacrati, Niccolo Perondoli, Niccolo Gozzadini, Alberto Bonacossi, Giovanni Novelli and his sons, Giacomino and Tommaso Riminaldi, Jacopo Caleffini and Cristoforo dell'Assassino. Some of these came from immigrant families: members of the Perondoli, from Florence, are found in Ferrara from the 1320s (their Florentine bank failed in 1342);[34] the

---

sons (ASM, Not. Cam., P. Sardi, E, fol. 60). Pietro Marocelli administered the property of Giglio Turchi when he was declared of unsound mind (ASF, Archivio Tassoni, vii/6 & 8). On the Marocelli: V. Vitale, 'Vita e commercio nei notai genovesi dei sec xii e xiii', *Atti della Società Ligure di Storia Patria*, 72 (1949), 30–1.

30 ASF, ANF, S. Todeschi, 16 Sept. & 23 Sept. 1408, 3 May 1409; Speroni, *Series*, p. 142; Bocchi, *Sede*, p. 17.

31 In 1422 Lucchino and Pietro di Marocello renewed investitures to 25 vassals holding small fiefs at Crespino: ASF, ANF, S. Todeschi, 28 Feb.–28 Apr. 1422. For their offices: Vicini, 'Podestà', pp. 193, 231; Vicini, 'Visconti', p. 32.

32 *Diario di Ugo Caleffini*, ed. G. Pardi, (3 vols. Ferrara, 1938–40), pp. 90–4. *Cf.* Jones, 'Mito', p. 29.

33 ASM, Leggi e Decreti, B iv, fols. 134–40; Sitta, 'Arti', p. 69; Dean, 'Venetian economic hegemony'.

34 A. Sapori, *Studi di storia economica* (2 vols., Florence, 1955), vol. i, p. 315; ASM, Investiture di Feudi, 10/28 & 55.

Gozzadini, as we have seen, were attracted to Ferrara in the late fourteenth century, as were the dell'Assassino. Of the others, a number formed part of the social and political élite: the Sacrati, as we have seen, maintained an unbroken presence in the Este estates office for over 25 years; Alberto Bonacossi was *fattore generale* from 1418 to 1438; members of the Riminaldi were frequent members of the communal council of twelve *savi*.[35]

If service was the chief means to nobility, the outward signs of new nobility were not just the political or administrative power that familiarity with the marquises brought. Nobility, as elsewhere, was largely a question of lifestyle and behaviour, of 'reputation'. It was seen in the possession of certain types of property, for example towers in the city: the Novelli acquired a tower in the fifteenth century, while the Marinetti had had a 'battlemented house' in Ferrara from the early fourteenth.[36] It was also shown in marriages into old noble families: Filippo Perondoli, for example, married Tiborga di Morbassano Turchi and Tiborga di Lodovico Marinetti married Bartolomeo Costabili.[37] Personal titles, such as knighthood and comital rank, further enhanced such individuals' standing. Giovanni Sala was an esquire (*scutifer*) in a tournament in 1392 and his son Alberto was knighted twice, once after the siege of Verona in 1404 in which he had taken part, then again in the Holy Land, which he visited in pilgrimage in 1413.[38] Jacopo Giglioli's son, Gigliolo, also became a knight.[39] Jacopo himself, along with Novello Novelli and Francesco Sacrati, became a count. Tax immunities were added to these privileges.[40] And ostentatious building was a further sign of eminence: the Avogari rebuilt the church of San Giuliano in the centre of the city,[41] while Jacopo Giglioli had a house fit for a prince at Corbola – when the marquis saw it, he immediately wanted to have it for himself, 'on account of its beauty, convenience and size'.[42] There was, of course, no inevitability in the connection

[35] ASM, Catastri, R and S, *passim*; ACF, Deliberazioni, Libri C and D, *passim*.
[36] Calura, 'Torri', p. 167; BCF, Archivio Pasi, b. 9.
[37] ASF, Archivio Tassoni, VI/17; ANF, U. Rossetti, 15 Apr. 1439.
[38] *Chron. Est.*, 527; *Ann. Est.*, 995–6; Campo, *Viaggio*, p. 125.
[39] Vicini, 'Podestà', p. 235.
[40] Jacopo Giglioli and Jacopo Sacrati and their heirs were given tax immunities by the commune of Adria (ASM, Leggi e Decreti, B IV, fol. 93), Gabriele Pendaglia for his *laboratores* at Copparo (ibid., fol. 87), Giovanni Gualengo in respect of his woods at Finale (Frizzi, *Memorie*, vol. 1, p. 51).
[41] *Ann. Est.*, 1036; *AMF*, 7 (1895) 25–31. For noble palaces in the Addizione in the 1490s, see *inter alia.*, Frizzi, *Memorie*, vol. 4, p. 168.
[42] 'propter pulcritudinem et aptitudinem ac magnitudinem suam nobis valde placuit': ASM, Catastri, Q, fol. 433.

between service and nobility: the chronology of each family's rise varied, their position remained open to challenge,[43] and many wealthy and influential citizens did not add nobility to whatever else they gained in Este service, for example the Mella, Caligi, Miazoli, Bellai and Barbalunga.[44]

### THE OLD NOBLE FAMILIES

As we have seen (above, pp. 95–6), Este patronage was not limited to 'new' noble families, but embraced the Ferrarese aristocracy as a whole. The most spectacular case of Este patronage of an 'old' noble family is found in Niccolo III's promotion of Uguccione Contrari. The Contrari had been powerful in Ferrara since the twelfth century and Mainardo was *massaro* of the commune in the 1380s and a temporary member of the regency council in the 1390s.[45] It was his son, Uguccione, who rose rapidly to power and favour in the early 1400s. In 1402, at the age of only twenty-one, he was entrusted with the government of the Este state and especially with military affairs, in which he showed a precocious talent: 'in his eighteenth year, Niccolo, in order to lighten the burden of his affairs, which were still heavy for his tender age, placed his administration and state and the care and government of his affairs in the hands of his beloved and trusted Uguccione Contrari, his relative by marriage'.[46] It was Uguccione who recovered Reggio in 1404 and again in 1409, who led the campaigns against Obizzo da Montegarullo in 1406, against the Terzi in 1409 and against Orlando Pallavicino in 1411.[47] He subsequently became the captain-general of Pope John XXIII and of the commune of Bologna.[48] And as Niccolo's right-hand man, his companion in government, he came to occupy an unparalleled

---

[43] In 1456 the wife of Lodovico Perondoli was prosecuted under the sumptuary laws on the grounds that she could not wear 'noble' attire as her husband engaged in trade: Brown, 'Magnificence', p. 437.

[44] Bartolomeo Mella built the monastery of S. Spirito (*Ann. Est.*, 1044); the Miazoli were gabelle and *valli* farmers (ASM, Not. Cam., J. Pavesi, A, fol. 59v; ASF, ANF, R. Jacobelli, 28 Mar. 1407); the Caligi were wealthy drapers among the most active members of the communal council (ACF, Deliberazioni, Libri B–D, *passim*) and frequently employed as administrators of the property of minors and absentee clerics (e.g. ASM, Not. Cam., P. Lardi, fols. 28, 30).

[45] 'satis potentes clientibus multis' according to Riccobaldo: *Chron. Parva*, 480. For Mainardo: ASM, Not. Cam., P. Arquada, fol. 1; J. Delaito, fol. 7 etc.; Leggi e Decreti, B II, fol. 238; *Ann. Est.*, 907.

[46] *Ann. Est.*, 974.

[47] Frizzi, *Memorie*, vol. 3, pp. 424, 431, 436, 440.

[48] Ibid., pp. 437–40.

position at the head of the Este state. Uguccione was formally given vicegerential powers in 1413 for the period of Niccolo's absence abroad, but continued to have authority to issue administrative orders in subsequent years.[49] As Uguccione himself declared: 'my affairs and those of my lord are one and the same'.[50] This close association was expressed in many ways: Uguccione's first will named Niccolo as his sole heir; Niccolo extended the coverage of the *crimen laesae maiestatis* to cover Uguccione; and after Niccolo's death, his sons treated Uguccione as a father.[51] All this suggests not just 'brotherhood in arms' and the nominal inclusion of favoured members of the nobility among the *signore*'s family, as we find elsewhere in Italy,[52] but also that Niccolo was looking for the help and support of his kinsmen in ruling, but since the Este family was itself divided and reduced in numbers, he promoted a kinsman by marriage to the position of a brother.

That promotion also took the form of expanding Contrari landed interests. In the thirteenth and fourteenth centuries, Contrari property seems to have been spread across a number of districts to the north-west of Ferrara beyond the Po (Gurzone, Ficarolo, Sariano and Occhiobello: see Map 6).[53] And it was in this area, along the Po from Castelmassa and Zelo to Stellata, that Uguccione and his brother, Tommaso, were given large estates by Niccolo, first in fief (1400), then in outright possession (1409) (see above, p. 62). By 1448, Uguccione had acquired further land, of almost equal size, from the nearby commune of Trecenta.[54] He also made acquisitions in other parts of the *contado*: at Porto (another gift from the marquis) and at Corlo (bought from Zaccaria Trevisan).[55] And his wills also refer to farms at Pontelagoscuro, Occhiobello and Gurzone.[56] In the

---

[49] e.g. his mandates to the *fattori generali*: ASM, Leggi e Decreti, A 5, fols. 228, 244, 254.

[50] 'i facti del mio signore e mei sum una medesima cosa': BEM, Documenti Campori, Appendice 1321–5; *cf.* Chittolini, 'Particolarismo', pp. 273–4.

[51] ASM, Not. Cam., J. Gualengo, fol. 43; BEM, Documenti Campori, Appendice 1313; 'De Rebus Estensium', ed. C. Antolini, *AMF*, 12 (1900), 59.

[52] Battistella, *Carmagnola*, p. 464; M. Keen, 'Brotherhood in arms', *History*, 47 (1962).

[53] For the Contrari fief in the fourteenth century, see above p. 93. For the fourteenth century: ASM, ASE, Giurisdizione sovrana, 250, fols. 6v, 8–v, 10, 33, etc.; ASF, ANF, N. Sansilvestri, 16 May 1377, 7 Oct. 1379.

[54] In 1448 the bishop invested Uguccione with 4,141 *starii* at Trecenta (acquired from Niccolo III) and with 10,165 *starii* (acquired from the commune of Trecenta), which Uguccione had hitherto held as allodial: ASM, Rettori dello Stato, Vignola.

[55] ASM, Not. Cam., A. Montani, fols. 56v–7v; ASF, Archivio Tassoni, v/20.

[56] ASM, Not. Cam., J. Gualengo, fols. 41–3 (10 Mar. 1423); ASF, ANF, U. Rossetti, 10 July 1442.

Ferrarese *contado* alone, recorded acquisitions by Uguccione and Tommaso amount to well over 2000 hectares – and this was in addition to their castles and lands in the Modenese which we shall examine in the next chapter. Through Este sponsorship, the Contrari became one of the most important families not just of Ferrara, but of the whole Este state.

Among the older Ferrarese families, however, the Contrari are exceptional: it was independence of the Este in terms of territorial status that was more usual. The Turchi, for example, had a landed base in the *contado* from at least the mid-twelfth century, based on grants by the archbishop of Ravenna of Crespino, Cologna, Alberone and neighbouring places (in emphyteusis), with jurisdiction and tithes in fief.[57] The Giocoli held land and tithe in fief of the bishop of Adria, leases and fiefs of the bishop of Ferrara, the archbishop of Ravenna and the monastery of S. Severo.[58] The Costabili could claim in the early fifteenth century that Viconovo was their allodial possession and that the marquis had no rights there.[59]

In the case of the Giocoli and Turchi, however, their landed base seems to have diminished over the centuries. Alberone passed from the Turchi to the Marocelli in the mid-fourteenth century and in 1381 Albertino Turchi surrendered to the archbishop one quarter of the villages and jurisdictions that he held, for Niccolo II's wife to be invested.[60] Part of the inheritance of Zarabino Turchi passed out of the family in the same year.[61] As for the Giocoli, much of their property was concentrated in the late fourteenth century in the hands of Albertino di Aldrovandino and his descendants: the death of his two grandsons in 1430 without male issue led to the reversion to the Este of the land they held in fief, although the rest of the inheritance passed to their uncle Bartolomeo. Bartolomeo's sons divided some of their joint property in 1439, consisting of land, *valli* and tithes at and around Guarda and Gradizola and houses in Ferrara, with vassals

---

[57] *Reg. Ch. Rav.*, vol. 1, nos. 31–2, 112; vol. 2, Appendix 1, p. 273; ASF, Archivio Tassoni, III/23, 31–2; Frizzi, *Memorie*, vol. 1, pp. 67–8. The Turchi are not listed by Riccobaldo, but are found as consuls in the twelfth century: Frizzi, *Memorie*, vol. 2, pp. 230, 267; vol. 3, pp. 33–4.

[58] ASM, Not. Cam., J. Sale, fol. 2; P. Lardi, fol. 88v; R. Codegorio, C, fols. 21–v; ASE, Giurisdizione sovrana, 250, fols. 33v, 86, 100v; *Reg. Ch. Rav.*, vol. 2, no. 741. ASF, Archivio Tassoni, IV/2.

[59] AV, RL, 146, fol. 41; ASM, Catastri, K, fol. 253.

[60] ASM, Not. Cam., R. Codegorio, A, fols. 97v–9.

[61] Zarabono appointed his uncle, Francesco Ariosti, as his heir: ASF, Archivio Tassoni, IV/4.

in the Polesine and patronage of the churches of Guarda and Cesta remaining in common.[62] Although obviously reduced since the twelfth century, this still constituted a small rural lordship embracing many of the sources of local power and wealth: land and vassals, control of the local church through receipt of tithes and appointment of the vicar. The same might be said of the Turchi, who retained demesne land and vassals at Crespino and Cologna,[63] jurisdiction (if only in part), the river crossings, tithes and patronage of the churches there,[64] lands in the Polesine,[65] and towers and houses in Ferrara[66] – none of which was held in any form of the Este.

### COUNTS AND COUNTIES

The social elevation and standing of a number of these families, both old and new, was assisted or consolidated by the acquisition, by papal or imperial grant, of the title of count. A group of Ferrarese counties was created in 1412–14 by Pope John XXIII in response to Este request: Guarda for Giocolo Giocoli; Viconovo for Antonio and Obizzo Costabili and their nephew Francesco; Marrara for Cristoforo Manfredini; Fossalta and Rottadola for Novello Novelli; and Perlo for the Carri (a family of household and court officials). In addition, Contrapo was later created a county for Francesco Sacrati by Pope Nicholas V.[67] By imperial creation, Jacopo Giglioli became

[62] On the concentration, see above pp. 95–6 and ASF, Archivio Tassoni, IV/2. In the division, Troilo di Bartolomeo received over 521 *starii*, 11,300 vines and the tithe at Guarda; Albertino and Giocolo di Bartolomeo received 1,317 *starii* and 3,900 vines at Cesta, Copparo and Gradizola, with tithe, 26 lessees, 2 *valli* and houses in Ferrara: ASF, ANF, U. Rossetti, 21 Mar. 1439. For joint feudal investitures in 1424: ibid., D. Dulcini, 2 Jan. 1424.

[63] The brothers Albertino and Gilio divided their property in 1430: Albertino took all property and fiefs in the Polesine and at Crespino, including the tithe and patronage of the church; Gilio took all property at Cologna and Brindola; while the river-crossings at Cologna and Crespino remained in common: ASF, Archivio Tassoni, VII/9.

[64] Ibid., III/16; ANF, D. Dulcini, 5 Sept. 1422.

[65] ASF, Archivio Tassoni, III/15, VI/8; ANF, S. Todeschi, 16 Sept. 1408.

[66] Calura, 'Torri', p. 165.

[67] Giocoli: ASV, Arm. xlvi, vol. 13, fol. 253 (Dec. 1412); Costabili: ASV, RL, 146, fol. 41 (May 1411); Manfredini: RL, 168, fol. 221 (Feb. 1414); Novelli: RL, 141, fol. 310v (Aug. 1414); Carri: RL, 175, fols. 82–3 (Nov. 1414); Sacrati: RV, 394, fol. 132v (Dec. 1449). Francesco and Albertino di Antonio Costabili were also created palatine counts by Emperor Sigismund in 1433: *Regesta Imperii xi: Die Urkunden Kaiser Sigmunds (1410–1437)*, vol. 2 (Innsbruck, 1897–1900), no. 9661. The three Carri brothers, Bartolomeo, Armanno and Giovanni were, respectively, Niccolò III's *factor*, physician and seneschal: ASM, Catastri, H, *passim*; N, fols. 110, 249, 520, 546, 576; Not. Cam., J. Delaito, fol. 106v.

count of Serravalle and Marocello Marocelli count of Riva.[68] What exactly did these counties signify? Most of them were hereditary and were limited to legitimate male succession.[69] They owed fealty to the church (or emperor) and were granted against a claim that the village elevated to a county was owned, wholly or in large part, by the new count.[70] But, unlike counties in other parts of northern Italy, they carried no territorial powers: they were largely honorific titles, palatine counties, conferring no more than the power to legitimate bastards and to create notaries. They were not, however, *purely* personal titles: they were still associated with particular places which, as we have seen, were declared to be in the recipients' 'ownership'. What that ownership comprised in terms of the powers of local lordship is not clear: there is certainly little other evidence at Ferrara for the existence of powerful rural lordships such as we find in other parts of northern Italy.[71]

Palatine counties were not highly regarded in some learned circles: Baldus dismissed them ('Note that a count properly so called is one who is invested with a county, therefore a count without a county, such as palatine counts, is incorrectly called a count') and the duke of Milan denied the validity of their acts of legitimation.[72] At Ferrara too, there were doubts whether legitimation by a count palatine was sufficient for succession to feudal property.[73] Nevertheless, counts palatine were created in large numbers in Italy from the mid-fourteenth century, with a wide range of powers, privileges and immunities, in addition to their usual powers of legitimation and authorisation.[74] And those powers were certainly used and the titles

---

[68] *Reg. Imp. xi*, no. 6737 (1426). On the Giglioli palace at Serravalle: Malagu, *Ville e delizie*, p. 69.

[69] The Giocoli county lapsed on the death without male issue of Giocolo's legitimate sons. Only the Manfredini county was created for heirs of both sexes, but 'de progenia de Manfredinis dumtaxat'.

[70] 'villam Madrarie . . . quam habere dinosceris' (Manfredini); 'locum ville vicinovi . . . ad vos ut asseritis iure proprio pertinentem' (Costabili); 'villas Fossalte et Rotadolle . . . ad te pro maiori parte iure proprietatis pertinentes' (Novelli); 'cum maior pars ville contrapadi . . . ad eum legitime pertinere noscatur' (Sacrati); 'cum accepimus loca Guardie et Guardizole . . . ad te pleno iure spectare noscantur' (Giocoli).

[71] Chittolini, 'Particolarismo', p. 57.

[72] *Opus aureum*, fol. 38; Tamassia, *Famiglia*, pp. 240–1.

[73] ASV, RL, 430, fol. 85v.

[74] Ercole, 'Impero e Papato', p. 330 n. 1; Ady, *Bentivoglio*, pp. 190–1; L. Simeoni, 'Federico della Scala, conte di Valpolicella', *Studi storici veronesi*, 11 (1961), 235, 239; d'Arco, *Studi*, vol. 7, pp. 180–2; *Libri Commemoriali*, xii, p. 152, no. 104.

were thought worth both displaying and fighting over in the courts.[75]

Such counties correspond to more general trends in late medieval Italy and Europe. The first is the eagerness of Italian *signori* to acquire new titles, whether of a personal or territorial nature: the Visconti became Dukes of Milan from 1395 and one of their Sforza successors looked for a royal title (perhaps in emulation of the Duke of Burgundy); both the Gonzaga and Sigismondo Malatesta pressed Emperor and Pope for the title of marquis; and the Este themselves became Dukes of Ferrara, by papal creation, and Dukes of Modena and Reggio, by imperial creation.[76] This is reflected in western Europe at large in the increasing stratification by title of the landed aristocracy in the same period.[77]

### KNIGHTHOOD

Another personal distinction much sought after in late medieval Europe was knighthood. At Ferrara, Este conferment of knighthood seems to have marked off the nobles of the court (the *nobiles curie*) from the rest of the Ferrarese nobility. Analysis of the knights created on various occasions by the Este and of those who are recorded in other documents reveals that, almost without exception, knighthood was limited to the political and military entourage of the Este: men such as Dondacio Fontana, Bichino da Marano and Filippo Guazalotti, who were appointed to military commands and embassies and who are recorded as counsellors,[78] and other outsiders of the Este entourage, for example, members of the Roberti,

[75] Ricciardo Cancellieri's immunities as palatine count included total fiscal and judicial exemption from all authorities save that of the Emperor: ASM, Not. Cam., B. Mella, fols. 49–50. His widow and grandson disputed possession of these privileges: ASF, ANF, G. Fiesso, 10 June 1430.

[76] Lubkin, 'Galeazzo Maria Sforza', p. 60; Jones, *Malatesta*, p. 209.

[77] McFarlane, *Nobility*, pp. 123, 268–78; A. Grant, 'The development of the Scottish peerage', *Scottish Historical Review*, 57 (1978); R. Cazelles, *Société politique, noblesse et couronne sous Jean le Bon et Charles V* (Paris, 1982), pp. 81–3.

[78] For Dondacio Fontana: *Chron. Est.*, 453, 470, 481; ASM, Not. Cam., M. Conte, fol. 121; R. Codegorio, A, fol. 57; A. Cavaleria, fol. 22 etc. For Bichino da Marano: ASM, Leggi e Decreti, A 1, fols. 1, 109; Not. Cam., M. Conte, fol. 124; J. Sanvitale, fols. 67, 127, 139; F. Tagliapetri, A, fol. 122; *Lettres secrètes Urbain V*, no. 1833; *Chron. Est.*, 495, 498; Grimaldi, *Signoria*, pp. 26ff; F. Novati, 'I codici francesi dei Gonzaga' in F. Novati, *Attraverso il medio evo* (Bari, 1905), pp. 276–9, 310–12. For Filippo Guazalotti da Prato: ASM, Leggi e Decreti, A 1, fols. 93, 140; Not. Cam., F. Tagliapetri, B, fol. 58v; B. Mella, fol. 39; ASE, Cancelleria, Carteggio dei Rettori, Ferrara, b. 6; Broilo, *Podestà*; P. G. Bonoli, *Storia di Lugo* (Faenza, 1732), p. 466.

Cancellieri, Boiardi, Savignano and Lambertini. These were nobles of long descent, whose position at Ferrara owed much to their martial prowess and their military resources. And as the Este drew their military captains more from 'foreign' nobles than from Ferraresi, so there are few Ferraresi among the knights: some members of the Costabili and Contrari, Alberto Sala, Gigliolo Giglioli and Brandelisio Boccamaiori,[79] but apparently none of the Giocoli, Trotti or Turchi, nor any of the new families of Gualengo, Sacrati and Marinetti (who were civil, not military servants). Knighthood was restricted to the marquis' military and political companions: those who took part in Este tournaments,[80] who formed the 'company of knights' (*comitiva militum*) that accompanied the Este on their travels to Rome, Venice and Jerusalem[81] and who discharged honorific offices such as escorting the Pope into Rome in 1367 or the Emperor into Ferrara in 1438.[82] The military and religious content of knighthood was still very much alive, as seen in a number of collective creations by the Este: in Rome in 1367, Niccolo II created twelve knights 'in the name and in memory of the twelve apostles';[83] after taking part in the siege of Verona in 1404, Niccolo III was himself knighted, along with Filippo da Pisa, Alberto Sala and Nanne Strozzi;[84] in Jerusalem in 1413 Niccolo III created five knights from among his companions and the whole occasion was marked by displays of religious piety (masses, vows and symbolic acts binding themselves, through knighthood, to Christ).[85] Knightings on the field of battle and in the Holy Sepulchre brought immeasurable esteem to those involved and Este creations there obviously bear some resemblance to the orders of knighthood founded by many northern European monarchs to bind more closely to themselves their companions-in-arms and others whom they wished to honour.[86]

---

[79] Uguccione and Tagliaferro Costabili were knighted in 1352 (*Chron. Est.*, 469), Tommaso Contrari and Alberto Sala in 1413 (Campo, *Viaggio*, p. 125) and there are references to Alberto Costabili as a knight in 1435, Gigliolo Giglioli in 1431 and Brandelisio Boccamaiori in 1418 (ASM, Not. Cam., reg. 68, fol. 23; Vicini, 'Podestà', pp. 228, 235).

[80] *Chron. Est.*, 488, 518–19, 522, 525–7, 530.

[81] Ibid., 413, 438, 492, 520–1.

[82] Ibid., 488; *Diario Ferrarese*, p. 22.      [83] *Chron. Est.*, 489.

[84] *Ann. Est.*, 995–6. For F. Pisa and N. Strozzi, see above, pp. 38, 97.

[85] Campo, *Viaggio*, p. 125; *Fr. Johannis Ferr.*, Appendix; G. Nori, 'La corte itineránte. Il pellegrinaggio di Niccolò III in Terrasanta', in *La corte e lo spazio: Ferrara esténse*, ed. G. Papagno & A. Quondam (Rome, 1982).

[86] P. Contamine, 'Points de vue sur la chevalerie en France à la fin du moyen âge', *Francia*, 4 (1976), 273, 281; J. Sumption, *Pilgrimage* (London, 1975), p. 266.

land to money or the promise of 'good lordship'. Lords and their clients ensured mutual support through non-feudal contracts which promised a cash fee or pension and protection in return for life service in peace and war. Yet the break between 'feudal' and 'non-feudal' was not a clean one: in several areas non-feudal contracts were reinforced by feudal grants (or vice versa), rather than replacing them.[16] And this state of affairs is clearly paralleled in Ferrara, where feudal and non-feudal contracts coexisted. The group of Este vassals looks very much like the 'affinity' of any magnate of late medieval Britain or France: counsellors, estate and household servants, lawyers and an 'indefinite circle of well-wishers and personal connections';[17] 'kin, friendis, allya and parttakaris'.[18] Or compare the Este affinity with that of the kings of England in the late fourteenth and early fifteenth centuries.[19] Richard II and Henry IV retained several hundred 'king's knights' and 'esquires', ranging from some men closely attached to the court and the king's person, to foreign knights not resident in England, but retained to support specific diplomatic manoeuvrings. Among such men, there is little evidence of service performed or required specifically by reason of being retained by the king: what evidence there is is coincidental – of king's knights serving in the king's wars or being appointed to parliament, shrievalties and judicial commissions. In general, their service remained '"personal and variable", rather than systematic and defined'.[20] So too in Ferrara: as outlined above, the Este affinity ranged from the marquis' intimates to the advisers of other princes; and their service too has to be deduced from the assertions of charter preambles and from the appearance of such men in office, at court and in Este armies. But whereas the king of England's affinity was retained by cash annuities, the marquis' affinity was enfeoffed with land (in addition to wages and pensions).

At the same time, the group of *raccomandati* (some of whom were also vassals) look very like French *alliés* or Scottish clients. There are

---

[16] P. S. Lewis, 'Of Breton *alliances* and other matters', in *War, Literature and Politics in the Late Middle Ages*, ed. C. Allmand (Liverpool, 1976); *Illustrations of the Topography and Antiquities of the Shires of Aberdeen and Banff*, vol. 4 (Aberdeen, 1862), pp. 395–6 contains a bond of manrent and a feudal grant of land concluded between the same parties on the same day in 1445 (I owe this reference to Dr A. Grant).

[17] C. Carpenter, 'The Beauchamp affinity: a study of bastard feudalism at work', *EHR*, 95 (1980), 516.

[18] Wormald, *Bonds of Manrent*, pp. 76ff.

[19] C. Given-Wilson, *The Royal Household and the King's Affinity: Service, Politics and Finance in England, 1360–1413* (New Haven and London, 1986), ch. 4.

[20] Ibid., pp. 245–6.

hood gave gentility only to the rich, reflects the increasingly rigid ideas of status in Renaissance Italy.

Knighthood in Ferrara, then, recovered or retained some of its military and religious connotations. It was also one sign, among others, of membership of the Este 'affinity' that stretched across the aristocratic world of north and central Italy. The marquis' 'company of knights' were also his 'companions and familiars' and 'companionship' (*societas*) was embodied also in grants of immunity from border tolls (*littere familiaritatis*) and of Este livery and devices.[93]

---

[93] For frequent issue of *littere familiaritatis*: ASM, Leggi e Decreti, A I, *passim*. In 1405, Niccolo III gave to Gianfrancesco Panciatichi da Pistoia, 'in signum societatis', 'divisiam calligarum nostrarum, unius totius rubee et alterius azurre et albe, ac cum arma nostra Worbas, cimeriumque nostrum de capite Aquile cum una ala supereminente': ASM, Leggi e Decreti, B III, fol. 193.

*Chapter 6*

# NOBLE SOCIETY IN THE PROVINCES

The construction of Este *signorie* in Modena, and later Reggio, posed quite different problems to those faced by the marquises in Ferrara. The political map, like the geographical, was very different. Unlike the flat Ferrarese, which was broken up, almost into an archipelago, by the Po delta and its *valli*, the *contadi* of Modena and Reggio were divided almost equally between hills and plain, with three smaller rivers running from south to north (the Enza, Secchia and Panaro). Large areas of these *contadi* in the later Middle Ages were held by territorial nobles whose landed bases formed rural lordships of a type not found in the Ferrarese: castles and jurisdictions, lands and powers of command. From such bases these families (again unlike the Ferraresi) often drew their name: thus the da Savignano, da Rodeglia, da Canossa and so on.[1] Such lordships, nominally subject to the city government, communal and signorial, in fact enjoyed considerable independence. Some of them were composed of only a single centre and its dependent area (for example, the Roberti at San Martino); others (for example, the Fogliani) comprised a string or block of castles and villages spread out across strategic zones, commanding the river or road routes down into the plain or over the Appennines into Tuscany. Such *signorie* were not, however, limited to the hills, but spread right over the plain as well. Modena was closely surrounded by the lordships of the Pio and Pico to the north (at Carpi and Mirandola), of the Boiardi to the west (Rubiera) and to the south by the da Sassuolo, the Rangone (Castelvetro, Marano and Spilamberto) and the Fogliani (a large number of castles, starting from Scandiano and Casalgrande in the plain and stretching far into the lower Reggiano along the Secchia) (see Map 7).[2] The picture at Reggio was similar, with the city surrounded by the lordships of the Roberti, Correggio, Boiardi, Fogliani, Manfredi and Canossa. And

---

[1] In general, see Chittolini, 'Particolarismo'.
[2] Tiraboschi, *Dizionario*, s.v.

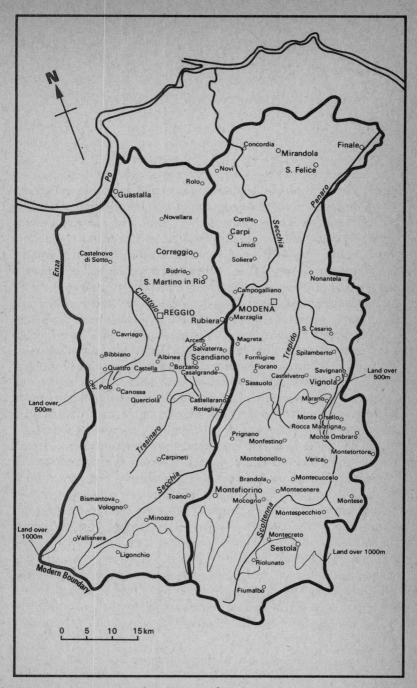

Map 7 The provinces of Modena and Reggio

151

the farther they were from the city, the stronger these lordships became: the northern Reggiano, for example, was appropriated by the Gonzaga, lords of Mantua, in the course of the fourteenth century and in the extreme south of the Modenese (the Frignano) government was almost completely controlled by the two families of the Montegarullo and Montecuccolo.

These families were not, however, wholly or even largely rural. Their property and political interests in the city were of equal or greater importance. For many of them, lands and lordship in the *contado* were the means to power in the city. Some of them did, indeed, achieve a temporary urban supremacy (the Pio at Modena, 1315–36; the Fogliani at Reggio, 1312–35). More numerous were those who aspired to it, for example the Correggio in the early fourteenth century. In these circumstances, the city's claim to exercise full governmental powers throughout its *contado* often rang hollow. Not only was the power of the city geographically limited, but in many cases it could be exercised at all only through negotiation with the local lord. This had serious consequences for the quality of government: as the commune of Modena itself commented in 1425, 'in every well-governed city, such as Bologna or Ferrara, the whole *contado* obeys the city', in contrast to Modena itself, which, 'because no castle anywhere obeys it, is desolated and without the means to sustain itself'.[3] The relative strength and density of rural lordships made obedience hard to enforce. It also meant that urban *signorie* in this part of Emilia were often little more than the nominal overlordship (sometimes not even that) of a volatile collection of partly autonomous and highly privileged local powers. In economic and financial matters, these rural lords offended city pretensions by holding unlicensed markets, obstructing the collection of taxes, impeding the movement of traffic, imposing tolls and exactions and harassing city landowners and their tenants.[4] More important to the city *signori* was the lack of political

---

[3] 'quod turpe est et preiudiciale civitati tenere comitatum abdicatum ab ipsa, quod accidit huic misere civitati, quia nullum castrum de mundo ei obedit quo fit ut desolata deficiat per se solam non valens sustentare et . . . quod cuicumque civitati bene recte, ut est civitas Bononie et Ferrarie, totus suus comitatus eis obedit': ASM, Leggi e Decreti, B IV, fol. 129v. *Cf.* Chittolini, 'Particolarismo', p. 262.

[4] Ibid., pp. 263–4; G. L. Basini, *L'uomo e il pane* (Milan, 1970), pp. 7–8; O. Rombaldi, 'La comunità reggiana nello stato estense nel sec. xv', *Annuario del Liceo-Ginnasio statale L.Ariosti di Reggio-Emilia*, 1965–7, p. 109. For specific examples: ASM, Leggi e Decreti, A 2, fols. 248, 273, 294; A 3, fol. 29; C. Campori, *Notizie storiche del Frignano* (Modena, 1886), p. 64.

control, the disorder of violent disputes among these rural lords and their separate interests and activities that weakened their attachment to the city. Noble society here looks very much like the clan-based societies faced by other rulers in late medieval Europe.[5] This can be seen in the way the central administration referred to such families as groups, as in 'i Fogliani' or 'i Boiardi'.[6] It can be seen in the common ownership within a family of property and jurisdiction.[7] And it can be seen in the way that *signori* sometimes tried to promote one member of a family to the position of clan-leader.[8] In rural Emilia, it was the clans, not the cities, that ruled.

However, the absorption of the cities and their ruling groups into regional states had profound effects on this society. Although the end result was the establishment of Visconti rule in western Emilia (Piacenza and Parma) and of Este rule in eastern Emilia (Reggio and Modena), that outcome was reached only after many decades of varying fortunes in peace and war. Periods of both conflict and stability had an impact on the local aristocracy. Wars between the Visconti and the Estensi broke up the old territorial unities and loyalties as each side sought to extend its sphere of influence into contested areas. The Fogliani, for example, at first Este supporters, split into opposing groups under pressure from Bernabo Visconti, lord of Reggio from 1371.[9] And this was not just a strategy for survival, but became a war to the death.[10] On the other hand, the stabilisation of Este rule brought greater signorial control over rural lords: some were dispossessed and their lands either ruled directly by the *signore* or granted out to his protégés; others were drawn into feudal and military dependence on the *signore* in return for recognition of their powers of jurisdiction and command. In both cases, the result did not please the city communes, as the unmistakable trend was towards the dismemberment of their *contadi* and the

[5] e.g., most recently, Wormald, *Manrent*, pp. 76–90.
[6] e.g. ASM, Leggi e Decreti, A 2, fol. 222.
[7] e.g. ASM, Rettori dello Stato, Guiglia (1378), and below pp. 165–6.
[8] In 1455 Borso d'Este declared that it was 'decens honestum et rationi consonum . . . ut qui in familia maior est natu et clarioribus gestis lucet huic honor, huic reverentia maior ab reliquia omni familia tribuatur eique demandetur rerum comunium summa ut ad se tanquam ad primorem domus et rerum in comuni possessarum moderatorem ac tanquam familie caput recursus habeatur' and accordingly appointed Guido Rangone head of the Rangone family: ASM, Leggi e Decreti, B VII, fol. 103.
[9] N. Grimaldi, *La signoria di Barnabo Visconti e di Regina della Scala in Reggio (1371–85)* (Reggio, 1921), pp. 132–48.
[10] Ibid., pp. 134–47; G. B. Venturi, *Storia di Scandiano* (Modena, 1822), pp. 55–63.

replacement of territorial 'obedience' to the city by personal 'obedience' to the regional lord. Whereas in the thirteenth century the communes had obtained recognition of their rule from the lords of the *contado*, now it was the regional *signore* who enforced that rule, but on his own terms, not on those of the city communes. As a result, communal petitions to the *signore* for lands and castles to be returned to their 'obedience' rarely had any effect. The *signori* made their own decisions about lands that they acquired in these *contadi*. Whether these led to the consignment of lands to protégés from the centre or their direct rule by officials appointed by the *signore*, the city communes had to accept and accommodate such arrangements.

Este strategy in dealing with the rural lords of Modena and Reggio was a simple one: territorial and political concessions at times of weakness (as in the 1390s), but at all other times, the unstinting reward of loyal friends and supporters at the expense both of those nobles whose loyalty was less than complete and of the city communes, which saw their powers of command in the *contado* being stripped away by signorial concession. This strategy was openly declared by Niccolo III d'Este in a grant to the Manfredi in 1423: 'we freely honour our subject nobles with our grace and favour, especially those whose faith and solid constancy has been made clear over a long stretch of time. And we accede to their requests, especially in those things which, through the private good of our nobles, bring fruit and benefit to the public good, such that, by the sheer number of favours and benefits they receive, their devotion and that of others by their example may grow.'[11] The same message is apparent in an instruction given to the Este governor of Modena in 1379 to advise the new captain of Sassuolo as to 'who are our friends and who are not our friends, of whom he has to beware and whom not'.[12] This was a region where friends were precious and had to be amply rewarded. As the papal legate wrote of the Fogliani in 1371, 'they are powerful, resourceful and loyal' and 'are to be handled and sup-

[11] 'Nobiles nobis subditos, eos maxime quorum sincera fides et solida constantia tractu longo temporis claruere, gratis et favoribus nostris libenter prosequimur et eorum votis annuimus in hiis maxime que cum privato eorum commodo reipublice frugem pariunt et commodum ut gratiarum multiplicitate et beneficiorum eorum devotio pariter et aliorum huius modi exemplo in dies augeatur': ASM, Leggi e Decreti, B iv, fol. 94.

[12] 'volumus quod predictum Jacobum advisetis de conditionibus modis et factis hominum terre predicte ut valeat aperte cognoscere qui sunt nostri amici et qui non sunt sic amici in terra predicta et a quibus haberit se precavere et qui non . . .': ASM, Leggi e Decreti, A i, fol. 397.

ported in every decent way possible'.[13] Priority was given to winning and rewarding those with local power and if they could not be won, then they had to be eliminated: as Niccolo III declared to the government of Bologna in 1394 regarding Atto da Rodeglia, who had rebelled after receiving for thirty years the 'honour and profit' of Este support: 'we say we have been cheated, offended and exhausted by his commission of every sort of betrayal, wherefore we utterly refuse to restore him to our favour and love, especially as we know him to be impudent, foolish and weak'.[14] Signorial anger of this sort, in the context of increasingly stable Este rule, could no longer be defied.

As in other regional states, for example Tuscany,[15] this restructuring of the old communal *contadi* went hand in hand with changes in the character of the territorial nobility. By the mid-fifteenth century, that of Modena and Reggio had changed greatly. Some old families, whose prominence went back to the early twelfth century (for example, the Pio) not only survived, but were raised in landed power through friendship and service to the Este. Other families of less antiquity but of no less power also survived (the Montecuccolo, Boiardi, Montetortore), but others were reduced to the ranks of the lesser nobility (for example, the Fogliani) or eliminated altogether (Montegarullo). In their place arose a number of native families (for example, the Cesi), but these were outnumbered by families from Ferrara and the Este court, for example the Contrari, Ariosti, Sala and Strozzi, who were deliberately promoted by the Este. A new territorial nobility was being created which originated from Ferrara and the court, but held lands throughout the Este state. The route to power in the provinces, for old and new nobility alike, lay increasingly through the court at Ferrara: a centre and a periphery were being created in territories which had many centres and many focal points of power.

---

[13] 'isti nobiles de Folliano . . . sunt tenendi et favendi viis et modis omnibus curialibus quibus fieri poterit, nam non restant nobis hodie in dispositione dampnificandi inimicos nisi illi qui sunt potentes, valentes et fideles': Theiner, *Codex*, vol. 2, p. 530.

[14] 'nos deceptos, nos offensos et per omnem proditionis speciem multipliciter ab eo fatigatos fuisse dicimus, unde pacem illi reddere gratiam concordium vel amorem penitus recusamus, ex hoc etiam potissime quia cognoscimus Attum ipsum protervum, fatuum et imbecilem . . . ob quod illius depositionem et exterminium . . . penitus perseverare intendimus': ASM, Leggi e Decreti, B II, fol. 223.

[15] Sestan, 'Guidi'; *I capitoli del comune di Firenze*, ed. C. Guasti (2 vols., Florence, 1866–93), vol. I, pp. 461ff.

## DISPOSSESSION

The most effective method of extending the lord's control in these provinces was dispossession of unruly nobles and the taking of lands into direct rule. As the Este regional lordship became more permanent and more stable, central control of the countryside hardened and new territorial loyalties were imposed. From the early fifteenth century, noble lawlessness and insurrection were severely dealt with. Jacopino da Rodeglia, after murdering his own uncle, was forced to surrender Castellarano to Niccolo III.[16] Alberto da Savignano, outlawed from Modena for murder in 1406, was seized and executed.[17] Francesco da Sassuolo's persistent involvement in rebellions from the 1390s led to his arrest in 1417 and subsequent death in a Ferrarese prison.[18] By confiscations and forcible dispossessions, Niccolo III acquired by 1433 a long list of castles and villages in the Modenese and Reggiano, as an imperial investiture to him in that year shows.[19] The main families thus displaced were the Montegarullo, Fogliani, Roberti, Dallo, Sassuolo and Rodeglia. Some of their lands were granted in fief or gift to other nobles, but much was retained by Niccolo III and reorganised into new administrative units: the Rodeglia and Sassuolo lands, for example, were arranged into new *podesterie* with centres at Castellarano and Sassuolo. These were henceforth governed by officials appointed by the Este, who were often not accountable to the city governments.[20]

Such dispossession was often the culmination of sustained and determined opposition to the Este. When this escalated to military confrontation, it was rarely resolved in favour of the rural lords.

[16] Tiraboschi, *Dizionario*, vol. 1, p. 185; vol. 2, pp. 226, 264–7; Schenetti, *Castellarano*, pp. 7, 31–4.

[17] Tiraboschi, *Dizionario*, vol. 1, pp. 35–7; vol. 2, pp. 296–302; G. Corni, *Il castello di Monfestino e il suo territorio* (Modena, 1950), pp. 35ff; A. Crespellani, *Compendio storico di Savignano* (Modena, 1873), pp. 19–31.

[18] Tiraboschi, *Dizionario*, vol. 2, pp. 58, 305–17; G. Bucciardi, *Fiorano nelle vicende storiche* (Modena, 1934), pp. 47–91; M. Schenetti, *Storia di Sassuolo* (Modena, 1966), pp. 21–52; Cerlini, 'Assedio', pp. 405–7.

[19] This included Sassuolo, Castellarano, Piolo, Ligonchio, Carpinete, Minozzo, Baiso, Sarzano, S. Cassiano, Rondinara, Rubiera, S. Martino in Rio and Montecchio: ASM, Casa e Stato, 24/11.

[20] A. Sorbelli, *Il comune rurale nell'Appennino emiliano nei sec. XIV e XV* (Bologna, 1910), pp. 99–100; Schenetti, *Castellarano*, p. 36; Crespellani, *Mem. stor. vignolesi*, p. 18; F. Milani, *Minozzo negli sviluppi storici della pieve e podesteria* (Reggio, 1938), pp. 160–70; N. Cionini, *I podestà di Sassuolo* (Pisa, 1879–81), pp. 7–8. Cf. Chittolini, *Formazione*, xvi–xvii; 'Particolarismo', p. 260; 'Ordinamento', pp. 296–8; Bertelli, *Potere*, pp. 33–6.

Although in the 1390s the marquis was unable effectively to over-come noble revolts in the periphery because of political disorder at the centre, from the early years of the fifteenth century, Este military intervention became more decisive. The Canossa family had never been friendly to the Este *signoria* and the rebellions of Simone da Canossa and of his uncle, Guido, led to the siege of Canossa itself in 1412 and the seizure of Castelnovo and Felina in 1414. Guido was imprisoned and all his property forfeited, while Simone went into exile and took military service with Niccolo III's enemies.[21] The Canossa family, whose lordship had comprised a large area on the border of Reggio around Quattro Castella, was thus dispersed, although one branch continued to hold lands in the Reggiano.[22] Another firm opponent of Niccolo III was Carlo Fogliani. His father, Guido Savina, had become a Visconti client in 1373 and Carlo remained a close supporter of the Visconti governor of Reggio, Ottobuono Terzi. Following the Este defeat of the Terzi, Carlo lost all his castles in the Reggian plain to Niccolo III (1409) and Carlo's son, Giovanni, later lost many of those in the hills (1426–8), declaring that he would rather die and lose his 'state' than submit to the marquis.[23]

The seizure of these lands was a major success for the Este *signoria* at Reggio, for the Fogliani was the local family that had most nearly succeeded in establishing its own lordship there.[24] From the mid-thirteenth century, they had been major leaders of faction in the city and had greatly expanded their lands in the *contado* after the expulsion of the Este in 1306. They became lords of Reggio and imperial vicars for a number of years, but were unable to maintain their position against an alliance of other north Italian lords and surrendered Reggio to the Gonzaga in 1335. Their treaty with the Gonzaga in that

[21] 'Vita del cavalier Feltrino Boiardo', BEM, Documenti Campori, 591, fol. 31; Tiraboschi, *Dizionario*, vol. 1, pp. 126, 181, 282; idem, *Mem. stor. mod.*, vol. 3, p. 94; Cerlini, 'Assedio', pp. 396–404; F. Milani, *Castelnovomonti* (Castelnovomonti, 1962), p. 38; G. Badini, 'Le carte dei Canossa nell'Archivio di Stato di Reggio', in *Quattro Castella nella storia di Canossa. Atti del convegno di studi matildici* (Rome, 1977), p. 124; Chron. P. Mattiolo, pp. 286–8; *Libri Commemoriali*, x, no. 170.

[22] Tiraboschi, *Dizionario*, vol. 1, pp. 50, 344; O. Rombaldi, 'Il potere e l'organizzazione del territorio di Quattro Castella', in *Quattro Castella*, pp. 31–2.

[23] 'Vita del cavalier Feltrino Boiardo', fol. 31; *Ann. Est.*, 1071; Tiraboschi, *Mem. stor. mod.*, vol. 3, pp. 96–7.

[24] Tiraboschi, *Dizionario*, vol. 1, pp. 263–4, 297–304; vol. 2, pp. 329–30; Venturi, *Scandiano*, pp. 38–68; Grimaldi, *Signoria*, pp. 132–48; O. Rombaldi, 'Matteo Maria Boiardo feudatario', in *Atti del convegno di studi su M. M. Boiardo*, ed. G. Anceschi (Florence, 1970), pp. 443–51.

157

year reveals how far they had gone in constructing a *signoria*: part of their vast dominion along the Secchia was confirmed and they retained administrative control of the bishop's lands, the right to appoint abbots to three major abbeys (Frassinoro, Canossa and S. Prospero) and the payment of a stipend by the commune. When the Gonzaga in turn gave way to the Visconti, Fogliani territorial power remained largely intact: Bernabo Visconti confirmed to Guido Savina Fogliani the dominion of twenty-four castles and their dependent villages. Much of this was seized by Niccolo III, though tne Fogliani later recovered or retained some castles: Niccolo and Cesare were enfeoffed in 1433 with Monteviano, Rondinara and Piagna.[25]

The region brought most closely under Este control by these means was the Frignano. Here already from the mid-fourteenth century, the marquises had a *podesteria* at Sestola from where they controlled a number of castles and villages.[26] But these were far outnumbered and outweighed by the territories commanded by the Montegarullo and Montecuccoli.[27] Indeed, in 1398, Este authority in the Modenese collapsed to the point where the marquis had to surrender Sestola to Obizzo da Montegarullo, although this was expressed as a governmental commission.[28] The marquis also had to deal with intervention in the area from other states. Throughout the second half of the fourteenth century, political instability in the central Po valley, especially the Visconti–Este conflict over Reggio and the disturbances of the 1390s, allowed both Bologna and Lucca to press their territorial ambitions in the Frignano. There were strong links of friendship and service binding the Montecuccoli to Lucca, which also came to hold some Montegarullo castles in the early fifteenth century.[29] Earlier, in the 1380s, Bologna had acquired some castles from Lanzalotto Montecuccoli and though the marquis

---

[25] ASM, Catastri, R, fol. 552; Venturi, *Scandiano*, p. 68; F. Milani, *Viano e il Querciolese nella storia* (Castelnovo ne' Monti, s.d.), p. 56.

[26] In the late fourteenth century the Este held Sestola, Fiumalbo, Riolunato, Fanano, Trentino, Lotta, Viano, Chiagnano and other places: G. Sercambi, *Cronache di Lucca*, ed. S. Bongi (Fonti per la storia d'Italia, Rome, 1892), vol. 2, p. 126; ASM, Not. Cam., P. Fabro, fols. 124, 128, 142, 151, 161; R. Codegorio, A, fols. 48v, 101v; Tiraboschi, *Dizionario*, vol. 1, pp. 273, 294; vol. 2, pp. 253, 345.

[27] For a list of over thirty places held by the Montecuccoli in the late fourteenth century and fourteen held by the Montegarullo: Sercambi, *Cronache*, vol. 2, pp. 127–33.

[28] ASM, Leggi e Decreti, B II, fol. 399.

[29] Sercambi, *Cronache*, vol. 2, pp. 130–3; ASM, Leggi e Decreti, B III, fol. 198; Tiraboschi, *Dizionario*, vol. 1, pp. 41, 73; vol. 2, p. 263; *Lucca regesti, passim.*

reacted aggressively against this incursion, he was not powerful enough to reverse the transaction unaided: his conflict with Lanzalotto and Bologna was arbitrated by Venice and Florence.[30] Nothing better illustrates the incomplete Este hold on distant loyalties than the resort to more powerful outside states to enforce it. Uncertain command was characteristic of this border region: although the main families there frequently reaffirmed their allegiance to the Este, they were also clients (*raccomandati*) of other states, for example Milan and Florence.[31] However, the early fifteenth century provided the opportunity for a reassertion of Este power: finally wearying of the 'continual perfidy and implacable treacheries of Obizzo da Montegarullo', Niccolo III seized all his castles (1406–8) and confined him to Ferrara.[32] By the mid-fifteenth century, three of the major families of the region had been eliminated (Montegarullo, Gomola and Gualandelli) and the extent of the Montecuccolo lordship had been reduced. Gomola was granted to the Cesi family, but other lands were added to the Este *podesterie* of Sestola and Montefiorino.[33] And this expansion of Este power in the Frignano facilitated the later conquest of part of the Garfagnana (1429–32) and the recovery, after two centuries, of Este properties in the Lunigiana.[34]

### ESTE RULE IN THE MODENESE AND REGGIANO

The constitution of Este *podesterie* was often accompanied by the granting of exemptions to the communities that comprised them. The Este, because more distant, had to show themselves to be lords more responsive to local circumstances and demands. All communities that came under Este rule for the first time received immunity from urban taxation for a number of years or a reduction in tax assessments, with concessions on a wide range of locally important matters, such as the guarding and repair of the castle, access to and ownership of the local mill and common grazing land, guarantees

---

[30] Tiraboschi, *Mem. stor. mod.*, vol. 3, p. 158.
[31] *Libri Commemoriali*, ix, no. 139; Sercambi, *Cronache*, vol. 2, p. 127; *Albizzi Commissioni*, vol. 1, p. 40.
[32] 'propter incessantem perfidiam et fraudulentias implacabiles Obbizonis de Montegaruleo': *Ann. Est.*, 1037–8, 1056–7.
[33] Tiraboschi, *Dizionario*, vol. 1, pp. 351–2; Campori, *Frignano*, pp. 48–53.
[34] D. Pacchi, *Ricerche istoriche sulla provincia della Garfagnana*, (Modena, 1785); C. de Stefani, 'Storia dei comuni di Garfagnana', *AMMo*, s. 7, 2 (1923); Tiraboschi, *Dizionario*, vol. 1, p. 408; vol. 2, pp. 178, 374, 393; M. Conti, 'Sulle tracce del diritto consuetudinario in Val di Magra', *ASPP*, s. 4, 23 (1971), 32.

regarding markets, salt prices and corvées, the return of property usurped by the previous lords.[35] The negotiation of such privileges was automatic on submission to the Este and charters embodying them were issued for all the castles and villages seized from Obizzo da Montegarullo, Carlo Fogliani, Andrea da Dallo and the Montecuccoli. Some received even wider privileges, such as political independence from the city and guarantees regarding local officials. Rubiera, for example, secured exemption from obedience to Reggio and a promise that Este officials there would come from Ferrara and not from Modena or Reggio.[36] The dominance of Ferrarese citizens in the government of these provinces would thus seem to respond to local aspirations to escape the harsher control of the city. Indeed, in granting such privileges, the Este made great play of the 'freedom' and 'protection' such communities would now enjoy in contrast to the 'tyranny' suffered under their previous lords.[37] Sometimes, it does seem that the lordship of a Fogliani or a Montegarullo was heavy-handed and cruel, but the language of freedom and tyranny was often just a rhetorical mask concealing reductions in urban rights and jurisdiction which could only be viewed uneasily from the city. City pressure against this dismemberment of the *contado* and for the subjection to city control of lands recovered from uncooperative nobles was rarely acceded to, despite its most eloquent expression.[38] And exemptions, once granted, tended to acquire a life and force of their own which the cities found they could not terminate.[39]

### THE NEW TERRITORIAL NOBILITY

What was taken from the old rural lords was redistributed, by gift and fief, to other noble families, mainly Ferrarese. Chief among these were the Contrari brothers, Uguccione and Tommaso, the first of a long line of Ferrarese nobles given lands and castles in the Modenese and Reggiano. In 1401, Uguccione, already the major political figure in Ferrara after the marquis, was given the important castle and town of Vignola with separate jurisdiction.[40] A few years

---

[35] ASM, Leggi e Decreti, B III, fols. 217–19, 228–9, 230, 234; B IV, fols. 143v–4, 153v–4v, 155v–6v, 157v, 159, 160v, 161–2v, 164, 171, 173, 206v–7, 220.

[36] Ibid., fols. 87v–8 (5 May 1423).      [37] Ibid., fols. 143v, 154v etc.

[38] Chittolini, *Formazione*, xix–xx, xxii–vii; *idem*, 'Particolarismo', pp. 261–3; Rombaldi, 'Comunità reggiana', pp. 55–8.

[39] e.g., that of the village of Marzaglia, maintained against repeated and reasonable challenge by Modenese officials: BEM, Documenti Campori, Appendice 1387.

[40] 'cum mero et misto imperio . . . necnon cum omnimoda exemptione . . . a

later, in 1409, he was given the neighbouring castles of Savignano, Monte Orsello, Montecorone, Monte Ombraro and Montebonello, as well as two castles in the Parmense taken from the Terzi (Guardasone and Montelugolo).[41] Uguccione also had possessions in adjacent parts of the Bolognese *contado*.[42] The political purpose of these gifts is clear: the Modenese castles, on the edge of the plain and in the foothills of the Appennines, controlled both the Panaro and the road into Tuscany.[43] And the assertion of Este power that they represent is aptly illustrated by the fresco painting executed at Vignola for the Contrari, which is full of Este emblems and devices.[44] The importance of the Contrari as leaders of local society was also made clear in 1429, when the government of Modena was trying to persuade the rural aristocrats (the *zentilhomini*) to provide labour for repairs to some dykes near Nonantola. Many of the 'gentlemen' were unwilling to contribute their full quota and went over the heads of the Modenese to the marquis in search of dispensations. The Modenese governors urgently warned the marquis of the damage and disorder being done by these refusals and urged him not to grant any exemptions, 'because by giving way once, all the rest is destroyed and wasted'.[45] At the same time, the governors sought the marquis' support in obtaining the full Contrari contribution, 'for we have found in the past that when Uguccione has made such a subvention, all the other gentlemen have done likewise and we are certain in the present case that if Uguccione contributes, every one of the gentlemen will too'.[46]

civitate et comuni Mutine a cuius civitatis et comunis Mutine jurisdictione dicta terra Vignole sit . . . exempta . . . totaliter': ASM, Not. Cam., A. Montani, fol. 74v. Vignola was neither given in fief, nor raised to a county at this stage, as is usually asserted: Crespellani, *Mem. stor. vignolesi*, p. 22; Chiappini, *Gli Estensi*, p. 101.

[41] ASM, Not. Cam., N. Abbatia, A, fols. 90–2. The castles in the Parmense were surrendered to F. M. Visconti in 1421 and returned by him to the Terzi: BEM, Documenti Campori, Appendice, 1321; *Fr. Johannis Ferrariensis*, Appendix 3; Pezzana, *Parma*, vol. 2, pp. 10, 131, 194; N. Pelicelli, *Pier Maria Rossi e i suoi castelli* (Parma, 1911), p. 10.

[42] Cossa promised Poggio Renatico and Castelfranco Emilia to Uguccione: Manni, 'Terzi', doc. 11; ASM, Casa e Stato, 22/27 (1403). It is not clear that either promise was fulfilled, but Uguccione did have possessions at Poggio: BEM, MSS Latini, 2, fol. 68 (1416).

[43] F. and S. Poggi, *Marano sul Panaro, dalle origini ad oggi* (Modena, 1962), pp. 20ff.

[44] L. Franchini, *Simboli, emblemi, impresi nel castello di Vignola* (Vignola, 1977).

[45] 'recordemo a la v. S. che compiasendo ad uno . . . tuto el resto è rotto e guasto': ASM, Rettori dello Stato, Modena, b. 1A, letter of 17 July 1429.

[46] 'perche nui havemo cognosciuto per lo passato che quando el Magnifico Uguzone ha facto simile subventione, tuti li altri zentilhomini hanno mandato, cussi de

In addition to their effect on local society, these grants to the Contrari also radically altered that family's territorial and political position. Hitherto they were a purely Ferrarese family; now, their Modenese possessions broadened their horizons and required considerable attention and expense: in the acquisition and management of land,[47] the rebuilding and decoration of Vignola castle,[48] the settling of relations with neighbouring nobles through a series of private treaties,[49] and the creation of a small group of administrators (many of them drawn from Ferrara).[50] Uguccione's large, but dispersed possessions placed his family in a new category of nobles, whose power and property were not limited to a single city, but were spread across the whole Este state. And there was more: Uguccione's power placed him at the forefront of north Italian politics, such that he was at times considered almost as a separate prince. Niccolo III's attitude to Uguccione was less that of ruler to subject and more that of one prince to another.[51]

During Niccolo III's reign, other Ferrarese nobles received grants, mainly in fief, of lands in the Modenese and Reggiano: the Sala brothers, Alberto, Niccolo and Baldassare, received the former Fogliani castles at Dinazzano, Casalgrande and Salvaterra, with jurisdiction and gabelle revenues;[52] Niccolo Ariosti received the castle at Magreda;[53] the Sacrati bought much former Boiardi property at Rubiera;[54] Alberto Costabili was given confiscated Montecuccoli property.[55] And this process was continued under Niccolo

---

     presente ne para esser certissimi che mandando dito Magnifico Uguccione, li altri zentilhomini tuti quanti mandarano': ibid., letter of 16 July 1429.

[47] In 1414 Uguccione acquired from the bishop of Modena 2,785 *biolche* in the territories of Vignola and Savignano: AV, Archivio Boncompagni, Prot. 713, no. 6, nos. 1 & 2; Crespellani, *Mem. stor. vignolesi*, p. 15.

[48] BEM, Documenti Campori, Appendix 1387, letter of 1419; A. Plessi, *Istorie vignolesi* (Vignola, 1885), pp. 32–42; Franchini, *Simboli*.

[49] Pacts with the Canossa, Rangoni, Savignano and with Alberto Pio: AV, Archivio Boncompagni, Prot. 714, nos. 13, 15, 17; Rombaldi, 'Quattro Castella', pp. 44–5.

[50] For references to his *factor generalis* and *canzellerii*: AV, Archivio Boncompagni, Prot. 713, nos. 6/5 and 7; BEM, Documenti Campori, 1313, letter of 21 Jan. 1404; ASM, Catastri, R, 5 May 1416. Among Uguccione's Ferrarese officials were Guglielmo Betto, Damiano Guidoberti, Gregorio Perondoli and Pietrobono Roti.

[51] ASM, N. Abbatia, A, fols. 122–7; BEM, Documenti Campori, 1313.

[52] These were donated (1413), later enfeoffed (1422), with 'merum et mixtum imperium' and all 'exactionibus tributis homagiis vassalis et valvassoribus ac datiis pedagiis et gabellis et quibuscumque honoranciis preheminenciis et regaliis' (but reserving the castle ditches): ASM, Not. Cam., N. Abbatia, A, fols. 99–100; Catastri, R, fol. 232.

[53] ASM, Leggi e Decreti, B IV, fol. 81.

[54] ASM, Catastri, R, fol. 543; Not. Cam., D. Dulcini, B, fol. 98.

[55] Tiraboschi, *Mem. stor. mod.*, vol. 3, p. 178.

III's successors, as the Calcagnini, Strozzi and Trotti acquired lands in these territories.[56]

## TERRITORIAL NOBLES IN FERRARA

The converse process was the granting of lands in the Ferrarese to nobles from Modena and Reggio, which has already been examined (above, chapter 3). The Este sought both to attract their territorial nobles to Ferrara and to install Ferrarese nobles in the periphery. Both the Savignano and Canossa, though later displaced, had in the fourteenth century been in Este service in Ferrara.[57] But the most successful of these provincial lords in Ferrara were the Roberti, lords of San Martino in Rio, to the north east of Reggio.[58] In the late thirteenth century, the Roberti had opposed the first Este *signoria* in Reggio, joining the faction that brought about its downfall; but with the revival of Este pressure on Reggio after 1336, the Roberti were quickly drawn into the Este orbit. They became Este *raccomandati* in 1346, undertaking to work for the re-establishment of the Este *signoria* in return for promises of lands and privileges when this was achieved. At the same time, the marquis 'granted' San Martino to them, although he had no title to do so, with high justice and immunity from city taxation.[59] This 'grant', in defiance of the Gonzaga lords of the city, was typical of the means by which political lordship was being extended in these years, as we shall see. In response, the Gonzaga expelled the Roberti from Reggio, attacked San Martino and forced it into submission. But the Roberti did not long remain obedient. From the 1350s they were aided against the Gonzaga first by the Visconti, and later by the Este, whose retainers they became.[60] Against Gonzaga and Visconti claims over San Martino, they again received it by Este 'grant' and finally in 1368 obtained imperial investiture in fief, with jurisdiction and immunity from city taxation. This ended their uncertain legal

---

[56] Ibid., vol. 1, pp. 104, 292, 335; vol. 2, pp. 15, 197, 226, 263.
[57] Zinello da Savignano resided at Ferrara as a *provisionatus* in the 1370s: ASM, Not. Cam., J. Sanvitale, fols. 9, 138; F. Tagliapetri, B, fols. 11v, 23; A. Cavaleria, fol. 5. Ugolino was a *provisionatus* in 1364 and *podestà* of Ferrara in 1371: ASF, ANF, N. Sansilvestri; J. Sanvitale, fol. 60. Albertino da Canossa was in Ferrara in the 1330s and early 1340s and his son, Cabriotto, was an Este military captain: ASM, Not. Cam., P. Fabro and B. Nigrisoli, *passim; Chron. Est.*, 463–4; Badini, 'Carte', p. 116.
[58] Tiraboschi, *Dizionario*, vol. 2, pp. 25–6; Cottafavi, *San Martino*.
[59] ASM, Not. Cam., B. Nigrisoli, fols. 31–v; Cottafavi, *San Martino*, pp. 14–15.
[60] See above, pp. 85–6.

position *vis-à-vis* the lords of Reggio.[61] Meanwhile, in these years the Roberti were building up their position in Ferrara, which they maintained until 1400, when a number were exiled or executed following an obscure political intrigue with Marco Pio. Even after this, however, Niccolo and Alberto Roberti remained close to the marquis, receiving a gift of Campogalliano (near Modena) in 1403.[62] And Roberti support remained important in Este campaigns to recover Reggio: when the sons of Filippo Roberti renewed their *accomandigia* with Niccolo III, they were promised further lands, tax privileges, pensions and military stipends.[63] But when Venice attacked Niccolo III's ally Francesco da Carrara in 1404–5, Niccolo and Alberto Roberti fought on the Venetian side and after the peace settlement of 1405 Roberti power in Ferrara was broken.[64] Rebellion in 1419 brought forfeiture of all their property in the Ferrarese and ten years later San Martino was taken from them as well. Some of this property, both in the Ferrarese and at San Martino, was later restored to them, but San Martino itself was kept firmly in Este hands, passing to a cadet branch of the Este family.[65] Like other families, the Roberti had been attracted to Ferrara by the prospects for power and profit that Este ambitions in Emilia offered; what they failed to realise, it seems, was that they remained valuable to the marquises only as long as Reggio eluded Este grasp.

Other families too transferred to Ferrara, among them the Boiardi. This family had held lands at Rubiera (midway between Modena and Reggio) from the twelfth century, but acquired political prominence only from the early fourteenth, seizing control of the

---

[61] ASM, Not. Cam., F. Tagliapetri, A, fols. 50–3, 91; BEM, Documenti Campori, Appendice 1251, fols. 96–8v; Cottafavi, *San Martino*, p. 20; R. Finzi, *Accordi e contese fra Correggio e S. Martino in Rio nella storia* (Correggio, 1935).

[62] ASM, Leggi e Decreti, B III, fol. 71.

[63] Promises to give them Budrio, to repay a loan of 6,000 ducats, to reduce Roberti tax assessments, to defend Ugo Roberti in his possession of certain benefices and to remove duty on salt imports to San Martino and on Roberti crop exports to Venice: ASM, Casa e Stato, 22/57.

[64] *Ann. Est.*, 1009; *Corpus Chron. Bon.*, vol. 3, pp. 511–12, 520, 526; Gatari, *Chron.*, vol. 1, pp. 501, 531; *Libri Commemoriali*, ix, nos. 301, 303.

[65] The property of Giovanni and Alberto was confiscated and disposed of in 1420–1 (ASM, Leggi e Decreti, A 5, fol. 335; B IV, fols. 46, 48, 58v, 67, 176). In 1430 Niccolo III cancelled all sentences against Ugo, Giovanni, Filippo and Francesco, released Giovanni from custody, returned some of their property in the Ferrarese and at San Martino, but refused to grant them pensions (ibid., fols. 196v–7). And see *Atti canc. viscontei*, vol. 2, 819; A. Affarosi, *Memorie istoriche del monastero di S. Prospero di Reggio* (3 vols., Padua, 1733–46), vol. 2, pp. 3–14.

castle of Rubiera in 1354 with Visconti assistance.[66] From the 1360s, they were loyal clients of the Papacy and of the Este: with Rubiera under papal protection, they served as papal *condottieri* (although paid, by default, by the Este).[67] The Boiardi provided, from the late fourteenth century, a series of Este courtiers and soldiers. Gherardo, who was also a friend and confidant of Francesco II da Carrara, was a councillor of Niccolo III from 1399, twice *podestà* of Ferrara, often an Este ambassador and for some years in the 1420s 'governor' of Niccolo's sons, Borso and Meliaduse.[68] Ugo Boiardi commanded Este forces in the Modenese in the early fifteenth century and was later the commendatory abbot of S. Bartolo near Ferrara.[69] But the closest to Niccolo III was Feltrino Boiardi.[70] Being about the same age as Niccolo, he was brought to court in 1396, where the two boys began what became a lifelong friendship. He was the marquis' companion in arms in his early military exploits and accompanied him in pilgrimage to the Holy Land in 1413. He was entrusted with some of the most difficult political tasks facing the marquis in these years: the negotiations with, for example, Ottobuono Terzi in 1409 and with Filippo Maria Visconti in 1420. In the late 1420s he led the Este assault on the Fogliani castles, taking almost thirty in a month, and under Niccolo III's successor, Leonello, he served as governor in turn of Modena and Reggio. Like most other members of the Este military entourage, he received some property in fief in and around Ferrara,[71] but the clearest sign of the favour he enjoyed was the rearrangement, in 1423, of Boiardi family property, which was assisted by Niccolo III. The object of this rearrangement was to exclude the other Boiardi from lordship in the Reggiano and to concentrate the family's seigneurial powers in the hands of Feltrino.[72] This expropriation took the following form: all Boiardi

---

[66] Tiraboschi, *Dizionario*, vol. I, pp. 373–84; Rombaldi, 'Matteo Maria Boiardo', pp. 452–4.
[67] ASM, Not. Cam., F. Tagliapetri, A, fols. 50–v, 91; Casa e Stato, 18/32 & 35; *Lettres secrètes Urbain V*, 1589.
[68] *Copialettere*, nos. 39, 72, 304, 753, 788; ASM, Not. Cam., J. Delaito, fol. 163v; N. Abbatia, A, fols. I, 28v; Catastri, R, fol. 302; Mandati, I, fols. 4, 28; ASF, Archivio Tassoni, V/20; F. di Broilo, 'I podestà di Ferrara'.
[69] ASM, Leggi e Decreti, B III, fol. 210; Not. Cam., P. Sardi, C, fol. 118v.
[70] 'Vita del cavalier Feltrino Boiardo'; G. Reichenbach, *Un gentiluomo poeta del Quattrocento: Matteo Maria Boiardo* (Ferrara, 1923), pp. 11–29; Tiraboschi, *Dizionario*, vol. 2, pp. 382–3; I. Mariotti, 'Tre epigrammi per casa Boiardo', in *Miscellanea Augusto Campana* (Padua, 1981).
[71] ASM, Catastri, N, fol. 577; R, fol. 517.
[72] 'Considerando . . . che non era possibile che tanti signori con longa concordia dominassero la giuriditione di un solo castello, [Feltrino] persuase a Niccolo che lo

rights at Rubiera were ceded to the marquis; in return Feltrino was enfeoffed with the former Fogliani castles of Scandiano, Gesso and Torricella, to add to Arceto, which he had received in fief in 1414, and with Scandiano being raised to the status of a county.[73] In addition, Feltrino was given Niccolo III's estates at Ostellato in the Ferrarese.[74] The other Boiardi, however, were given lands, totalling fewer than 200 hectares, near Porto Maggiore, to the south of Ferrara.[75] It is not difficult to see who the main beneficiary of this rearrangement was: here was another example of the strategy of heavily rewarding the marquis' friends.

### FEUDAL AND 'POST-FEUDAL' BONDS

Este relations with the old noble families of Modena and Reggio were complicated by their possession of imperial fiefs, lands that were held directly from the Emperor and were separate from the jurisdiction of the city communes.[76] Some families had held lands by imperial grant from the twelfth or thirteenth centuries (for example, the Montecuccolo, Sesso or Canossa),[77] others had had *de facto* lordship legitimated by imperial or papal grant in the course of the fourteenth century (for example, the Pio, Manfredi and Correggio).[78] Real political relations between *signori* and rural lords, however, did not coincide with the legal ones. An imperial fief was not proof against dispossession by the *signore* (as the Roberti and Montecuccoli discovered) and with the imperial creation of the duchies of Modena and Reggio for Borso d'Este in 1452, the Este secured overlordship of the imperial fiefs in those territories.[79] But

---

pigliasse per se . . . mentre con li contanti comprasse la parte de fuorosciti et seco permutasse la sua con qualche altro castello': 'Vita di Feltrino', fol. 30.

[73] ASM, Catastri, N, fol. 577; R, fol. 269; Tiraboschi, *Dizionario*, vol. 2, p. 383; G. Pagliani, *Notizie storiche civili e religiose di Arceto e della antica contea di Scandiano* (Reggio, 1907), pp. 11–17.

[74] ASM, Catastri, Q, fols. 468–79 (7 June 1423).

[75] Ibid., fols. 489–513, 544–64.

[76] Chittolini, 'Infeudazioni'.

[77] Tiraboschi, *Dizionario*, vol. 1, p. 344; vol. 2, pp. 92, 229–30, 268.

[78] The Manfredi held Borzano, Montericco and Mucciatella in imperial fief (granted 1368: Tiraboschi, *Dizionario*, vol. 1, p. 8) and Albinea as a papal county, created in 1412 by John XXIII (Tacoli, *Memorie*, vol. 2, pp. 353–4, vol. 3, pp. 539–40; Tiraboschi, *Dizionario*, vol. 1, p. 9). On the Correggio, see O. Rombaldi, *Correggio città e principato* (Modena, 1979).

[79] The marquis' relations with the Reggio feudatories were complicated by the fact that he held Reggio in fief of the Visconti, who had reserved to themselves direct dominion of the castles held by the Gonzaga, Correggio, Pico, Roberti, Simone

even earlier in the fifteenth century, the Este were already assuming direct control, in more or less legal form, of fiefs originally granted to rural lords by local bishops and abbots: the Fogliani, for example, were invested by Niccolo III with Querciola, although they had previously been invested by the bishop; Arceto and Gesso, previously held of the bishop by the Malapresi family, were given in fief by Niccolo to the Boiardi; Leonello d'Este invested Albertino Boschetti with San Cesario which he had earlier been granted in perpetual lease by the papal legate.[80] There was also a trend, mirroring that in contemporary Milan, to transform the territorial nobles into vassals. A dozen such fiefs are recorded in the *Catastri* between 1394 and 1436. Some of these, as we might expect, rewarded service to the marquis: Gasparo Montecuccoli was invested in 1406 with Cadriana in reward of his loyalty and personal service in Niccolo III's recent war against Obizzo da Montegarullo; Sforza degli Attendoli, Niccolo's captain-general, was rewarded for his military achievements with Montecchio and other castles in the Parmense.[81] Others reflected the territorial status of existing lordships: in 1412, the Dal Verme, having previously been vassals of the Visconti when lords of Parma, now became vassals of the Este on similar terms.[82] Some fiefs expressed the marquis' will to be obeyed or the wishes of the nobles for the marquis' protection: in 1433 Cesare and Niccolo Fogliani were invested with Monteviano and Rondinara on the specific undertaking that they were to be 'always loyal and obedient to the marquis and his successors'; in 1414 Francesco da Palu declared to Niccolo III his desire to live 'under the shade of the wings of your lordship' and to enjoy his 'tutelage and defence', by becoming Niccolo's vassal.[83]

However, the form of control most favoured by the Este was not enfeoffment, but *accomandigia*,[84] a loose, non-feudal contract of

---

Canossa and Andriolo da Dallo: Tiraboschi, *Mem. stor. mod.*, vol. 3, p. 95; and see U. Petronio, 'Giurisdizioni feudali e ideologia giuridica nel ducato di Milano', *Quaderni storici*, 26 (1974), 363–4 and n. 32.

[80] Tiraboschi, *Dizionario*, vol. 1, pp. 23, 87, 344–6; vol. 2, p. 235.

[81] ASM, Catastri, N, fols. 376, 489; also enfeoffments to Feltrino Boiardi, Alberto Sala and the Bismantova: ibid., N, fol. 577; R, fols. 232, 578.

[82] Ibid., N, fol. 517.      [83] Ibid., N, fol. 583; R, fol. 552.

[84] On *accomandigia*, see G. Soranzo, 'Collegati, raccomandati, aderenti negli stati italiani dei sec. XIV e XV', *ASI*, 99 (1941); Chittolini, 'Infeudazioni', pp. 47, 60–1, 75; *idem*, 'Particolarismo', pp. 259, 269; *Capitoli*, vol. 1, pp. 452ff; Sestan, 'Guidi', p. 374; Cherubini, 'Ubertini', pp. 203–4; Jones, *Malatesta*, pp. 98, 106, 108, 111, 121, 167; T. Dean, 'Lords, vassals and clients in Renaissance Ferrara', *EHR*, 100 (1985).

protection and military aid. The simplest way to introduce and explain *accomandigia* is possibly to describe one bond in particular, which comes as close to being typical of such bonds as is possible. This is the contract made between Niccolo III d'Este and three members of the Pico della Mirandola in 1406. The contract took the form of letters patent in which the Pico declared 'we have passed into adherence and become the adherents of Niccolo d'Este and . . . for ourselves and our heirs promise to the marquis that we . . . shall henceforth in perpetuity be good, true and faithful adherents, friends and servants of the marquis and shall recognise, hold and treat him as our true and only lord . . . To the utmost of our power we shall obey his every order . . . Whenever he orders, we shall make war and peace and truce with all men . . . with all our lands, castles, villages and subjects we shall have his friends as our friends and his enemies as our enemies . . . We shall receive in our lands and castles all the marquis' troops, horse and foot, at his every request, and shall provide them with victuals at a reasonable price, make war with them against the marquis' enemies and allow them to deposit any booty in our territory. And we promise that we shall never treat nor, as far as is possible, allow to be treated anything either secretly or openly which might turn to the prejudice of the marquis' honour and estate, rather shall we maintain and defend his honour and estate to the utmost of our ability. We shall, however, be allowed at any time, but with the marquis' prior knowledge, to take up service with any other lord, community or person . . . provided that such lord, community or person is not hostile to the marquis, with the condition that we shall not ride or be with any person against the marquis or against any of his adherents or subjects . . . And with the further condition that we shall be obliged to serve the marquis rather than any other person in the world if he wants us'. In return, the marquis declared that he had received the Pico as his adherents and promised 'to defend to the utmost of our power and with all our strength their lands, castles, fortresses, territories and places, men and subjects against anyone seeking to attack them . . . And we shall include them and their lands and subjects in every alliance, con-federation or peace that we make . . . and we promise that hence-forth we shall pay them every month as provision 150 ducats and that henceforth they and all their Modenese friends may enjoy all offices and honours in the city of Modena which other nobles and their friends enjoy in Modena'. (Appendix 4).

This is one of the simpler bonds of *accomandigia*: others were much more elaborate, but this one is typical in much of its wording and in the type of obligations it created. Essentially, these were: extensive and exclusive loyalty, obedience to the lord's orders (especially military orders), and the opening of the client's military activities to the lord's control. In return, clients received pensions, privileges and promises of protection. In the Este state, as elsewhere in north and central Italy, *accomandigia* of this type seems to appear, fully formed, during the 1330s and 1340s. In the period to 1440, bonds of *accomandigia* were made and renewed by most of the territorial nobles of Modena and Reggio. More bonds were made than survive: whenever Este *raccomandati* were listed, families and individuals were included whose bonds are not to be found in surviving Este records. Both the lists and the existing examples of bonds make it very clear that *accomandigia* was a highly flexible means of formulating relationships of dependence between lords and their clients. Bonds were made with both the old nobility, whose rights predated the Este *signoria*, and the new nobles promoted by the Este. Bonds could be made for a period of years or for life. *Raccomandati* could be petty rural nobles or major *signori* from outside the Este state (Este *raccomandati* often included lords from central Emilia, the Lunigiana and the Romagna), just as the Este themselves became the *raccomandati* of Venice. Above all, the content of the bonds shows that *accomandigia* was a combination of various relations between lords and their clients. In part, bonds were military contracts, envisaging an exchange of military resources between lord and *raccomandato*; in part they were diplomatic instruments, constructing a protected sphere of influence around the lord in his relations with other states; and in part they were financial agreements, involving payments both by clients to lords (recognitory dues) and, more often, by lords to clients (pensions, tax concessions etc.). In some bonds, like those of the Pico, the emphasis was on the personal commitment of the *raccomandati* to the lord; in others the stress lay on the status of the client's territories: loyalty was attached to specified castles, possession of which was confirmed and publicly accepted by the lord. This territorial dimension often went further and included a formal grant to the *raccomandato* of powers of jurisdiction (*merum et mixtum imperium*) and command (*gubernatio*). Each bond of *accomandigia* was different, responding to the specific circumstances of each family and of their relationship to the Este. Some bonds look more like *condotte*, with additional clauses to protect the recipients' territorial position; others look more like formal delegations of governmental powers.

*Accomandigia* could be a temporary wartime alliance, part of a settlement of a political dispute or a permanent definition of the powers and rights of territorial lordships. All this made *accomandigia* very different to fiefs. As we have seen, fiefs rewarded and expected service in only very general terms. *Accomandigia* was loaded with the highly specific terms of noble loyalty and of Este protection. *Accomandigia* certainly *looks* feudal, but the language is different. Some early Este bonds did have some feudal elements (the oath of fealty, an oath sworn 'in manibus') and the term *accomandigia* itself has obvious feudal connotations (*commendatio*). But the language of 'commendation' was used too generally and loosely in late medieval Italy for these connotations to be insisted upon. And in general the vocabulary of *accomandigia* is not feudal: *adherentia, adherentes, amici et servitores, gubernatio, superioritas*. Still less was *accomandigia* subject to the rules of feudal tenure. Nothing changed hands when a bond of *accomandigia* was made: only a relationship was created.

It was the military character of *accomandigia* that was uppermost at first. *Accomandigia* seems to have developed specifically in response to Italian states' military and diplomatic needs during regional warfare in the mid- to late-fourteenth century. For the *raccomandati*, attachment to one state brought much-needed stability and protection in a period of almost constant conflict; for the major states, *accomandigia* defined spheres of influence and created the forward bases which they needed in contested territory in order to realise their expansive ambitions. This meant that the bargaining for the adherence of strategic rural lords was sometimes akin to bargaining for *condotte*. This was shown in the 1370s in the efforts of the Este and the papal legate to secure the adherence of nobles in the Reggiano in their campaign against Bernabo Visconti. The Este and the legate targeted two families to be won over: the Boiardi and the Correggio, 'who are great and powerful in the territory of Parma and have many friends there and can do considerable harm to Bernabo'. Together, their castles close to Reggio (at Rubiera and Correggio) 'are well-placed to damage Reggio and large enough to hold a thousand lances'.[85] The Este needed these families, who could also pose a powerful threat to Modena, should they come to terms with Bernabo Visconti instead. Hence the Este readiness to grant the Correggio and Boiardi demands for the supply of munitions, for pensions, *condotte* and the deployment of Este troops at their castles.

[85] ASM, Leggi e Decreti, A 1, fols. 152–3 insert.

But the Boiardi needed more than this: *condotte* and garrison troops would be removed at the end of campaigning, leaving the Boiardi exposed to attack. It was *accomandigia* which provided a more lasting form of protection: their agreement with the Este in 1371 not only met their military and financial demands, but also obliged the marquis and his ally, the Pope, to defend them and their lands and to include them in all peace negotiations. By the same agreement, the Este secured the sworn loyalty of the Boiardi and the use of their military resources and abilities.[86] This sort of *accomandigia* was an extension of *condotta* to accommodate the needs of *condottieri* who had territorial interests in the theatre of war itself.

However, *accomandigia*, unlike a *condotta*, was not (usually) a fixed-term contract. It was entered into without restriction of time ('from this day forward') and was often by 1400 envisaged as a permanent bond between lord and client. *Condotta* was a contract of hire; there was honour in *accomandigia*. This was demonstrated in 1417, when the honour engaged by both the Este and the Visconti to their *raccomandati* complicated their peace negotiations regarding Parma.[87] When, therefore, the new *raccomandato* undertook to hold his castles 'to the estate and honour of the marquis', this was not merely formulaic, but described precisely the sort of relationship that was being created. This was why the passage of a *raccomandato* from one lord to another created such a stir.[88] Honour involved reciprocal obligations which continued after the immediate occasion of the bond had passed. The lord's protection thus extended to a general assumption of the client's interests and the promotion of the client's advantage. What this meant in terms of local power was often spelt out in the bonds themselves. Some bonds protected the position of one branch of a family against another: to Feltrino, Bartolomeo and Giorgio da Bismantova, Niccolo III promised not to favour the claim of Franceschina and Caterina da Bismantova to Vologno; to Carlo Fogliani, Niccolo III promised to give all the territories held by Giberto and Pietro Anglico Fogliani.[89] The Pio and Roberti were promised rights of appointment to some minor

---

86 ASM, Casa e Stato, 18/32 & 35.
87 ASM, Ambasciatori, Venezia, 1, 2, fol. 4. On honour, see in general and recently: Arnold, *German Knighthood*, p. 135; Wormald, *Manrent*, p. 98; K. M. Brown, *Bloodfeud in Early Modern Scotland, 1573–1625* (Edinburgh, 1986), pp. 23–6.
88 e.g. the transfer to Venetian adherence of Rolando Pallavicino: ASVe, Senato, Secreta, reg. 10, fols. 85ff.
89 ASM, Leggi e Decreti, B III, fols. 160–1; Tacoli, *Memorie*, vol. 3, pp. 397–401.

offices in the city.[90] The Fogliani at one point were even promised
the bishopric of Reggio.[91] Pensions, for fixed periods or for life,
were commonly provided; and some of these could be large, for
example, the 150 ducats per month awarded to the Pio. Other
financial concessions included loans, the cancellation of tax arrears
and tax immunities.[92] Nobles' territorial ambitions were also
satisfied or fuelled: the Roberti were twice promised Budrio; the Pio
were offered military aid in the recovery of their ancient patrimonial
rights in the Corte di Quarantola.[93] Gherardino da Gomola and
Obizzo da Montegarullo were given licence to engage in private
wars to recover lands that they had lost.[94]

These promises were not always fulfilled, but there is substantial
evidence that the Este took seriously their obligations to their
*raccomandati*. The Pio and their servants received a number of
financial and judicial favours, including the remission of a fine for
assault.[95] For the Manfredi, Niccolo III interceded with Ottobuono
Terzi to mollify his attitude towards them.[96] Above all, the Este
intervened to arbitrate their clients' quarrels. Within a few years of
the Pio becoming Este *raccomandati* (1374), Niccolo II d'Este
supervised a settlement between Marsiglio and Giberto Pio.[97] In
1407, Niccolo III and Gianfrancesco Gonzaga arranged a settlement
of a border dispute between their respective clients, the Fogliani and
Sesso.[98] Niccolo III also arbitrated a quarrel between the Dallo and
Bismantova.[99] Signorial arbitration of noble quarrels was certainly
nothing new – the Este were arbitrating among the Rodeglia in 1336
and between the Montegarullo and Gualandelli in 1347, for example,
– but *accomandigia* possibly made such intervention easier and the
results of intervention more lasting. There is also the possibility that
the Este tried to promote themselves as the arbiters of quarrels
within their own state, much as they did within Italy as a whole.

*Accomandigia* was thus also a vehicle for extending Este control
over noble behaviour. The Este camera instituted the rule that taxes

[90] ASM, Not. Cam., B. Nigrisoli, fols. 30–3; Muratori, *Antichità*, vol. 2, pp. 89–95.
[91] Tacoli, *Memorie*, vol. 3, pp. 397–401.
[92] ASM, Leggi e Decreti, B II, fol. 209; B III, fols. 264–5; A 3, fol. 123.
[93] ASM, Not. Cam., B. Nigrisoli, fols. 30–3; Casa e Stato, 22/57; Investiture di Feudi, 13/18.
[94] ASM, Leggi e Decreti, B II, fols. 141–2; B III, fols. 264–5.
[95] ASM, Leggi e Decreti, A I, fols. 243, 338; B III, fols. 175–6.
[96] ASM, Leggi e Decreti, B III, fol. 159.
[97] ASM, Not. Cam., A. Cavaleria, fols. 12–16.
[98] ASM, Not. Cam., P. Bononia, fol. 71v.
[99] ASM, Leggi e Decreti, B v, fol. 18.

uncollected through noble obstruction should be deducted from their pensions.[100] *Accomandigia* often involved the temporary surrender of castles to the marquises by clients. The Este had some success in removing castles from noble hands and this was often associated with the making of a bond of *accomandigia*. The Fogliani surrendered Budrione for a year in 1370, but did not recover it.[101] The Canossa surrendered San Polo for a year in 1371 and Canossa and Gesso in 1409.[102] Alberto Balugola, on becoming an Este adherent in 1406, agreed to release the 'curia Balugola', with all its castles at the marquis' request, for it henceforth to be subject to the Este *podestà* at Montefestino.[103] Under pressure from Niccolo III, the Bismantova surrendered the castle of Bismantova in 1422, so that it could be 'better and more safely guarded' under Este garrison.[104] In 1367, the Roberti and Manfredi briefly resigned their castles to Este agents, before receiving them in imperial fief the following year – a procedure clearly indicating that it was only through the Este that these rural lords could remove themselves from nominal subordination to the city of Reggio.[105] Moreover, a common, though not always explicit condition of *accomandigia* seems to have been residence in Ferrara. The bonds of the Correggio, for example, included the gift of a house in Ferrara and, as we have seen, many nobles of Modena and Reggio possessed houses there.[106] Some clients were even specifically exempted from a residence requirement: it was stated in the Fogliani pacts of 1404 that Carlo Fogliani was not obliged, by reason of a pension of L. 120 per month, to reside outside his castles; the Pio were granted a pension of 300 florins per month with exemption from residence at Ferrara.[107]

The strict terms of *accomandigia*, when observed, established some

---

[100] This order was questioned by the *massaro* of Modena, but confirmed by the *fattori generali*, in order that 'nobiles et potentes remaneant continuo creditores camere': ASM, Leggi e Decreti, A 2, fols. 265, 274 (1396).

[101] Tiraboschi, *Dizionario*, vol. 1, pp. 75–6; *cf.* the surrender or sale of castles by Florentine *raccomandati: Capitoli*, vol. 1, pp. 269–71, 334–9, 454, 459 etc.

[102] Tiraboschi, *Dizionario*, vol. 1, p. 126; vol. 2, p. 186; ASM, Leggi e Decreti, A 1, fol. 87.

[103] Ibid., B III, fol. 227.     [104] Ibid., B IV, fol. 67v.

[105] ASM, Not. Cam., F. Tagliapetri, A, fols. 50–3v, 91.

[106] The Correggio were given a house 'in qua pro libito habitare possunt sine aliqua pensione': ASM, Leggi e Decreti, B III, fols. 281–3. *Cf.* the licence granted by Bernabo Visconti to his client Guido Savina Fogliani to acquire a house in Milan: Grimaldi, *Signoria*, p. 147; and Florentine *raccomandati* of the Aretino, who were given licence to reside in Florence, but not in Arezzo: *Capitoli*, vol. 1, pp. 464, 476, 486, 546.

[107] Tacoli, *Memorie*, vol. 3, pp. 397–401; ASM, Investiture di Feudi, 13/18.

restraints on the autonomous military activity of the territorial nobility and strengthened state loyalties. But some independence of action was sometimes explicitly permitted. Clients were allowed, with the prior consent of the marquis, to enter the civil or military service of other lords or communes, provided that this did not lead them into opposition to the marquis or any of his other clients.[108] With the same reservation, the Montecuccoli were permitted to use their military power to assist any of their *amici*.[109] Some bonds established liege adherence to the Este[110] and others included a permanent licence to build and repair castles.[111]

If clients' political independence was curtailed, their territorial power was often extended by *accomandigia*, which defined and augmented noble privileges, conferring jurisdictions and immunities, guaranteeing supplies of salt, corn and munitions. Such concessions made bonds of *accomandigia* more like bilateral agreements between equals than terms of subjection. For, with the emergence from the mid-fourteenth century of increasingly stable foreign *signorie* in Reggio and Modena, the direction of noble ambitions shifted. Nobles who had previously themselves aspired to city lordship now sought recognition of their territorial power from the new *signori*. Bonds of *accomandigia* defined the terms of alliance, of protection and privilege, between lord and nobility. But, at the same time, *raccomandati* recognised in some form the sovereign authority of the Este. Bonds confirmed their possessions and their local lordship, but granted them 'in custody and in government', to be held in the name of the marquis, and to his 'honour and estate'. The territorial nobility thus accepted a role as subordinate military and political governors. And this subordination was not merely nominal: the commissions of lands to *raccomandati* to govern ('ad

---

[108] In 1418 Antonio da Rodeglia offered his military services to the Guinigi, but saving the licence of the marquis 'cum sit castellanus et ad petitionem domini Marchionis': *Lucca regesti*, vol. 3, pt. 1, b. 1236. For members of the Fogliani in the service of other states: Tiraboschi, *Dizionario*, vol. 1, p. 302. And see Dean, 'Venetian economic hegemony'.

[109] 'quod ipse Lanzalotus possit iuvare quemcumque suum amicum dummodo hoc non procedat et fiat contra statum ipsius domini Marchionis': ASM, Not. Cam., Z. Coadi, fols. 44–5v. There was a similar clause in the bonds of Gasparo Montecuccoli in 1394: ASM, Not. Cam., A. Cavaleria, fols. 87–9.

[110] See above, p. 168. Lanzalotto Montecuccoli was allowed to take up service elsewhere 'dummodo non sit dicto domino [Marchioni] necessarius pro factis suis': ASM, Not. Cam., Z. Coadi, fols. 44–5v.

[111] Thus the Bismantova and Fogliani bonds: ASM, Leggi e Decreti, B III, fols. 160–1; Tacoli, *Memorie*, vol. 3, pp. 397–401.

gubernandum') were clearly seen as revocable. San Martino, for example, which the Roberti held as an imperial fief, was regarded by the Este as land which they had committed to the Roberti to govern and it was taken back from them when their rule could no longer be trusted.[112]

Recognitions of noble power and commissions of government probably changed the local distribution of power very little, amounting to no more than the confirmation of *de facto* rule; but they were clear attempts by the *signore* to extend some overlordship (*superioritas*) over the lands held by the nobility, despite his lack of direct legal authority. The problem was that of extending state authority when the legal basis of that authority was challengeable or uncertain. Imperial vassals could dispute the *signore*'s claim to demand from them loyalty and obedience, even where the *signore* himself held imperial powers as vicar or duke.[113] Against this background, bonds of *accomandigia* were *de facto* arrangements, overlapping and disregarding, if not replacing, the rights of the direct lord, whether Emperor, bishop or abbot, of whom the *raccomandato* nominally held his lands. The Montecuccoli, for example, recognised Este *superioritas* over lands that they had previously received by imperial investiture.[114] We have seen the same process in the case of the Roberti. *Accomandigia* thus formalised or created a relationship of political, not legal, dependence and became the means by which the *signore* extended his political authority over semi-independent nobles. As we have seen, expropriation of *raccomandati* was based on their obligations as clients and was not impeded by their immunities as imperial vassals.

Most clearly illustrating this basic political nature of *accomandigia* are the bonds of the Montecuccoli, who ruled much of the Frignano for the Este. Despite a number of rebellions in the late fourteenth century (1388, 1391, 1394), Montecuccoli privileges were extended, with life pensions and wide tax immunities. The commissions to their rule of a large number of castles and villages contained the usual clauses of *accomandigia*, but reserved to the Este some form of overlordship (a 'ius superioritatis'). This was defined in the following way: the inhabitants were to be subject to the jurisdiction of the marquis' *podestà*, but the fines were to be shared with the Montecuc-

[112] ASM, Leggi e Decreti, BIV, fol. 196v.
[113] Magni, *Tramonto*, pp. 57–81; Chittolini, 'Infeudazioni', pp. 51–8.
[114] Campori, *Frignano*, p. 40; ASM, Not. Cam., J. Mizino, fols. 2–5v; A. Cavaleria, fols. 87–9.

coli; the Montecuccoli were to pay L.2,100 each year 'in recognition of the marquis' superiority and dominion', but they were to receive monthly pensions; it was forbidden to them to alienate any of the castles, but they could take up military service elsewhere.[115] Particular importance seems to have been attached to the large recognitory payment, which was paid regularly and in full for many years, until cancelled in 1387.[116]

Montecuccoli power remained largely intact in the fifteenth century,[117] and this was also true of most of the rural lordships to the north of Modena and Reggio. Here the Pico and Correggio, despite their bonds of *accomandigia*, resisted absorption into the exclusive orbit of one principality.[118] Both were descended from powerful members of the entourage of Countess Matilda in the early twelfth century, the Pico being one of a number of related families 'dei figli di Manfredo'.[119] The Correggio were politically the more ambitious: Giberto in the early fourteenth century attempted to create a large *signoria* stretching from Reggio to Cremona and based on the Correggio lands in the northern Reggiano and Parmense.[120] Both families secured imperial investiture or confirmation of their territorial power: the Pico for Mirandola in 1311 and for Concordia (also raised to a county) in 1432; the Correggio in 1350 and 1452.[121] Even more independent were the Sesso, who had held Rolo in imperial fief since the twelfth century and also owned lands throughout the northern Reggiano. From the early fourteenth century, they became highly active in Veronese public life, holding lands and office there both under the Scaligeri and later under Venice.[122]

---

[115] Lanzalotto received government of Semese, Ranocchio, Montese, Brandola, Cereto, Frassinete, Montespecchio, 'turris Montisfortis' and 'turris Nicoleti'; Gasparo that of Montecuccolo, Renno, Camatta, Padrisio, Olina, Sassostorno, Sassoguldano, Castagneto, Montefolignano, Montespecchio, 'Saxumrossum' and 'Borbonum'. *Cf.* similar pacts between Florence and the Guidi in 1385: *Capitoli*, vol. 1, pp. 481–3.

[116] ASM, Casa e Stato, 16/1, 17/17, 19/14. *Cf.* the annual recognitory due of a *palio* of silk owed by all Florentine *raccomandati*: *Capitoli*, vol. 1, *passim*.

[117] C. Campori, 'Cesare Montecuccoli', *AMMo*, 5 (1870).

[118] Rombaldi, *Correggio*; D. M. Bueno de Mesquita, 'Niccolo da Correggio at Milan', *Italian Studies*, 20 (1965).

[119] On the 'figli di Manfredo': Tiraboschi, *Mem. stor. mod.*, vol. 4, pp. 123–33. On the Pico: ibid., pp. 173–91.

[120] F. Manzotti, 'Giberto da Correggio e la mancata signoria del medio corso del Po', *AMMo*, s. 8, 7 (1955); Rombaldi, *Correggio*, pp. 37–42.

[121] Tiraboschi, *Mem. stor. mod.*, vol. 4, pp. 173–91; Rombaldi, *Correggio*, pp. 45, 55.

[122] The Sesso were *podestà* and military captains of the Scaligeri and of Venice, received lands in the Vicentino and resided at Verona: Tiraboschi, *Dizionario*, vol.

Independence for some nobles thus remained the preferred course, but for others alliance with the Este brought great rewards. Of the old *contado* lords, those who most successfully profited from this alliance were the Pio. Linked by common ancestry to the Pico, the Pio had been prominent in Modena throughout the twelfth and thirteenth centuries, taking a large part in fights for power in Modena from the late thirteenth.[123] Egidio Pio was a leader of the faction which expelled the Este in 1306 and his son, Guido, was briefly lord of the city (1331–36). In 1319, Manfredo Pio had seized Carpi, a small town to the north of Modena, and this was later confirmed to the family by the Emperor, who also granted him jurisdiction and immunity from the city.[124] When Guido and Manfredo Pio surrendered Modena to Obizzo d'Este in 1336, the price of their surrender was Este recognition of their lordships at Carpi and San Felice, with large pensions, immunities and detailed guarantees of the property and position of their supporters.[125] Moreover, Este power in Modena was heavily mortgaged with concessions to the Pio: named exiles were not to be allowed to return to the city; Pio supporters, for example the Adelardi, were confirmed in their lordships; the Pio themselves were promised a full political and administrative indemnity, the payment of all their creditors and guarantees regarding the canal from the Secchia to Carpi. This treaty recognised the existence, under the Este *signoria*, of a privileged and almost separate group, that of the Pio and their affinity. In the following decades, the Pio repeatedly underlined their independence of the new *signori* by aligning with the Visconti against them. Their return to obedience in both 1358 and 1374 was the occasion for further concessions: in 1358 the extension of previous immunities; in 1374 the feudal grant of a number of villages near Carpi and favourable bonds of *accomandigia*.[126] These bonds, apart from the usual promises of defence and loyalty, awarded large pensions to the Pio brothers, Giberto and Marsiglio, renewed immunities to the Pio and their supporters (the Papazzoni and

2, p. 268; G. Mantovani, *Storia di Rolo* (Carpi, 1977); ASVe, Senato, Secreta, reg. 2, fol. 96; reg. 3, fols. 80, 102v.

[123] Tiraboschi, *Mem. stor. mod.*, vol. 4, pp. 133–50.

[124] P. Guaitoli, *Bibliografia storica carpigiana* (Carpi, 1882), pp. 154, 163, 168, 196, 230.

[125] Muratori, *Antichità*, vol. 2, pp. 89–95.

[126] ASM, Not. Cam., F. Sale, fols. 61v–2; Investiture di Feudi, 13/18; Guaitoli, *Bibliografia*, pp. 209–13. The villages around Carpi had long been disputed between the Pio and the Este: in 1374 the Pio were forced to renounce their claims to all of them in return for feudal investiture of some of them.

Adelardi), deployed thirty lances of papal troops at Carpi and made promises of support for Pio territorial claims against the Pico. The terms of this contract were confirmed in 1420, with further concessions on milling and salt.[127] From the 1370s, the Pio moved into closer personal and political alliance with the Este, becoming their retainers and residing for long periods at Ferrara. This new-found loyalty was soon rewarded with a substantial extension of Pio power, chiefly into the southern Modenese. From 1374, they held Marano, on the Panaro near Vignola.[128] In 1395, Marco Pio seized Spezzano and Formigine, on the edge of the plain near Sassuolo, which Niccolo d'Este confirmed to them in 1405, along with a grant of Soliera (near Carpi) and a number of former Montecuccoli castles in the Frignano.[129] It was in these years that the Pio treaties with the Este were transformed into *accomandigia*: the treaties of 1336 and 1358 were limited almost wholly to tangible concessions to the Pio, with no reciprocal obligations; but that of 1374 for the first time created a fully reciprocal contract.

The Pio, like the Boiardi, clearly illustrate the benefits to be gained from loyalty to the Este. Such families entered a more or less permanent alliance with the *signore*, becoming familiar figures in the Este entourage. Other families can be seen moving in the same direction, attracted to Ferrara and into Este service, either rather briefly (as with the Savignano) or for some decades (the Roberti). Their presence at the centre underpinned Este power in the periphery. At times of crisis or instability, when the personal political authority of the marquis declined, the local ambitions of these nobles came to the fore: family disputes erupted into violence and Este power was openly defied. But, as Este power in the hills and plain of central Emilia expanded and as Italy moved into a period of greater political stability, so the opportunities for independent action by the territorial nobility were severely reduced. Through fiefs and *accomandigia*, their relations with the centre were set on an increasingly firm and clearly defined basis.

[127] ASM, Leggi e Decreti, B IV, fols. 24–6.
[128] Tiraboschi, *Dizionario*, vol. 2, p. 16; Poggi, *Marano*, p. 43.
[129] *Ann. Est.*, 918. In 1420 the marquis confirmed Pio possession of the castles of Marano, Spezzano, Formigine, Soliera, Guiglia, Rochetta, Brandola, Mocogno, Malatigna, Monterastello, Samone, Sasso di Verica, 'Frassaneta' and 'Marcii': ASM, Leggi e Decreti, B IV, fols. 24–6.

# CONCLUSION

Until recently, the history of late medieval principalities was conceived largely as the history of their central institutions. This was the picture of the 'Renaissance state', 'unitary, absolute and secular' (Jones), with centrally-directed administrative, diplomatic and military organisations. Much attention has remained fixed on central institutions, on the prince and his court as the signs of a transition from medieval to modern government. Most recently, the court has been propounded as the instrument of cultural and political unification.[1] This transition from lordship (*seigneurie*) to principality has long been familiar in French late-medieval historiography. The chief features are rapidly rehearsed: the use of new titles (*Dei gratia*) and ceremonies (coronations), the claim to regalian rights (coinage, rights over vacant churches), judicial autonomy and the construction of appellate jurisdictions, taxation and institutions of government such as a chancery, archive, treasurers and auditors (*chambre des comptes*), a professional council with judicial functions and a court.[2] Much of this can be found in the Italian principalities, as we have seen: the pursuit of titles (of duke or marquis and the use of *Dei gratia*); the appropriation and invention of ceremonies and rituals;[3] the claim to imperial status and rights;[4] the establishment of courts and jurisdictions and the creation of central institutions.[5] The Italian princes' construction of new forms of government has also been seen in their assertive building programmes: both in the city (new castles

---

[1] A. Tenenti, 'La corte nella storia dell'Europa moderna', in *Le corti farnesiane di Parma e Piacenza (1545–1622)*, ed. M. A. Romani (2 vols., Rome 1978).

[2] J. Le Patourel, 'The king and the princes in fourteenth-century France', in *Europe in the Late Middle Ages*, ed. J. Hale *et al.* (London, 1965); F. Lot and R. Fawtier, *Histoire des institutions françaises au Moyen Age*, vol. 1, *Institutions seigneuriales* (Paris, 1957); Lewis, *Later Medieval France*, pp. 233–5.

[3] See above, p. 127.

[4] See above, p. 146 and C. Mozzarelli, 'Lo stato gonzaghesco: Mantova dal 1382 al 1707', in *Storia d'Italia*, vol. 17 (UTET, Turin, 1979), pp. 379–80.

[5] See above, pp. 22–3; Mozzarelli, 'Lo stato gonzaghesco', pp. 381–2; Brown, *Magnificence*, pp. 133–246.

and palaces, new churches associated with the dynasty) and in the countryside (villas).[6] However, an alternative picture has also been built up in recent years, one which questions the effectiveness of much 'central' government and stresses the autonomy and strength of local power structures. In England and France, as well as in Italy, attention is now trained on local communities and their relations with the centre. On the one hand, the interventions of central government in the localities are found to be misinformed and disruptive, provoking resistance and protest;[7] on the other, we are encouraged to recognise the power of lobbyists and 'fixers', adept at 'playing the system' in the interests of their local constituents and employers.[8] The result is a recognition that the 'state' was not unitary and was far from absolute: rather is it seen as pluralistic, with many centres of power;[9] with autonomous territories and privileged groups; with complementary and duplicated functions serving to maintain local participation in government.[10]

The history of feudalism is important in several ways to this revision of views about the medieval 'state'. First, because fiefs in many cases defined the relations of periphery to centre. Secondly, because, as we have seen, fiefs were used to reward members of the lord's entourage. That fiefs could still denote both territorial hierarchy and personal dependence upsets the picture of 'modernisation' painted for Renaissance Italy. Yet, between *signoria* and principality, it is clear that the role of feudal grants changed in many ways. The real value of feudal bonds to lords in the twelfth and thirteenth centuries cannot be doubted: feudal courts, assemblies of vassals, political and military service are all well attested.[11] The

[6] See above, p. 64; Mozzarelli, 'Lo stato gonzaghesco', pp. 362–4, 389–90.
[7] M. T. Clanchy, 'Law, government and society in medieval England', *History*, 59 (1974), esp. p. 78; M. Knapton, 'Capital city and subject province: financial and military relationships between Venice and Padua in the later fifteenth century', Oxford D.Phil. thesis, 1978, pp. 74–5, 89–146; Chittolini, 'Particolarismo', pp. 261–5.
[8] P. S. Lewis, 'The centre, the periphery and power distribution of fifteenth-century France', in *The Crown and Local Communities in England and France in the Fifteenth Century*, ed. J. R. L. Highfield (Gloucester, 1981).
[9] Ibid., p. 46; E. Fasano Guarini, 'Gli stati dell'Italia centro-settentrionale tra quatro e cinquecento: continuità e trasformazioni', *Società e Storia*, 21 (1983), 629–30.
[10] Ibid., pp. 626–8; G. Chittolini, 'Le "terre separate" nel ducato di Milano in età sforzesca', in *Milano nell'età di Ludovico il Moro* (Milan, 1983); J. E. Law, 'Verona and the Venetian state in the fifteenth century', *BIHR*, 52 (1979).
[11] A. Castagnetti, 'La famiglia veronese degli Avvocati (secoli XI–XIII)', in *Studi sul medioevo cristiano offerti a R. Morghen* (Rome, 1974), pp. 268–9; A. Castagnetti, 'Le due famiglie comitali veronesi, i San Bonifacio e i Gandolfingi-di Palazzo',

Cancellieri, Boiardi, Savignano and Lambertini. These were nobles of long descent, whose position at Ferrara owed much to their martial prowess and their military resources. And as the Este drew their military captains more from 'foreign' nobles than from Ferraresi, so there are few Ferraresi among the knights: some members of the Costabili and Contrari, Alberto Sala, Gigliolo Giglioli and Brandelisio Boccamaiori,[79] but apparently none of the Giocoli, Trotti or Turchi, nor any of the new families of Gualengo, Sacrati and Marinetti (who were civil, not military servants). Knighthood was restricted to the marquis' military and political companions: those who took part in Este tournaments,[80] who formed the 'company of knights' (*comitiva militum*) that accompanied the Este on their travels to Rome, Venice and Jerusalem[81] and who discharged honorific offices such as escorting the Pope into Rome in 1367 or the Emperor into Ferrara in 1438.[82] The military and religious content of knighthood was still very much alive, as seen in a number of collective creations by the Este: in Rome in 1367, Niccolo II created twelve knights 'in the name and in memory of the twelve apostles';[83] after taking part in the siege of Verona in 1404, Niccolo III was himself knighted, along with Filippo da Pisa, Alberto Sala and Nanne Strozzi;[84] in Jerusalem in 1413 Niccolo III created five knights from among his companions and the whole occasion was marked by displays of religious piety (masses, vows and symbolic acts binding themselves, through knighthood, to Christ).[85] Knightings on the field of battle and in the Holy Sepulchre brought immeasurable esteem to those involved and Este creations there obviously bear some resemblance to the orders of knighthood founded by many northern European monarchs to bind more closely to themselves their companions-in-arms and others whom they wished to honour.[86]

---

[79] Uguccione and Tagliaferro Costabili were knighted in 1352 (*Chron. Est.*, 469), Tommaso Contrari and Alberto Sala in 1413 (Campo, *Viaggio*, p. 125) and there are references to Alberto Costabili as a knight in 1435, Gigliolo Giglioli in 1431 and Brandelisio Boccamaiori in 1418 (ASM, Not. Cam., reg. 68, fol. 23; Vicini, 'Podestà', pp. 228, 235).

[80] *Chron. Est.*, 488, 518–19, 522, 525–7, 530.

[81] Ibid., 413, 438, 492, 520–1.

[82] Ibid., 488; *Diario Ferrarese*, p. 22.　　　　　[83] *Chron. Est.*, 489.

[84] *Ann. Est.*, 995–6. For F. Pisa and N. Strozzi, see above, pp. 38, 97.

[85] Campo, *Viaggio*, p. 125; *Fr. Johannis Ferr.*, Appendix; G. Nori, 'La corte itinerànte. Il pellegrinaggio di Niccolò III in Terrasanta', in *La corte e lo spazio: Ferrara estense*, ed. G. Papagno & A. Quondam (Rome, 1982).

[86] P. Contamine, 'Points de vue sur la chevalerie en France à la fin du moyen âge', *Francia*, 4 (1976), 273, 281; J. Sumption, *Pilgrimage* (London, 1975), p. 266.

land to money or the promise of 'good lordship'. Lords and their clients ensured mutual support through non-feudal contracts which promised a cash fee or pension and protection in return for life service in peace and war. Yet the break between 'feudal' and 'non-feudal' was not a clean one: in several areas non-feudal contracts were reinforced by feudal grants (or vice versa), rather than replacing them.[16] And this state of affairs is clearly paralleled in Ferrara, where feudal and non-feudal contracts coexisted. The group of Este vassals looks very much like the 'affinity' of any magnate of late medieval Britain or France: counsellors, estate and household servants, lawyers and an 'indefinite circle of well-wishers and personal connections';[17] 'kin, friendis, allya and parttakaris'.[18] Or compare the Este affinity with that of the kings of England in the late fourteenth and early fifteenth centuries.[19] Richard II and Henry IV retained several hundred 'king's knights' and 'esquires', ranging from some men closely attached to the court and the king's person, to foreign knights not resident in England, but retained to support specific diplomatic manoeuvrings. Among such men, there is little evidence of service performed or required specifically by reason of being retained by the king: what evidence there is is coincidental – of king's knights serving in the king's wars or being appointed to parliament, shrievalties and judicial commissions. In general, their service remained '"personal and variable", rather than systematic and defined'.[20] So too in Ferrara: as outlined above, the Este affinity ranged from the marquis' intimates to the advisers of other princes; and their service too has to be deduced from the assertions of charter preambles and from the appearance of such men in office, at court and in Este armies. But whereas the king of England's affinity was retained by cash annuities, the marquis' affinity was enfeoffed with land (in addition to wages and pensions).

At the same time, the group of *raccomandati* (some of whom were also vassals) look very like French *alliés* or Scottish clients. There are

[16] P. S. Lewis, 'Of Breton *alliances* and other matters', in *War, Literature and Politics in the Late Middle Ages*, ed. C. Allmand (Liverpool, 1976); *Illustrations of the Topography and Antiquities of the Shires of Aberdeen and Banff*, vol. 4 (Aberdeen, 1862), pp. 395–6 contains a bond of manrent and a feudal grant of land concluded between the same parties on the same day in 1445 (I owe this reference to Dr A. Grant).

[17] C. Carpenter, 'The Beauchamp affinity: a study of bastard feudalism at work', *EHR*, 95 (1980), 516.

[18] Wormald, *Bonds of Manrent*, pp. 76ff.

[19] C. Given-Wilson, *The Royal Household and the King's Affinity: Service, Politics and Finance in England, 1360–1413* (New Haven and London, 1986), ch. 4.

[20] Ibid., pp. 245–6.

some very close similarities of form, vocabulary and content here.[21] *Accomandigia* did, however, make much more explicit the relationship between lord and client and the rewards and benefits that each was to enjoy. *Accomandigia* was also territorial in character, where *alliance* and manrent were more personal. In their simplest forms, bonds of manrent consisted of bald statements of maintenance and service: the lord undertook to take his client's part in all his 'actions, causes and quarrels lawful and honest', while the client undertook to advise and attend ('ride and gang' with) his lord, to take his part in all his actions, causes and quarrels and to warn him of any imminent attacks on his person or interests.[22] Very similar were French *alliances*, which promised assistance and advice in all ways and means and whenever requested and which provided for the maintenance, defence and advancement of each party's 'good, honour, estate, rights, *preheminenses*, offices, liberties, *noblesses*, prerogatives and profit'.[23] On the whole, *alliances* left 'the nature of the client's interest, like that of the lord . . . in general terms'.[24] The profits of good-lordship and 'good-servantship' did not need to be made explicit. *Accomandigia*, too, includes general promises of support and maintenance, of intangible and unspecific protection, couched, as we have seen, in much the same vocabulary; but *accomandigia* differs in the level of specific additional detail – the provision of pensions, political guarantees, concessions of territory, jurisdiction and immunity. It is difficult to see why this should have been so and what conditions, specific to Italy, might account for this divergence; but the answer probably lies in the strength of the rural nobility (the Pio, Pico, Boiardi and so on) and in the need of the 'states' which were aiming to absorb them to define fiscal, judicial, territorial and political relationships. As far as the Este were concerned, *accomandigia* was possibly the best deal they could make with powerful local families, but they supplemented it where they could by attracting such men to Ferrara, by employing them at court and in military service and by rewarding them with fiefs of land in the Ferrarese *contado*.

This reflects a basic distinction in the *type* of lordship exercised by the Este at the centre and in the periphery. At Ferrara, as we have

---

[21] Both in the use of terms (*adherens, adherer, valledeur*) and in phrasing ('to have his enemies as our enemies and his friends as our friends'): Lewis, 'Decayed and non-feudalism', pp. 180, 182–3; *cf.* Lünig, *Codex*, vol. 3, 278–82.

[22] Wormald, *Bonds of Manrent*, pp. 53ff.

[23] Lewis, 'Decayed and non-feudalism', p. 180.      [24] Ibid., p. 165.

seen (chapter 2), the Este were not only lords of the city but also lords of vast urban and rural properties, which were accumulated over a long period. Here the Este could be liberal, using those estates to reward servants and supporters and to enrich newcomers. In Modena and Reggio, the situation was different: though they were lords of the city and *contado*, the Este actually *owned* very little. This meant that they had to use their Ferrarese resources to promote themselves as lords of men, rather than territory, in these outlying areas.

# APPENDICES

## 1. (ASM, Casa e Stato, 8/21, 24 Feb. 1308)

In 1308, Aldrovandino ceded to his sons, Rinaldo and Obizzo, the following property: in the Padovano, 298 *campi*, a few houses, half of the lake at Ponso and a *valle* at Megliadino; in the territory of Lendinara, unspecified property in 'terris et villis . . . Cavacane, Longalis, Bornii, Rami de Palo et ville nove'; in the Polesine di Rovigo, 'castella' at Fratta, Arqua and Pontecchio, a 'palacium merlatum' in Rovigo, tithes of Roverdicre, S. Apollinare, Buso, Sarzano and Mardimago, *valli* at Fratta, Arqua, Pontecchio, Ceregnano and Adria, woods at Rovigo and Mardimago; in Ariano, a 'castrum . . . cum quadam turre . . . supra Padum' and, in its territory, a 'magnum nemus'; in Ferrara, two 'palacia', two houses and the tithe of S. Luca; in the Ferrarese, unspecified pieces of land throughout the province, a 'castellum' at Copparo, 116 *mansi* at S. Niccolo and Bozoleto 'cum omnibus terris vassallorum', and 'omnes terras valles boschas prata et decima . . . terre Figaroli et tocius eius comitatus'. Aldrovandino also ceded 'jurisdictiones' of 'Rodigii et comitatus eiusdem . . . pollicinum Fratte, Coste et Arquade et aliarum villarum positarum in ipso pollicino . . . civitatis Adrie . . . Papocce et Villanove . . . terrarum de Este, Montagnane et aliarum omnium terrarum positarum in . . . districtibus dictarum terrarum et tocius Scodosie . . . terrarum castrorum Cerri, Calaonis et Baonis . . . plebatus ville et curtis Solexini . . . terrarum Cavacane, Saguedi, Raxe'; and the *ius patronatus* of churches in Ferrara (S. Alessio and the priory of S. Maria 'ultra padum'), in Rovigo (S. Maria 'de Sablonibus') and in the Padovano (S. Maria di Carceri, Este; S. Andrea, Villa; S. Giustina, Calaone; the priory of S. Elena; S. Maria, Solesino; S. Trinità, Tricontai); and all other property which Aldrovandino held *pro indiviso* with his brother, Francesco, 'exceptis depositis que habet Veneciis, Florencie et alibi'.

## 2. (ASM, Casa e Stato, 9/13, 9 Aug. 1310)

Following the defeat of Folco d'Este in 1310, Aldrovandino and Francesco divided between themselves part of the inheritance of Obizzo II. Documentation of only Aldrovandino's share seems to survive. This comprised: 2,170 *starii* 'in villa Porti et plebatus'; 313 *starii* 'in Cavalaria'; 307 *starii* 'ultra brellum'; 218 *starii* 'in Manoriis'; 90 *starii* 'in Gorgobonello'; 103 *starii* at Consandolo and 2,320 *starii* 'in Comuna'; also 'omnes possessiones Bozoleti exceptis terris infeudatis', 'totum Recane cum Recanella, Pelosella, Lytigia et Guandiario' (but the tavern,

# Appendices

river crossing (*passus*) and port there to remain in common), 'omnes valles de Trecenta et totum boscum Rucani et valles de Gurzono', a *valle* and property at Migliaro, property at Quinta, S. Giovanni and Paiero, 'valles que vocantur valles rupte cum canale que vocatur canal marchionum', half of the 'bosci Adriani' and two houses in Ferrara. (Cf. Muratori, *Antichità*, vol. 2, pp. 70–1).

### 3. (*ASM, Casa e Stato, 16/15, 16/16, 16/17: 1364*)

Between 9 and 22 June 1364, Francesco d'Este's agent repossessed the following property: at Marrara, 852 *starii* and 30,400 vines in lieu of all property and revenues that Francesco held there 'ante recessum eius de civitate Ferrarie et subsequenter conducta fuerunt ad affictum per . . . dominum Aldrovandinum . . . ab ipso domino Francisco'; half of 'tocius terre . . . et fundi Miliarii' and of S. Giovanni, Paiero, la Rotta and Quinta, the 'castrum Coparii' ('nomine potestarie et iurisdictionis') and four 'possessiones' there; of 'tocius terre Adriani . . . nomine capitaneatus eiusdem . . . meri et misti imperii . . . et portus Gauri et omnium possessionum terrarum . . . valium et boschium necnon aquarum padi et maris Mensularum' and of 'tocius ville Seravalis et eius fundi', with all lands and jurisdictions; a house at Corbola ('in qua habitat . . . custos Corbule superioris') 'nomine . . . potestarie ac jurisdictionis elligendi . . . potestatem in villa Papociarum' and the inn at Corbula 'nomine . . . tocius dicti policini Corbule'; eight 'possessiones' at Paviole and the inn and a 'possessio' at 'Guandiario' in lieu of all Francesco's property there; 'casamenta' and 'possessiones' at Villamana, 'Catinaria' and 'villa Ponticellorum' and half *pro indiviso* of 'dominii et proprietatis' of Villamana.

### 4. (*ASM, Leggi e Decreti, B III, fols. 232–3, 17 Dec. 1406*)

'Yaches' di Tommasino and Giovanni and Francesco di Francesco Pico della Mirandola announced 'Quod in adherentiam transivimus et adherentes facti sumus . . . domini Nicolai Marchionis Estensi et perinde obligantes nos et bona nostra presentes et futura per nos et heredes nostros promittimus eidem domino Marchioni quod nos . . . erimus deinceps perpetuo boni veri et fideles adherentes, amici et servitores ipsius domini Marchionis et ipsum pro vero et singulari domino nostro recognoscemus tenebimus et tractabimus . . . ac toto posse nostro in omnibus parebimus et obediemus omnibus mandatis eiusdem domini . . . Guerram pacem treuguam et sufferentiam cum omnibus et singulis . . . quandocumque et quotienscumque fieri voluerit ordinaverit et mandebit nobis ipse dominus Marchio faciemus . . . cum omnibus terris castris villis et subditis nostris, amicos suos pro amicis nostris et inimicos suos pro inimicis nostris habebimus . . . Et omnes et singulos gentes equestres et pedestres ipsius domini Marchionis ad omnem requisitionem . . . eiusdem domini intra terras nostras fortilitia et loca receptabimus et eis victualia prestabimus et prestari faciemus possibiliter pro precio condecenti et eas guerram facere cum inimicis ipsius domini et omnem predam in terras et territoria nostra eas gentes reducere permittemus. Et promittimus quod nunquam tractabimus nec aliquo modo palam vel occulte tractari quantum in nobis fuerit permittemus aliquid quod in preiuditium vergat aut vergere possit honoris et . . . status ipsius domini, quinimo honorem et statum eius manutenebimus et tuebimur toto posse. Ita tamen quod possimus et nobis . . . licitum sit quandocumque facta tamen prius conscientia dicto domino Marchioni nos et quemlibet nostrum aptare cum quocumque domino . . . comunitate et . . . persona tam ad stipendium quam ad provisionem et alio quocumque modo dummodo talis dominus comunitas et persona non sit inimicus sive inimica dicti domini Marchionis, Cum hoc quod cum quacumque persona simus non possimus equitare venire vel esse contra ipsum dominum Marchionem nec contra aliquem suum adherentem aut subditum cum personis vel brigatis nostris, cum hoc etiam quod teneamur potius servire dicto domino Marchioni quam alii cuicumque persone de mundo si nos voluerit. Et generaliter omnia alia . . . faciemus . . . que facere . . . debet quilibet bonus verus et legalis adherens amicus et servitor suo vero et singulari domino. Et versa vice Nos Nicolaus Marchio . . . acceptavimus in adherentiam nostram . . . spectabiles viros dominos Yaches militem et Johannem et Franciscum de la Mirandula et perinde obligantes nos et nostra bona presentes et futura per nos et heredes nostros promittimus . . . quod ipsos . . . deinceps perpetuo habebimus tractabimus et reputabimus pro bonis veris et fidelibus adherentibus amicis et servitoribus nostris Et ipsorum terras castra fortilitia territoria et loca et homines et subditos ipsorum ab omnibus ipsos offendere volentibus toto posse nostro et totis viribus defendemus Et in suis terris fortilitiis et dominio possibiliter manutenebimus . . . Et in omni liga confederatione et pace quam cum quacumque persona faciemus ipsos et eorum terras et subditos includemus Et etiam . . . promittimus quod deinceps singulo mense dabimus eis pro provisione de introitibus nostris cl ducatis auri Ac etiam eis promittimus quod deinceps ipsi et amici sui omnes de Mutina gaudere poterunt et gaudebunt omnibus illis officiis et honoribus ac suis honorantiis civitati et districtu Mutine quibus et quemadmodum gaudent alii nobiles et amici eorum dicte nostre civitatis Mutine.

5.

Before the division of the Abbey of Pomposa's property in 1491, a survey was prepared of revenues received by the abbey in the early 1480s.[1] This survey was divided into three parts: receipt and issue accounts for 1485–7, a 'compendio' of all revenue 'before the time of the war' (presumably 1482) and a 'figurato' (estimate) of the 'income of the abbey after the war' (the latter two compiled by the abbey's 'factor et governator', Alberto de' Fanti).

Receipts were divided into two broad groups: income from dues and rents and income from the sale of produce from the abbey's demesne farms (the 'castalderie'). The communes subject to the abbey (Codegoro, Lagosanto, Mezzogoro and Massenzatica) all owed certain tributary dues: Codegoro owed a 'colta' of L. 120 and the 'bracenti' (workers) there owed a quota of works ('per ogni casa opere sei'); at Mezzogoro and Massenzatica the communes were

---

[1] BEM, Documenti Campori, Appendice 1342 and see C. Morbio, *Storie dei municipi italiani*, vol. 1 (Milan, 1836), pp. 94–8.

'obligati ali donicati che accade per labba in quelli loci' ('liable to the corvées that arise there for the abbey'); Mezzogoro also owed L.7 'for the monks' vestments'. More important were the rents which these communes owed for *valli* (Codegoro owed L.200 for 'la valle di Trebba'), for inns, tithes and watercourses. The abbey also had a number of named lessees ('affictuarii'): 10 at Codegoro, 60 at Lagosanto, 19 at Comacchio, 13 at Mezzogoro, 21 at Baura and 31 at Valcesura-Ostellato. These included a number of prominent Ferrarese families: the Marocelli, Strozzi, Sacrati, Canali and Tempesta. The most important rental properties were the inns ('hostarie') and the abbey's property in Venice. The 'hostarie' yielded L.723 in 1485 (and more in 1486), the most profitable being that at Volano (yielding L.465 in 1485). Other 'hostarie' were at Goro and Vacolino. The profitability of such hostelries at the mouths of the Po reflects, of course, the continuing vitality of the Po river traffic. The abbey's houses in Venice yielded L.902. The abbey also had receipts from tithes at Codegoro, Garofalo and Vacolino, from fines (L.100), from wood-cutting (L.600) and from payments made by the Estensi.

The abbey had 'castalderie' at Codegoro, Lagosanto and Baura. That at Codegoro was by far the largest. These produced a variety of crops (mainly corn and wine, but also barley, maize, linseed, hay, 'legumi' and livestock). Sales of produce realised nearly L.400 in 1485, although the 'compendio' put such receipts at a much higher level (L.1,800).

Total revenue in 1485 was L.3,921, in 1486 L.5,523 and in 1487 L.5,486. The 'compendio' arrived at a total of L.5,534. But the 'figurato' revealed the dilapidated state of much of this property: woodland had been burned during the war, there was a lack of oxen on the estates, the 'hosteria' at Vacolino 'saffitta hora pocho', the houses in Venice required expenditure and the revenues had been appropriated by the Venetian government, reclamation work was needed at Codegoro and possessions throughout the *isola* and outside it had been usurped 'per modo che li sera molto da sbatere'.

# BIBLIOGRAPHY

## A: MANUSCRIPT SOURCES

I: BOLOGNA, BIBLIOTECA COMUNALE DELL'ARCHIGINNASIO
**Archivio Gozzadini,** buste 41, 109.

II: FERRARA, ARCHIVIO COMUNALE
**Deliberazioni,** Libri A-F.

III: FERRARA, ARCHIVIO DI STATO
**Archivio Tassoni,** buste III–VIII
**Archivio notarile di Ferrara, protocolli** of F. Santi, L. Villa, N. Sansilvestri,
J. Pavesi, R. Jacobelli, S. Todeschi, P. Sardi, D. Dulcini, U. Rossetti.

IV: FERRARA, BIBLIOTECA COMUNALE ARIOSTEA
**Collezione Antonelli,** busta 966
**Cl. I,** 126 (Statuta Rhodigii)

V: LONDON, BRITISH LIBRARY
MS 25595, Statuta daciorum et gabellarum comunis Argente

VI: MODENA, ARCHIVIO DI STATO
**Archivi privati,** Archivio d'Espagnac, buste 2, 18, 19, 25, 40.
**Camera Ducale,**
Amministrazione finanziaria dei paesi, Ferrara e Ferrarese: Casaglia, Migliaro,
Camarlengheria di Este.
Cancelleria, Pomposa Chiesa e Monastero, buste 3, 8.
Catastri delle Investiture, registri A, B, H, I, K-S, U, V, X, Y, BC and
Appendice (Strumenti d'acquisti di terreni a Belriguardo).
Feudi Usi Affitti Livelli:
   22: Usi ed affitti, 1414
   23: Feudi, usi e livelli, 1430
   117: Investiture di livelli dell'Abbazia di Marola
   151: Investiture di terre in Padova, Rovigo ecc.
   152: Liber feudorum, 1410
Investiture di Feudi, buste 7–14
Mandati, registro i, 1422–4

# Bibliography

Notai camerali ferraresi,
 I A–B, N. Abbatia; III, P. Arquada; VII, M. Benintendi; VIII A–B, N. Bonazoli;
 IX, P. Bononia; XI, N. Camarlenghi; XIV, L. Casella; XV, A. Cavaleria; XVI, Z.
 Coadi; XVII A–C, R. Codegorio; XVIII, J. Gualengo; XIX, M. Conte; XX, A.
 Cordoani; XXII, N. Delaito; XXIII, J. Delaito; XXIV A–D, D. Dulcini; XXV, F.
 d'Este; XXVI, P. Fabro; XXX, A. Florano; XXXIII A, C. Lardi; XXXIV, P. Lardi;
 XXXV, F. Libanori; XL, F. Maroni; XLII, A. Villa; XLIII, B. Mella; XLIV, J.
 Mizino; XLV, A. Montani; XLVII, B. Nigrisoli; XLVIII, J. Pavesi; XLIX, J.
 Pelizari; LIV, F. Sale; LV, J. Sanvitale; LVI A–F, P. Sardi; LIX A–B, F. Taiapetri;
 LXIII Diversorum Instrumenta.

**Cancelleria**
Ambasciatori, Venezia, I.
Carteggio di Referendari ecc, busta I.
Gride Manoscritte
Leggi e Decreti (Registra epistolarum decretorumque), serie A, registri I–6; serie
 B, registri I–VII.
Rettori dello Stato
 Ferrara: buste 6 (Ferrara), 12 (Adriano), 32 (Codigoro), 41 (Crespino), 56
 (Porto).
 Modena and Reggio: Albinea, Bismantova busta 3, Campogalliano, Gom-
 bola, Guiglia, San Martino in Rio busta I, Vallisniera, Vignola busta IA.
Statuti Capitoli Grazie, busta I.
**Documenti riguardanti la Casa e lo Stato**, cassette 8–24 and buste 324, 511
 (Controversie di Stato).
**Giurisdizione sovrana,** Vescovado di Ferrara, no. 250.
**Manoscritti della biblioteca:**
133: P. Prisciani, Historiae Ferrariae liber ix.
136: P. Prisciani, Collectanea.


VII: MODENA, BIBLIOTECA ESTENSE
**Documenti Campori**
591: Vita del Cavalier Feltrino Boiardo
Appendice 1251, 1261 (Roberti), 1313–16 (Estensi), 1321–5 (Ferrara), 1342
 (Introitus tocius Abbacie Pomposie ante divisionem), 1383–7 (Modena).
**Manoscritti italiani**
265: Mario Equicola, Genealogia de'signori da Este
**Manoscritti latini**
2: Aristoteles, Oeconomicorum (with attached letters)
651: Statuta Sancti Martini
1271: Possessiones dominorum Azonis et Franceschini Estensium
1272: Liber possessionum domini Leonelli in districtu paduani.


VIII: VATICAN, ARCHIVIO SEGRETO VATICANO
A.A. Arm. i–xviii, 4796, 4799.
Arm, xlvi–xlviii.

# Bibliography

Registri Laterani, 141, 146, 168, 175.
Registri Vaticani, 253–4, 256, 365, 385, 394, 410.

IX: VATICAN, ARCHIVIO VATICANO
**Archivio Boncompagni**, Prot. 587, 599, 713, 714.

X: VENICE, ARCHIVIO DI STATO
**Avogaria del Comun,** Raspe 3643
**Dieci**, Misto, reg. 22
**Procuratori di San Marco,** Commissarie miste, 98A (Verde della Scala).
**Provveditori sopra camere**
A I, 2: Catastico dei beni feudi e livelli di Obizzo II nel Padovano
A I, 18: Statuti del Polesine (1440)
A I, 19: Privilegi feudi e livelli del vescovado di Adria
**Senato**, Miste, registri 30, 32, 35.
**Senato**, Secreta, registri, 2–4, 10.

## B: PRINTED PRIMARY SOURCES

*Annales Forolivienses, RIS²*, vol. 22, pt. 2.
*Gli atti cancellereschi viscontei*, ed. G. Vittani, Inventari e regesti dell'Archivio di Stato in Milano, vol. 2, Milan, 1929
Baldus de Ubaldis, *Opus aureum . . . super feudis cum additionibus doctissimi domini Andree barbacia necnon aliorum clarissimorum dominorum*, Venice, 1500.
Benvenuti de Rambaldis de Imola, *Comentum super Dantis Aldigherii Comoediam*, ed. J. P. Lacaita, 5 vols., Florence, 1887.
Bratti, I. 'Cronaca della Mirandola', *Memorie storiche della Mirandola*, vol. 1 (1872).
Caleffini, U. 'Cronaca in Rime', ed. A. Capelli, *AMMo*, s. 1, 2 (1865).
*Diario di Ugo Caleffini 1471–94*, ed. G. Pardi, Monumenti della Deputazione ferrarese di Storia Patria, 1–3 (1938–40).
da Campo, L. 'Viaggio a Gerusalemme di Nicolo da Este', in G. Ghinassi (ed.), *Collezione di opere inedite e rare dei primi tre secoli della lingua*, Turin, 1861.
*I capitoli del comune di Firenze*, ed. C. Guasti, 2 vols., Florence, 1866–93.
di Chinazzo, Daniele, *Cronica de la guerra da veniciani a zenovesi*, ed. V. Lazzarini, Deputazione di Storia Patria per le Venezie, Monumenti storici, n. s., 11 (1958).
*Chronica parva ferrariensis, RIS*, 8.
*Chronicon Estense, RIS*, 15.
*Commento alla Divina Commedia d'anonimo fiorentino del secolo XIV*, 3 vols., ed. P. Fanfani, Bologna 1866–74.
*Commissioni di Rinaldo degli Albizzi per il comune di Firenze dal 1399 al 1433*, 3 vols., ed. C. Guasti, Florence, 1867–73.
*Corpus Chronicorum Bononiensium, RIS²*, vol. 18, pt. 1.
Corrain, C. 'Alcuni registri di terratici ed affitti del Monastero della Vangadizza', *Atti e Memorie del Sodalizio vangadiciense*, 1 (1972–3), Badia Polesine, 1975.

# Bibliography

de Delayto, Jacobus, *Annales Estenses, RIS*, vol. 18.

*Le deliberazioni del consiglio dei XL della repubblica di Venezia*, ed. A. Lombardo, Deputazione di Storia Patria per le Venezie, Monumenti storici, n.s., 12 (1958), 20 (1967).

'De Rebus Estensium', ed. C. Antolini, *AMF*, 12 (1900).

'Diario di Palla di Nofri Strozzi', *ASI*, s. 4, 12–14 (1883–4).

*Diario ferrarese dall'anno 1419 sino al 1502 di autori incerti, RIS²*, vol. 24, pt. 7.

*Dispacci di Pietro Cornaro, ambasciatore a Milano durante la guerra di Chioggia*, ed. V. Lazzarini, Deputazione veneta di Storia Patria, Monumenti storici, s. 1, Documenti, 20 (1939).

*Documenti per la storia delle relazioni diplomatiche fra Verona e Mantova nel sec. XIII*, ed. C. Cipolla, Milan 1901.

B. Fontana, 'Documenti Vaticani di un plebiscito in Ferrara sul principio del sec. xiv', *AMF*, 1 (1886).

G. and B. Gatari, *Cronaca Carrarese, RIS²*, vol. 17 pt. 1.

Gloria, A. *Monumenti della Università di Padova*, Padua, 1888.

Griffoni, M. *Memoriale historicum de rebus bononiensium, RIS²*, vol. 18, pt 2.

Guaitoli, P. *Bibliografia storica carpigiana*, Carpi 1882.

'Hugolini Summa super usibus feudorum', ed. J. B. Palmieri, *Bibliotheca iuridica medii aevi*, vol. 2, Bologna 1892.

Lehmann, K. *Das Langobardische Lehnrecht*, Göttingen, 1896.

*Lettres secrètes et curiales du Pape Urbain V (1362–70) se rapportant à la France*, ed. P. Lecacheux & G. Mollat, *Bibliothèque des Ecoles françaises d'Athènes et de Rome*, s. 3. 1955.

*Libri Feudorum*, see Lehmann, K.

*Lucca Regesti dell'Archivio di Stato*, vol. 3, ed. L. Fumi & E. Lazzareschi, Lucca, 1925–33.

Lünig, J. C. *Codex Italiae Diplomaticus*, 4 vols., Frankfurt & Leipzig, 1725–35.

Marri, G. C. *I documenti commerciali del fondo diplomatico mediceo nell'Archivio di Stato di Firenze*, Biblioteca dell'Archivio Storico Italiano, 3 (1951).

Mattiolo, P. 'Cronaca bolognese', ed. C. Ricci, in *Scelta di curiosità letterarie inedite e rare*, Bologna 1885.

Minotto, A. S. *Documenta ad Ferrariam, Rhodigium, Policinium ac Marchiones Estenses spectantia*, 2 vols., Venice 1873–4.

Muratori, L. A. *Antiquitates Italicae Medii Aevi*, 6 vols., Milan, 1738–42.

Mussato, A. *Sette libri inediti del 'De Gestis Italicorum post Henricum VII' di Albertino Mussato*, ed. L. Padrin, Venice, 1903.

*Orlandini Rodulphini bononiensis doctoris in utroque iure consumatissimi in artem notariae ordinatissime summule*, Venice, 1565.

Pastorello, E. *Il copialettere marciano della cancelleria carrarese 1402–3*, Venice, Deputazione veneta di storia patria, Monumenti storici, Documenti, s. 1, 19 (1915).

Pendaglia, B. *Quattro canti . . . ne' quali si contiene brevemente la genealogia di tutti gli huomini e honorati della nobil casata sua*, Ferrara, 1563.

Piccolomini, Aeneas Sylvius, *De viris illustribus*, Stuttgart, 1842.

# Bibliography

Del Piazzo, M. 'Il carteggio 'Medici-Este' dal sec. xv al 1531', *Quaderni della Rassegna degli Archivi di Stato*, 34 (1964).

Predelli, R. *I Libri Commemoriali della Repubblica Veneta*, Venice, Deputazione veneta di storia patria, 1876–1901.

Della Pugliola, B. *Historia miscella bononiensis*, *RIS*, 18.

Rangoni Machiavelli, L. *Liber memorialis familiae Rangoniae*, Città di Castello, 1913.

*Regesta Imperii XI. Die Urkunden Kaiser Sigmunds (1410–1437)*, Innsbruck, 1897–1900.

*Regesto della Chiesa di Ravenna*, ed. V. Federici and G. Buzzi, Rome, Regesta Chartarum Italiae, 7 (1911) and 15 (1931).

*I Registri Viscontei*, ed. C. Manaresi, Milan, 1915.

Rucellai, G. *Il Zibaldone Quaresimale*, ed. A. Perosa, London, 1960.

Riccobaldo, see *Chronica parva ferrariensis*.

Sanudo, M. *Vite de' Duche di Venezia*, *RIS*, 22:

Sercambi, G. *Cronache*, ed. S. Bongi, Fonti per la storia d'Italia, Rome, 1892.

*Statuta civitatis Ferrariae*, Ferrara 1476.

*Statuta civitatis Mutine*, ed. C. Campori, Parma, Deputazione di storia patria per le provincie modenesi, Monumenti, Statuti, 1 (1864).

*Statuta Ferrariae anno MCCLXXXVII*, ed. W. Montorsi, Ferrara, 1955.

'Statuta Pomposiae annis MCCXC et MCCCXXXVIII–LXXXIII', ed. A. Samaritani, *AMF*, Monumenti, 4 (1958).

'Statuti di Massafiscaglia', ed. P. Antolini, *AMF*, 5 (1893).

*Gli statuti veronesi del 1276*, ed. G. Sandri, Venice, Deputazione di storia patria per le Venezie, Monumenti storici, n.s., 3 (1940).

Stella, A. 'Testi volgari ferraresi del secondo trecento', *Studi di filologia italiana*, 26 (1968).

Tacoli, N. *Memorie istoriche della città di Reggio*, 3 vols., Reggio, Parma and Carpi, 1742–9.

Tarlazzi, A. *Appendice ai Monumenti Ravennati de' secoli di mezzo del conte M. Fantuzzi*, Ravenna, 1872–4.

Theiner, A. *Codex diplomaticus Dominii temporalis Sanctae Sedis*, 3 vols., Rome, 1861–2.

*Viazo al Sancto Sepolcro per lo marchese Nicolo da Este* and *Viaggio di S. Antonio de Viene in Franza*, appendices to *Fr. Johannis Ferrariensis ex annalium libris Marchionum Estensium Excerpta*, *RIS*², 20 pt. 2.

## C: PRINTED SECONDARY SOURCES

Ady, C. M. *The Bentivoglio of Bologna: A Study in Despotism*, Oxford 1937.

Affarosi, C. *Memorie istoriche del monastero di S. Prospero di Reggio*, 3 vols., Padua, 1733–46.

Affo, I. *Istoria della città e ducato di Guastalla*, 4 vols., Guastalla, 1785–7.

Alessi, I. *Ricerche istorico-critiche delle antichità di Este*, vol. 1, Padua, 1776.

Allmand, C. T. *Lancastrian Normandy, 1415–50*, Oxford, 1983.

# Bibliography

Ammirato, S. *Delle famiglie nobili fiorentine*, Florence, 1615.

Anselmi, S. 'Organizzazione aziendale, colture, rese nelle fattorie malatestiane, 1398–1456', *QS*, 39 (1978).

Antolini, C. 'Una questione cronologica: la morte di Guglielmo Marchesella', *AMF*, 9 (1897).

Antonelli, M. 'Di alcune infeodazioni nell'Umbria nella seconda metà del secolo XIV', *BU*, 13 (1907).

*L'Appennino modenese*, ed. V. Santi and D. Pantanelli, Rocca S. Casciano, 1895.

d'Arco, C. *Studi intorno al municipio di Mantova*, 7 vols., Mantua 1871–4.

Arnaldi, G. 'Il feudalesimo e le "uniformità" nella storia', *SM*, s. 3, 4 (1963).

Arnold, B. *German Knighthood 1050–1300*, Oxford, 1985.

Aston, M. '"Caim's Castles": poverty, politics and disendowment', in *The Church, Politics and Patronage in the Fifteenth Century*, ed. B. Dobson, Gloucester, 1984.

Atti, G. *Sunto storico della città di Cento*, Cento, 1853.

Badini, G. 'Le carte dei Canossa nell'Archivio di Stato di Reggio', in *Quattro Castella nella Storia di Canossa. Atti del Convegno di Studi Matildici*, Rome 1977.

Balboni, D. 'Le fonti storiche di Pomposa', *AMF*, n.s., 29 (1964).

Baldoni, U. *Podestà e vicari nella cronaca di Finale nell'Emilia*, Bologna, 1927.

Balletti, A. *Storia di Reggio nell'Emilia*, Reggio 1925.

Bandi, D. *Memorie storico-cronologiche di Argenta*, Argenta 1868.

Barni, G. 'La formazione interna dello stato visconteo', *ASL*, n.s., 6 (1941).

Barotti, L. *Serie dei vescovi e arcivescovi di Ferrara*, Ferrara, 1781.

Basini, G. L. *L'uomo e il pane: risorse, consumi e carenze alimentari della popolazione modenese nel cinque e seicento*, Milan, 1970.

Battistella, A. *Il conte Carmagnola*, Genoa, 1889.

Bean, J. M. W. *The Decline of English Feudalism*, Manchester, 1968.

Bellini, L. 'La legislazione speciale delle valli di Comacchio nella sua genesi storica, nelle fonti e nell'applicazione', *AMF*, s.3, 1 (1965).

'Sul territorio della diocesi di Comacchio', *AMF*, n.s., 8 (1953).

Bellini, V. *Delle monete di Ferrara*, Ferrara, 1761.

Berengo, M. 'Patriziato e nobiltà: il caso veronese', *RSI*, 87 (1975).

Bertelli, S. *Il potere oligarchico nello stato-città medievale*, Florence, 1978.

Bertoldi, F. L. *Memorie storiche d'Argenta*, 3 vols., Ferrara, 1787–1821.

Bertoni, G. *La biblioteca estense e la cultura ferrarese ai tempi del duca Ercole I (1471–1505)*, Turin, 1903.

*Guarino da Verona fra letterati e cortigiani a Ferrara 1429–60*, Geneva, 1921.

Bizzocchi, R. 'La dissoluzione di un clan familiare: i Buondelmonti di Firenze nei secoli XV e XVI', *ASI*, 140 (1982).

'Chiesa e aristocrazia nella Firenze del Quattrocento', *ASI*, 142 (1984).

Bocchi, F. A. 'Dei dominatori di Adria veneta', *AV*, 20 (1880).

*Della sede episcopale di Adria veneta*, Adria, 1858.

Il patrimonio bentivolesco alla metà del quattrocento, Bologna, 1970.

'Patti e rappresaglie fra Bologna e Ferrara dal 1193 al 1255', *AMRo*, n.s., 23 (1972).

# Bibliography

*Uomini e terra nei borghi ferraresi: il catastro parcellare del 1494*, Ferrara, 1976.

Bock, F. 'Der Este-Prozess von 1321', *Archivum fratrum praedicatorum*, 7 (1937).

Bognetti, G. 'Per la storia dello stato visconteo', *ASL*, 54 (1927).

Bonoli, G. *Storia di Cotignola*, Ravenna, 1734–1880.

Bonoli, P. G. *Storia di Lugo*, Faenza, 1732.

Bordone, R. 'Lo sviluppo delle relazioni personali nell'aristocrazia rurale del regno italico', in *Structures féodales* (see below).

'Tema cittadino e "ritorno alla terra" nella storiografia comunale recente', *QS*, 52 (1983).

Borgogno, A. 'Prime indagini sulla cancelleria mantovana al tempo della signoria', *Ricerche medievali*, 1 (1966).

Borsari, L. *Il contratto d'enfiteusi*, Ferrara, 1850.

*Collezione di leggi e ordinamenti per servire all'opera 'Il contratto d'enfiteusi'*, Ferrara, 1854.

Boutruche, R. *Seigneurie et féodalité*, 2 vols., Paris, 1959–70.

Bowsky, W. M. 'City and contado: military relationships and communal bonds in fourteenth-century Siena', in *Renaissance Studies in Honor of Hans Baron*, Florence, 1970.

Branchi, E. *Storia della Lunigiana feudale*, 3 vols., Pistoia, 1898.

Brancoli Busdraghi, P. 'La formazione storica del feudo lombardo come diritto reale', *Quaderni di 'Studi senesi'*, 11 (1965).

Di Broilo, F. 'I podestà di Ferrara', *Rivista del Colleggio Araldico* (1906).

Brown, E. 'The tyranny of a construct: feudalism and historians of medieval Europe', *AHR*, 79 (1974).

Brown, R. G. 'The Politics of Magnificence in Ferrara, 1450–1505', Ph. D. thesis, University of Edinburgh, 1982.

Brucker, G. *The Civic World of Early Renaissance Florence*, Princeton, 1977.

Brunetti, M. 'Nuovi documenti viscontei tratti dall'Archivio di Stato di Venezia: figli e nipoti di Bernabo Visconti', *ASL*, s. 4, 11 (1909).

Bucciardi, G. *Fiorano nelle vicende storiche*, Modena, 1934.

Bueno de Mesquita, D. M. 'Ludovico Sforza and his vassals', in *Italian Renaissance Studies*, ed. E. F. Jacob, London, 1960.

Busmanti, S. *Pomposa*, Imola, 1881.

Cahen, C. *Le régime féodal de l'Italie normande*, Paris, 1940.

Calura, M. 'Torri pubbliche e gentilizie medioevali nella città di Ferrara', *AMF*, 2 (1944).

Cammarosano, P. 'Aspetti delle strutture familiari nelle città dell'Italia comunale (secoli XII–XIV)', *SM*, 16 (1975).

Campi, G. 'Cenni storici intorno l'Archivio Segreto Estense ora Diplomatico', *AMMo*, 2 (1864).

Campori, C. 'Cesare Montecuccoli', *AMMo*, 5 (1870).

*Notizie storiche del Frignano*, Modena, 1886.

Capasso, C. 'I "provvisionati" di Bernabo Visconti', *ASL*, s. 4, 15 (1911).

Capelli, A. 'Niccolo di Lionello d'Este', *AMMo*, 5 (1868).

Cardini, F. 'Una signoria cittadina "minore" in Toscana: i Casali di Cortona', *ASI*, 131 (1973).

# Bibliography

Carpenter, C. 'The Beauchamp affinity: a study of bastard feudalism at work', *EHR*, 95 (1980).

Carreri, F. C. 'Del feudo onorifico rispetto alla nobiltà', *RA*, 11 (1913).

Castagnetti, A. 'Enti ecclesiastici, Canossa, Estensi, famiglie signorili e vassalatiche a Verona e Ferrara', in *Structures féodales* (see below).

'La famiglia veronese degli Avvocati (secoli XI–XIII)', in *Studi sul medioevo cristiano offerti a R. Morghen*, Rome, 1974.

'Le due famiglie comitali veronesi: i San Bonifacio e i Gandolfingi-di Palazzo', *Passatopresente*, 1 (1981).

*L'organizzazione del territorio rurale nel medioevo*, Turin, 1979.

*Società e politica a Ferrara dall'età postcarolingia alla signoria estense*, Bologna 1985.

Castignoli, C. 'Il comune di Piacenza nel 1300: organi comunitativi e signorili', in *Studi storici in onore di E. Nasalli Rocca*, Piacenza, 1971.

Cazelles, R. *Société politique, noblesse et couronne sous Jean le Bon et Charles V*, Paris, 1982.

Cerlini, A. 'Un assedio a Canossa nel secolo XV', *Studi storici*, 14 (1905).

Cessi, B. 'Un trattato fra Carraresi ed Estensi (1354)', *NAV*, 7 (1904).

*Venezia, Padova e il Polesine di Rovigo*, Città di Castello, 1904.

Cessi, R. *La Repubblica di Venezia e il problema adriatico*, Naples, 1953.

Chenon, E. *Etude sur l'histoire des alleux en France*, Paris, 1888.

Cherubini, G. 'Aspetti della proprietà fondiaria nell'aretino durante il XIII sec', *ASI*, 121 (1963).

*Una comunità dell'Appennino dal XIII al XV sec. Montecoronaro dalla signoria dell'abbazia del Trivio al dominio di Firenze*, Florence, 1972.

'La signoria degli Ubertini sui comuni rurali casentinesi di Chitignano, Rosina e Taena all'inizio del Quattrocento', *ASI*, 126 (1968) and in his *Signori, contadini, borghesi*, Florence, 1974.

Chiappini, L. *Gli Estensi*, Varese, 1967.

Chittolini, G. 'I beni terrieri del capitolo della cattedrale di Cremona fra il XIII e il XIV sec.', *NRS*, 49 (1965).

'Città e contado nella tarda età comunale', *NRS*, 53 (1969).

'La crisi delle libertà comunali e le origini dello stato territoriale', *RSI*, 82 (1970) and in *La formazione*.

*La formazione dello stato regionale e le istituzioni del contado*, Turin, 1979.

'Infeudazioni e politica feudale nel ducato visconteo-sforzesco', *QS*, 19 (1972) and in *La formazione*.

'Il particolarismo signorile e feudale in Emilia fra Quattro e Cinquecento', in *Il Rinascimento nelle corti padane: società e cultura*, ed. P. Rossi et al., Bari, 1977, and in *La formazione*.

'Ricerche sull'ordinamento territoriale del dominio fiorentino agli inizi del secolo XV', in *La formazione*.

'La signoria degli Anguissola su Riva, Grazzano e Montesanto fra Tre e Quattrocento', *NRS*, 78 (1974) and in *La formazione*.

'Le "terre separate" nel ducato di Milano in età sforzesca', in *Milano nell'età di Ludovico il Moro*, Milan, 1983.

Ciaccio, L. 'Il Cardinale legato Bertrando del Poggetto in Bologna (1327–1334)', *AMRo*, s. 3, 23 (1904–5).

# Bibliography

Cionini, N. *I podestà di Sassuolo*, Pisa 1879–81.

Cipolla, C. M. 'Une crise ignorée. Comment s'est perdue la propriété ecclésiastique dans l'Italie du nord entre le XIe et le XVe siècle', *Annales E.S.C.*, 2 (1947).
'Per la storia della crisi del sistema curtense in Italia. Lo sfaldamento del manso nell'Appennino bobbiese', *BISI*, 62 (1950).

Cittadella, L. N. *Notizie amministrative, storiche ed artistiche di Ferrara*, Ferrara, 1868.

Collodo, S. 'Per la storia della signoria carrarese: lo sfruttamento dei benefici canonicali di Padova nel XIV secolo', *Passatopresente*, 1 (1981).

Coniglio, G. *Mantova. La storia*, vol. 1, *Dalle origini a Gianfrancesco primo marchese*, Mantua, 1958.

Contamine, P. 'Points de vue sur la chevalerie en France à la fin du moyen âge', *Francia*, 4 (1976).

Conti, M. N. 'Sulle tracce del diritto consuetudinario in Val di Magra', *ASPP*, s. 4, 23 (1971).

Cordani, E. 'La famiglia dei da Mandello di Caorso (secc. XIII–XV)', Tesi di Laurea, Università di Milano, 1978–9.

Corni, G. *Il castello di Monfestino e il suo territorio*, Modena, 1950.

Corrain, C. 'Alcuni registri di terratici ed affitti del Monastero della Vangadizza', *Atti e Memorie del Sodalizio Vangadiciense*, 1 (1972–3).

Costa Giana, P. *Memorie storiche di San Felice sul Panaro*, Modena, 1890.

Cottafavi, C. *San Martino in Rio. Ricerche storiche dal 1050 al 1859*, Reggio, 1885.

Crespellani, A. *Memorie storiche vignolesi*, Modena, 1872.
*Compendio storico di Savignano*, Modena, 1873.

Cristiani, E. *Nobiltà e popolo nel comune di Pisa. Dalle origini del podestariato alla signoria dei Donoratico*, Naples, 1962.

Curis, G. 'Feudo', in *Nuovo Digesto Italiano*, ed. M. d'Amelio, vol. 5, Turin, 1938.

Dean, T. 'Lords, vassals and clients in Renaissance Ferrara', *EHR*, 100 (1985).
'Venetian economic hegemony: the case of Ferrara, 1200–1500', *Studi Veneziani*, forthcoming.

Dillay, L. 'Le service annuel en deniers des fiefs de la région angevine', *Mélanges P. Fournier*, Paris, 1929.

Dondi Orologio, F. S. *Dissertazioni sopra l'istoria ecclesiastica di Padova*, 9 vols., Padua, 1802–17.

Duby, G. *La société aux XIe et XIIe siècles dans la région mâconnaise*, Paris, 1953.

Dumas, A. 'Encore la question: "Fidèles ou vassaux?"', *NRHD*, 44 (1920).

Dunham, W. H. *Lord Hastings' Indentured Retainers, 1461–83*, New Haven, 1955.
Review of Lyon, *From Fief to Indenture*, *Speculum*, 33 (1958).

Durazzo, G. *Dei rettori veneziani in Rovigo*, Venice, 1865.

Ercole, F. 'La lotta delle classi alla fine del medio evo', *Dal Comune al Principato*, Florence, 1929.
'Comuni e signori nel Veneto', *NAV*, 19 (1910) and in *Dal Comune al Principato*.

Evergates, T. *Feudal Society in the Bailliage of Troyes under the Counts of Champagne, 1152–1284*, Baltimore, 1975.

# Bibliography

Fanfani, A. 'Le prime difficoltà finanziarie di Giovanni Maria Visconti', *RSI*, s. 5, 4 (1939).

Fasano Guarini, E. 'Gli stati dell'Italia centro-settentrionale tra quattro e cinquecento: continuità e trasformazioni', *Società e Storia*, 21 (1983).

Fasoli, G. 'Città e feudalità', in *Structures féodales*, below.

'Feudo e castello', in *Storia d'Italia Einaudi*, vol. 5, Turin, 1973.

'Lineamenti di politica e di legislazione feudale veneziana in terraferma', *RSDI*, 25 (1952).

'Lineamenti di una storia della cavalleria', in *Studi di storia medievale e moderna in onore di E. Rota*, Rome 1958.

'Ricerche sulla legislazione anti-magnatizia nei comuni dell'alta e media Italia', *RSDI*, 12 (1939).

'Signoria feudale ed autonomie locali', in *Studi Ezzeliniani*, Rome 1963.

Ferraresi, G. *Il beato Giovanni Tavelli da Tossignano e la riforma di Ferrara nel Quattrocento*, vol. 1, Brescia, 1969.

*Storia di Bondeno raccolta di documenti*, Rovigo, 1963.

Ferrer i Mallal, M. T. 'Mercenaris catalans a Ferrara (1307–17)', *Anuario de estudios medievales*, 2 (1965).

Ferretti, A. *Canossa studi e ricerche*, 2nd edn., Turin, 1884.

Fichtenau, H. *The Carolingian Empire*, Oxford, 1957.

Filippini, F. *Il Cardinale Egidio Albornoz*, Bologna, 1933.

Finzi, R. *Accordi e contese fra Correggio e San Martino in Rio nella storia*, Correggio, 1935.

Fiumi, E. 'Fioritura e decadenza dell'economia fiorentina', *ASI*, 115–7 (1957–9).

*Storia economica e sociale di San Gimignano*, Florence, 1961.

Forti, F. 'Bologna e Ferrara nel 1465 in un dialogo di Ludovico Carbone', *AMRo*, n.s., 22 (1971).

Fourquin, G. *Seigneurie et féodalité au moyen âge*, Paris, 1970.

Franceschini, A. *I frammenti epigrafici degli statuti di Ferrara del 1173*, Ferrara, 1969.

'Nuovi frammenti epigrafici degli statuti di Ferrara del 1173', *AMF*, s. 3, 11 (1972).

'Curie episcopali ferraresi nella traspadana (sec. x–xiv): Trecenta', *Ravennatensia*, 5 (1976).

Franchini, L. *Simboli, emblemi, imprese nel castello di Vignola*, Vignola, 1977.

Frassoni, C. *Memorie di Finale*, Modena, 1778.

Frizzi, A. *Memorie storiche della famiglia Ariosti di Ferrara*, Ferrara, 1779.

*Memorie storiche della nobile famiglia Bevilacqua*, Parma, 1779.

*Memorie per la storia di Ferrara*, 2nd edn., 5 vols., Ferrara, 1847–50.

Galli, G. 'La dominazione viscontea a Verona, 1387–1404', *ASL*, 54 (1927).

Gallo, R. 'Una famiglia patrizia, i Pisani ed i palazzi di S. Stefano e di Stra', *AV*, s. 5, 24–5 (1944).

Ganshof, F. L. *The Carolingians and the Frankish Monarchy*, London, 1971.

*Feudalism*, 3rd edn., London, 1964.

Gardner, E. G. *Dukes and Poets in Ferrara*, London, 1904.

Gaudenzi, A. 'Il testamento di Azzo VIII d'Este e la pace del 1326 tra Modena e Bologna', in *Miscellanea Tassoniana*, Bologna, 1908.

Ghetti, B. *I patti tra Venezia e Ferrara dal 1191 al 1313*, Rome, 1907.

# Bibliography

Ghidoni, E. 'Agricoltura nel xv secolo: le castalderie estensi' *AMMo*, s. 11, 4 (1982).

Gibbon, E. *Antiquities of the House of Brunswick*, London, 1814.

Giordanengo, G. 'Vocabulaire et formulaires féodaux en Provence et en Dauphiné (xiie–xiiie siècles)' in *Structures féodales*, below.

Given-Wilson, C. *The Royal Household and the King's Affinity: Service, Politics and Finance in England, 1360–1413*, New Haven and London, 1986.

Le Goff, J. 'Le rituel symbolique de la vassalité', *Pour un autre moyen âge*, Paris, 1977.

Gorreta, A. *La lotta fra il comune bolognese e la signoria estense (1293–1303)*, Bologna, 1906.

Gothein, P. 'Zaccaria Trevisan', *AV*, s. 5, 21 (1937).

Gozzadini, G. *Delle torri gentilizie di Bologna*, Bologna, 1875.

*Nanne Gozzadini e Baldassare Cossa poi Giovanni XXIII*, Bologna, 1880.

Grant, A. 'The development of the Scottish peerage', *Scottish Historical Review*, 57 (1978).

'Extinction of direct male lines among the Scottish noble families in the fourteenth and fifteenth centuries', in *Essays on the Nobility of Medieval Scotland*, ed. K. J. Stringer, Edinburgh, 1985.

'The Higher Nobility in Scotland and their Estates, 1371–1424', Oxford D.Phil thesis, 1975.

Green, J. 'William Rufus, Henry I and the royal demesne', *History*, 64 (1979).

Grimaldi, N. 'Di alcuni feudatari reggiani del secolo xiv', in *Studi in onore di N. Campanini*, Reggio, 1921.

*La signoria di Barnabo Visconti e di Regina della Scala in Reggio (1371–1385)*, Reggio, 1921.

Guidoni, E. 'Residenza, casa e proprietà nei patti tra feudalità e comuni (Italia sec xii–xiii)', in *Structures féodales*, below.

Gundersheimer, W. *Ferrara: the Style of a Renaissance Despotism*, Princeton, 1973.

Gurrieri, G. 'Notizie e problemi della storia economica di Pomposa nei sec x–xiv', *AMF*, n.s., 29 (1964).

Heers, J. *Le clan familial au Moyen Age*, Paris, 1974.

Herlihy, D. *The History of Feudalism*, New York, 1970.

Housley, N. *The Italian Crusades*, Oxford, 1982.

Hyde, J. K. *Padua in the Age of Dante*, Manchester, 1966.

'Lendinara, Vangadizza e le relazioni fra gli Estensi e il comune di Padova', *Bollettino del Museo Civico di Padova*, 52 (1963).

James, M. E. 'The first earl of Cumberland (1493–1542) and the decline of northern feudalism', *Northern History*, 1 (1966).

Jones, P. J. 'Communes and despots: the city-state in late medieval Italy', *TRHS*, 15 (1965).

'Economia e società nell'Italia medievale: il mito della borghesia', *Economia e società nell'Italia medievale*, Turin, 1980.

'From manor to mezzadria: a Tuscan case-study in the medieval origins of modern agrarian society', in *Florentine Studies*, ed. N. Rubinstein, London, 1968.

'An Italian estate, 900–1200', *EcHR*, s. 2, 7, (1954–5).

# Bibliography

'Italy', in *Cambridge Economic History of Europe*, vol. 1, 2nd edn., Cambridge, 1966.

*The Malatesta of Rimini and the Papal State*, Cambridge, 1974.

'La storia economica', in *Storia d'Italia Einaudi*, vol. 2, Turin, 1974.

Keen, M. 'Brotherhood in arms', *History*, 47 (1962).

*Chivalry*, New Haven and London, 1984.

Kent, F. W. '"Più superba de quella de Lorenzo": Courtly and family interest in the building of Filippo Strozzi's palace', *Renaissance Quarterly*, 30 (1977).

Kohl, B. G. 'Government and society in Renaissance Padua', *JMRS*, 12 (1972).

Lane, F. C. *Venice – A Maritime Republic*, Baltimore, 1973.

Larner, J. *Italy in the Age of Dante and Petrarch 1216–1380*, London, 1980.

*The Lords of Romagna: Romagnol Society and the Origins of the Signorie*, London, 1965.

Laurent, J. K. 'The Este and their vassals: a study in signorial politics', Brown University D.Phil. thesis, 1976.

'Feudalesimo e signoria', *ASI*, 137 (1979).

'The signory and its supporters: the Este of Ferrara', *JMH*, 3 (1977).

Law, J. E. 'Popular unrest in Ferrara in 1385', in *The Renaissance in Ferrara and its European Horizons*, ed. J. Salmons and W. Moretti, Cardiff and Ravenna, 1984.

Lazzari, A. 'Il padre dell'Ariosto', *AMF*, s. 1, 30 (1936).

'Il signor di Ferrara al tempo del concilio del 1438–9, Niccolo d'Este', *AMF*, n.s., 10 (1954).

'Origini della signoria estense a Ferrara', *AMF*, n.s., 10 (1954).

Lazzarini, V. 'Antiche leggi venete intorno ai proprietari nella terraferma', *NAV*, n.s., 38 (1920).

'Beni carraresi e proprietari veneziani', in *Studi in onore di G. Luzzatto*. Milan, 1949.

'Marino Falier e un feudo dei Falier nel Ferrarese', *AV*, 38–41 (1946–7).

'Possessi e feudi veneziani nel ferrarese', in *Miscellanea in onore di R. Cessi*, Rome 1958.

Leguai, A. 'Un aspect de la formation des états princiers en France à la fin du Moyen Age: les réformes administratives de Louis II, duc de Bourbon', *MA*, 70 (1964).

Leicht, P. S. 'L'omaggio feudale in Italia', *RSDI*, 26–7 (1953–4).

*Storia del diritto italiano. Il diritto pubblico*, 2nd ed., Milan, 1940.

*Studi sulla proprietà fondiaria nel medio evo*, Milan, 1964.

Le Patourel, J. 'The king and the princes in fourteenth-century France', in *Europe in the Late Middle Ages*, ed. J. Hale et al., London, 1965.

Lewis, N. B. 'The organisation of indentured retinues in fourteenth-century England', *TRHS*, 27 (1945).

Lewis, P. S. 'Decayed and non-feudalism in later medieval France', *BIHR*, 37 (1964–5).

*Later Medieval France: the Polity*, London, 1968.

Leyser, K. 'The German aristocracy from the ninth to the early twelfth century', *Past and Present*, 41 (1968).

Litta, P. *Famiglie celebri italiane*, Milan, 1819–74, Naples, 1902–23.

# Bibliography

Lockwood, D. P. *Ugo Benzi Medical Philosopher and Physician, 1376–1439*, Chicago, 1951.

Lombardi, P. T. *I Francescani a Ferrara*, 4 vols., Bologna, 1974–5.

*Lordship and Community in Medieval Europe*, ed. F. Cheyette, New York, 1968.

Lot, F. and Fawtier, R. *Histoire des institutions françaises au Moyen Age*, vol. 1, *Institutions seigneuriales*, Paris, 1957.

Lubkin, G. P. 'The Court of Galeazzo Maria Sforza, Duke of Milan (1466–1476)', University of California, Berkeley, Ph. D. thesis, 1982.

Luzzatto, G. 'Le sottomissioni dei feudatari e le classi sociali in alcuni comuni marchigiani (secoli XII e XIII)', *Dai servi della gleba agli albori del capitalismo*, Bari, 1966.

'Tramonto e sopravivenza del feudalismo nei comuni italiani del Medio Evo', *SM*, s. 3, 3 (1962).

*Storia economica di Venezia dall' XI al XVI secolo*, Venice, 1961.

Lyon, B. D. 'The money fief under the English kings, 1066–1485', *EHR*, 66 (1951).

*From Fief to Indenture*, Cambridge, Mass., 1957.

McFarlane, K. B. '"Bastard Feudalism"', *BIHR*, 20 (1943–5).

*The Nobility of Later Medieval England*, Oxford, 1973.

Magni, C. *Il tramonto del feudo lombardo*, Milan, 1937.

Malanima, P. 'A proposito degli "Annali" della "Storia d'Italia": Dal feudalesimo al capitalismo', *Società e Storia*, 7 (1980).

Malagu, U. *Guida del Ferrarese*, Verona, 1967.

*Ville e 'delizie' del Ferrarese*, Ferrara 1972.

Mallett, M. E. *Mercenaries and their Masters: Warfare in Renaissance Italy*, London, 1974.

'Venice and its condottieri, 1404–54', in *Renaissance Venice*, ed. J. R. Hale, London, 1973.

Mallett, M. E. and Hale, J. R. *The Military Organisation of a Renaissance State: Venice c. 1400 to 1617*, Cambridge, 1984.

Manini Ferranti, G. *Compendio della storia sacra e politica di Ferrara*, 6 vols., Ferrara, 1808–10.

Manni, A. *L'età minore di Niccolo III d'Este marchese di Ferrara (1393–1402)*, Reggio, 1910.

*Un ramo della famiglia estense in esilio e le sue relazioni coi signori di Ferrara*, Novara, 1919.

'Terzi ed Estensi 1402–21', *AMF*, 25 (1925).

Mantovani, G. *Storia di Rolo*, Carpi, 1978.

Manzotti, F. 'Giberto da Correggio e la mancata signoria del medio corso del Po', *AMMo*, s. 8, 7 (1955).

Marchetti Longhi, G. 'La legazione in Lombardia di Gregorio da Monte Longo', *Archivio della Società Romana di Storia Patria*, 36 (1913).

Marini, L. 'Lo stato estense', in *Storia d'Italia*, vol. 17 (UTET, Turin, 1979).

Massera, A. F. 'La data della morte di Guglielmo III degli Adelardi', *AMF*, 22 (1915).

Mate, M. 'Profit and productivity on the estate of Isabella de Forz (1260–92)', *EcHR*, s. 2, 33 (1980).

# Bibliography

*Memorie storiche e documenti sulla città e sull'antico principato di Carpi*, Carpi, 1877–1905.

Menant, F. 'Les écuyers ("scutiferi") vassaux paysans d'Italie du nord an xɪɪe siècle', in *Structures féodales*, below.

Milani, F. *Castelnovomonti*, Castelnovomonti, 1962.

*Minozzo negli sviluppi storici della pieve e podesteria*, Reggio, 1938.

*Viano e il Querciolese nella storia*, Castelnovo ne'Monti s.d.

Milsom, S. F. C. *The Legal Framework of English Feudalism*, Cambridge, 1976.

Montanari, P. 'La formazione del patrimonio di una antica famiglia patrizia bolognese: i Lambertini', *L'Archiginnasio*, 62 (1967).

Montorsi, W. 'Considerazioni intorno al sorgere della signoria estense', *AMMo*, s. 8, 10 (1958).

Mor, C. G. 'La cavalleria', in *Nuove questioni di storia medievale*, Milan, 1964.

'Conte di Savoia, feudali e comunità in Valle d'Aosta nei sec. xɪ–xv', *XXXI Congresso storico subalpino* (1959).

'I "feudi di abitanza" in Friuli', *Memorie storiche forogiuliesi*, 54 (1974).

Morbio, C. *Storie dei municipi italiani*, vol. 1, Milan, 1836.

Mozzarelli, C. 'A proposito degli Annali della "Storia d'Italia": Dal feudalesimo al capitalismo', *Società e Storia*, 7 (1980).

'Lo stato gonzaghesco: Mantova dal 1382 al 1707', in *Storia d'Italia*, vol. 17, UTET, Turin, 1979.

Mueller, R. C. 'The Procurators of San Marco in the thirteenth and fourteenth centuries', *Studi Veneziani*, 13 (1971).

Muratori, L. A. *Delle Antichità Estensi ed Italiane*, 2 vols., Modena, 1717–40.

Nicolio, A. *Historia . . . dell'orgine e antichità di Rovigo*, Brescia, 1584.

Nobili, M. 'L'equazione città antica – città comunale ed il 'mancato sviluppo italiano' nel saggio di Philip Jones', *Società e Storia*, 10 (1980).

Nori, G. 'La corte itinerante. Il pellegrinaggio di Niccolo III in Terrasanta', in *La corte e lo spazio: Ferrara estense*, ed. G. Papagno and A. Quondam, Rome, 1982.

Novati, F. 'I codici francesi dei Gonzaga', *Attraverso il medio evo*, Bari, 1905.

Nuvolato, G. *Storia di Este e del suo territorio*, Este, 1851.

Olivi, L. 'Del matrimonio del M. Nicolo III con Gigliola figlia di Francesco Novello da Carrara', *AMMo*, 5 (1890).

Ortalli, G. 'Comune e vescovo a Ferrara nel sec. xɪɪ: dai "falsi ferraresi" agli statuti del 1173', *BISI*, 82 (1970).

Ostoja, A. 'Vicende dela commenda pomposiana in relazione al piano di assorbimento della signoria estense', *Analecta pomposiana*, ed. A. Samaritani, Codegoro, 1965.

Pacchi, D. *Ricerche istoriche sulla provincia della Garfagnana*, Modena, 1785.

Pagliani, G. *Notizie storiche civili e religiose di Arceto e della antica contea di Scandiano*, Reggio, 1907.

Pagnin, B. 'I beni della chiesa di S. Giustina di Ferrara alla fine del sec. xɪɪɪ e principio del xɪv', *AMF*, n.s., 14 (1955).

Palmieri, A. 'La congiura per sottomettere Bologna al conte di Virtu', *AMRo*, s. 4, 6 (1916).

# Bibliography

'Feudatari e popolo della montagna bolognese (periodo comunale)', *AMRo*, s. 4, 4 (1913–14).

*La montagna bolognese del medio evo*, Bologna, 1929.

Pansini, G. 'Per una storia del feudalesimo nel Granducato di Toscana durante il periodo mediceo', *QS*, 19 (1972).

Pardi, G. 'Dal comune alla signoria in Orvieto', *BU*, 13 (1908).

'Nomi locali del ferrarese', *AMF*, 1 (1942).

'La suppellettile dei palazzi estensi in Ferrara nel 1436', *AMF*, 19 (1908).

Partner, P. *The Papal State under Martin V*, London, 1958.

Pasini Frassoni, F. *I conti Trotti di Zenzalino e i conti Avogli-Trotti e Canestri-Trotti*, Pisa, 1888.

'Della nobiltà ferrarese', *Giornale araldico*, 1886.

*Dizionario storico-araldico dell'antico ducato di Ferrara*, Rome, 1914.

'Le famiglie medioevali ferraresi', *Giornale araldico*, 1897–8.

Patetta, F. 'Studi storici e note sopra alcune iscrizioni medievali', *Accademia di Scienze, Lettere ed Arti in Modena*, s. 3, 3 (1907).

Pazzi, G. Le *'Delizie Estensi' e l'Ariosto. Fasti e piaceri di Ferrara nella Rinascenza*, Pescara, 1933.

Pelicelli, N. *Pier Maria Rossi e i suoi castelli*, Parma, 1911.

Pertile, A. *Storia del diritto italiano*, 2nd edn, 6 vols., Turin, 1892–1903.

Petronio, U. 'Giurisdizioni feudali e ideologia giuridica nel ducato di Milano', *QS*, 26 (1974).

Pezzana, A. *Storia della città di Parma*, 5 vols., Parma, 1837–59.

Picotti, G. B. *I Caminesi e la loro signoria in Treviso dal 1283 al 1312*, Livorno 1905.

Pieri, P. *Il Rinascimento e la crisi militare italiana*, Turin, 1952.

di Pietro, P. 'La cancelleria degli Estensi nel periodo ferrarese (1264–1598)', *AMMo*, s. 10, 10 (1975).

Pivano, S. *Contratti agrari in Italia nell'alto medio evo*, Turin, 1904.

Plessi, A, *Istorie Vignolesi*, Vignola, 1885.

Pocquet de Haut-Jussé, 'Les pensionnaires fieffés des ducs de Bourgogne de 1352 à 1419', *Mémoires de la société pour l'histoire du droit des anciens pays bourguignons*, 8 (1942).

Poggi, F. and S. *Marano sul Panaro, dalle origini ad oggi*, Modena, 1962.

Polica, S. 'Basso Medioevo e Rinascimento: "rifeudalizzazione" e "transizione"', *BISI*, 88 (1979).

Pollard, A. J. 'The Richmondshire community of gentry during the Wars of the Roses', in *Patronage, Pedigree and Power in Later Medieval England*, ed. C. Ross, Gloucester, 1979.

Powicke, M. R. 'Distraint of knighthood and military obligation under Henry III', *Speculum*, 25 (1950).

Prestwich, J. O. 'The military household of the Norman kings', *EHR*, 96 (1981).

Prosperi, A. 'Le istituzioni ecclesiastiche e le idee religiose', in *Il Rinascimento nelle corti padane. Società e cultura*, Bari, 1977.

Rangoni Machiavelli, L. *Piccolo sunto storico della famiglia Rangone di Modena*, Rome, 1908.

# Bibliography

Reichenbach, G. *Un gentiluomo poeta del Quattrocento: Matteo Maria Boiardo,* Ferrara, 1923.

Reynolds, S. *Kingdoms and Communities in Western Europe, 900–1300,* Oxford, 1984.

Ricci, B. 'Il canonico Obizzo de Domo Estense', *AMF,* 24 (1919).

'Di Aldobrandino d'Este, vescovo di Modena', *AMMo,* s. 5, 3 (1904).

Richardot, H., 'Le fief roturier à Toulouse aux xiie et xiiie siècles', *RHDF,* s. 4, 14 (1935).

'Francs-fiefs', *RHDF,* s. 4, 27 (1949).

Righini, G. 'Due donne nel destino di Casa d'Este: Marchesella degli Adelardi', *AMF,* n. s., 28 (1964).

Rigon, A. *San Giacomo di Monselice nel Medio Evo,* Padua, 1972.

Rippe, G. 'L'évêque de Padoue et son réseau de clientèles en ville et dans le contado (xe siècle – 1237)', in *Structures féodales,* below.

'Feudum sine fidelitate'. Formes féodales et structures sociales dans la région de Padoue à l'époque de la première commune (1131–1236)', *MEFR,* 87 (1975).

Roberti, M. 'Pomposa', *Annuario della libera università di Ferrara,* 1905–6.

Rocca, P. 'Filippo, vescovo di Ferrara, arcivescovo di Ravenna nelle grandi vicende del Duecento', *AMF,* s. 3, 2 (1966).

Rombaldi, O. *Correggio città e principato,* Modena, 1979.

'La comunità reggiana nello stato estense nel secolo. xv', *Annuario del Liceo-Ginnasio statale L. Ariosti di Reggio-Emilia,* 1965–7.

'Matteo Maria Boiardo feudatario', in *Atti del convegno di studi su Matteo Maria Boiardo,* ed. G. Anceschi, Florence, 1970.

'Il potere e l'organizzazione del territorio di Quattro Castella', in *Quattro Castella nella storia di Canossa. Atti del convegno di studi matildici,* Rome 1977.

Roncaglia, C. *Statistica generale degli stati estensi,* Modena, 1849.

de la Roncière, C. M. 'Fidélités, patronages, clientèles dans le contado florentin au xiv siècle. Les seigneuries féodales, le cas des comtes Guidi', *Ricerche storiche,* 15 (1985).

Saccani, G. 'L'Abbazia', in *Marola. Notizie storiche dell'abbazia e del seminario,* Reggio, 1924.

*Cronotassi dei vescovi di Reggio-Emilia,* Reggio, 1898.

Sagredo, A. and Berchet, F. *Il Fondaco dei Turchi in Venezia,* Milan, 1860.

Salvemini, G. 'La dignità cavalleresca nel comune di Firenze', Florence, 1896 and in *Magnati e popolani in Firenze dal 1280 al 1295,* Turin 1960.

Samaritani, A. 'L'estimo del clero a Ferrara nel 1410', *AMF,* s. 3, 29 (1980).

'Il regesto di Cella Volana antitesi permanente di Pomposa', *Rivista di Storia dell'Agricoltura,* (1963).

'I vescovi ferraresi di Comacchio nella storia della civiltà estense', *Palestra del Clero,* 1963.

Sandri, G. 'I Bevilacqua e il commercio del legname tra la val di Fiemme e Verona nel sec. xiv', *AV,* s. 5, 26 (1940).

Saul, N. *Knights and Esquires: The Gloucestershire Gentry in the Fourteenth Century,* Oxford, 1981.

# Bibliography

Scalabrini, G. A. *Memorie istoriche delle chiese di Ferrara e de'suoi borghi*, Ferrara, 1773.

Schenetti, M. *Castellarano*, Castellarano, 1976.

'I signori da Gorzano', in *La Valle del Tiepido*, Modena, 1973.

*Storia di Sassuolo*, Modena, 1966.

Scufflaire, A. *Les fiefs directs des comtes de Hainaut de 1349 à 1504*, Brussels, 1978.

Sestan, E. 'I conti Guidi e il Casentino', *Italia Medievale*, Naples, 1968.

'Le origini delle signorie cittadine: un problema storico esaurito?', *BISI*, 71 (1962) and in *Italia medievale*.

'La storia dei Gonzaga nel Rinascimento', in *Mantova e i Gonzaga nella civiltà del Rinascimento*, Mantua, 1977.

Settia, A. 'Motte e castelli a motta nelle fonti scritte dell'Italia settentrionale', *Mélanges d'archéologie et d'histoire médiévale en l'honneur du Doyen Michel de Bouard*, Geneva, 1982.

Simeoni, L. 'L'azione del comune nel comitato', in *Verona e il suo territorio*, vol. 2, Verona, 1954.

'Il comune rurale nel territorio veronese', *NAV*, 43 (1921).

'L'elezione di Obizzo d'Este a signore di Ferrara', *ASI*, 93 (1935).

'Ricerche sulle origini della signoria estense a Modena', *AMMo*, s. 5, 12 (1919).

Sisto, A. *Banchieri-feudatari subalpini nei secoli XII–XIV*, Turin, 1963.

Sitta, P. 'Saggio sulle istituzioni finanziarie del ducato estense nei secoli XV e XVI', *AMF*, 3 1891.

'Le università delle arti a Ferrara dal secolo XII al XVIII', *AMF*, 8 (1896).

Soranzo, G. 'Collegati, raccomandati, aderenti negli stati italiani dei sec. XIV e XV', *ASI*, 99 (1941).

*La guerra fra Venezia e la Santa Sede per il dominio di Ferrara (1308–1313)*, Città di Castello, 1905.

Sorbelli, A. *Il comune rurale nell'Appennino emiliano nei sec. XIV e XV*, Bologna, 1910.

Soriani, G. A. *Notizie storiche di Fusignano*, Lugo, 1819.

Speroni, A. *Adriensium Episcoporum Series*, Padua, 1788.

Steer, L. A. 'Landownership and rural conditions in the Padovano during the later Middle Ages', Oxford University D.Phil. thesis, 1967.

de Stefani, C. 'Storia dei comuni di Garfagnana', *AMMo*, s. 7, 2 (1923).

Storey, R. L. *The End of the House of Lancaster*, London, 1966.

*Storia di Milano*, 16 vols., Fondazione Treccani degli Alfieri, Milan, 1953–62.

*Structures féodales et féodalisme dans l'occident méditerranéen (Xe–XIIIe siècles)*, Collection de l'Ecole française de Rome, 44 (1980).

Tabacco, G. 'Fief et seigneurie dans l'Italie communale', *MA*, 75 (1969).

review of Keller, H. *Adelsherrschaft und städtische Gesellschaft in Oberitalien*, *RSI*, 93 (1981).

Tabanelli, M. *La Romagna degli Estensi*, Faenza, 1976.

Tamassia, N. *La famiglia italiana nei secoli decimoquinto e decimosesto*, Milan, 1910.

Tangheroni, M. 'Il feudalesimo in Sardegna in età aragonese', *Annali della scuola normale superiore di Pisa*, s. 3, 3, (1973).

# Bibliography

*Politica, commercio, agricoltura a Pisa nel trecento*, Pisa, 1973.

'La Sardegna prearagonese: una società senza feudalesimo?' in *Structures féodales*, above.

Tenenti, A. 'La corte nella storia dell'Europa moderna (1300–1700)', in *Le corti farnesiane di Parma e Piacenza*, ed. M. A. Romani, Rome, 1978.

Tiraboschi, G. *Dizionario topografico-storico degli stati estensi*, 2 vols., Modena, 1824–5.

*Memorie storiche modenesi*, 4 vols., Modena, 1793–5.

*Storia dell'augusta badia di S. Silvestro di Nonantola*, 2 vols., Modena, 1784–5.

Tirelli, V. 'Sulla crisi istituzionale del comune a Lucca (1308–12)', in *Studi per E. Fiumi*, Pisa 1979.

Torelli, P. *Un comune cittadino in territorio ad economia agricola*, Mantua, 1930.

Tristano, R. M. 'Ferrara in the Fifteenth Century: Borso d'Este and the Development of a New Nobility', D.Phil. thesis, New York University, 1983.

Trombetti Budriesi, A. L. 'Beni estensi nel Padovano: da un codice di Albertino Mussato del 1293', *SM*, 21 (1980).

'Vassalli e feudi a Ferrara e nel Ferrarese dall'età precomunale alla signoria estense (sec. XI–XIII)', *AMF*, s. 3, 28 (1980).

Valenti, F. 'I consigli di governo presso gli Estensi dalle origini alla devoluzione di Ferrara', *Studi in onore di R. Filangieri*, Naples, 1959.

'Il fondo pomposiano nell'Archivio di Stato di Modena', *Analecta pomposiana*, ed. A. Samaritani, Codegoro, 1965.

'Note storiche sulla cancelleria degli Estensi a Ferrara dalle origini alla metà del secolo XVI', *Bollettino dell'Archivio Paleografico Italiano*, n.s., 2–3 (1956–7).

Varanini, G. M. 'Un esempio di ristrutturazione agraria quattrocentesca nella bassa veronese: il monastero di S. Maria in Organo e le terre di Roncanova', *Studi Storici Veronesi*, 30–1 (1980–1).

Vasina, A. 'L'abbazia di Pomposa nel duecento', in *Analecta Pomposiana*, ed. A. Samaritani, Codegoro, 1965.

'Il territorio ferrarese nell'alto medioevo', in *Insediamenti nel Ferrarese*, Florence, 1976.

'La Romagna estense', *SR*, 21 (1970).

'La società riminese nel tardo medioevo', *Romagna medievale*, Ravenna, 1970.

Vaughan, R. *Philip the Good*, London, 1970.

Ventura, A. *Nobiltà e popolo nella società veneta del '400 e '500,* Bari, 1964.

Venturi, G. B. *Storia di Scandiano*, Modena, 1822.

Verci, G. B. *Storia della marca trivigiana e veronese*, 20 vols., Venice, 1786–91.

de Vergottini, G. 'Di un vicariato imperiale degli Estensi a Ferrara sotto Ludovico IV', *RSDI*, 11 (1938).

Vicini, E. P. 'I podestà di Modena dal 1336 al 1796', *AMMo*, s. 5, 10 (1917).

'Visconti estensi in Modena', *AMMo, Studi e documenti*, n.s., 1 (1942).

Vitale, V. *Il dominio della parte guelfa in Bologna (1280–1327)*, Bologna, 1902.

'Vita e commercio nei notai genovesi dei secoli XII e XIII', *Atti della Società Ligure di Storia Patria*, 72 (1949).

Waley, D. P. 'La féodalité dans la région romaine dans la 2e moitié du xiiie siècle et au début du xive', in *Structures féodales*, above.

*The Italian City-Republics*, 2nd edn., London, 1978.

*The Papal State in the Thirteenth Century*, London, 1961.

Waller, E. M. L. 'The Diplomatic Relations of the Gonzaga, 1328–1407', Oxford, B. Litt. thesis, 1953.

Wormald, J. *Lords and Men in Scotland: Bonds of Manrent, 1442–1603*, Edinburgh, 1985.

Zanella, G. *Riccobaldo e dintorni*, Ferrara, 1980.

Zennari, J. *Adria e il suo territorio attraverso i secoli*, Adria, 1931.

Zorzi, E. *Il territorio padovano nel periodo di trapasso da comitato a comune*, Venice, 1929.

Zorzi, M. A. 'L'ordinamento comunale padovano nella seconda metà del sec. xiii', *Deputazione di Storia Patria per le Venezie, Miscellanea di storia veneta*, 5 (1931).

Zucchini, M. *L'agricoltura ferrarese attraverso i secoli*, Rome, 1967.

'Pomposa e la bonifica ferrarese', *AMF*, n.s., 29 (1964).

# INDEX

# Index

# Index

Galluzzi, 83–4
Garfagnana, 26, 159
Gavello, 39
Geri, Filippo, 77, 91n., 103
Giglioli
  Gigliolo, 140, 147
  Jacopo, 59, 61, 67, 77, 91n., 135, 136–7, 138, 140, 144–5
Giocoli, 15, 65, 93, 95–6, 143, 144–5
  Aldrovandino, 60, 67, 95
  Giocolo, 61, 95
Gomola, 172
Gonzaga, 19, 20, 25, 53n., 85, 132n., 152, 157, 163, 172
Gozzadini, 39, 82–3, 96, 139
Guarda, 139, 143, 144
Gualengo, 135–6, 137–8
  Giuliano, 61n., 92, 98
Guazzalotti, Filippo, 146
Guidizzoni, Aliprando, 61n.
Guidoberti, 94, 162n.

homage, 111, 129–30
hunting, 64, 101, 127

illegitimacy, 51, 56, 96, 118–19, 120–1, 145

John XXIII, Pope, see Cossa

knighthood, 84, 87, 140, 146–9

Lagosanto, 35, 37, 187–8
Lambertini, 77, 83–5, 90n., 126n., 147
  see also Poggio Renatico
Lendinara, 17, 40, 51, 58, 106
Leon, 77, 79–80, 103
Lonato, Francesco da, 77, 87–8
Lunigiana, 50, 159
Lupi, 105

Macaruffi, 60n.
Mainardi, 15, 93–4
Malaspina, 50, 88
Malatesta, 19–20, 27, 38, 57
Mandello, Otto da, 77, 87
Manfredi (Faenza), 20, 24–5, 132n.
Manfredi (Reggio), 166, 172–3
Manfredini, 103–4, 144–5
Marano da, 90n., 146n.
Marinetti, 65, 136–7, 140
Marocelli, 65, 100–2, 138–9, 144–5, 188
Marola, 102

Massafiscaglia, 40, 116
Mazzoni, 77, 92
Medici (Ferrara), 42, 58, 60
Mella, Bartolomeo della, 61, 65, 91n., 100–2, 135, 141n.
Mellara, 25, 42, 69
Menabuoi, 18, 41, 58
Mesola, 37, 103, 186
Milan, 6, 118, 131, 145–6
  see also Visconti
Mirandola, see Pico
Modena, 16–17, 18, 19, 51, 69, 86, 115, 150–78
money fiefs, 7, 75, 118
Monselice, 32, 46, 48, 50, 106
Montecuccolo, 24, 127, 155, 158–9, 162, 166, 167, 174, 175–6
Montegarullo, 24, 155, 158–9, 172
Morosini, 77, 79–80
multiple lordship, 116, 130

Nonantola, 24–5, 39
Novelli, 40, 61n., 91n., 98, 138, 139, 140, 144

Obizzi, 77, 79
Orgogliosi, 85
Ostellato, 35, 37, 38, 166

Padovano, 14, 17–18, 20, 32, 39, 46–50, 87, 104–6, 123–4, 185
Padua, 17–18, 48–50, 132
  see also da Carrara, Cumani, Forzate, Macaruffi
Pagani, 15, 58, 93–4, 96
Pallavicino, Rolando, 25, 141
Panico da, 85
Papacy, 14, 18, 20, 26, 37, 38, 44, 58
  see also Boniface IX, Eugenius IV, John XXIII, vicariate
Parma, 19, 25, 26, 83n., 87, 97, 132, 167, 170
  see also Castiglione, Lupi, Rossi
Pendaglia, 60, 61, 91n., 136
Perondoli, 43, 61, 91n., 139, 140, 141n., 162n.
Piacenza, 25
  see also Fontana
Pico, 20, 150, 168, 176
Pio, 20, 76, 86–7, 150, 152, 166, 171, 172, 173, 177
  Marco, 76, 86, 178
Pisa, Filippo da, 61n., 88, 147
Po, 10, 35, 37, 65, 69, 138, 188

# Index

Polesine di Rovigo, 13, 14, 24–5, 26, 40, 51, 54, 56, 63, 72, 75, 80–1, 92, 103, 123–4, 126, 139, 185
Poggio Renatico, 84–5, 161
Pomposa, 32, 35–9, 80, Appendix 5
Portomaggiore, 32, 43, 99, 142
primogeniture, 51, 53–4, 56
Pritati, Pietro, 39, 62, 89, 98
*provisionati*, 78, 80, 82n., 88, 163n.

Querini, 65, 67

Ramberti, 15, 18, 41
Rangoni, 16–17, 61, 86–7, 150, 153n.
Ravenna, archbishop, 12, 20, 26, 30, 42–3, 46n., 65, 143
reclamation, 65, 67, 100, 137–8
recognition dues, 125n., 126–8
Reggio, 6, 16, 18, 20, 25, 69, 85, 132n., 150–78
revenues, 19, 58, 68–9, 128–9
Roberti, 61, 76, 79, 85–6, 134, 146, 150, 163–4, 171, 172, 173, 175
  Filippo, 85–6
  Niccolo, 25, 61n., 85–6
  Niccolo, bishop of Ferrara, 40, 86
  Ugo, 40, 164n.
Rossi, 25, 77, 105–6
Roteglia da, 24, 155, 156, 172, 174n.
Rovigo, 32, 34, 40, 53, 63, 116–17, 185
Rubiera, 150, 160, 164–5
  *see also* Boiardi
rustic fiefs, 99–102, 104–5

S. Giorgio, 38, 40
S. Maria di Belfiore, 27, 63
S. Martino in Rio, 85, 163–4, 175
Sacrati, 83n., 135–9, 144–5, 162, 188
Sala, 136, 155, 162
  Alberto, 134–5, 137, 138, 140, 147
  Baldassare, 38
  Giovanni, 83n., 98, 140
salt, 19, 44, 160, 164n., 174
Sassuolo da, 20, 24, 150, 156
Savignano, 24, 77, 86–7, 147, 156, 160, 163
Sesso da, 166, 172, 176

Sestola, 24, 158
sharecropping, 48, 65
Signorelli, 15, 93–4
Strozzi, 97, 155, 163, 188
  Nanne, 61, 62n., 147
subinfeudation, 93, 121n.
substitution, 120, 121–2

Tavola, Camilla a, 60n.
tax immunities, 44n., 60–1, 62, 65, 67n., 68, 93, 95, 104, 116n., 140, 159–60, 172
Terzi, Ottobuono, 24–5, 89, 165, 172
tithe, 40–2, 44n., 58, 62, 65, 67, 75, 106, 138, 143, 144, 185, 188
Torelli (Ferrara), 13, 14, 18, 41, 57n.
Torelli (Guastalla), 89
Trecenta, 42, 62, 142
Trevisan, Zaccaria, 62, 77, 80–1
Trotti, 94, 96n., 139, 163
Turchi, 15, 42, 65, 79, 93–4, 96, 100–2, 103n., 138, 140, 143–4

university, 21, 22, 27

Vangadizza, 32–4, 46n.
Venice, 10, 12, 14, 18, 24–6, 32, 37, 48, 49–50, 53, 54–5, 65, 69n., 79n., 80–1, 86, 124, 128n., 137, 159, 164, 169, 185, 188
  *see also* Corner, Leon, Morosini, Querini
vicariate, 19, 39, 53, 55
Vighizzolo, 20, 46, 48, 54
Vignola, 160–2
Villanova, 67, 85, 100–2
villas, 64
Visconti, 19, 20, 21, 26, 49n., 54–5, 59, 60n., 83, 87, 89n., 118, 132, 157–8, 163, 165, 166n., 170–1, 173n., 177
Visdomini, 94
Volano, 35, 188

women (as vassals), 16, 109–10, 111, 113, 120–1, 122, 124
woodland, 35, 37, 40, 48, 103, 137, 185–6, 187–8